Oxford
Practice Grammar
(Advanced)

牛津高级
英语语法

[英] George Yule 编著

外语教学与研究出版社
FOREIGN LANGUAGE TEACHING AND RESEARCH PRESS
北京 BEIJING

京权图字：01-2022-1122

图书在版编目（CIP）数据

牛津高级英语语法 ／（英）乔治·尤尔（George Yule）编著. —— 北京：外语教学与研究出版社，2022.3（2022.11 重印）
书名原文：Oxford Practice Grammar (Advanced)
ISBN 978-7-5213-3455-5

Ⅰ. ①牛… Ⅱ. ①乔… Ⅲ. ①英语－语法－自学参考资料 Ⅳ. ①H314

中国版本图书馆 CIP 数据核字（2022）第 050619 号

出版人　王　芳
项目策划　刘　旭
责任编辑　许圆圆
责任校对　王　晶
封面设计　李　高
出版发行　外语教学与研究出版社
社　　址　北京市西三环北路 19 号（100089）
网　　址　http://www.fltrp.com
印　　刷　廊坊十环印刷有限公司
开　　本　787×1092　1/16
印　　张　18
版　　次　2022 年 6 月第 1 版 2022 年 11 月第 2 次印刷
书　　号　ISBN 978-7-5213-3455-5
定　　价　49.00 元

购书咨询：（010）88819926　电子邮箱：club@fltrp.com
外研书店：https://waiyants.tmall.com
凡印刷、装订质量问题，请联系我社印制部
联系电话：（010）61207896　电子邮箱：zhijian@fltrp.com
凡侵权、盗版书籍线索，请联系我社法律事务部
举报电话：（010）88817519　电子邮箱：banquan@fltrp.com
物料号：334550001

记载人类文明
沟通世界文化
www.fltrp.com

目 录

iii

v

前言

　　"牛津英语语法"系列包含初级、中级和高级三个级别，不同学习阶段的英语学习者均可找到适合自己水平的级别。本系列图书可供课堂教学使用，也可供自学者使用。

　　本书中，每单元涵盖一个重要的语法项目。每个单元均以先进行语法讲解，再进行一系列相关练习的形式呈现。每单元结尾的测验以及全书最后的"学习成果评测"为学习者提供了更多练习机会，学习者可据此检验自己的学习效果。书后附有所有试题的答案。

　　学习者可以自行决定学习顺序。你或许希望先学习那些给你造成了困扰的语法项目。（本系列每册书的目录和书后索引列出了具体的语法项目。）你也可以选择从头至尾学习每册书。

用作备考材料

　　本系列的第一册是《牛津初级英语语法》，适合英语水平处于初级至中级阶段的学习者，以及备考牛津英语测试（Oxford Test of English）和"剑桥通用五级考试"中 A2 Key 考试、B1 Preliminary 考试的学习者。第二册是《牛津中级英语语法》，读者对象是具有中等英语水平的学习者。该水平的学习者已经不再是初学者，但尚不能熟练使用英语。第二册适合备考牛津英语测试和"剑桥通用五级考试"中 B2 First 考试的学习者。第三册《牛津高级英语语法》适合中级水平以上且希望进一步拓展英语语法知识、能更加自如地使用英语的学习者。第三册能够帮助学习者备考"剑桥通用五级考试"中的 C1 Advanced 考试和 C2 Proficiency 考试，以及托福、雅思等其他高级水平的英语考试。

本书适合我吗?

　　本书为具有高级水平的英语学习者设计，处于该水平的学习者已经学过中级水平的英语语法。本书适合学习者在自学时或在学习小组中学习时使用，也可在课堂上用来参考。

本书包含哪些内容?

本书包含 17 个单元，全面讲解了当代英语语法知识。每单元包含数个独立小节，讲解具体的语法应用特点（如"被动式的用法"）或语法难点（如"现在完成时还是一般过去时？"）。每小节均由语法点讲解、相应例句和配套练习构成（练习题可能与讲解在同一页上，也可能在讲解的对侧页面上）。每单元的结尾有一套测验，篇幅为两页。练习题和测验题的答案在书后的答案部分（见第 220 页）。本书后还附有术语表（见第 260 页），解释了书中出现的语法术语的含义。

如何使用本书?

本书有多种使用方法。

• 你可以将本书用作参考指南，查找关于某个语法点清晰简明的讲解。书中的每段语法讲解均配有例句，展示相应语法点在语境中的正确用法，并提醒应避开哪些常犯错误。为方便读者查阅，各语法话题会被列在当页开头的标题中。所有的单元标题和每单元中的语法话题均可在目录（见第 iii 页）和书后索引（见第 270 页）中找到。

• 你可以将本书用作练习册，通过做题完成书中的练习。对照参考答案来检查自己的答案是否正确。如果发现某道题答错了，可以看看相关页面上与此题涉及的语法点有关的讲解，以及讲解下展示了正确用法的示例。

• 你可以将本书用作课本，从第一页开始，按照自己的节奏一直学到最后。这让你在全面审视英语语法时，把每个语法项目都视为同等重要。虽然本书中的语法项目不是按照由易到难的顺序编排的，但这样的顺序与很多教材采用的语法讲解顺序相似。

• 你也可以用本书创建自己的语法学习课程。你可以学习某小节或某单元的全部或部分内容，然后选择性地完成练习或测验。可以参看讲解页最下面的语法点参照注释，这些注释可指导你找到其他相关小节。由于本书的语法项目不是按照难度编排顺序的，所以你可以自由选择学习顺序。

本书特色

除了传统题型以外，本书还设置了一些新颖的语法练习，专为英语水平较高的学生设计。

· **概述练习**：从一篇较长的文本中选择恰当的语法形式来补全一篇关于该文本的简短概述。这些练习有助于提升使用准确的语法结构汇报所读内容的能力（如第 2 页的练习 B）。

· **词典释义练习**：选择恰当的语法形式填空，完成单词和短语的释义。这些练习可帮你扩大词汇量，并且提高以准确的语法结构作出清晰描述的能力（如第 7 页的练习 H）。

· **匹配练习**：以恰当的语法形式补全句子（有可能是问句）或部分句子，使其与另一个句子或句子的另一部分语意连贯、呼应。这些练习可帮你提高英语口语和写作能力，让你能够在表达较复杂内容的同时保证语法的准确性（如第 7 页的练习 I）。

· **改错练习**：通读一段文本，找出其中的语法错误并进行必要的修改。这些练习可帮你掌握以更准确的语法写较长英语文章的能力（如第 9 页的练习 M）。

· **填序号练习**：找出最能体现某条语法讲解的示例，把它的序号填在讲解后的方格里，从而将讲解与示例匹配起来。这些练习增强了学习的互动性，能让你更好地把自己的英语理解能力和关于语法规则的知识结合起来（如第 12 页的练习 Q）。

在每单元末的测验中，你可以练习各种不同的题型。这些题型来自一些英语水平测试，如雅思考试、美国密歇根英语考试和 C2 Proficiency 考试。这些练习能使你更加熟悉高级水平的英语考试，并更好地理解选自各种真实英语素材的文本，包括报刊文章以及布鲁斯·查特文（Bruce Chatwin）、T. S. 艾略特（T. S. Eliot）、马格努斯·米尔斯（Magnus Mills）等作者的作品。

牛津高级英语语法

Oxford Practice Grammar
(Advanced)

简单句（simple sentence）只含一个分句（clause）。该分句可仅由一个主语（subject）和一个动词（verb）构成（*Jenny laughed.*）。该分句也可含有助动词（auxiliary verb，包括 **be**, **do**, **have** 和情态动词）——作为动词短语的一部分，动词之后可以有状语（*She was sitting at the table.*）。动词之后可以有一个宾语（object）（*She was drawing a picture.*），两个宾语（*She showed me the picture.*），或没有宾语（*She giggled.*）。简单句也可由系动词（linking verb）和补语（complement）构成（*It looked very silly.*）。

并列复合句（compound sentence）由 **and, but, or** 等并列连词（coordinating conjunction）连接两个或更多分句构成（*I made some coffee, but Jenny wanted orange juice.*）。主从复合句（complex sentence）由 **after, because, if, while** 等从属连词（subordinating conjunction）连接两个或更多分句构成（*We chatted in the kitchen while I cooked breakfast.*）。

A 阅读下面这篇新闻报道，并找出：

1 一个简单句；
2 一个含有两个连词的主从复合句。

A young English teacher saved the lives of 30 students when he took control of a bus after its driver suffered a fatal heart attack. Guy Harvold, 24, had collected the students and
5　three course leaders from Gatwick airport and they were travelling to Bournemouth to meet their host families. They were going to start a course at the International Language Academy in Bournemouth where Harvold works as a
10　teacher.

Harvold, who has not passed his driving test, said, 'I realized the bus was out of control when I was speaking to the students on the microphone.' The bus collided with trees at
15　the side of the road and he noticed the driver was slumped over the wheel. The driver didn't move. He was unconscious.

'We hit a barrier and swerved to the other side of the road and I grabbed the wheel,'
20　Harvold explained. 'The driver's legs were over the pedals and I had difficulty reaching the brake. We hit a lamp post and it shattered the glass on the front door before I managed to bring the bus to a halt.' Police praised the young teacher's quick
25　thinking. If he hadn't reacted quickly, there could have been a terrible accident.

The bus driver never regained consciousness. He was later pronounced dead at East Surrey hospital. He had worked regularly with the
30　school and was very well regarded by staff. Harvold said, 'I was so relieved that no one else was hurt, but I hoped the driver would survive. It was only later I heard he had died. That's a terrible tragedy.'

35　The Language Academy's principal told the Gazette that the school is going to send Harvold on a weekend trip to Dublin with a friend, as a gesture of thanks for his bravery. A local driving school has also offered him six free
40　driving lessons.

B 用上面新闻报道中的动词和连词，完成以下概述。

English teacher Guy Harvold, 24, •*saved* _____ the lives of 30 students on a bus from Gatwick to Bournemouth ¹ _____ the driver ² _____ a heart attack. The bus went out of control. It ³ _____ trees, a barrier and a lamp post ⁴ _____ Harvold could stop it. The driver ⁵ _____ , ⁶ _____ no-one else ⁷ _____ hurt. Harvold, who hasn't passed his driving test, was ⁸ _____ by police ⁹ _____ was ¹⁰ _____ free driving lessons by a local driving school.

简单句和动词

1 简单句

简单句由一个分句构成，含一个主语和一个动词。

1 *Mary sneezed.* • *Somebody coughed.* • *The train didn't come.* • *People were waiting.*

简单句也可含有宾语（2）和 / 或状语，状语可以是副词（3）或介词短语（4）等。

2 *Mr Owen made lunch.* • *I brought some cakes.* • *We drank tea.* • *Everyone enjoyed it.*
3 *Suddenly the weather changed.* • *We quickly closed the windows.* • *It often rains there.*
4 *Shakespeare married Anne Hathaway in 1582.* • *He moved to London in 1588.*

在使用了 **be, look** 等系动词的简单句中，有描述主语的补语。

5 *Cathy is a nurse.* • *She wasn't ready.* • *Her hair looked wet.* • *The room felt like an oven.*

2 动词

大多数动词是行为动词（action verb），用于描述行为（做了什么）或事件（发生了什么）。

6 *Richard eats a lot of pasta. It gives him energy. He runs every night. I saw him in the park.*

有些动词是状态动词（state verb）而不是行为动词，用于描述状态：思维活动（7）；感受（8）；关系，特别是包含和所属关系（9）。

7 *I know what you mean.* • *My parents understood everything.* • *They believe in fate.*
8 *I appreciate all your help.* • *Some people hate cucumber in sandwiches.*
9 *The city guide contains useful information.* • *That old suitcase belongs to me.*

状态动词通常不使用进行时形式。（不说 ~~That suitcase is belonging to me.~~）
其他状态动词如：**consist of, exist, include, matter, own, prefer, realize, remember, resemble**。

也可用系动词（**be, seem** 等）来描述状态，即事物是什么样的或看起来如何。

10 *These flowers are beautiful.* • *Everything seems fine.* • *Your friend appears to be nervous.*

有些动词，例如 **taste** 和 **weigh**，可以用作状态动词（11），也可用作行为动词（12）。

11 *Flowers don't usually taste very good.* • *The box weighs two kilos.*
12 *Have you tasted this soup?* • *They carefully weighed the flour.*

助动词 **be, do** 和 **have** 与其他动词连用，可以构成不同的时态（13），可以构成疑问句和否定句（14），还可以表示强调（15）。

13 *The boys have been waiting for you. I think they've gone outside. They're playing football.*
14 *What did Josh say?* ~ *He didn't say anything.* • *Does he want coffee?* ~ *I don't think so.*
15 *You aren't working very hard.* ~ *I AM working hard!* • *You don't miss me.* ~ *I DO miss you!*

be, do 和 **have** 也可用作主要动词（main verb）：*He is lazy. He does nothing. He has no money.*

can, must, should, will 等情态动词与其他动词连用可以表达许可、义务、必要性、预测等含义。

16 *Can I leave now?* • *You shouldn't go yet.* • *I must catch the next bus or I'll be late for work.*

C 再读一读第 **2** 页的新闻报道，就下列描述各找出一个例子。

1 含一个系动词的简单句：_____
2 含一个行为动词和一个副词的分句：_____
3 含一个情态动词的分句：_____

→ 并列复合句和主从复合句 12 系动词 10 情态动词 28 介词短语 125

主语和动词

3 主语

一个句子的主语通常是句中第一个名词（短语）或代词，指明了执行动词所示行为的人或事物（1）。它可以指明是什么人或事物经历了某事或某情况（2），也可以是描述的对象（如补语描述的对象）（3）。

1 *Anthony lost his keys.* • *The dog ate my homework.* • *You are working too hard these days.*
2 *The children heard a loud noise.* • *The audience enjoyed the concert.* • *Megan doesn't like coffee.*
3 *Lions are large and powerful.* • *Her new classmates seem friendly.* • *Your hair looks great.*

主语一般位于动词之前，除非是在疑问句（4）和倒装句（5）中。

4 *Where has she been?* • *Does this bus go to the university?* • *Isn't Oslo in southern Norway?*
5 *In front of us and blocking the way stood a large dog. Never had I seen such a fierce animal.*

主语也可以是动名词（6）、动词不定式（7）或分句（8）。

6 *Reading comics is her favourite thing.* • *Studying always makes me sleepy.*
7 *Just to complete the classes has become my new goal.* • *To go without you wouldn't be any fun.*
8 *That she would win the election was never in doubt.* • *What he said wasn't very polite.*

4 主谓一致（subject-verb agreement）

主语决定动词用单数形式还是复数形式（9）。注意，是主语中的中心名词，而非介词短语，决定了动词是单数形式（10）还是复数形式（11）。

9 *Adam's sister lives in Scotland. His parents live near London.*
10 *A new pair of shoes doesn't cost a lot.* • *A woman with three children was waiting outside.*
11 *New shoes don't always feel comfortable at first.* • *The children were crying.*

不定代词（**everybody, nobody** 等）作主语时，后面使用单数动词（12）。主语以 **none of** 或 **neither of** 开头时，在正式语言中后面通常用单数动词（13），在非正式语言中有时也用复数动词（14）。

12 *Everybody in the country wants one of these.* • *Nobody except his parents was willing to help.*
13 *None of the candidates has much support.* • *Neither of King Henry's sons was born in France.*
14 *She shouted, 'None of you have a chance.'* • *He's complaining that neither of them were asked.*

有的主语看上去是复数形式，但后面使用单数动词，比如：某些以 -s 结尾的名词（15），描述数量的短语（16），某些用 **and** 连接的词组（17）。而有些名词，例如 **people** 和 **police**，看上去是单数形式，但要使用复数动词（18）。

15 *The news wasn't too bad.* • *Cards is more than a game for some people.* • *Measles is a disease.*
16 *£200 is too much.* • *20 miles was too far and two days wasn't enough time.*
17 *Tom and Jerry is a rather old cartoon.* • *Sausage and beans doesn't cost very much.*
18 *The police are trying to stop speeding in the city, but people are still driving too fast.*

集体名词用作主语时可以指若干人，此时搭配复数动词（19）；也可以把这些人视作一个整体单位，此时搭配单数动词（20）。使用哪种动词形式取决于要表达什么。

19 *The Welsh team are getting tired.* • *The committee have not expressed all their views.*
20 *The Welsh team is in second place.* • *The committee hasn't reached a decision yet.*

其他集体名词如：**audience, class, crowd, enemy, family, government, orchestra, staff**。

注意，在美式英语中，集体名词之后通常使用单数动词：*My wife's family always has a big get-together with a barbecue on July 4th.*

→ 集体名词 75　不定代词 98　动词不定式和动名词 139　倒装 216

D 再读一读第 **2** 页的新闻报道，就下列描述各找出一个例子。

1 含一个不定代词的分句： _____

2 含一个表示群体的名词的分句： _____

E 选择合适的动词，添加到下列句子中的正确位置。

> ~~does~~ doesn't has have is isn't are aren't was wasn't won't

♦ Excuse me, but this train *does* stop at Croydon?

1 To get an A in every class be easy.

2 *Lord of the Flies* the name of the book we had to read last year?

3 My new pair of jeans pockets on the side of the legs.

4 What they're doing in Parliament interest me.

5 Being absent from class a lot going to improve his chances of passing.

6 Jess got really angry with us and screamed, 'None of you my friends any more!'

7 Never I had to listen to so many boring people!

8 I watched *Dances with Wolves*, which about dancing at all.

9 Statistics more difficult than Economics?

10 These new sunglasses made of glass or plastic or anything like that.

F 为句子的前半句（1—5）选择合适的后半句（a—e），并在横线处补充形式恰当的 be 动词。

♦ *The Simpsons is* _____ (*f*)

1 *Romeo and Juliet* _____ ( )

2 Last night's news _____ ( )

3 25 kilos _____ ( )

4 Billy as well as all his friends _____ ( )

5 The audience _____ ( )

a a lot to carry by yourself, don't you think?

b usually in their seats before the play starts.

c written by Shakespeare.

d going camping this weekend.

e rather exciting, I thought.

f the name of a television programme.

G 选择合适的词并搭配 has 或 have，补全下列句子。

> committee darts ~~diabetes~~ eggs everybody
> nobody orchestra police teachers

♦ *Diabetes has* _____ become a more common disease, mainly because of the way we eat.

1 The conductor and the _____ had very little time to rehearse for the concert.

2 Security is just something that _____ to go through in airports nowadays.

3 _____ from the new student group _____ volunteered to help with the Christmas party.

4 The planning _____ all been given individual copies of the agenda for the meeting.

5 _____ always been a popular game in English pubs.

6 According to the rules, none of the _____ the right to make students stay after school.

7 The _____ no idea how the robbers got into the bank.

8 Bacon and _____ been the Sunday breakfast in our house for years.

动词和宾语

5 接宾语的动词（及物动词 [transitive verb]）

及物动词后面接宾语，宾语通常是名词短语或代词。

   1 *He kicked a small stone. It hit me. • We discussed the problems. They affected all of us.*

及物动词用于描述影响宾语的行为（2），或描述由宾语引起的感受或体验（3）。

   2 *Are they building a wall? • I'll cut the grass. • Elizabeth bought an old Volkswagen.*

此类及物动词还有：**carry, catch, fix, heat, prepare, protect, rob, scratch, sell, trim**。

   3 *Did you enjoy the concert? • One of our old teachers remembered us. • I don't like onions.*

此类及物动词还有：**admire, believe, fear, hate, hear, love, need, please, prefer, receive**。

只有及物动词可以用于被动语态。

   4 *Someone stole my bag.* → *My bag was stolen. • They caught the thief.* → *The thief was caught.*

put 等某些及物动词的宾语后面通常跟一个介词短语。

   5 *He put the keys <u>in the drawer</u>. • We crammed all our boxes <u>into the back of Jasmine's car</u>.*

6 不接宾语的动词（不及物动词 [intransitive verb]）

不及物动词在使用时不带宾语。

   6 *I can't sleep. • Everyone was waiting, but he didn't care.*（不说 ~~He didn't care it.~~）

其他不及物动词如：**arrive, depart, disappear, happen, hesitate, occur, pause, rain**。

不及物动词用于谈论简单的事件、行为或声音。

   7 *The roof collapsed. • She sighed and yawned. • A lot of people were shouting.*

此类不及物动词还有：**cough, faint, fall, growl, moan, scream, shiver, sneeze**。

不及物动词不能用于被动语态。

   8 *The thief escaped.*（不说 ~~The thief was escaped. / The police were escaped by the thief.~~）

不及物动词之后经常跟介词短语（9），尤其是描述移动行为的不及物动词之后（10）。

   9 *Darwin died in 1882. • I slept until noon. • They are kneeling on mats and praying to God.*

  10 *It came from Argentina. • Let's go to bed. • We walk to the park and then we run round it.*

7 有及物和不及物双重用法的动词

一些动词，如 **eat** 和 **read**，可以带宾语（11），也可以不带宾语（12）。

  11 *She read his message. • I don't eat fish. • We won the match. • Do you speak English?*

  12 *He always reads when he's eating. • Did you win? • She was so upset she couldn't speak.*

此类动词还有：**cook, draw, dress, drink, drive, hurt, paint, spread, study, write**。

有些动词，如 **die** 和 **smile**，通常不带宾语（13），但可以搭配某个或某类特定的宾语（14）。

  13 *Miss Reynolds smiled and said she was quite certain that none of us would ever die.*

  14 *Nina smiled her bright smile. She seemed unconcerned that she might die a painful death.*

此类动词还有：**dance, dream, laugh, live, sigh**。

一些动词，如 **fight** 和 **meet**，可以带宾语（15）。当它们位于复数主语之后时，也可以不带宾语，可理解为省略了宾语 **each other**（16）或 **with each other**（17）。

  15 *When I met Sergio in Madrid, he embraced me like a brother. • John had to fight two thugs.*

  16 *We met in Rome. • Our fingers touched. • The old women embraced. • They hugged and kissed.*

  17 *John and I always fight. • Two of Australia's major wine producers have merged.*

→ each other 100　被动 57　介词短语 125

H 选择合适的名词或动词填空，补全下列释义，动词形式要使用恰当。在须带宾语的动词后补充单词 things。如有必要请查词典。

hallucination	hinge	behave	close		go	seize	~~hassle~~	holdall	carry
demand		pretend	swing	hijacker	hypocrite	~~cause~~	~~do~~	see	travel

A ♦ *hassle*＿＿＿＿ is something that is annoying because it ♦ *causes*＿＿＿ problems or difficulties when you try to ♦ *do things*＿＿＿＿ .

A ¹＿＿＿＿ is a large soft bag in which you can ²＿＿＿＿ when you ³＿＿＿＿ .

A ⁴＿＿＿＿ is a small piece of metal on which a door ⁵＿＿＿＿ as it opens and ⁶＿＿＿＿ .

A ⁷＿＿＿＿ is a feeling or belief that you are ⁸＿＿＿＿ when nothing is there.

A ⁹＿＿＿＿ is a person who ¹⁰＿＿＿＿ to have high values that are not matched by the way he or she ¹¹＿＿＿＿ .

A ¹²＿＿＿＿ is a person who ¹³＿＿＿＿ control of a vehicle, especially an aircraft, in order to ¹⁴＿＿＿＿ to a new destination or to ¹⁵＿＿＿＿ from a government in return for the safety of those in the vehicle.

I 为问题（1—4）选择合适的答语（a—d），再选择合适的动词并用其恰当形式填空。在必要的地方补充代词 it 和 / 或一个介词。

believe	go	hear	like	put	shiver	take	wait

1 Did Andreas ＿＿＿＿ the key? ( ) a Yes, but I don't ＿＿＿＿ .
2 Do you ＿＿＿＿ old towns? ( ) b Yes, he ＿＿＿＿ his pocket.
3 Could you ＿＿＿＿ outside? ( ) c Yes, that's why I'm ＿＿＿＿ Edinburgh.
4 Have you ＿＿＿＿ the latest rumour? ( ) d No, it's too cold and I'm ＿＿＿＿ .

J 为每句选择一组正确的不及物动词，将句子补全。注意应使用动词的恰当形式。

breathe / snore	~~dream / sleep~~	eat / hibernate	fall / lie
get / move	go / sing	happen / talk	nap / rest

♦ When you *dream*＿＿＿ , you see and experience things while you are *sleeping*＿＿＿ .

1 Someone who ＿＿＿＿ up and ＿＿＿＿ around while asleep is called a sleepwalker.
2 When people in hot countries ＿＿＿＿ or ＿＿＿＿ after lunch, it's called having a siesta.
3 Animals that ＿＿＿＿ don't ＿＿＿＿ at all while they spend the winter in a deep sleep.
4 When you ＿＿＿＿ awake at night and you can't ＿＿＿＿ asleep, you have insomnia.
5 If someone ＿＿＿＿ about a place as 'sleepy', it means that nothing much ＿＿＿＿ there.
6 When you ＿＿＿＿ softly to help a child ＿＿＿＿ to sleep, you are singing a lullaby.
7 People who ＿＿＿＿ very noisily when they are sleeping.

动词后接间接宾语（indirect object）或从句

8 动词后接间接宾语

有些动词后面有两个宾语：间接宾语和直接宾语（direct object）。在使用 **send** 之类的动词时，间接宾语可以紧跟在动词之后（1），或跟在介词 **to** 之后（2）。间接宾语（如 **you, Joe, everyone**）是直接宾语（如 **message, note, form**）的接收者。

   1   *I'll send you a message. • She handed Joe the note. • Did you give everyone a form?*
   2   *I'll send a message to you. • She handed the note to Joe. • Did you give a form to everyone?*

此类动词还有：**bring, lend, offer, pass, post, read, sell, show, teach, tell, throw, write**。
不要把 **to** + 间接宾语放在直接宾语之前。（不说 *Did you give to everyone a form?*）

在使用 **buy** 之类的动词时，间接宾语可以紧跟在动词之后（3），或跟在介词 **for** 之后（4）。间接宾语（如 **him, me, you**）表示动词（如 **buy, do, make**）所示行为的受益者。

   3   *She bought him a tie. • Can you do me a favour? • I'll make you a sandwich.*
   4   *She bought a tie for him. • Can you do a favour for me? • I'll make a sandwich for you.*

此类动词还有：**build, cook, cut, draw, fetch, find, get, keep, leave, order, pick, save**。
不要把 **for** + 间接宾语放在直接宾语之前。（不说 *I'll make for you a sandwich.*）

把较短的宾语，尤其是代词，放在较长的宾语之前（5）。在动词后使用两个代词作为双宾语（不使用介词）时，间接宾语在前（6）。

   5   *Show me the prize you won. • Show it to everyone who said you couldn't do it. • Show it to them!*
   6   *Show me it.* （不说 *Show it me.* ） *• I'll make you one.* （不说 *I'll make one you.* ）

有些动词，如 **describe** 和 **explain**，其间接宾语要跟在介词之后，不能直接跟在动词之后。也请注意与本页最后一部分的例句（14）进行比较。

   7   *He described the man to them. • He explained the plan to us.* （不说 *He explained us the plan.* ）

类似的动词还有：**admit, announce, mention, murmur, report, shout, suggest, whisper**。
注意，这类动词通常与说话有关：*He said 'Hello' to me.* （不说 *He said me 'Hello'.* ）

还有一些动词，如 **cost**，其间接宾语必须紧跟在动词之后。

   8   *The mistake cost us a lot of money. • They fined him £250. • I bet you £5.* （不说 *I bet £5 to you.* ）

此类动词还有：**forgive, grudge, refuse**。

9 动词后接从句

that 从句可以用作直接宾语，跟在 **believe** 或 **think** 等用于表达想法的动词之后（9），以及 **say** 或 **explain** 等转述动词之后（10）。

   9   *They believed that the sun went round the earth. • He thinks that the students are lazy.*
  10 *She said that she would be late. • He explained that there was no money left.*

注意，**that** 常被省略：*He thinks the students are lazy.*

在转述疑问的动词之后，可以用 **if, whether**（11）或 **wh-** 疑问词（12）引导从句。

  11 *The teacher asked if anyone was absent. • They enquired whether it was legal or not.*
  12 *We should ask what it costs. • I wonder when they'll make the decision.*

在 **remind, tell** 等某些转述动词之后，必须先加间接宾语，再加从句。

  13 *I'll remind him that you're here. • You told me that he was ill.* （不说 *You told that he was ill.* ）

此类转述动词还有：**assure, convince, inform, notify, persuade**。

在 **admit** 等某些转述动词之后，要在从句前面的间接宾语之前加 **to**。

  14 *He admitted to the police that he had stolen the money.* （不说 *He admitted the police that he had stolen the money.* ） *• She mentioned to me that she hated her job.* （不说 *She mentioned me that she hated her job.* ）

此类转述动词还有：**boast, confess, declare, hint, propose, reveal**。

→ 转述疑问句 154　转述动词 152　that 从句 161　动词和宾语 6

K 完成下列句子，使其与所给句子的意思尽可能接近。

♦ They had it. Now we have it.
  They gave it to us. (OR They gave us it.)

1 She quietly wished him, 'Good luck.'
  She whispered _____.

2 She was ordered by the judge to pay £700 for speeding.
  The judge fined _____.

3 The farmer wouldn't give permission to us to walk across his field.
  The farmer refused _____.

4 James took Caroline's book. He told me.
  James confessed _____.

L 选择合适的动词并用其恰当形式填空，在必要的地方补充恰当的代词和介词。如有必要请查词典。

| find | offer | reserve | sell | spread | transmit |
| keep | require | retrieve | ~~send~~ | transfer | ~~transport~~ |

♦ Your boxes will be *transported* _____ by air. We will *send them to* _____ you soon.

1 In a restaurant, if a table is _____, that means the restaurant is _____ a special person or group.

2 Contagious diseases are easily _____. People with contagious diseases can easily _____ the rest of the population.

3 Those computer files that I thought I had lost were _____ by Andrew. I was so glad that he _____ me.

4 In football, when a player is _____, it means that one team _____ another team.

5 In a university, if certain courses are _____, it means that all students must take those courses and the university must _____ students every year.

M 改正下文中的错误。

During the psychology class, one student reported ~~us~~ her experiment ˄*to us* She explained us that it was about communication between husbands and wives. The researcher gave the following information half of the husbands. 'Your wife has described you a holiday trip to China. One of her friends told to her about it. You think sounds like a really good idea, so you ask to her some questions about the cost.' The other group of husbands heard the following information. 'Your wife has suggested you a holiday trip to China. You don't like. You believe is a really bad idea, so you ask some questions her about the cost.' The researcher didn't tell to the wives she said to the husbands. She asked the wives to listen to the recording of their husbands' questions and decide the husbands thought it was a good idea or not. A significant number of the wives couldn't decide. That was very surprising.

系动词

⑩ 系动词和补语

一些系动词，如 **be** 和 **seem**，后接用来描写或说明主语的补语。补语可以是形容词（1）、名词（短语）（2）或介词短语（3）。

1 *His parents were Welsh.* • *That isn't funny!* • *It doesn't seem possible.* • *You sound unhappy.*
2 *I am a student.* • *Anna became my best friend.* • *Despite the scandal, he remained president.*
3 *She said she was on a diet.* • *He seemed in a good mood.* • *Sometimes I feel like an idiot.*

"系动词"在英语中的对应词一般为 linking verb，但也可以用 copula 或 copular verb 表示。

seem 和 **appear** 可用作系动词，并与动词不定式连用（4）。使用 **seem** 时，也可以省略 **to be**，直接用形容词或名词短语作补语（5）。**seem** 不如 **appear** 正式。

4 *Bill seems to have no friends.* • *There appears to be a problem.* （不说 ~~There appears a problem.~~）
5 *The old man seemed (to be) lost.* • *Equal pay for everyone seems (to be) the best solution.*

在美式英语中，不省略 **seem** 之后的 **to be**：*He seemed to be a hard-working student.*

描述感官体验的动词（如 **feel, smell, taste**）和形容看法的动词（如 **look, sound**）可以用作系动词，后跟形容词（6），或与 **like** 搭配并后接名词短语（7）。

6 *I feel great!* • *You look much better.* • *The food didn't smell good and it tasted terrible.*
7 *Her suggestion sounded like a good idea.* • *Your drawing looks like a cat.* （不说 ~~Your drawing looks a cat.~~）

使用某些动词（如 **make, find, call**）时，可以在宾语之后使用形容词或名词短语作宾语的补语，描述宾语的情况或补充与宾语相关的信息。

8 *That makes me angry.* • *They found the exam difficult.* • *She called him a fool.*

注意语序：*Let's paint the wall white.* （不说 ~~Let's paint white the wall.~~）

⑪ 用系动词表达变化

become 和 **get** 可用作系动词，谈论变化的结果。

9 *The world is becoming / getting more crowded.* • *Everything will get worse before it gets better.*

become（不是 **get**）用作系动词时，后面可以跟名词性的补语（10）。**get**（不是 **become**）则用在很多常见的描述行为的短语中（11）。**get** 不如 **become** 正式。

10 *Traffic delays have become a problem.* • *We became friends.* （不说 ~~We became to be friends.~~）
11 *They won't get married.* • *He got dressed quickly.* • *Let's get ready.* （不说 ~~Let's become ready.~~）

可用 **go** 和 **turn** 来谈论变化（12）。**turn into** + 名词短语用于说明状态的彻底改变（13）。

12 *I'll go crazy if I have to wait.* • *Our dog is going blind.* • *She turned pale.* • *The light turned green.*
13 *Joe turned into a health fanatic.* • *The caterpillar turned into a butterfly.* （不说 ~~The caterpillar turned a butterfly.~~）

come 和 **grow** 作系动词时，可与形容词构成常用于形容较慢变化的短语，有 **suddenly** 或 **unexpectedly** 等副词修饰时除外（14）。**come** 和 **grow** 也可以用在动词不定式之前，描述逐渐发生的变化（15）。

14 *Dreams come true.* • *People grow old.* • *The days grew warmer.* • *The knot suddenly came loose.*
15 *As we came to know her better, we grew to like her a lot. We came to see things as she did.*

一些动词（如 **keep, remain, stay**）可用作系动词，谈论保持不变的状况。

16 *Please keep quiet.* • *She kept busy.* • *Everything remained the same.* • *We tried to stay warm.*

注意，此类系动词不与 **to be** 连用。（不说 ~~I'll keep to be quiet~~ • ~~We stayed to be awake.~~）

→ 形容词 111　动词不定式 139　含有 get 的被动式 65

N 为问题（1—5）选择合适的答语（a—f），再选择合适的系动词并用其恰当形式填空。

> appear   ~~be~~   feel   look   sound   taste

◆ What _is_ he like?　　　　　　　(_d_)　a　Angry and impatient.
1　Who does she _____ like?　　( )　b　I'm sure he was smiling.
2　How does it _____?　　　　( )　c　No, it's more like chicken.
3　Did he _____ to be happy?　( )　~~d~~　He's kind and generous.
4　How did he _____?　　　　( )　e　Soft and comfortable.
5　Does it _____ fishy?　　　( )　f　The actor Scarlett Johansson.

O 为每个段落选择一组合适的动词，将段落补全，动词形式要使用恰当。

> appear / be / look / turn　　~~seem~~ / smell / taste / ~~think~~
> become / get / make / seem　　feel / get / stay / turn

A　The writer of the guide book ◆_seemed to think_____ that the Maharani restaurant had the best Indian food. In her description, she wrote, 'All the dishes were full of fragrance and flavour.' In other words, she thought the food ¹_____ wonderful and ²_____ delicious.

B　In her late teens, Hannah fell in love with James Covington and wanted to ³_____ married, but that topic always ⁴_____ him uncomfortable. To her intense disappointment, he later decided to ⁵_____ a priest.

C　Elena was reading a novel with a red dragon on the cover. It ⁶_____ like a large lizard with wings. The novel was a horror story, she said, full of people who ⁷_____ living normal lives, but were actually vampires, and one character who ⁸_____ into a werewolf during the night of a full moon.

D　I didn't want the bananas to ⁹_____ too ripe and then ¹⁰_____ soft or squishy when I wanted to eat them, so I put them in the fridge. I was just hoping that they would ¹¹_____ firm, but I didn't realize that the skins would ¹²_____ black.

P 改正下文中系动词用法有误的地方。

One Saturday afternoon when my younger sister Mona and I were teenagers, I was ~~becoming~~ _getting_ ready to go to a party. Mona hadn't been invited. It appeared a big problem for her. She went to be crazy because of it. She found some hair dye and she just decided to make blonde her hair, but she didn't do it right and her hair turned into bright orange. It also became orange her face, so she looked like really strange. When my mother saw her, she said Mona looked an orange balloon. After that, Mona got to be very upset and she started screaming with her hands over her ears. I just kept to be quiet during all that. My mother eventually calmed her down and we got some darker hair dye to make it look like better.

并列复合句和主从复合句

Q 将恰当例句的序号填入对应的方格中。

12 并列复合句

一个并列复合句包含两个 □2 或更多 □1 分句，分句由并列连词 **and, but, or** 等连接。

1 *You can take the bus or stay here and I'll drive you tomorrow, but I'm not driving tonight.*
2 *Dave slept and I read. • It wasn't cold, but I was shivering. • You must help us or we will fail.*

在并列复合句中，后面的分句通常略去与第一个分句相同的主语 □，相同的主语和动词 □，或相同的主语和助动词 □。

3 *They played well, but _ lost. (They played well, but they lost.) • Martin smiled, _ shrugged his shoulders and _ said nothing. (Martin smiled, he shrugged his shoulders and he said nothing.)*
4 *She will come and _ get those later. • You can take it or _ leave it. • I am waiting and _ hoping.*
5 *They have a cat or _ a dog. • I like swimming, _ football and _ watching TV.*

略去句中主语和 / 或其他部分的语法现象被称为省略。

通常省略后面分句中的助动词之后与第一个分句相同的动词和宾语 □；但倾向于略去前面分句中与后面重复的宾语和 / 或介词短语 □。

6 *I'll wash _ and peel the potatoes. • The McGregors have lived _ and died in Crieff for centuries.*
7 *I wasn't making a noise and the others were _. • They may forget you, but I never will _.*

在并列复合句中，可使用不同的连词组合强调两个分句之间的关系。它们可以表示补充 □、选择 □、并列 □ 或否定意思的并列 □。

8 *They not only clean houses, but also do repairs, painting and other odd jobs.*
9 *You can both turn the TV on and change channels with the remote control.*
10 *I will neither sleep nor rest until this is over. • He neither speaks English nor understands it.*
11 *You can either go with us or stay here alone. • They must either pay you or give you time off.*

13 主从复合句

使用从属连词，如 **because, before, that, which** 等，连接两个或更多分句，可以构成主从复合句。

12 *I couldn't sleep because I was thinking about all the work that I had to do before I could leave.*

注意，在上面的例句中，同一个主语在几个分句中重复出现。(不说 ~~I couldn't sleep because was thinking.~~)

其他从属连词如：**although, as, if, in order that, since, when, who**。

主从复合句包含关系从句 □、名词性从句 □ 或状语从句 □。可将状语从句置于主从复合句句首，后面加一个逗号 □。

13 *I didn't realize that Noah wasn't feeling well. • Did you know that he was married?*
14 *She liked the women with whom she worked, but she hated the dirty jobs which they had to do.*
15 *I had a shower after I ran. • He's still working although he's 79. • We won't play if it rains.*
16 *If it rains, the ground will be too muddy. • Although he's 79, he still walks to work every day.*

14 并列–主从复合句（compound-complex sentence）

同时使用并列连词和从属连词连接三个或更多分句，可以构成并列–主从复合句。

17 *We hit a lamp post and it shattered the glass on the front door before I managed to bring the bus to a halt.*
18 *Harvold said, 'I was so relieved that no one else was hurt, but I hoped the driver would survive.'*

→ 状语从句 197　either 和 neither 89　省略 106　名词性从句 161　关系从句 173

R 为句子的前半句（1—4）选择合适的后半句（a—d），并在横线处补充连词 and, but 或 or。

1 You can leave now   (......)   a _____ she can also read _____ write it.
2 He says he needs a knife   (......)   b _____ dries them straight away.
3 She not only speaks Arabic,   (......)   c _____ stay _____ help us finish the job.
4 Rob usually washes the dishes   (......)   d _____ scissors to open the package.

S 选择合适的动词或"主语 + 动词"填空。

| came | got | had | seemed | ~~stopped~~ | talked |
| she came | he got | we had | it seemed | it stopped | we talked |

◆ Police allowed protests outside the meeting, but *stopped* _____ people trying to get inside.
1 When _____ about religion or politics, _____ very excited.
2 After _____ home from her trip, we sat and _____ for hours.
3 _____ easier in the past because people just met, _____ married and _____ kids.
4 If she got up early enough and _____ downstairs, _____ breakfast together.
5 The dog ran over to the door where _____ and _____ to be waiting for us to open it.

T 选择合适的词填空，补全下列释义。

| ~~heartache~~ | heartbeat | heartburn | and (×2) | because | or | | who |
| heart attack | heartbreak | heart-throb | as | ~~or~~ | which (×2) | whom |

◆ *Heartache* _____ is a feeling of great sorrow, anxiety ◆ *or* _____ worry.

Your [1] _____ is the action [2] _____ sound of your heart [3] _____ it pumps blood through your body.

[4] _____ is a feeling of great sadness [5] _____ something bad has happened, such as the end of a love affair or the loss of a life.

A [6] _____ is a famous actor or singer [7] _____ is very attractive [8] _____ with [9] _____ people fall in love.

A [10] _____ is a sudden illness in [11] _____ the heart beats violently. It causes great pain [12] _____ sometimes death.

[13] _____ is a burning sensation in the chest [14] _____ is caused by indigestion.

U 选择合适的词或短语填空，补全下面这段描述。注意应使用动词的恰当形式。

| and | because | but | if | ~~which~~ | who | live | not like | see | tell |

A Neighbourhood Watch is an arrangement by ◆ *which* _____ people [1] _____ [2] _____ in a particular street or area watch each other's houses [3] _____ [4] _____ the police [5] _____ they [6] _____ anything suspicious. Many people have formed local Neighbourhood Watch groups to try to prevent crime, [7] _____ others have refused to join them [8] _____ they [9] _____ the idea of being watched by their neighbours.

This is a NEIGHBOURHOOD WATCH AREA

测验

A 选出最恰当的词或短语完成下列句子。

1 He couldn't rest or sleep because ＿＿＿＿ too much coffee.
   a drinking **b** been drinking **c** had been drinking **d** he had been drinking

2 My brother, together with his friends, always ＿＿＿＿ round collecting wood for bonfire night.
   a go **b** goes **c** going **d** gone

3 Some of the girls in my group are surprised that I don't wear make-up, but I don't ＿＿＿＿.
   a wear **b** care **c** do **d** like

4 The team all wanted coffee so I made ＿＿＿＿.
   a it them **b** some it **c** some them **d** them some

5 The director ＿＿＿＿ to us that there had been financial problems earlier in the year.
   a concluded **b** offered **c** revealed **d** told

B 从每句标有下划线的部分（A，B，C，D）中选出错误的一项。

1 The tour of the palace included a visit to the old kitchen where they were baking bread and the
huge underground wine cellar which was containing thousands of bottles and felt like a prison.

2 None of the children wants to be in the group that has to stay inside because everyone prefer to
go outside and play.

3 The old ladies were collecting money for people who needed some help at Christmas so, after
my wife and I discussed it, we decided to put £20 their collection box.

4 Elaine handed Michael the letter that someone had sent her and told him to read it to me, but I
asked him to show it me because I wanted to see the signature.

5 When Fox became president, this seemed to be the first thing that made happy all the young
people, especially those who had felt angry with the old government leaders.

C 选择合适的动词并用其恰当形式填空。将剩余的词或短语也填入横线处适当的位置。

begin	catch	give	include	sneeze	fever	in November	it	the flu

Anyone who has a history of health problems and people who are 65 or older should get
a flu vaccination every year before the flu season [1] ＿＿＿＿＿＿＿＿＿＿＿＿＿＿＿＿.
Flu, or influenza, is a serious infection of the nose, throat and lungs. Symptoms
[2] ＿＿＿＿＿＿＿＿＿＿＿＿＿＿＿＿, cough, runny nose, sore throat, headache and tiredness.
Anyone can [3] ＿＿＿＿＿＿＿＿＿ and [4] ＿＿＿＿＿＿＿＿＿ to others.
It is spread when an infected person coughs or [5] ＿＿＿＿＿＿＿＿＿＿＿＿.

D 完成下列句子，使其与所给句子的意思尽可能接近。

1　Nick told one of the detectives that he had taken the cash box.
Nick admitted ....

2　The police said it was too dangerous and we were convinced.
The police persuaded ....

3　After the princess kissed the frog, he suddenly became a prince.
The frog suddenly turned ....

4　Two hours won't be enough to finish the job, he said to us.
He told ....

5　The wall is white. Someone did it yesterday.
Someone painted ....

E 选择合适的动词并搭配选项中合适的补语填空，注意应使用动词的恰当形式。

> be (×2)　become　seem　stand　alone　better　clear　quite satisfied　ready

Donald's presence certainly made a big difference to the speed we arose that day. There was no question of Tam lounging about in bed until the last minute, and we
[1] .... for work by half past seven. Donald had his own map of the job, with all the fences marked out in red ink, and the first thing he did was go for a tour of inspection, accompanied by me. We followed the hill up to the summit, and then came down by way of the cross-fence, Donald all the time checking for wire tension and, of course, straightness. When we got to the encircling fence he [2] .... with what he'd seen.

'Hmm, quite professional,' he said.

After a while we came to the gateway that [3] .... Donald looked at it for a moment, and then said, 'Yes, I always think it [4] .... to do the gate first and build the fences round it.'

Donald had put on some overalls, and it soon [5] .... that he intended to work alongside us during his visit.

2 时态 (tense)

时态是动词形式和动词表示的行为或状态发生的时间之间的关系。常通过将助动词 **be, have** 与其他动词连用来构成不同的时态。关于时态和相关的动词形式，参见第 **17** 页的表格。

A 阅读下文中的第一段，并找出：

1 一个含助动词 be 的句子；

2 一个含助动词 have 的句子。

A This October 31st is a scary day for Jake Barnes, not just because it is Halloween, but because it is a special anniversary for him. For several years he will have been trying
5 to turn a good idea into a successful online business. He won't be doing anything special to celebrate the occasion, mainly because his business venture won't have made any money for most of the past year.
10 Like his two business partners before him, he will soon need to do something else.

B When they started, it had seemed like such a great idea. Jake and his friend, Michael Underwood, had been writing up their
15 lecture notes as complete sets, with review sheets and sample tests, and selling them to other students. They had used that money to pay for complete sets of notes from other big lecture classes, which they then sold
20 to an eager population of new students. They were starting to make a small steady profit when they met Isaac Lloyd. Isaac had been creating free blogs for his friends, then larger websites, and he showed them how
25 to do it too. Using the initials of their last names, they created 'Bullnotes', established a website, and set out to become entrepreneurs of the information age.

C They soon found that students were
30 looking for more than lecture notes. They needed to do other things that they weren't learning in their classes. Imagine that you are applying for a scholarship. You have been trying to write a letter of application
35 and you can't get it right. You need an example of the kind of letter you are trying to write. Or maybe someone has asked you to write a letter of recommendation. From the website you could download the basic form
40 of the letter with spaces in it for your own details. 'I am writing this letter in support of .... whom I have known for .... years', and so on.

D Soon there were all kinds of forms available
45 from Bullnotes, from passport application forms to those for making a will. Jake was working day and night to make the material available, but he didn't think about what he was doing in terms of a business.
50 The big problem, they soon discovered, is that everyone wants these things, but no one wants to pay for them. In what turned out to be a common experience for many people who tried to create businesses,
55 they had a successful website, but they didn't really make any money from it.

E Then one of the giants of the Internet created an app that did many of the same things. Isaac quickly found a highly paid job
60 with an investment company and Michael went off to work for a software manufacturer. Jake is still looking for a way to make Bullnotes work as a business, but these days he is always counting his pennies and
65 he is having a hard time paying his bills. He has thought about taking a teaching job after seeing an ad for a teacher of business writing with business experience. He has lots of experience now and there really won't
70 be a problem with the letter of application.

B 选择合适的句子作为上文各段（A—E）的结尾句，将对应段落的字母序号填入括号。

1 They were ready to become millionaires. (.......)
2 He also knows where to find some good lecture notes. (.......)
3 Everyone acted as if the information was free. (.......)
4 He will have to find a job. (.......)
5 Writing was a couple of clicks, then a fill-in-the-blanks exercise. (.......)

16

动词、助动词和时态

词典中列出的动词形式为原形（base form），可用于祈使语气（imperative）和动词不定式。

  1 *Stop! • Please wait. • Don't be impatient. • Ask someone to help you. • Let's try to find a solution.*

动词原形有时也叫不带 **to** 的动词不定式（infinitive without *to* 或 bare infinitive）。

大多数动词用于描述行为或事件（2），一些动词用于描述状态（3）。

  2 *Do you play chess? • I'll open a window. • Someone has taken my book. • The crowd is cheering.*
  3 *Do you know Mark? • Anil seems really nice. • Her parents own a shop. • I believe you.*

状态动词通常不使用进行时（continuous / progressive）形式。（不说 *I'm believing you.*）

使用一般现在时或一般过去时时，将助动词 **do** 与动词原形连用，构成疑问句和否定句。

  4 *What did Anna want for lunch? ~ She didn't want anything. • Does she feel better? ~ I don't know.*

助动词 **be** 与动词的现在分词（present participle，也称为 -ing 形式）连用，构成进行时形式（5）；助动词 **have** 与动词的过去分词（past participle，也称为 -ed 形式）连用，构成完成时（perfect）形式（6）。助动词 **have** + **been** 与现在分词连用，构成完成进行时形式（7）。

  5 *Are you waiting for me? • William isn't using his computer. • They were working all night.*
  6 *Have you finished already? • The parcel hasn't come yet. • Andy had forgotten to bring the keys.*
  7 *Have you been sleeping? • It hasn't been raining recently. • We had been studying for hours.*

情态动词与动词原形连用，或与助动词 **be** 和 **have** 连用。

  8 *They will help us. • I'll be waiting for you. • We won't have finished.* （不说 *We won't finished.*）

C 再读一读第 16 页的文章，就下列关于动词形式的描述各找出一个例子，完成列表。

祈使语气或动词不定式：动词原形	*play*
一般现在时：动词原形 　　　　　第三人称单数形式	*play* *plays*
现在进行时：**be** 的现在式 + 现在分词	*am / is / are playing*
现在完成时：**have** 的现在式 + 过去分词	*has / have played*
现在完成进行时：**have** 的现在式 + **been** + 现在分词	*has / have been playing*
一般过去时：动词原形 + **-ed**（常见形式）	*played*
过去进行时：**be** 的过去式 + 现在分词	*was / were playing*
过去完成时：**have** 的过去式 + 过去分词	*had played*
过去完成进行时：**have** 的过去式 + **been** + 现在分词	*had been playing*
表示将来：**will** + 动词原形	*will play*
将来进行时：**will** + **be** + 现在分词	*will be playing*
将来完成时：**will** + **have** + 过去分词	*will have played*
将来完成进行时：**will** + **have** + **been** + 现在分词	*will have been playing*

关于规则动词和不规则动词的词形变化，参见第 **258** 页和第 **259** 页。

→ 情态动词 29　行为动词和状态动词 3

现在时（present）和现在完成时（present perfect）

1 一般现在时（present simple）和现在进行时（present continuous）

一般现在时主要用于表示一直存在的情况（1）和总体上真实的情况（2）。

1　*Giraffes live in Africa. They have very long legs and necks. They feed on acacia leaves.*
2　*It rains more in winter. • Birds don't sing at night. • Do women live longer than men?*

一般现在时也用于谈论习惯（3）和定期发生的事（4），描述当前的状态（5），或用在非正式的报告或指示中（6）。

3　*I bite my nails. • She smokes cigars. • Does he usually wear white socks with black shoes?*
4　*They play tennis on Monday nights. • Her parents go to Majorca every summer.*
5　*She loves chocolate. • They don't believe us. • He owns his flat.*（不说 *He is owning his flat.*）
6　*It says here the strike is over. • Baker passes to Cook who shoots. • You go to the end and turn left.*

通过言语实施的行为，如承诺做某事，通常用一般现在时，而不是现在进行时。

7　*I accept their decision. • I promise to be more careful.*（不说 *I'm promising to be more careful.*）

此类动词还有：**admit, apologize, bet, deny, insist, regret**。

现在进行时用于描述正在发生的行为，或谈论正在进行的活动。

8　*Hi. I'm calling to let you know I'm coming, but it's snowing and the traffic is moving slowly.*

在描述当前情况时，如果想描述长期存在的情况，用一般现在时（9）；如果想描述暂时的情况，则用现在进行时（10）。

9　*My brother Oliver lives in London and works for a magazine. He writes about economics.*
10　*My sister Fiona is living with Oliver just now. She isn't working yet. She's looking for a job.*

可用 **be** 和 **have** 的一般现在式表述一贯的情况或状态（11），用它们的现在进行式表述暂时的或特殊的情形（12）。

11　*Emilia's normally a quiet person. She has a gentle voice.*（不说 *She's having a gentle voice.*）
12　*Emilia's being wild tonight. She's having a graduation party.*（不说 *She has a party.*）

2 （一般）现在完成时和现在完成进行时（present perfect continuous）

一般现在完成时可用于谈论或描述开始于过去并与现在有联系的行为或情况（13），也可用于表达"迄今为止的任意时间"的含义（14）。可以与状态动词搭配使用（15）。

13　*How long have you worked here? ~ I've worked here since 2007.*（不说 *I work here since 2007.*）
14　*This is the best coffee I have ever tasted. • I haven't been to an opera, but I've seen one on TV.*
15　*I have known Anthony for about five years.*（不说 *I know him for five years. / I've been knowing him for five years.*）

现在完成进行时用于谈论到现在为止一直在进行的活动（16），或用于询问或描述到现在为止持续了一段时间的行为（17）。

16　*They've been repairing our street and it's been causing a lot of traffic problems.*
17　*Have you been waiting long? ~ I've been sitting here for an hour.*（不说 *Are you waiting long?*）

用现在完成进行时描述到目前为止仿佛在持续不断发生的行为（或情况）（18）。用一般现在完成时描述一系列独立的行为（19）。

18　*He's been calling for you. • It has been raining a lot recently.*（不说 *It's raining a lot recently.*）
19　*He has called four times and he has asked for you each time.*（不说 *He has been calling four times.*）

可用现在完成进行时将某行为描述为一个从过去一直持续到现在的过程（20），或用一般现在完成时来体现现在某事是过去的行为带来的结果（21）。

20　*We've been making chicken soup. That's why the kitchen is hot and steamy.*
21　*We've made chicken soup. That's what everyone is eating. Would you like some?*

→ 状态动词 3

D 将三组动词分别填入下列各段中，动词应使用一般现在式或现在进行式。

> know / look / not be / repair / use   ~~be~~ / be / have / say / tell
> be / live / look / move / resemble

A My computer ♦ *is being* _____ very irritating right now. Every time I ¹ _____ it to save something, it ² _____ it ³ _____ no free memory, which ⁴ _____ ridiculous.

B Whales and dolphins ⁵ _____ like fish, but they ⁶ _____ mammals that ⁷ _____ in the ocean and ⁸ _____ through water in ways that ⁹ _____ the movements of a dog rather than those of a shark.

C **Man:** Excuse me. I ¹⁰ _____ for Mrs Adamson, but she ¹¹ _____ in her usual classroom. ¹² _____ you _____ where she is?
  Woman: Oh, they ¹³ _____ her classroom ceiling this week so she ¹⁴ _____ the library as her classroom.

E 选择合适的名词和动词填空，动词应使用现在完成式。如有必要请查词典。

> also-ran   hat-trick   buy   not come   say   train
> has-been   no-show   hear   not finish   take   win

1 Colin _____ the race for the second year in a row and he _____ that he will come back and try to make it a _____ next year.

2 An '_____' is an informal expression for a person or a horse that _____ part in a competition or a race, but _____ first, second or third.

3 Wilson says he _____ people describe him negatively as a '_____', but he _____ hard this year to prove that he's still one of the best.

4 A '_____' is an informal expression for someone who _____ a ticket for an event, a journey, etc., but who _____ to the event.

F 为问题（1—4）选择合适的答语（a—d），再选择合适的动词并用其（一般）现在完成式或现在完成进行式填空。

> be   complete   do   know   read   show   swim

1 How long _____ she and Mark _____ each other? ( )
2 Why is your hair all wet? ( )
3 _____ you _____ an application form? ( )
4 _____ you _____ Joseph the report yet? ( )

a Yes, he _____ it for the past hour.
b I _____ just _____.
c They _____ friends since school.
d Yes, I _____ already _____ that.

G 改正下文中的错误。

My neighbour is called Jeanine. She ~~is coming~~ *comes* from Belgium. She is living here since 2012 and she says she has been going back to visit her family in Belgium only once. She's having an accent that is the same as people who are coming from France, but I never ask her if she is speaking French. She is really liking to go to the theatre and she is inviting me to go with her one Saturday. In the short time I am knowing her, we become good friends.

过去时（past）和过去完成时（past perfect）

3 一般过去时（past simple）和过去进行时（past continuous）

一般过去时用于谈论过去已完成的行为（1）或过去的状态（2）。

1　*Dickens wrote* Oliver Twist. • *Edison invented the light bulb.* • *The Beatles sang 'Yesterday'.*

2　*Life seemed easier then.* • *That ring belonged to my mother.* （不说 *It was belonging to my mother.*）

一般过去时用于谈论在过去先后发生的两个或多个行为，尤其是在记叙中。

3　*I tripped and landed on my knees.* • *He knocked her down, grabbed her purse and ran off.* • *He took off his hat and came forward. The floorboards creaked under his boots.*

谈论过去的习惯或突出与现在的反差，可使用 **used to**（4）。其否定形式是 **didn't use to** 或（更正式的）**used not to**（5）。也可用 **would** 谈论过去某段时间内经常发生的行为或活动（6）。

4　*There used to be a shop on the corner.* • *He used to smoke a lot.* （不说 *He was used to smoke a lot.*）

5　*Didn't they use to hang people?* • *We didn't use to have a car.* • *They used not to be enemies.*

6　*In summer, we would take trips to the country. We would sometimes buy fresh strawberries.*

过去进行时用于描述过去某个具体时间正在发生的行为。

7　*What were you doing at 8.30 last night? ~ I wasn't doing anything special. I was just reading.* • *During the 1890s, many people were leaving the south and moving to the north to look for work.*

某些动词（如 **wonder, hope**）使用过去进行时以后可以更加礼貌地表达请求。

8　*I was wondering when I could talk to you.* • *We were hoping you might have a free moment.*

若想把过去的活动描述为一系列单独的行为，可用一般过去时（9）；若想描述为仿佛在持续不断发生的行为，可用过去进行时（10）。许多情况下，一般过去时和过去进行时可以相互替换。

9　*Usually she went to the library about once a week and only studied occasionally for tests.*

10　*Before the final exam, however, she was going to the library and studying every single day.*

在含 **when / while** 分句的句子中，可在一个分句中用过去进行时描述一种活动，该活动在另一个分句的行为发生前就开始了（11）。后发生的行为可能导致已发生的活动中断（12）。

11　*While he was driving, I fell asleep.* • *We saw Henry while we were walking in the park.*

12　*I was listening to the news when she phoned.* • *When I was running, I slipped and fell.*

注意这两个句子的不同：*When she came back, we were watching TV*（她回来之前，我们已经在看电视了）和 *When she came back, we watched TV*（她回来之后，我们才看电视）。

4 （一般）过去完成时和过去完成进行时（past perfect continuous）

过去完成时也称为 pluperfect。如果在用一般过去时描述一个行为时，想谈及此行为之前发生的另一个行为，用一般过去完成时（13）。如果转述动词或表示思维活动的动词使用了过去时，该动词引导的分句用一般过去完成时描述更早发生的事件（14）。

13　*We went to his office, but he had left.* • *Lucy didn't have the money because she had spent it.*

14　*Joe told me our team had scored twice.* • *I thought we had won.* （不说 *I thought we have won.*）

过去完成进行时用于表述在过去某事发生之前持续进行的另一件事。

15　*I had been thinking about that before you mentioned it.*

状态动词不使用过去完成进行时。（不说 *I had been knowing about that before you mentioned it.*）

可用过去完成进行时将某行为描述为一个在过去某事发生之前一直持续的过程（16），或用一般过去完成时来体现过去某事是更早发生的行为带来的结果（17）。

16　*We had been making chicken soup so the kitchen was still hot and steamy when she came in.*

17　*We had made chicken soup and so we offered her some when she came in.*

→ 转述动词 152　状态动词 3　when / while 引导的从句 198　would 33

H 为每个段落选择一组合适的动词，用其一般过去式或过去进行式将段落补全。

> miss / not get / wonder   break / see / steal / teach
> come / ~~listen~~ / make / say   explain / talk / understand

A   We ✦ _were listening_ _____ to music when one of the neighbours [1] _____ to the door and [2] _____ she couldn't sleep because we [3] _____ too much noise.

B   Someone [4] _____ into Hannah's office and [5] _____ her laptop yesterday afternoon while she [6] _____ her history class. No one [7] _____ the thief.

C   Because he never [8] _____ anything very clearly, none of us [9] _____ what the science teacher [10] _____ about most of the time.

D   I'm sorry. I [11] _____ here on time and I [12] _____ the beginning of your presentation, but I [13] _____ if you might have an extra handout left.

I 选择合适的动词填空，动词应使用（一般）过去完成式或过去完成进行式。

> be   catch   live   plan   take   break   have   make   remove   worry

The phone call from the police was a shock, but not a complete surprise. Molly ✦ _had been worrying_ (OR _had worried_) constantly about the old house lying empty during the two months since her mother went into hospital. She [1] _____ to go round and check the empty place, but she [2] _____ extra busy at work recently. According to the police, a squatter [3] _____ into the house. They [4] _____ him one morning as he was leaving the building with one of her mother's large paintings. When Molly walked into the house, it was obvious that the man [5] _____ there for quite a while. He [6] _____ food from the cupboards and throwing empty tins and packages all over the floor. He [7] _____ quite a mess. He [8] _____ also _____ several paintings from the walls. Molly decided not to tell her mother because she [9] _____ already _____ enough pain in recent weeks and really didn't need any more bad news.

J 改正下文中时态用法有误的地方。

A few years ago, when my friend and I were ~~hitchhike~~ _hitchhiking_ through France, we sometimes stop for the night in a park or a field. If it wasn't rain, we just sleep outside in our sleeping bags under the stars. We really enjoying that. If it was rain, we put up our small tent and crawl inside for the night. One night, while we sleep in the tent, I think that the ground moving under me. I sit up and I realize that the tent was try to move and only the weight of our bodies was hold it in place. When we get outside, we discover that we stand ankle-deep in a small stream and our tent slowly floats away. At first, we really surprised and worried, but then we think it is very funny.

现在完成时还是一般过去时?

现在完成时用于表示某情况尚未终止（1），一般过去时表示该情况已经终止（2）。

1　*I have lived in London for a year.* • *She has known him since school.* • *Has Jason been ill?*

2　*I lived in London for a year.* • *She knew him in school.* • *Was Jason ill?*

现在完成时经常与表示"到现在为止的一段时间"的词或短语（如 **lately, so far**）搭配（3）。
一般过去时经常与表示"已经过去的一段时间"的词或短语（如 **last night, yesterday**）搭配（4）。

3　*Have you seen any good films lately?* • *So far the new teacher hasn't given us any homework.*

4　*Did you see that film last night?* • *I didn't do the homework yesterday.*
　（不说 *Have you seen that film last night?* • *I haven't done the homework yesterday.*）

现在完成时用于谈论持续到现在并有可能再次发生的行为（5），一般过去时用于谈论说话者认为不会再发生的行为（6）。

5　*He has written two bestsellers and we hope his next book will do well.* • *He's been on TV; he's famous!* • *He has often had health problems.*

6　*She wrote several books of poetry in the last years of her life.* • *She was a teacher in Zambia.*
　• *She had three children.*

在由 **after, as soon as** 或 **when** 引导的从句中，可用现在完成时表述在将来完成的行为（7），
用一般过去时表述在过去完成的行为（8）。

7　*After / As soon as / When he has made his copies, I will do mine.*（他尚未完成复印，我也没有）

8　*As soon as he made his copies, I did mine.*（他先完成了复印，然后我完成了复印）

K 将三组动词分别填入下列各段中，动词应使用现在完成式或一般过去式。

> have / not come / tell　　become / have / hear　　~~know~~ / meet / start

A　I ♦ *'ve known* _____ Laura Palmer since we both [1] _____ work on the same day
at Thames College about five years ago. She is one of the smartest people I [2] _____
ever _____ .

B　[3] _____ you _____ the good news yet? Jenny and Michael
[4] _____ just _____ parents! Jenny [5] _____
a baby girl last night.

C　The plumber [6] _____ me this morning, 'I'll be back to finish the work as
soon as I [7] _____ some lunch.' But now it's past three o'clock and he still
[8] _____ back.

L 选择合适的动词并用其现在完成式或一般过去式填空，补全下列对话。

> ask　　be　　have　　make　　not call　　not eat
> not know　　not seem　　say　　tell

It's Monday afternoon. Ron is at home, phoning Lucy at the office where they both work.

Ron:　Hi Lucy, it's me.

Lucy:　Well, hello! Where ♦ *have* _____ you *been* _____ all day? The boss
[1] _____ me this morning where you [2] _____ , but he
[3] _____ to be looking for you or anything.

Ron:　What [4] _____ you _____ ?

Lucy:　I [5] _____ him that I [6] _____ . Are you okay?

Ron:　I'm sorry I [7] _____ you this morning. I [8] _____ the flu since
Saturday. I [9] _____ anything for two days and it [10] _____ me
feel really weak. But I'll probably be there tomorrow.

　　　　　　　　　　→ after 等引导的从句 199　一般过去时 20　现在完成时 18

过去完成时还是一般过去时？

谈论过去发生的行为，使用一般过去时（如 **won**）；若想谈论在过去更早的时间发生的行为，使用过去完成时（如 **had won**）。

1 *Jenny Fisher won her first gold medal in 2016. She had won two silver medals in previous Olympics, but this was her first gold.*

若 **when** 从句使用了一般过去时（如 **arrived**），则主句可以用过去完成时（如 **had started**）来描述更早发生的行为（2），或用一般过去时（如 **started**）描述之后发生的行为（3）。

2 *When he arrived in the morning, we had started work.*（他到达之前，我们已经开始工作了）

3 *When he arrived in the morning, we started work.*（他到达之后，我们才开始工作）

注意，主句和从句都使用一般过去时，有时可暗示一种因果关系：*When I called, he came.*

在条件句中，用过去完成时谈论过去实际上没有发生的事情（4），一般过去时则可用于谈论有可能发生（也许可能性不大）的事情（5）。

4 *If you had come, you could have stayed with us.* • *If I'd known, I certainly would have helped.*

5 *If you came, you could stay with us.* • *If I saw anyone doing that, I certainly would try to stop it.*

过去完成时，而不是一般过去时，通常会与一些副词（如 **already, still, just**）搭配。

6 *An ambulance came quickly, but the crash victim had already died.*（不说 ~~The crash victim already died.~~）

7 *The books still hadn't arrived when I left.*（不说 ~~They still didn't arrive when I left.~~）

8 *The students had just opened their books when the fire alarm went off.*

M 为句子的前半句（1—4）选择合适的后半句（a—d），再选择合适的动词并用其过去完成式或一般过去式填空。

come	give	need	not finish	say	talk	work

1 He _____ the money last week, (　) a that you _____ about that already.

2 You _____ during the meeting (　) b so I _____ it to him then.

3 When he _____ back later, (　) c if she _____ harder.

4 Ashley could have done much better (　) d they still _____ writing their reports.

N 选择合适的动词或动词短语填空。

was (×2)	explained	didn't eat	have gone	had cooked	hadn't eaten
were	went	didn't lock	~~have heard~~	had reached	hadn't locked

One of the four-year-olds in the reading group suddenly said, 'This is the silliest story I *'ve* ever *heard* !' I ¹ _____ in the middle of reading Goldilocks and the Three Bears to the group. We ² _____ just _____ the part in the story where Goldilocks goes into the bears' house and eats some of the food from bowls on the table.

'Where ³ _____ the bears?' he asked.

'Maybe outside or playing in the woods,' I suggested.

'And their house was wide open? They ⁴ _____ even _____ the door before going out?'

'Well, in the old days, people ⁵ _____ their doors.'

'And their food was on the table, but they ⁶ _____ it before they ⁷ _____ outside?'

'Maybe they ⁸ _____ it because it ⁹ _____ too hot .'

'If you ¹⁰ _____ that meal, you wouldn't ¹¹ _____ out and left it, would you?'

'Probably not, but it's just a story,' I ¹² _____ rather weakly.

→ already 等副词 116　非真实条件句 186　过去时和过去完成时 20

将来

⭕ 将恰当例句的序号填入对应的方格中。

5 将来：will 和 shall

没有哪种单一的形式被用作将来时态。**will**＋动词原形可用于给出或询问与将来有关的信息 2，或在许诺、提出请求或进行威胁时说明未来可能出现的行动 ☐。其缩约形式（contracted form）常用在代词后（**'ll**）或否定式中（**won't**），但不用于正式表达或表示强调时。

  1　*We'll help you clean up.* • *I won't tell anyone.* • *Will you please go?* • *Stop or I'll call the police.*
  2　*Christmas will be on a Friday.* • *The meeting won't start until 9.30.* • *When will you leave?*

shall 与 **I** 或 **we** 连用，可用于表示决心，或在问句中主动提出做某事或提建议。

  3　*We will forgive, but we shall never forget.* • *Shall I make some tea?* • *Let's talk later, shall we?*

在美式英语中，**I** 和 **we** 与 **will / won't**（不是 ~~shall / shan't~~）连用。

6 将来进行时（future continuous），将来完成时（future perfect）和将来完成进行时（future perfect continuous）

will + be + 现在分词（将来进行时形式）可用来谈论在将来某特定时间正在进行的行为 ☐，也可用来表达计划或打算 ☐。

  4　*I'll be sending in my application tomorrow.* • *Will you be using the car later or can I have it?*
  5　*Next week at this time, you will be lying on the beach and we'll all still be slaving away here.*

will + have + 过去分词（将来完成时形式）用于表示某事在未来某个时间将已经完成或表示说话者认为某事很可能或肯定已经完成 ☐。**will + have been +** 现在分词（将来完成进行时形式）用于展望未来的某个时间，设想某种情况从某一时间开始一直持续到该时间 ☐。

  6　*On the 10th of this month, I'll have been living here for exactly two years.*
  7　*By next summer I'll have finished my degree.* • *It's 5.30. Will Jay have left work already?*

7 will 还是 be going to？

will 用于表述根据过去的经验或已有知识作出的预测 ☐，尤其是用在预测条件句中 ☐。**be going to** 用于表述根据现在的感受或想法作出的预测 ☐。**would** 或 **was / were going to** 可用于表述在过去作出的预测 ☐。

  8　*Oh, no, I think I'm going to be sick.* • *We've just heard that Kim's going to have a baby.*
  9　*If you eat too much ice cream, you'll be sick.* • *We'll do okay if the test isn't too difficult.*
  10　*As soon as the victorious British team lands at Heathrow, thousands of fans will start celebrating.*
  11　*When I was a teenager, I thought I was going to be a rock star and I would never have to work.*

be going to 还可用于表述已经作好的决定 ☐，**will** 则可用于表述说话当时作出的决定 ☐。

  12　*Her parents have said they're going to pay for her tuition.* • *I've decided I'm going to get a new phone.*
  13　*I need someone to take this to the post office. ~ I'll go!* • *That's the doorbell ~ I'll get it!*

8 用一般现在时和现在进行时表示将来

一般现在时可用于表述按计划表、时间表将会发生的事 ☐，也可用于由从属连词引导的从句，表述将来的行为 ☐。现在进行时可用于表述已经计划好或安排好将要做的事 ☐。

  14　*I'm seeing the doctor on Friday.* • *We're playing tomorrow.*（不说 ~~It's snowing tomorrow.~~）
  15　*It won't matter what he says later.* • *I'll see you when I get back.*（不说 ~~I'll see you when I will get back.~~）
  16　*The new course starts in January.* • *I think Kate's flight arrives tomorrow morning.*

→ 预测条件句 185　从属连词 12　will, would, be going to, shall 32

P 为左侧的句子（1—4）选择合适的下文（a—d），并在横线处补充 will, will be 或 will have been。

1 Next April 21st .... my parent's silver anniversary. (......)

2 I'm sure everyone .... want to get an early start. (......)

3 Mr Russell .... teaching his last English classes during May. (......)

4 My life as a student .... over at the end of this term. (......)

a By then, he .... working here for 40 years.

b That means they .... married for 25 years.

c Do you realize that I .... in school for most of my life so far?

d .... you ready to leave at about 6 a.m.?

Q 用下列动词最恰当的形式填空。可搭配 will 或 be going to 的某种形式，或使用动词的一般现在式。

| be | give | ~~have~~ | make | not start | not stop |

I was standing at the bus stop reading my horoscope in the newspaper. It said, 'You ♦ *will have* .... good moments and bad moments today.' I looked up and saw the bus coming. Then I realized it ¹ .... because it was already full. 'Oh, no,' I thought. 'If I ² .... walking fast, I ³ .... late for my first class!' I had just started walking when a car pulled up beside me and one of my classmates leaned out. 'Hey Julia, get in, we ⁴ .... you a lift.' It's amazing how the bad moments ⁵ .... the good moments feel so much better.

R 改正下列句子中的错误。

♦ An imminent event is one that/~~happens~~ *will happen* soon.

1 Please stop making so much noise or I report you to the supervisor.

2 As I was about to leave his office, Rob said, 'Let's get together for lunch sometime, will we?'

3 They came and asked for people to help immediately, so Jenny jumped up and said, 'I do it!'

4 When he is released next week, Matt McGuire will spend almost five years in prison for a crime he didn't commit.

5 I'm going to work on the report at home last night, but I had left all my notes in the office.

6 It's probably too late to call Maddie. Do you think she'll go to bed already?

7 I'm not certain, but I guess it's raining later this afternoon.

8 Forthcoming books are those that we think about to be available soon.

9 I can't believe that you'll sit on a plane to Malta while I'm driving to work tomorrow morning.

10 If I'll find the files, I download them for you.

11 Will Stefan to get these boxes later or is to take them now?

12 I must get to the post office before it'll close or the parcel doesn't arrive in time for Joy's birthday.

测验

A 选出最恰当的词或短语完成下列句子。

1 I think Mr Wilson _____ in this school since 2005 or maybe earlier.
   a teaches **b** is teaching **c** has taught **d** taught

2 I stopped watching the game before the end, but I thought we _____.
   a had won **b** have won **c** have been winning **d** will have won

3 That's very sad news. If _____ sooner, I would have tried to help.
   a I know **b** I'll know **c** I knew **d** I'd known

4 My sister _____ me once or twice since she's been living in Athens.
   a was messaging **b** has messaged **c** has been messaging **d** had messaged

5 According to the memo, we're _____ the meeting at noon tomorrow.
   a having **b** have **c** going have **d** will have

B 从每句标有下划线的部分（A，B，C，D）中选出错误的一项。

1 My next door neighbour, who is usually shy and doesn't say much, is being very friendly this
   morning and has a big party tonight for all his friends.

2 Martin was used to smoke a lot when he was studying, but since he has been working in the
   bank, he hasn't been smoking as much.

3 People were slipping on the wet floor because no one had cleaned up the water that all of us
   were knowing had leaked from the coffee machine.

4 When you will make a promise, you tell someone that you will definitely give them something
   or that you definitely will or won't do something.

5 As we were entering the building, I noticed a sign that someone has put above the door
   which said, 'Be alert.'

C 从每对动词（短语）中选择恰当的一个填空。

| had decided | was walking | hadn't changed | thinking |
| decide | walk | wasn't changing | thought |

| were looking | whispered | saw | wasn't wearing |
| are looking | was whispering | see | didn't wear |

I had a very embarrassing moment last Monday. I ¹ _____ to school and
² _____ about the weekend when I noticed that people ³ _____
at me in a strange way. I couldn't understand it, and just when I ⁴ _____
I was imagining things, I ⁵ _____ my best friend. 'Look down!' he
⁶ _____ to me. Then I understood. I ⁷ _____ any shoes. I
⁸ _____ out of my fluffy slippers.

D 完成下列句子，使其与所给句子的意思尽可能接近。

1 We are spending £300 on repairs before we sell the car.
   By the time we sell the car, we _____.

2 I never had to think about my health before this.
   This is the first _____.

3 Juliet started working here about six years ago.
   Juliet has _____.

4 I didn't think it would be good, but it's really bad.
   It's even worse _____.

5 I haven't talked to my parents since Christmas.
   It was Christmas when _____.

E 选择合适的动词或动词短语填空。

believe	holds	be experiencing	had	have been changing
will keep	lets	is happening	have been	have created

The world is getting warmer and the oceans are rising. Why [1] _____

this _____? One answer is that it could simply be part of a natural

process. After all, there [2] _____ ice ages and long periods of warmth in

the past, so we could just [3] _____ another warming trend. This kind of

answer [4] _____ more supporters a few years ago. What scientists now

[5] _____ is that human activity is the cause. For more than 200 years,

humans [6] _____ gradually _____ the atmosphere, mainly

as a result of industrial pollution. We [7] _____ an atmosphere around the

earth that, like a giant glass container, [8] _____ heat from the sun through

and then [9] _____ it in. [10] _____ temperatures and sea levels

_____ rising? The general answer is unfortunately, yes.

情态动词是一类助动词，如 **can, could, may, might, must, ought, shall, should, will, would**。这类助动词可以与其他动词连用，表示可能性、许可、必要性等。

短语情态动词（phrasal modal）是一些可以代替情态动词使用的动词短语，如 **be able to, be allowed to, be going to, be supposed to, have to, have got to**。

A 阅读下面这篇文章，并找出：

1 一个否定形式的情态动词；
2 一个含有三个不同的情态动词的句子。

A Superstitions are beliefs that some things can't be explained by reason and that there are certain objects or actions that bring good or bad luck. Most superstitions are old and people
5 usually have no idea where they came from. We may be told, for example, that we should never open an umbrella indoors because that will bring bad luck. We aren't told why or what kind of bad thing might happen to us, but few
10 of us are going to try to find out.

B Everyone knows that 13 is an unlucky number. Other things that can bring bad luck include breaking a mirror, walking under a ladder or spilling salt. At least when you spill salt,
15 you can avoid the bad luck by immediately throwing some of the salt over your left shoulder with your right hand. Unfortunately, the man sitting behind you at that moment will suddenly get a shower of salt all over him.
20 Obviously, he must have done something earlier that brought him bad luck.

C If you ask people why it is bad luck to walk under a ladder, they usually say that it's because something might fall on your head.
25 It could be a hammer, a brick, a piece of wood, paint or water. It is interesting that the superstition is explained in terms of such ordinary things. The origin of the superstition is much darker and more scary. According
30 to the *Oxford Guide to British and American Culture*, 'this idea may have developed out of the practice in medieval times of hanging criminals from ladders.'

D More confusing are those superstitions
35 that seem to have different meanings for different people. Some people will tell you that it is bad luck if a black cat walks in front of you. Others will say that seeing a black cat is supposed to be lucky. Other tokens of
40 good luck are a rabbit's foot (not lucky for the rabbit, obviously), a special coin, a four-leaf clover and a horseshoe. If you hang the horseshoe over your front door to bring luck to your house, you must be careful to have the
45 open end pointing upwards. If you hang it the other way, your good luck will just drop out through the gap. You can also wish for good luck by crossing your fingers. You don't have to cross all of them, only the middle finger
50 over the index finger.

E There are special phrases that people use to bring luck. There's 'Good luck', of course. Another expression is 'Touch wood' or 'Knock on wood'. This is usually heard when people
55 talk about their good luck or when they are hoping that they will be able to get or do something they want. By using the expression, the speaker tries to avoid having any bad luck that might be caused by talking about having
60 good luck. If there isn't anything wooden to touch, some people will tap themselves on the head as they say 'Touch wood'. However, acting as if you have a wooden head, touching it with your fingers crossed and saying 'Knock
65 on wood' all at once won't necessarily increase your luck.

B 选择合适的句子作为上文各段（A—E）的结尾句，将对应段落的字母序号填入括号。

1 People will just think you're very superstitious or possibly crazy. (......)
2 That explanation makes the superstition much easier to understand. (......)
3 With your fingers like this, however, it may be hard to nail that horseshoe over your door. (......)
4 We just don't open one until we are outside. (......)
5 Perhaps he had opened an umbrella indoors. (......)

情态动词和短语情态动词

1 情态动词

情态动词（又称"情态助动词"［modal auxiliary verb］）是形式固定的单个单词。

1 *We should wait for David. He may come soon.* （不说 *He mays come soon.*）

其他情态动词：**can, could, might, must, ought, shall, will, would**。

在情态动词之后使用其他动词的原形。

2 *I can wait for him.* • *You must leave.* （不说 *I can waiting for him.* • *You must to leave.*）

ought 之后总跟着 **to**：*You ought to go home.* （不说 *You ought go home.*）

用情态动词构成疑问句（3）或否定句（4）时，不使用助动词 **do**。

3 *Will it work?* • *Can you play the piano?* （不说 *Do you can play the piano?*）

4 *She might not want it.* • *I couldn't swim very fast.* （不说 *I didn't could swim very fast.*）

情态动词 **shall**, **will** 和 **would** 通常以缩约形式出现（5），被强调时除外（6）。

5 *I'll bring you one, shall I?* • *He'll be there, won't he?* • *She'd like to stay, wouldn't she?*

6 *Do not forget! We will leave at 8 a.m. precisely. We will not wait for latecomers.*

在由采用过去时态的动词引导的从句中（7），特别是在间接引语中（8），通常用 **could, might** 和 **would**。

7 *I didn't know she could speak Spanish.* • *I was hoping you might give me some advice.*

8 *('Can I help?') She asked if she could help.* • *('I'll be late.') He said he would be late.*

在一个动词之前不能同时用两个情态动词。另见本页下面的示例（11）。

9 *We can win this game and we will win it!* （不说 *We will can win this game!*）

2 短语情态动词

短语情态动词是以 **be** 或 **have** 开头，可以代替情态动词使用的动词短语。

10 *Most old people are able to look after themselves.* （= … *can look after themselves.*）
   However, we have to make sure that they can cope. （= …*we must / should make sure …*）

其他短语情态动词：**be allowed to (can / may)**, **be going to (will)**, **be supposed to (should)**, **have got to (must)**。

在以下五种情况下，要使用短语情态动词而不是情态动词：在情态动词之后（11），需要使用动词不定式（12）或动名词（13）时，以及在完成式（14）或进行式（15）中。

11 *We will be able to win this game!* • *They may be going to increase tuition next year.*

12 *He seems to be able to do everything* • *I hope to be allowed to stay.*

13 *I love being able to sit outside in the sun.* • *I hate having to repeat everything.*

14 *They have had to wait for hours.* • *They haven't been allowed to leave the building.*

15 *She is having to pay extra.* • *We aren't being allowed to take the test early.*

可以连用两个短语情态动词：*I'm going to have to go to the shop for more bread.*

C 在第 28 页的文章中找出三个同时包含一个情态动词和一个短语情态动词的句子。

1 ....

2 ....

3 ....

→ 间接引语 150　动词不定式和动名词 139　否定句和疑问句 45

情态动词的复杂用法

情态动词完成式的结构是：情态动词 + **have** + 过去分词。

1 *Nick may have taken your book. He shouldn't have done that.*（不说 *He shouldn't done that.*）·*Obviously, he must have done something earlier that brought him bad luck.*

情态动词进行式的结构是：情态动词 + **be** + 现在分词。

2 *Alex shouldn't be acting so confident. He should be studying.*（不说 *He should studying.*）

情态动词完成进行式的结构是：情态动词 + **have been** + 现在分词。

3 *I called, but she didn't answer. She must have been sleeping.*（不说 *She must been sleeping.*）

情态动词被动式的结构是：情态动词 + **be** + 过去分词（4）或情态动词 + **have been** + 过去分词（5）。

4 *Some things cannot be explained by reason.* · *This shirt should be washed by hand.*

5 *People could have been injured by falling branches.*（不说 *People could have injured …*）

D 用 be, have 或 have been 填空。

◆ She shouldn't *have* _____ taken Tom's dictionary. I'm sure he'll *be* _____ looking for it later.

1 I was glad that my old laptop could _____ repaired. I would _____ hated to have to buy a new one.

2 Children may not _____ left alone in the playground. They must _____ accompanied by an adult.

3 Where's Anthony? He should _____ helping you clear out the garage. I guess he must _____ forgotten about it.

4 We weren't tired. We could easily _____ chatted for another hour. But we would probably _____ asked to leave the restaurant. It was getting late.

E 将练习 D 中八个补全后的句子填入下面对应的横线处。

预测：will, would, be going to, shall ◆ *I'm sure he'll be looking for it later.*
1 _____

意愿、习惯和偏好：will, would
2 _____

能力：can, could, be able to
3 _____

许可：can, could, may, might, be allowed to
4 _____

可能性：may, might, can, could
5 _____

必要性：must, have to, have got to, need to, needn't
6 _____

推论：must, have to, have got to, can't, couldn't
7 _____

义务和建议：should, ought to, be supposed to, had better ◆ *She shouldn't have taken Tom's dictionary.*
8 _____

→ 进行时 17 情态动词的被动式 58 过去分词 258 完成时 17

F 为句子的前半句（1—4）选择合适的后半句（a—d），再选择合适的词或短语填空。

able to | ~~will be~~ | must be | ought | going to
can't | won't | must have | ~~should be~~ | may have been

♦ You know there *will be* _____ a test tomorrow (*e*) a so that we _____ be late.

1 Samantha isn't _____ study at all (___) b so I _____ left them somewhere.

2 I _____ find my glasses (___) c so she _____ feeling very confident.

3 We _____ to check the timetable (___)

4 Mark's arm _____ injured (___) d so he probably isn't _____ write.

e so you *should be* _____ studying tonight.

G 选择合适的形容词或情态动词填空。如有必要请查词典。

advisable | inconceivable | ~~regrettable~~ | can't | ~~should~~ | will
hypothetical | inevitable | reluctant | might | shouldn't | wouldn't

♦ Someone who says, 'It is *regrettable* _____ that the police didn't do something sooner' feels that the police *should* _____ have acted sooner.

1 If someone says it is _____ to wait, it means that you _____ act immediately.

2 When you describe something as _____, you are certain that it _____ happen.

3 It was clear that he was _____ to talk and we _____ get any information from him.

4 If you say that something is _____, you mean that you _____ imagine it at all.

5 When something is described as _____, it is based on an idea about what _____ happen and not on a real situation.

H 改正下文中情态动词用法有误的地方。

A dilemma is a situation in which you have a choice and you are not sure what you should t̶o̶ *do*. In my dilemma, I had a good job as a secretary for a big company, but I really wanted to become a teacher and I didn't could do that without going to university. If I decided to do that, I knew I will have to quit my job and, as a student, I have much less money. I talked about my dilemma with one of the other secretaries and she warned me that I don't should give up such a good job. It really was a dilemma and I couldn't decided what I ought do. But then I talked to my aunt Maria. She told me that she should go to university when she was younger. She decided not to go and she regretted it. She thought that I should to give it a try. She said I didn't should be afraid and that she may can help me pay for things with some money she had saved. That was the end of my dilemma.

预测：will, would, be going to, shall

will 可用于表示对未来的预测（1），也可表示说话者认为现在最有可能是什么情况（2）。

1 *It will be cold tomorrow. • I won't finish this before Friday. • Who do you think will win?*
2 *My phone's ringing. It will be Harry. • Don't call them now. They'll be sleeping.*

will 用于可预见的情况（3），**would** 用于假设的情况（4）。

3 *He'll look better without that scruffy beard.* （我认为他将会把胡子刮掉）
4 *He'd look better without that scruffy beard.* （我认为他不会把胡子刮掉）

will + 动词完成式可用于预测在未来某个时间已经发生的事（5）。**would** + 动词完成式用于就假想的过去事件或情况进行预测（6）。

5 *It's no good phoning at midnight. Everyone will have gone to bed.*
6 *Life in the Middle Ages was harsh and cruel. You would have hated it.*

will 通常用于表述根据过去的经验或已有知识作出的预测（7），**be going to** 则用于表述根据现在的感受或想法作出的预测（8）。

7 *There will be delays because of bad weather. • Too much coffee will give you a headache.*
8 *Oh, no, I think it's going to rain. • He's going to get a headache from drinking all that coffee.*

be going to 还可用于表示已经作好的决定（9）或表示某事正要发生（10）。

9 *We're going to spend Christmas at home. • Paul and Angela are going to get married in May.*
10 *Be careful – you're going to drop it! • Close your eyes. I'm going to give you a big surprise.*

was / were going to（不是 ~~would~~）可用于表示过去作出的打算：*I was going to do law, but changed my mind.*

在疑问句中将 **shall** 和 **I** 或 **we** 连用，可表示主动提出做某事、提建议或征求建议（11）。**shall** 或 **will** 也可用于表示决心（12）。

11 *Shall I close the door? • Let's try again, shall we? • Where shall we go for lunch today?*
12 *I shall / I'll finish this if it kills me! • We lost a battle, but we shall / we'll never give up!*

I 选择合适的词或短语填空，补全下面的对话。

~~will~~	I'll	I'm going to	I'd	would
shall	you'll	I was going to	won't	would have

It's 7.30 a.m. on Thursday morning. Grace and James are awake, but still in bed. A phone rings.

Grace: Oh, that * *will* _____ be mine. Hello?

Mum: Hello dear. I was hoping it wasn't too early for you. I have to come into town today and I was wondering if you ¹ _____ be able to meet me for lunch.

Grace: Oh, ² _____ love to, Mum, but ³ _____ get my hair done at lunchtime. I ⁴ _____ been free, but Jessica called yesterday and changed my appointment from Friday to today. ⁵ _____ get it cut on Friday so that it would be nice for Dad's birthday this weekend.

Mum: Ah, the birthday party! That's why I have to come to town. ⁶ _____ we just have a coffee later? When do you think ⁷ _____ be finished at the hairdresser's?

Pam: Oh, she ⁸ _____ have finished before 1.30 or 2.00. And then I have to get back to the office.

Mum: It's okay. I understand. ⁹ _____ talk to you later.

→ will, shall 和 be going to（将来）24 条件句中的 will 和 would 185—186

意愿、习惯和偏好：will 和 would

3 意愿：will 和 would

will 用于表示当前的确定意愿（1），而 **would** 用于表示将来的意愿，或用在条件句中表示意愿（2）。**would** 也用于表示自己主观上愿意但实际上无法做到（3）。

1 *I will give you one more chance. • There are advisers here who will help and guide you.*
2 *Most people would pay more for better health care. • I would stay longer if they asked me to.*
3 *Can you help us carry these boxes? ~ Oh, I would help you, but I've injured my back.*

可用 **won't**（= isn't willing to）或 **wouldn't**（= wasn't willing to）表示某人不愿意做某事（4），或表示某物，如机器，像人那样"不愿意"做某事，即无法实现某功能（5）。

4 *He's ill, but he won't go to the doctor's. • She had a lot of money, but she wouldn't lend us any.*
5 *The door isn't locked, but it won't open. • My car wouldn't start this morning.*

4 习惯和偏好：will 和 would

可用 **will** 描述现在的习惯或常有的行为（6）。可用 **would** 描述过去的惯常行为（7）。

6 *Her children will break everything they touch. • Tim will just sit watching TV for hours.*
7 *I would try to stay awake every Christmas to see Santa. • Each summer we would visit my cousins.*

表示过去的状态时用 **used to**（不是 ~~would~~）：*I used to have a dog.*（不说 ~~I would have a dog.~~）

would（不是 ~~will~~）可以和 **like, love, prefer** 等用于表达偏好的动词连用（8），特别是用在表示愿意提供某物的句子中（9）。

8 *I would prefer an early class. • I'd love to go on a cruise.*（不说 ~~I'll love to go on a cruise.~~）
9 *Would you like some tea or would you prefer coffee?*（不说 ~~Will you like some tea?~~）

在由动词 **wish** 引导的从句中谈论希望某行为发生时，用 **would**（不是 ~~will~~）。

10 *I wish she wouldn't smoke. • Don't you wish they would make it easier to recycle things?*

would 不用于描述状态：*I wish I had a car.*（不说 ~~I wish I would have a car.~~）

J 为每个段落选择一组合适的动词，在适当的地方搭配 will 或 would 的恰当形式，将段落补全。动词形式应恰当。

be / hate	be / say	eat / need	~~give / go~~	have / like	play / stay	push / start

◆ Even when she gets the flu, my friend Alice _won't (OR will not) go_ to see the doctor because she's afraid that he _'ll (OR will) give_ _____ her an injection. She is terrified of needles.

1 We had an old car that _____ on cold mornings unless we got out and _____ it.

2 **Amy:** Carla wants to know if you _____ a slice of her home-made chocolate cake.

   Rob: Tell her I _____ normally _____ two slices, but not while I'm on this strict diet.

3 When we were young, we _____ always _____ outside during the summer holidays, but nowadays children _____ just _____ inside watching TV or playing computer games all day.

4 I hope I _____ never _____ asked to work on a night shift because I _____ having to go to sleep for most of the following day.

5 I'm sure we _____ to cook anything for them because they _____ lunch before they come here.

6 When people asked Annie's dad if he had children, his typical answer _____ 'And how!' Her mother usually murmured, 'I wish he _____ things like that.'

→ 行为动词和状态动词 3

能力: can, could, be able to

can 用于谈论一般的能力，could 用于谈论过去的一般能力。

    1 *Can you play chess? • Ostriches can run very fast. • Their son could swim before he could walk.*

在否定句中，**can't** 比 **cannot**（写作一个单词）更常用，后者是非常正式的用法。（不说 ~~I can not go.~~）

can 和 **could** 常与表示心理过程（2）和感知（3）的动词连用。

    2 *I couldn't decide. • Can you remember her name?* （不说 ~~Are you remembering her name?~~）

    3 *We could hear a cat, but we couldn't see it. • I can smell onions.* （不说 ~~I'm smelling onions.~~）

这类动词有时可用一般现在时（*I smell onions*），但不用现在进行时。这类动词还有：**believe, feel, guess, taste, understand**。

be able to（不是 can 或 ~~could~~）可用在以下四种结构中：在动词不定式或动名词中（4），在情态动词之后或在完成式中（5）。

    4 *They want to be able to practise. • She left without being able to talk to the teacher.*

    5 *I won't be able to finish. • He hasn't been able to study.* （不说 ~~He hasn't could study.~~）

be able to 不用于进行式：*He isn't able to walk.*（不说 ~~He isn't being able to walk.~~）

在正式表达中，有时用 **am / is / are able to** 代替 **can** 来谈论一般能力（6）。用 **was / were able to**（不是 ~~could~~）来谈论在过去做成了某件困难的事（7）。

    6 *Is the child able to tie his or her shoelaces without help?*

    7 *We had a flat tyre, but we were able to fix it and carry on.* （不说 ~~… but we could fix it.~~）

可以用 **couldn't** 来表达没有做成某件困难的事：*We couldn't fix it.*

可用 **could**（不是 ~~can~~ 或 ~~be able to~~）+ 动词的完成式谈论过去没有发挥的能力或没有利用的机会。

    8 *He could have done very well, but he was lazy.* （不说 ~~He can have done very well.~~）

注意 *I was able to win* 和 *I could have won* 的区别，前者表示取得了胜利，后者表示本可以取胜但并未取胜。

K 为每句选择一组合适的词，搭配 can, could 或 be able to 的恰当形式，将句子补全。如有必要请查词典。

difficult / managed	fly / swimming	stay / unflappable
feel / numb	illiterate / read	successful / tried

1 Penguins are birds that _____, but _____ use their wings for _____.

2 An _____ person is someone who _____ calm in difficult situations.

3 It was so cold that my fingers were _____ and I _____ anything.

4 When people are _____, they _____ or write.

5 A _____ person is someone who has _____ do what he or she _____ to do.

6 If you _____ to finish a task, it means you _____ do it, even though it was _____.

L 用 can 或 could 的恰当形式填空，补全下面这则笑话。

Did you hear about the boy who went fishing, but [1] _____ catch anything?
On his way home, he stopped at the market so that he [2] _____ buy two fish.
He then stepped back a few paces and asked the fish seller if she [3] _____ throw them to him. The puzzled seller asked, 'Why?' The boy answered, 'So that I [4] _____ tell my mum that I caught a couple of fish today!'

→ 短语情态动词 29

许可: can, could, may, might, be allowed to

can 和 **could** 可用来征求许可，用 **could** 比用 **can** 更礼貌（1）。**can**（不是 ~~could~~）也用于表示给予许可或不予许可（2）。

> 1 *Can I borrow your dictionary?* • *Can the dog come into the house?* • *Could we leave early today?*
> 2 *Yes, you can.* • *No, it can't.* • *I'm sorry, but you can't.*（不说 ~~I'm sorry, but you couldn't.~~）

在正式表达中，可以用 **may** 来征求许可（3），给予许可或拒绝给予许可（4）。

> 3 *May we come in?* • *May I take this chair?* • *May I use one of these pens?*
> 4 *Yes, you may.* • *No, you may not, because I need it.* • *Of course, you may use any of these pens.*

might 可用来征求许可，但不用于给予许可：*Might I take one? ~ Yes.*（不说 ~~Yes, you might.~~）

谈论法律和规定时，通常用 **can**（不是 ~~may~~）（5）。**may**（不是 ~~might~~）有时被用在正式规定中（6）。

> 5 *You can't park here. ~ Why not? ~ I think only buses and taxis can park here.*
> 6 *No food or drinks may be brought inside.* • *Pedestrians may not enter this way.*

be allowed to（不是 ~~may~~ 或 ~~might~~）可用于强调在某个特定的时候获得许可（7），并且可用在各种短语情态动词结构中（8）。

> 7 *That day was the first time I was allowed to make my own breakfast.*（不说 ~~… I might make …~~）
> 8 *No one has been allowed to see the test results.* • *We aren't being allowed to go in yet.*

注意，**may** 或 **might** 可以与 **be allowed to** 连用：*You may / might be allowed to go.*（"你可能会被准许离开。"）

M 为句子的前半句（1—5）选择合适的后半句（a—f），并在横线处补充 can, may 或 be allowed to。

◆ New students *may* ___ not register	(*c*)	a	as if he was interested in my drawing.
1 Children shouldn't ___	(___)	b	because there's no more work to do.
2 He casually asked, '___ I see that?'	(___)	c	for more than three classes.
3 You might not ___ go in	(___)	d	eat or drink during a test.
4 You ___ all leave early today	(___)	e	if you're under 21.
5 They are unlikely to ___	(___)	f	play with matches.

N 改正下文中的错误。

My friend Dana ~~can not~~ ^can't^ say 'No'. If another student asks her, 'Can I borrow your pen?', she always says, 'Of course you could,' and hands it over, even when she only has one pen and it means she isn't being able to do her own work. After I heard her do that one day, I told her that she can have said, 'Sorry, but you can not, because I only have one pen.' In reply, she said, 'But how do they could do their work without a pen?' I knew that I can have tried to answer that question, but somehow I didn't think I'll can change how she behaved, no matter what I said.

→ can't, couldn't（推论）40　may, might, can, could（可能性）36

可能性：may, might, can, could

5 可能性：may 和 might

可用 **may** 或 **might** 来表述某事在现在或以后有可能发生（1）。可用 **may** / **might** + 动词的完成式表述以前有可能发生了某事（2）。

1 *Taking these pills may / might cause drowsiness. You might / may fall asleep at the wheel.*
2 *I may / might have lost my key. • Tanya might / may have met James when she was in London.*

在否定句中，可以说：*It may not / might not / mightn't happen.*（不说 ~~It mayn't happen.~~）

may（不是 ~~might~~）可用于谈论普遍存在或经常发生的可能情况（3）。**might**（不是 ~~may~~）可用于描述在过去有可能发生了什么（4），也可用于由使用过去时的动词转述的话语或想法（5）。

3 *Peppers may be green, yellow, orange or red. • Measles may cause a fever and small red spots.*
4 *In those days, people might spend their entire lives in the village where they were born.*
5 *('I may be late.') He said he might be late. • I was wondering if you might have time to read this.*

6 可能性：can 和 could

can 和 **could** 可用在一般性的陈述中，表示现在（**can**）或过去（**could**）有可能存在的情形。

6 *Some dogs can be very dangerous. • The old house could be quite cold, even in summer.*

could（不是 ~~can~~）可用于推测，表示有可能是某情况（= It's possible that …）（7），或询问是否有可能是某情况（= Is it possible that …?）（8）。

7 *Your bag could be in the car. • It could rain this weekend.*（不说 ~~It can rain this weekend.~~）
8 *Peter is late. Could he be stuck in traffic?*（不说 ~~Can he be stuck in traffic?~~）

could（不是 ~~can~~）+ 动词的完成式可用于谈论某事在早些时候发生的可能性。

9 *The bank could have closed already. • You could have fallen.*（不说 ~~You can have fallen.~~）

7 may / might 还是 can / could？

may, might 和 **could**（不是 ~~can~~）可用于表示某一特定事件有发生的可能性（10），可用在短语情态动词之前（11），也可用在动词的进行式或完成式之前（12）。**might** / **could** + 动词的完成式也可用于就某人未做某事表达气恼（13）。

10 *Anna may arrive later. • There could be a storm tonight.*（不说 ~~There can be a storm tonight.~~）
11 *It may be going to rain. • We might have to leave soon.*（不说 ~~We can have to leave soon.~~）
12 *The economy may be showing signs of recovery. • Lani might have borrowed the hairdryer.*
13 *You might have thought to take the dog when you went for a walk!*

may 或 **might**（不是 ~~can~~ 或 ~~could~~）可用在 **but** 之前的分句中，表示让步。

14 *She may be 90, but she still likes to dance. • We might have lost a battle, but not the war.*

注意，*It may be old, but it works* 在意思上与 *Although it's old, it works* 很相似。

can 或 **could**（不是 ~~may~~ 或 ~~might~~）可用于就可能采取的行动提出建议（15），也可用于请求他人做某事（16）。

15 *We have a simple choice. We can / could wait here for a bus or we could / can start walking.*
16 *Can you show me where it is? • Could you take this away?*（不说 ~~May you take this away?~~）

may not 或 **might not** 用于表示"可能不"（17）。表示"不可能"，要用 **can't** 或 **couldn't**，**can't** 用于谈论现在的情况，**couldn't** 用于谈论过去的情况（18）。

17 *It may / might not be true.*（可能不是真的）*• This bill may / might not be right. It seems too high.*
18 *That story can't be true.*（我确定那不是真的）*• This bill can't be right. We only had two coffees.*
    • I knew the rumour about your accident couldn't be true because I'd seen you that morning.

→ can, could（能力）34 can, could, may, might（许可）35
   can't, couldn't（推论）40 短语情态动词 29

O 为每句选择一个形容词和一个情态动词（短语），将句子补全。如有必要请查词典。

| ~~absurd~~ | feasible | theoretical | may | may be | might |
| disqualified | potential | undecided | may not (×2) | ~~may have~~ | might not |

- Your uncle *may have* _____ run in a marathon when he was younger, but it's *absurd* _____ to keep describing him as 'one of the top runners'.
1 She _____ breaking the rules and will possibly be _____ from the rest of the competition.
2 If someone is _____ about an action, they _____ or _____ do it.
3 We knew about the _____ problems and the workmen had said they _____ finish on time.
4 Your plan _____ be approved because people don't think it's economically _____.
5 From a _____ perspective, that _____ happen, but nobody thinks it will.

P 选择合适的动词，用其恰当形式搭配 can 或 could 的恰当形式，补全下文。

| avoid | be | not imagine | ~~pick~~ | save | not send |

These days, when we ◆*can pick* _____ up our phone and call anywhere in the world, we really don't realize, and often [1] _____ how difficult long-distance communication [2] _____ for people in the past. In the early 19th century, the Treaty of Ghent brought an end to the War of 1812 between Britain and the United States. But the news [3] _____ across the Atlantic fast enough to stop General Andrew Jackson attacking and defeating the British forces in New Orleans a full two weeks after the treaty was signed. With better communication, the battle [4] _____ and the lives of more than 2000 people [5] _____.

Q 用 may, might, can 或 could 改正下列句子中的错误。

- It was a bad accident. We/~~can~~ *could* have been killed.

1 They can be going to increase airport fees to pay for increased security.

2 Don't turn off the computer yet. George can still need it.

3 In late 18th-century Scotland, you may be hanged for stealing a sheep.

4 These people can have a lot of money, but it doesn't make them interesting.

5 May someone tell me where the main office is?

6 We know he doesn't tell the truth, so we really might not believe any of his stories.

7 He asked me last night if you may be willing to talk to Maddie for him.

8 According to the forecast, the weather can be a bit warmer today.

9 This switch isn't working. May the children have broken it?

必要性：must, have to, have got to, need to, needn't

8 必要性：**must** 和 **mustn't**

must 可用于表示必要性（1），特别是用来表达命令或规定（2）。其否定式 **mustn't / must not** 用于告诫他人不要做某事，或表示做某事是坏主意（3）。

1　*Plants must have light.* • *Your basic needs are the things you must have to live a normal life.*
2　*You must come to class on time.* • *Safety helmets must be worn.* • *All visitors must sign in.*
3　*You mustn't come late.* • *Empty boxes must not be stacked in front of the emergency exit.*

must 也可用于鼓励他人做你认为重要的事（4），或强调某种强烈的态度或观点（5）。

4　*We must have a party at the end of term.* • *You and I must get together for lunch soon.*
5　*I must disagree with that. We must not accept new regulations that restrict our civil rights.*

9 必要性：**have to, don't have to** 和 **have got to**

当表示不由自己掌控地必须或需要做某事时，通常用 **have to** 而不用 **must**。

6　*My mother has to have an operation on her knee.* • *I have to wear glasses for reading.*

在疑问句中，通常用 **have to**（搭配助动词 **do**）而不用 **must**。

7　*Why does everyone have to sign?* • *Don't you have to wear a seat belt?* • *Do I have to do it again?*
must 可以用来构成疑问句，但听起来更正式：*Must I do it again?*

have to（不是 ~~must~~）可用于询问或谈论在过去需要或有必要做的事（8），并且可用在各种短语情态动词结构中（9）。

8　*Did you have to wear uniform in school? Matthew had to wear a blazer, a cap and a tie.*
9　*You will have to change.* • *I don't want to have to fight.* • *Nobody likes having to wash dishes.* •
　I have had to complete three forms already. Now I'm having to complete another one.

don't have to（不是 ~~mustn't~~）的意义与 **must** 相反，表示不必做某事。

10　*It's free – you don't have to pay.* • *The gate was open so we didn't have to wait outside.*

在非正式表达中，可以用 **have got to** 代替 **have to**，但只用于现在时（11）。构成否定句和疑问句时，将 **have**（不是 ~~do~~）作为助动词与 **got to** 连用（12）。

11　*We have got to find a better way to do this.* • *I've got to see Ben.*（不说 ~~I had got to see Ben.~~）
12　*She hasn't got to wait long.* • *Have we got to buy tickets?*（不说 ~~Do we have got to buy tickets?~~）

10 必要性：**need to, don't need to** 和 **needn't**

need to 的用法和 **have to** 类似，用于表示有必要做某事（13）或没必要做某事（14）。

13　*James needs to / has to leave soon.* • *I'll need to / have to take an umbrella.*（不说 ~~I'll need take an umbrella.~~）
14　*We don't need to / have to wait.* • *Because it rained, I won't need to / have to water the garden.*

也可用 **needn't** 或 **need not**（没有 **to**）表示在某个特定的时候不必做某事，而 **don't need to** 通常用于表示在一般情况下不必做某事。

15　*You needn't pay me now.* • *It's still early so we needn't rush.*（不说 ~~We needn't to rush.~~）
16　*Students don't need to pay to use the library.*（不说 ~~Students needn't pay to use the library.~~）
在美式英语中，只用 **don't need to**（不用 ~~needn't~~）。

didn't need to 用于表示在过去没有必要做某事（17）。**needn't have** + 过去分词表示在过去做了本来没必要做的事（18）。

17　*I knew there wouldn't be a test, so I didn't need to study. I watched TV instead.*
18　*I studied all night, then found out the test was cancelled. I needn't have studied at all.*

→ 助动词 17　must, have to, have got to（推论）40　短语情态动词 29

R 选择合适的词和 must 或 have to 的恰当形式，补全下列各句。如有必要请查词典。

| command | duty-free | evil | ~~extra~~ | fruit | obligation | step | taboo |

♦ An optional *extra* _____ in a new car is something that is available, but you *don't have to* _____ get it.

1 An essential _____ is a part of a procedure you'll _____ do in order for it to be successful.

2 Forbidden _____ is something that you _____ touch or have, even though you really want it.

3 In the army, soldiers _____ always obey a _____ given by a senior officer.

4 If you are under no _____ to do something, you _____ do it.

5 When you buy things that are _____, you _____ pay tax on them.

6 If a topic is _____ in a particular culture, it means that you _____ talk about it because it is considered offensive.

7 A necessary _____ is something you don't like or want, but which you may _____ accept in order to achieve your goal.

S 选择合适的动词（短语）或形容词填空。

| ~~didn't have to~~ | must | need to | allowed | official | significant |
| having to | mustn't | needn't have | impossible | ~~required~~ | unnecessary |

♦ I *didn't have to* _____ wear a jacket and tie last night. Formal attire was not *required* _____.

1 You _____ made so much noise. All that shouting was quite _____.

2 People _____ have dogs in their rooms. Pets are not _____ in the hotel.

3 You won't _____ fill in forms. All the _____ paperwork will be complete.

4 Not _____ pay to use the pool is a _____ benefit of being a student here.

5 Everyone _____ have a valid passport because it will be _____ to enter the country without one.

T 改正下列句子中的错误。

1 We have already washed all the dinner dishes so you mustn't clean them tonight.

2 Everyone will have got to go through metal detectors every time they enter the building.

3 I'll need get some aspirin because I've got a terrible headache and I have to keep working.

4 The part that broke is a crucial component and I must to find a replacement immediately.

5 Whenever service is included in a bill, customers needn't to leave a tip for the waiter.

6 Our train arrived rather late and so we had got to take a taxi to get to our meeting on time.

7 I don't want to be the one to must have to tell him that he failed the entrance exam again.

8 I'm sure you don't need be over 21 to go into a pub here, but we must ask someone.

9 When we stayed with my grandmother, we must go to church with her every Sunday.

10 We didn't know that our friends had already gone into the theatre so we needn't have to wait all that time for them outside in the cold.

推论：must, have to, have got to, can't, couldn't

must 可用于表示，根据证据某一想法或推论很有可能或肯定是真实的（1）。**must** + 动词的进行式可用于对现在正在发生的事作出推论（2）。

1 *You're shivering – you must be cold.* • *Look at that car! Ali's parents must have a lot of money!*
2 *Listen. It must be raining outside.* • *I think I must be getting the flu.*（不说 *I must get the flu.*）

若想对已发生的事情作出推论（3），或当表述推论的分句跟在使用过去时的动词之后时（4），使用 **must** + 动词的完成式。

3 *Someone must have taken the key because it isn't here.*（不说 *Someone must take the key.*）
4 *We realized he must have lied.* • *I thought at first that someone must have made a mistake.*

must 可用在间接引语中，此时表示被转述的信息现在仍然是真的：*He said she must be Italian.*

在非正式语言中，可以用 **have to** 或 **have got to** 代替 **must** 来表述推论。

5 *I didn't order ten books. This has to be a mistake.* • *These aren't mine – they've got to be yours.*

can't 和 **couldn't**（不用 **mustn't**）用在表示否定意义的推论中，意思与 **must** 相反（6）。**can't** / **couldn't** + 动词的完成式用于对早些时候的事表达否定性推论（7）。

6 *The bill is over £50 – that can't be right.* • *You can't be 21!*（不说 *You mustn't be 21!*）
7 *You can't have finished already!* • *If he wasn't there, he couldn't have committed the murder.*

U 为左侧的句子（1—5）选择合适的下文（a—e），并在横线处补充 must 或 can't 的恰当形式。

1	Julia goes to Malta every summer.	(　)	a	She _____ started school yet.
2	What she's asking for is ridiculous.	(　)	b	If one is correct, the other _____ be.
3	The hands on the clock weren't moving.	(　)	c	It's crazy. She _____ joking.
4	Their daughter was only three this year.	(　)	d	She _____ really like it there.
5	Those are two contradictory statements.	(　)	e	It _____ stopped working.

V 将 must 或 couldn't 与所给动词的恰当形式搭配，补全对话。

be　carry　do　lose　put　take

Mum (putting on her coat): I'm going to have to go down to the shop for more bread.

Oliver: Why?

Mum: I'm not sure what happened. I made some sandwiches earlier and left them on the table when I went to answer the doorbell. But someone ¹ _____ them because they're gone.

Oliver: Oh, it ² _____ Dad. I'm sure he was in the kitchen earlier.

Mum: No, he went off to his tennis match before I finished making them, so he ³ _____ it. Anyway, he ⁴ _____ a plate of sandwiches as well as all his tennis stuff, so I'm sure it wasn't him.

Oliver (opening fridge door): Well, it wasn't me. But Mum, look! Are these your sandwiches here on the bottom shelf of the fridge?

Mum: Are they in there? Oh, my goodness. I ⁵ _____ them in there when the doorbell rang. Oh, dear. I really ⁶ _____ my mind. Now, why did I put on my coat?

→ 间接引语 150　can, could 34—36　must, have to, have got to（必要性）38

义务和建议: should, ought to, be supposed to, had better

11 义务和建议: should

should 可用于表达义务（1），谈论期望某人做某事（2），或笼统地表达自己觉得好或恰当的主意（3）。

1　*The police should crack down on speeding. • At election time, everyone should vote.*
2　*You're a student. You should be studying! • Nurses and doctors shouldn't smoke.*
3　*Teachers should get more pay. • Children should learn to say 'Please' and 'Thank you'.*

should 可用于征求或给出建议（4），或提出警告（5）。

4　*What should I do? • You should take notes during lectures. • You should get to the airport early.*
5　*You shouldn't go swimming right after eating. • You shouldn't go through the park at night.*

should 可以用来表达某事应该会发生，因为这件事已经计划好了或说话者是这样预期的。

6　*If all goes well, we should be there before it gets dark. • The bus should come soon.*

should + 动词的完成式可用于表示某件好事或值得去做的事在过去没有发生（7），常用来表达后悔（8）。

7　*They should have rehearsed before playing. • We should have left a tip for our waiter.*
8　*We should have been more careful with our money. • I shouldn't have told anyone about it.*

12 义务和建议: ought to, be supposed to, had better

ought to 可用来代替 should，两者在意义上没有差别。

9　*Neighbours ought to / should help each other. • You really ought to / should be more careful. • He should / ought to have completed the work before he left.*（不说 ~~He ought have completed the work …~~）

ought to 的否定式是 **oughtn't to** 或 **ought not to**：*You ought not to wait.*（不说 ~~You ought not wait.~~）

也可以用 **be supposed to** 代替 should，这种用法通常出现在非正式语言中（10）。**be supposed to**（不是 ~~should~~）也可用于转述被其他一些人相信的事（11）。

10　*You are supposed to / should be sleeping.*（不说 ~~You supposed to be sleeping.~~）
11　*Killing a spider is supposed to be unlucky.*（不说 ~~Killing a spider should be unlucky.~~）

建议某人做某事（12）或警告某人不要做某事（13）时，可以用 **had better** 代替 should，**had better** 表达的意思更强烈。

12　*You have failed two tests. You had better start working harder or you won't pass the course.*
13　*Johnny's going to take your bike. ~ He'd better not do that!*（不说 ~~He'd not better do that!~~）

W 选择合适的名词或动词（短语）填空。

cat	mirror	shoulder		had better	ought not	should be
ladder	~~person~~	umbrella		is supposed to	shouldn't	should have

If you listen to the advice of a superstitious ♦ *person*_____, you [1] _____ be ready to pay a lot of attention to what you're doing each day. Be careful with that [2] _____. You'll be told that you [3] _____ open it indoors. When you're walking along the street, watch out for a [4] _____. You [5] _____ careful not to walk under one. Did you spill any salt recently? You know that you [6] _____ immediately thrown some of it over your [7] _____, don't you? And remember that you [8] _____ to be careless with a [9] _____, because if you break one, you'll have seven years of bad luck. However, if you see a black [10] _____, that's good, because it [11] _____ be lucky.

→ 在名词性从句中使用 should 167

测验

A 选出最恰当的词或短语完成下列句子。

1 You're 18! You're ＿＿＿＿＿ to be able to look after yourself by now.
   a have **b** ought **c** should **d** supposed

2 A permit is a document which states that you ＿＿＿＿＿ to do something.
   a are allowed **b** cannot **c** may **d** shall

3 He ＿＿＿＿＿ have helped us if he'd really wanted to.
   a could **b** may **c** must **d** will

4 My laptop ＿＿＿＿＿ be old, but it still works really well.
   a can **b** could **c** may **d** would

5 ＿＿＿＿＿ someone please tell me where the library is?
   a Can **b** May **c** Must **d** Should

B 从每句标有下划线的部分（A，B，C，D）中选出错误的一项。

1 They say it <u>can</u> <u>be going to</u> rain later so you <u>should</u> take an umbrella or you <u>might</u> get wet.
   A   B   C   D

2 I <u>was going to ask</u> you if you <u>would read</u> over my essay before I <u>have to hand</u> it in, but when you
   A   B   C
   read it, you <u>ought not be</u> too critical or negative.
   D

3 His right hand <u>may have been</u> badly injured and he probably <u>won't be able to</u> type, so I thought
   A   C
   that I <u>will</u> offer to do some typing for him.
   D

4 Andy was so generous. If I asked him, 'Could I borrow your car?', he <u>would</u> always say,
   A   B
   'Of course, you <u>could</u>!', and he <u>would</u> immediately start looking for the keys.
   C   D

5 I really wish I <u>would have</u> a car of my own so that I <u>could</u> go for a drive in the country and I
   A   B
   <u>would be able to</u> go when I want to and not <u>have to</u> wait for a bus or a train.
   C   D

C 将左框中的一个情态动词和右框中的一个动词短语搭配起来，填入下文中的横线处。

| can   may not   must | be charged   be paid   be used |
| will   won't | be familiar   be required |

Note: Credit cards are used instead of cash, interest is charged and part payment is allowed. Charge cards are used instead of cash, but no interest is charged and full payment is required.

As a new customer of the bank, you [1] ＿＿＿＿＿ with the difference between a charge card and a credit card. Both cards [2] ＿＿＿＿＿ instead of cash in most places to pay for goods and services. Later, when you receive your charge card bill, the total [3] ＿＿＿＿＿ in full every time. However, when you receive your monthly credit card bill, you [4] ＿＿＿＿＿ to pay the total amount. If you choose to pay only part of the bill, you [5] ＿＿＿＿＿ interest on the amount not paid.

D 完成下列句子，使其与所给句子的意思尽可能接近。

1 Students may not park here.
Students are _____ .

2 It's possible that his trip was cancelled at the last minute.
His trip may _____ .

3 She had to get up at five o'clock every morning and she didn't enjoy it.
She didn't enjoy _____ .

4 It was impossible for him to have committed the crime, according to the report.
He _____ .

5 It was a bad idea to put this shirt in the washing machine.
This shirt _____ .

E 选择合适的词或短语填空。

be able to	couldn't	might	was able to	would (×2)
be willing to	had to	should	was going to	

'Hello! Mr Appleton!'

The voice was some distance behind him. He stopped raking the leaves and turned to see two women struggling up the driveway towards him. They were wearing identical white T-shirts which had MADD in large black letters across the front. He had a sudden strange thought that they [1] _____ be crazy people who [2] _____ spell. But they didn't look crazy. As they came closer, he [3] _____ make out smaller letters under each of the big letters, spelling out the words 'Mothers Against Drunk Driving'.

'I'm so glad we found you. I'm Nettie Albright and this is Agnes Miller.'

He shook their outstretched hands. Agnes was wearing thin gloves.

'We talked to your wife this morning and she's the one who told us we [4] _____ [5] _____ find you here. She said she hadn't really witnessed the accident, but you had. We were hoping you [6] _____ [7] _____ testify.' She [8] _____ stop and take a deep breath.

'You mean the car crash?'

'Yes, exactly, the crash. We need witnesses. That awful man says it wasn't his fault. He [9] _____ be jailed immediately! He's a menace to society. We need your help to put him away.'

'It had happened one early evening in July. I [10] _____ just _____ cross the street when a car came racing through the red light, narrowly missing me, but smashing into another car in the middle of the junction. The woman in that car died. When the man who hit her turned out to be very drunk, it all changed from being an accident to being a criminal case.'

4 否定句（negative）和疑问句（question）

否定句的构成方式通常是把助动词（**be, do** 或 **have**）/ 情态动词和 **not / n't** 连用，放在主要动词前（*I am not crying; you don't care; he hasn't gone; we shouldn't wait*）。

疑问句的构成方式通常是把助动词（**be, do** 或 **have**）或情态动词放在主语和主要动词前（*Has he gone? Should we wait?*）。

疑问句的类型包含 **yes / no** 疑问句（'yes / no' question）（*Are you crying? Do they care?*）和 **wh-** 疑问句（*wh-*question）（*Where has he gone? Why should we wait?*）。

A 阅读下面这篇采访并找出：

1　一个 yes / no 疑问句；

2　一个含有两个否定动词的句子。

A **Why did you start the 'Protect Yourself' programme?** A good friend of mine was attacked and robbed last year on her way home from work. She wasn't seriously
5　injured, but it really frightened her and she wouldn't go out alone. I started talking to her about protecting herself and she thought it would be a good idea to form a group. Eventually we had so many people that it
10　turned into a regular kind of night class.

B **Who can take part?** Anyone who wants to, but mostly it's young women. We meet in an old building that's next to the big church on Wilder Avenue, from 6 to 7 on Mondays.

15 **C** **Do you teach karate and stuff like that?** Not really. We tried some of that at first, but it wasn't very successful. There is a real karate class in the same building on Thursdays for people who want that. We still use some of
20　the movements from karate when we talk about ways to escape, but we focus more on avoiding risky situations and being prepared.

D **What do you mean?** It's really more about awareness. There are some statistics about
25　assault victims that we talk about. For example, women with longer hair are more likely to be attacked than women whose hair is shorter or in a style that can't be grabbed.

E **Is there anything else?** Clothing is another
30 thing. Statistically, women in skirts and dresses are attacked more than those wearing jeans or trousers.

F **When and where do most attacks occur?** At night, of course. But surprisingly, a large number
35　of assaults occur in the early morning, before 8.30. They happen in isolated areas, parks, outside schools and office buildings before and after regular working hours. We advise people not to go alone to parking areas and garages in
40　the morning or in the evening. But, if you must, you should carry an umbrella or something like that and, if you're going to your car, have your keys ready.

G **What's the umbrella for? Is it a weapon?**
45　Well, it isn't much of a weapon, is it? But we think it helps you feel more confident. We actually practise using the umbrella to keep someone at a distance while you shout and scream as loud as you can to discourage any
50　attacker who wants you to be an easy victim.

H **What should you do if you're actually attacked?** Be a problem. Grab fingers and bend them backwards. Bite hands. Stomp your foot down hard on the attacker's toes. Grab the
55　skin under the arm above the attacker's elbow and squeeze as hard as you can. Move, twist, kick, scratch, fall down, scream and yell. Be hard to hold and make a lot of noise.

B 选择合适的句子作为上文最后五段（D—H）的结尾句，将对应段落的字母序号填入括号。

1　We want you to be a difficult problem.　(.....)

2　Maybe that's why there are also more attacks in warmer weather.　(.....)

3　You may be fighting for your life.　(.....)

4　It isn't wise to stand out there searching for something in your bag.　(.....)

5　A ponytail can make you very vulnerable.　(.....)

否定句和疑问句的语序

① 否定句

对于使用了助动词 **be, have** 和情态动词的句子，加 **not / n't** 构成其否定形式。在正式语言中要用非缩约形式（*We are not*）（1）。在非正式语言中，通常将 **not** 变为缩约形式（*We aren't*）（2），或将助动词（*We're not*）或情态动词（*We'll not*）变为缩约形式（3）。

1 *Dogs are not allowed in supermarkets.* • *Guests must not eat or drink outside.*
2 *They aren't listening.* • *We haven't forgotten the meeting.* • *Her parents won't let her go.*
3 *We're not ready yet.* • *I've not been given any instructions.* • *He'll not go unless you ask him.*

如果使用的是其他动词，要在该动词的原形前用 **do** 和 **not / n't**，构成否定形式。

4 *Some people do not understand.* • *It does not work.* • *I did not refuse to pay.* • *They don't remember.* • *It doesn't help us.* • *We didn't see it.*（不说 ~~We didn't saw it.~~）

do 的否定形式不与情态动词连用：*I can't swim.*（不说 ~~I don't can swim.~~）

在含有动词不定式和动名词的句子中，要把 **not** 置于不定式或动名词之前。

5 *He pretended not to see us.* • *I enjoyed not going to school for a few days.*

可以在名词之前用 **no**（6），在动词之前用 **no longer** 或 **never** 等否定副词（negative adverb）（7）。

6 *There were no problems.* • *We'll have no money for rent.*（不说 ~~We'll no have money for rent.~~）
7 *She's no longer working there.* • *They will never be free.*（不说 ~~They will be never free.~~）

② 疑问句

对于使用了助动词 **be, have** 和情态动词的句子，在构成疑问句时，把助动词或情态动词置于主语之前。主要动词位于主语之后。

8 *Are you coming?* • *Have they finished?* • *Why must you leave?*（不说 ~~Why you must leave?~~）• *How can I help?* • *Where was your watch made?*（不说 ~~Where was made your watch?~~）

如果使用的是其他动词，在构成疑问句时，要在主语前用 **do**，在主语后用该动词的原形。

9 *Do you know the answer?* • *What does she want?* • *Did he break it?*（不说 ~~Did he broke it?~~）

yes / no 疑问句以 **be, do, have** 或情态动词开头，这类问句的回答通常是 **yes** 或 **no**（10）。如果想给出两个可能的答案供对方选择，可以用 **yes / no** 疑问句，并在句中用 **or** 将两种选择连接起来（11）。

10 *Am I the first to arrive?* • *Are you feeling okay?* • *Do you like it?* • *Does it work?* • *Have you got a minute?* • *Has it stopped raining?* • *May we come in?* • *Can you play the piano?*
11 *Do we go now or wait until later?* • *Would you like something hot or something cold to drink?*

wh- 疑问句以 **wh-** 疑问词（*wh-word*）开头，询问特定的信息。

12 *What's your name?* • *How much does it cost?* • *When and where do most attacks occur?*
其他 **wh-** 疑问词：**which, who, whom, whose, why**。

what 或 **who** 作主语时，通常把主要动词（不是 ~~do~~）置于它们之后。

13 *What's making that noise?* • *Who used my mug?*（不说 ~~Who did use my mug?~~）
注意，**whose** 和 **which** 与名词连用时也有类似的用法：*Whose phone is ringing?* • *Which team won?*

C 再读一读第 **44** 页的采访，就下列描述各找出一个例子，将相应的句子写在横线上。

1 一个否定形式的情态动词：......
2 一个否定形式的动词不定式：......
3 一个作主语的 wh- 疑问词：......

否定疑问句（negative question）和附加疑问句（question tag）

3 否定疑问句

yes / no 否定疑问句通常以 **be, do, have** 或情态动词的否定形式开头（1）。在 **wh-** 否定疑问句中，否定结构位于 **wh-** 疑问词之后（2）。

1 *Aren't those books mine?* • *Doesn't he speak any English?* • *Didn't she get married last year?* • *Hasn't the lecture finished yet?* • *Haven't we seen that film?* • *Can't you open the window?*

2 *Everyone was invited to the party. Why didn't you go?* （不说 ~~Why you didn't go?~~） • *There are only ten players on the field. Who isn't here yet?* （不说 ~~Who isn't he here yet?~~）

回答 yes / no 否定疑问句时，yes 表示正面含义为真，no 表示反面含义为真。

3 *Aren't they French?* ~ *Yes.* （他们是法国人） / *No.* （他们不是法国人）

在否定疑问句中，把 **never** 等否定副词和用于强调的 **not** 置于主语（不是助动词）之后。

4 *Have you never eaten meat?* • *Did he not understand the text?* （不说 ~~Did not he understand the text?~~）

yes / no 否定疑问句可用于向他人核实信息（5），也可用来表达惊讶（6）。

5 *Isn't 4th July a big American holiday?* • *Haven't we already paid for the tickets?*

6 *Doesn't she like any music at all?* • *Haven't you ever seen snow?*

Why don't you …? 和 **Why not …?** 用于主动提出帮助或提建议。

7 *Why don't you come with us?* • *Why not have the party on Saturday instead of Friday?*

在 **Why not …?** 这一句型中，why not 之后没有主语。（不说 ~~Why not you have the party on Saturday?~~）

4 附加疑问句

附加疑问句（也称"疑问尾句"）指跟在陈述句之后的简短疑问句。

常见用法为肯定陈述句 + 否定附加疑问句（8）或否定陈述句 + 肯定附加疑问句（9）。

8 *We're late, aren't we?* • *Mark really loves her, doesn't he?* • *She lost it, didn't she?*

9 *I can't win, can I?* • *They don't like it, do they?* • *You haven't studied at all, have you?*

附加疑问句的非缩约形式（如 **are we not?** 和 **does he not?**）是非常正式的。

在附加疑问句中，代词与主句主语一致，动词与主句中的助动词（如果有的话）或 **be** 动词（作为主要动词）一致，或使用 **do** 的恰当形式。

10 *You haven't talked to Mary since she went on holiday, have you?* （不说 ~~didn't she?~~） • *He was guilty, wasn't he?* • *The evidence showed he was guilty, didn't it?* （不说 ~~wasn't he?~~）

注意，在以 **no one** 或 **nobody** 为主语的句子后，用 **they** 来构成肯定附加疑问句：*Nobody likes it, do they?*

在表达请求或提议的祈使句之后使用附加疑问句时，使用情态动词。

11 *Don't say anything, will you?* • *Pass me that knife, could you?* • *Let's leave, shall we?*

可以在肯定句（常常是对之前某人所说内容的重复）之后使用肯定附加疑问句来确认信息。在否定句之后使用否定附加疑问句的情况非常少见。

12 *That's your new car, is it?* • *So, the students are planning a protest, are they?*

D 在第 **44** 页的采访中，找出一个含有附加疑问句的句子。

→ 否定词 48　主谓一致 4　wh- 疑问词 45

E 选择合适的词填空。如有必要请查词典。

isn't	doesn't	no	nondescript	non-refundable	~~non-stick~~
~~aren't~~	won't	not	non-event	non-resident	non-stop

♦ There usually *aren't* _____ any problems cleaning a pan if it's the *non-stick* _____ kind.

1 When someone _____ living permanently in a country, he or she is a _____ .

2 If something is expected to be big or dramatic, but it's _____ , it can be described as a _____ .

3 _____ means the money won't be returned, _____ it?

4 The word _____ is used for something which has _____ special or unusual features.

5 If your journey is _____ , you _____ be able to visit any of the places along the way.

F 从左框和右框中各选一个词搭配起来，补全下列句子。

What	Where	Whose
When	~~Who~~	Why

are	do	~~isn't~~
did	don't	were

♦ I have 20 names and only 19 students. *Who isn't* _____ here today?

1 We have an extra room in our place. _____ you stay with us?

2 Everyone was looking for Mr Kidd. _____ you tell them he was?

3 There must be hundreds of people working there. _____ they all do?

4 My parents worked in Saudi Arabia too. _____ you there?

5 Some things were left in class yesterday. _____ books _____ these?

G 改正下文中否定句和疑问句用法有误的地方。

In our group, we had to write down questions before a discussion of the topic: 'What kind of pet is best?' That was difficult because some of us ~~didn't~~ *hadn't* ever had a pet, so we didn't really could say much about this topic. I asked Michel, 'What you think is the best pet?' He answered, 'I not care about pets.' Then he said, 'Why we have pets? We not need them for anything, don't we? And some people think dogs not clean, so they not good pets.' I asked him, 'Aren't some pets cleaner than dogs? For example, no one thinks a cat makes more mess than a dog, does he?' He didn't answered. Then Paola explained that she could have not a cat in her house because cats made her mother sneeze a lot. So she suggested that an important question was: 'Why do some people can't have pets?' I wrote down three other questions from our group: 'Do some pets more expensive to keep than others?' 'How will be trained the pet?' 'Who is take care of the pet?'

否定词

5 no, none, nobody, no one 和 nothing

虽然通常用否定动词（如 wasn't, haven't）来表达否定概念（1），但也可以将肯定动词与 no, none, nobody, no one 和 nothing 等否定词连用来表达否定概念（2）。可将这些否定词用作主语并与肯定动词连用（3）。

1　*There wasn't anything to eat in the hotel room, so we haven't had breakfast yet.*
2　*There was nothing to eat in the hotel room, so none of us has had breakfast yet.*
3　*No one complained. • Nobody told us.* （不说 ~~Not anybody told us. / Nobody didn't tell us.~~）

no 可用在名词之前，而 **none** 可代替名词。

4　*Didn't you bring any money? ~ I have no money. / I have none.* （不说 ~~I have none money.~~）

通常不使用双重否定。（不说 ~~I don't have no money. / I don't have none.~~）

none of 用在代词和限定词（the, those, our 等）之前。

5　*None of them understood it. • None of our friends will come. • None of the lights is working.*

在非正式语言中，**none** 有时与复数动词连用：*None of them are working.*

no 可以与单数形式的名词、复数形式的名词或动名词连用来强调否定意义。这类结构可用来代替否定动词（6），或在正式语言中作为 is / are not allowed 的简略形式（7）。

6　*One class doesn't have a teacher. → One class has no teacher.*
　　Cameras aren't permitted inside the court. → No cameras are permitted inside the court.
7　*No dogs. No skateboards. • No talking during the examination. • No parking.*

在非正式语言中，用 **Don't** + 动词而不是 **No** + 动名词：*Don't park there.*

可以将 **no** 或 **not / n't any** 与形容词（8）或副词（9）的比较级连用。

8　*These seats are no better than the others. / These seats aren't any better than the others.*
9　*We should leave no later than eight-thirty. / We shouldn't leave any later than eight-thirty.*

not（不是 ~~no~~）可用在简化的否定句（reduced negative）中（10），也可用在不定冠词 a / an 之前（11），以及 **all** 或 **a lot** 这类数量词之前（12）。

10　*Do you want to keep these boxes or not? If not, I'll just throw them out.*
11　*Not a single drop of blood was spilt. • A whale is a mammal, not a fish.*
12　*Not all Americans are rich. • There is not a lot to be gained by being rude to people.*

6 否定词和否定短语后的倒装 (inversion)

当 never, nowhere 等否定副词位于句首起强调作用时，后面使用倒装结构，即将主语置于助动词（**be, do, have**）或情态动词之后。

13　*I have never heard such nonsense. → Never have I heard such nonsense.*
　　They couldn't find a bottle opener anywhere. → Nowhere could they find a bottle opener.

含有 **no**（14）或 **not**（15）的否定短语位于句首时，后面也使用倒装结构。

14　*The children weren't in danger at any time. → At no time were the children in danger.*
　　You shouldn't go under any circumstances. → Under no circumstances should you go.
15　*I didn't realize what she meant until later. → Not until later did I realize what she meant.*
　　Mark is not only single, but he is also clever. → Not only is Mark single, but he is also clever.

倒装一般用于正式语言或文学语言，但也可用在非正式回答中的 **neither, nor** 或 **no way** 之后。

16　*I don't understand. ~ Neither do I. • We didn't like the film. ~ Nor did most people. • I think Mr Atkins should let us leave early. ~ No way will he agree to that.*

→ 比较级 120　限定词 83　倒装 216　否定副词 45　数量词 84

H 为句子的前半句（1—4）选择合适的后半句（a—d），并在横线处补充 no, none 或 not。

1 I wrote to several people,   ( )   a so you must ____ eat in there.
2 We needed some glue,   ( )   b and we have ____ emergency funds.
3 ____ food is allowed in that room, ( )   c but ____ of them has replied yet.
4 There's ____ much money left   ( )   d but there was ____ in the house.

I 选择合适的词或短语填空。如有必要请查词典。

carefree	indifferent	~~infrequent~~	doesn't	no	not
careless	infallible	invisible	never	no one	nothing

If something is ♦ _infrequent_____, it [1] ____ happen very often.
When you are [2] ____, you have [3] ____ to worry about,
but the word [4] ____ isn't the same. It means [5] ____ paying
enough attention to detail.
An object is [6] ____ if [7] ____ can see it.
If people or things are [8] ____, they [9] ____ make mistakes or
go wrong.
When people are [10] ____ to something, they have [11] ____
interest in it.

J 将下面的句子改写为非正式的语言。

♦ Nowhere else do they make this bread. _They don't make this bread anywhere else._
1 Never has there been a better chance to make money on the stock market.

_____

2 Not until the next morning did we notice that she had not come home.

_____

3 At no time did anyone warn us about polluted water.

_____

4 The janitor will say, 'No smoking in here,' will he not?

_____

K 选择合适的词或短语填空。

no idea	not only	nor	did I	had I	were they
~~no sooner~~	not until	nothing	did we	I had	they were

Have you ever arrived at work thinking something was wrong? It recently happened to me.
On Saturday morning, when I arrived at the City Concert Hall, there were a lot of musicians
waiting outside. ♦_No sooner_ [1] ____ opened the front door than
the musicians started to come in and complain. [2] ____ [3] ____
unhappy that their next concert had been cancelled, but [4] ____ also very angry
that they hadn't been paid for weeks. I tried to explain that I only looked after the Concert
Hall and [5] ____ [6] ____ to do with money or music. They said that
a lot of tickets had been sold, but they had [7] ____ where the money had gone.
[8] ____ [9] ____, I kept telling them. [10] ____ two
days later [11] ____ all find out that the concert organizer had run off with all the
money.

疑问词

7 what 还是 which?

what 和 which 可用在名词之前或用作代词（1）。如果认为所问的问题有无数种可能的答案，用 what（2）；如果认为可能的答案数目有限，则用 which（3）。

1 *What bus / Which bus should I take?* • *What / Which do you want?*
2 *What are you doing?* • *What's her home phone number?* • *What would you like to drink?*
3 *There are three numbers listed here. Which is her office phone number?* • *We have both red wine and white wine. Which would you prefer?*

which（不是 ~~what~~）可用在 one 或 ones 之前（4）。针对数量有限的一系列人或事物提问时，用 which of（不是 ~~what of~~），将其置于限定词（the, these, my 等）（5）或代词（6）之前。

4 *There are a lot of cups of tea here. Which ones already have sugar? Which one is mine?*
5 *Which of these books haven't you read?* （不说 ~~What of these books haven't you read?~~）
6 *Edberg had four sons. Which (one) of them was the famous artist?* • *Which of you is first?*

who 可用于就范围不明确的对象提问：*Who is first?*（不说 ~~Who of you is first?~~）

L 为左侧的陈述句（1—6）选择可跟在后面的问句（a—f），并在横线处补充 what 或 which。

1 I'm one of the girls in that old photo. (　) a ＿＿＿＿＿＿＿＿ was your score?
2 'Flunk the test' is an American phrase. (　) b ＿＿＿＿＿＿＿＿ one did you get wrong?
3 He gave us our exam results. (　) c ＿＿＿＿＿＿＿＿ are you waiting for?
4 I'd like to leave soon. (　) d ＿＿＿＿＿＿＿＿ is you?
5 I got 19 out of 20 correct. (　) e ＿＿＿＿＿＿＿＿ of them have you read?
6 I haven't read all his books. (　) f ＿＿＿＿＿＿＿＿ does it mean?

8 疑问词与介词 / 副词连用

wh- 疑问句可用来对介词宾语提问，通常把介词放在 wh- 疑问句的末尾（7）。在正式语言中，有时把介词放在句首（8）。

7 *He's going to fill the hole with something.* → *What is he going to fill the hole with?*
　You gave your old laptop to someone. → *Who did you give your old laptop to?*
8 *With what is he going to fill the hole?* • *To whom did you give your old laptop?*

在介词之后要用 whom（不是 ~~who~~）。（不说 ~~To who did you give your old laptop?~~）

在某些 wh- 疑问句中（如 **What … for?**，**What / Who … like?**），介词总是位于句尾。

9 *What are you doing that for?* • *Who does she look like?* （不说 ~~Like whom does she look?~~）

某些介词用在 wh- 疑问句的开头，不用在句尾。

10 *During which period were the French in control?* • *Since when have these records been kept?*
这种用法的介词还有：**above, after, before, below**。

副词通常位于 wh- 疑问词之后（11），但某些副词也可用在 wh- 疑问词之前（12）。

11 *How often do you exercise?* • *What else did he say?* • *When exactly did he leave Cyprus?*
12 *Precisely where did you last see the keys?* • *Exactly when did he leave Cyprus?*

含 ever 的 wh- 疑问词（如 **wherever, whoever**）可用于表达惊讶或不敢相信。

13 *Wherever did you find that?* • *However did she do it?* • *Whoever told you such nonsense?*
whichever 没有这种用法：*Whatever do you mean?*（不说 ~~Whichever do you mean?~~）

→ 副词 118　限定词 83　one 和 ones 104　代词 97　介词 125

M 选择合适的词填空，补全下列知识问答题的问题，并试着选出正确回答。

> by for how often where who with
> ~~during~~ from (×2) of what (×2) which whom

◆ *During which* century did the French Revolution begin? （*B*）
   A 17th **B** 18th **C** 19th

1 .... does an annual meeting take place? （_）
   A every week   **B** every month   **C** every year

2 Cider is a type of drink. .... is it made .... ? （_）
   A apples   **B** grapes   **C** oranges

3 .... did Paul McCartney write many of the Beatles' hit songs? （_）
   A Mick Jagger   **B** Elton John   **C** John Lennon

4 .... these countries is not in South America? （_）
   A Bolivia   **B** Nicaragua   **C** Paraguay

5 Cate Blanchett is a well-known actor. .... is she .... ? （_）
   A Australia   **B** Canada   **C** Scotland

6 *War and Peace* is the title of a famous book. .... was it written .... ? （_）
   A Charles Dickens   **B** William Shakespeare   **C** Leo Tolstoy

7 .... is a whisk used .... ? （_）
   A cleaning floors, etc.   **B** playing cellos, violins, etc.   **C** stirring eggs, cream, etc.

N 选择合适的词或短语填空，补全下面的对话。对话选自一部美国犯罪惊悚小说。

> how ever   what … about   where   where … from   ~~who~~
> how long   whatever   where exactly   which … in   who else

The phone woke me up. I automatically reached over and picked it up.

'Good morning, darling. I guess you're not coming to get me, are you?'

'What? ◆*Who* .... is this?

'It's me. Charles. [1] .... were you expecting?'

'Sorry. I'm still asleep. Aren't you in New York?'

'[2] .... are you talking .... ? [3] ....
gave you that idea?'

'You're not? Oh, no, I can't think straight. [4] .... are you?'

'I'm at the airport. I just got back from Glasgow.'

'Oh, goodness. [5] .... have you been waiting? I'm so sorry.'

'It's okay. Don't panic. I'm just about to pick up my bag.'

'I'm up. I'll be there. [6] .... are you? [7] .... terminal are you
?'

'It's okay. I'll catch the train into town. Can you meet me at the station?'

'Yes. It'll be quicker that way. I'll see you in about 45 minutes.'

'Okay. Bye.'

I started to put the phone down, but there was something wet and sticky on it. Was it
blood? [8] .... had it come .... ? There was more of it on
the sheet. [9] .... did it get there?

其他类型的疑问句

9 疑问句套疑问句

可以在 **wh-** 疑问句中的 **wh-** 疑问词（如 **what, who**）之后加一个 **yes / no** 疑问句来就他人的想法（1）或说的话（2）提问。

1 Do you think something is wrong? → *What do you think is wrong?*（不说 *What you think is wrong?*）

2 Did he say someone was waiting outside? → *Who did he say was waiting outside?*

将 **yes / no** 疑问句放在 **wh-** 疑问句中时，在 **yes / no** 疑问句部分使用疑问句语序（即倒装语序），在 **wh-** 疑问句部分不使用疑问句语序。

3 Does he believe the fighting will end? → *When does he believe the fighting will end?*
（不说 *When does he believe will the fighting end?*）

10 陈述式疑问句

可把陈述句用作 **yes / no** 疑问句，向他人确认某事（4），或重复他人刚说过的话——通常意在表达惊讶（5）。若想让对方再讲清楚一点，或想针对对方刚才所说内容的某一部分获得更多信息，可在陈述句中使用一个 **wh-** 疑问词，构成疑问句（6）。

4 *Monday is a holiday?* • *Mr. Jones was your teacher too?* • *David doesn't know about this?*

5 *Paul won first prize.* ~ *He won first prize?* • *I had a ticket, but didn't go.* ~ *You didn't go?*

6 *She zapped it.* ~ *She did what to it?* • *I met Pip.* ~ *You met who?*（不说 *Did you meet who?*）

11 修辞性疑问句（rhetorical question）

修辞性疑问句具有问句的形式，但可用于明确肯定某事（7），也可用来引入话题（8），或在回答先前提出的某问题前再强调一次问题（9）。

7 *Mike isn't here yet.* ~ *Who cares?*（= I don't care.）*Isn't he always late?*（= He is always late.）

8 *Do you remember the oil crisis? We were sure then that cars would have to become smaller.*

9 *What do you think of it?* ~ *What do I think of it? I think it's just too expensive.*

12 简化的疑问句

在非正式表达中，有时可以略去 **yes / no** 疑问句句首的 **Are you** 或 **Do / Did you**（10），**wh-** 疑问句可以简化为单个的 **wh-** 疑问词（11）或短语（12）。

10 *Feeling okay?* • *Tired?* • *Going out?* • *Need some help?* • *Like it?* • *Have fun last night?*

11 *We must buy that piano.* ~ *How?* ~ *I'll find the money.* ~ *Where?* ~ *I know someone.* ~ *Who?*

12 *You have to do it.* ~ *Why me?* • *Your plan won't work.* ~ *Why not?* • *Bring a knife.* ~ *What for?*

可将 **How about …?**（13）和 **What about …?**（14）与名词、动名词连用（不使用动词），来提出建议或引起听者对某事物的注意。

13 *How about a cup of tea?* • *How about watching TV?*（不说 *How about shall we watch TV?*）

14 *What about your homework?* • *What about playing 'Go'?*（不说 *What about we play 'Go'?*）

13 间接疑问句（indirect question）

间接疑问句用于转述问题，句中不使用疑问句语序，句末不使用问号（15）。间接的 **yes / no** 疑问句以 **if** 或 **whether** 开头（16）。

15 Why did you start the programme? → *I asked her why she (had) started the programme.*
What do you mean? → *I asked her what she meant.*（不说 *I asked her what did she mean?*）

16 Do you teach karate? → *I asked if they taught karate.*（不说 *I asked did they teach karate?*）
Is it an umbrella or a weapon? → *I asked whether it was an umbrella or a weapon.*

→ 动名词 139　间接疑问句 154　疑问句的语序 45

O 将下面的陈述句改写为以 what, when, where 或 who 开头的疑问句。

◆ They think something is wrong. *What do they think is wrong?*

1 You believe someone is responsible for the current conflict.

2 Her father thought she might have gone somewhere.

3 The weather forecaster said the rain should stop at some time.

4 You imagine their new house is going to look like something.

P 为左侧的句子（1—5）选择合适的下文（a—e），再选择合适的词填空。

did	didn't	do	does	how	which	who	why

1 Will it be sunny tomorrow? (　) a _____ he? With _____ part?
2 Mary, you have to crawl through the tunnel. (　) b _____ about studying?
3 I understood nothing he said. (　) c _____ knows?
4 I don't know how I'll pass the exam. (　) d You _____? Neither _____ I!
5 He says there is a problem with the contract. (　) e _____ I have to? _____ me?

Q 下面是亚当斯太太和侦探格里姆肖在警察局的一段对话。选择合适的词或短语填空。

he did	he's	he was	I do	you're	you don't
did he	is he	was he	do I	~~are you~~	don't you

Mrs Adams: Can we leave now or ◆*are you* _____ going to start paying us for all the time we're spending here?

Detective: Your son isn't going anywhere, Mrs Adams. [1] _____ in deep trouble this time.

Mrs Adams: [2] _____ really? Maybe you're the one who's in trouble, detective. My son has done nothing. This is police harassment.

Detective: I asked your son what [3] _____ doing in John Mansfield's house last night and what do you think he said?

Mrs Adams: What [4] _____ think? I think [5] _____ making all this up because [6] _____ have a clue. You're just trying to blame my Tommy for something he didn't do. He worked for Mr Mansfield. That's all.

Detective: Listen. I didn't tell your son that Mansfield was killed with a knife. He told me. He wasn't just helping us make this up, [7] _____?

Mrs Adams: Oh, [8] _____ make you think he was going to confess? I don't know what you think [9] _____. One thing [10] _____ know for sure is that he was at home with me all last night. Why [11] _____ just leave him alone and go find the real killer?

测验

A 选出最恰当的词或短语完成下列句子。

1 What do you think _____ me?
   a told **b** they told **c** didn't tell **d** did he tell

2 Why not _____ the meeting for Monday morning?
   a schedule **b** scheduling **c** you schedule **d** do you schedule

3 They explained that she couldn't take the course, _____?
   a could she **b** couldn't she **c** did she **d** didn't they

4 _____ real work was done in the office while the boss was away.
   a Not a **b** Not any **c** No **d** None

5 Good morning, gentlemen. _____ of you is first in line?
   a Which **b** Whose **c** Who **d** Whom

B 从每句标有下划线的部分（A，B，C，D）中选出错误的一项。

1 My neighbour used to say, 'How about helping me carry this?' or 'Give me a hand with this, would you?', but at no time he asked me if I ever needed help with anything.

2 I'm not trying to work more, but quite often I have no time for lunch or I don't have much of an appetite, and so I take no longer a whole hour for my lunch break.

3 I told Sarah that it wasn't my party. I explained that it was my brother's party, so none of my friends had been invited. I guess she didn't believe me because her first question was, 'Why you didn't invite me to the party?'

4 'Did you see those students cheating during the exam?' ~ 'No, but didn't you tell the teacher?' 'I decided not to tell her because I didn't really think it was my business and no one wants to be a telltale, does he? Don't say anything about this to anyone, will you?'

5 Not many people realize that a spider is no insect because insects don't have eight legs and none of them make webs.

C 补全下面对话中缺失的词语。

A 'Isn't window-shopping fun? Look at these lovely vases. ¹_____ they beautiful?'

B 'They're okay.'

A 'Let's buy one!'

B 'With ²_____?'

A 'Oh, come on, just one.'

B 'No, I don't think so. They're ³_____ nicer than the ones we already have at home.'

A 'Oh, you're such a spoilsport!'

B 'No, ⁴_____. I'm simply trying to avoid spending money that we haven't got!'

A '⁵_____ we buy anything at all?'

B 'No. But you can enjoy looking. That, after all, is what window-shopping means.'

D 完成下列句子，使其与所给句子的意思尽可能接近。

1 The room wasn't only cold, it was also very damp.
Not _____.

2 Your sister said she gave the money to someone.
Who _____?

3 Andreas thinks that something has been stolen.
What _____?

4 She suggested that I take the train instead of driving.
She said, 'Why _____?'

5 'What's his name and where does he live?'
They asked me _____.

E 选择合适的词填空，补全短文和后面的问题，然后根据短文内容回答这些问题。

did	how	never	no	nothing	what	where	which	who	why

Your parents have sent you a ticket to fly to New York where they are planning to celebrate their wedding anniversary. ¹_____ much is happening at work, you've ²_____ been to New York and you've had ³_____ holiday trips for more than a year, so you've quickly packed a couple of large suitcases and headed to the airport. You are now sitting on board flight YZ-23, non-stop from London to New York, waiting to take off. The flight attendant hands you a questionnaire. You decide to complete it.

⁴_____ is your flight number? _____

⁵_____ are you taking this flight? Business ☐ or Leisure ☐

⁶_____ paid for your flight? Myself ☐ or Somebody else ☐

⁷_____ you check in bags for this flight? _____

At ⁸_____ airport did you board this flight? _____

⁹_____ will you leave this flight? _____

¹⁰_____ many flights have you made in the last 12 months? _____

5 被动（passive）

动词的被动式由动词 **be** 和及物动词的过去分词构成（*My car was stolen.*）。动词的被动式用于表示主语承受的动作（*Two men were arrested.*），而主动式用于表示主语执行的动作（*The police arrested two men.*）。

A 阅读下面的新闻报道，再找出两个动词（即 find 和 move）各自的主动用法和被动用法。

For as long as people can remember, small towns like Stone Creek and Pineville in northern Alabama have been hit by storms every spring. They are as predictable as the apple blossoms
5 that are always shaken loose from the trees and blown along the country roads. Some trees may be knocked over or the roof of a building might be slightly damaged, but usually the effects of the storms are more inconvenient than deadly.
10 This year was different.

Last night, a powerful storm roared into the area, sending devastating tornadoes spinning through the small farming communities. It destroyed farms, schools and churches, and
15 buried people in the ruins of their own homes. It transformed the landscape. Herds of cattle that had been moved into barns for safety are nowhere to be seen, nor are the barns. Other buildings where tractors and equipment were
20 being stored seem to have been completely blown away.

The scenes of devastation this morning are described by one rescue worker as 'like the end of the world'. Since first light, rescue crews
25 have been moving through the countryside, looking for survivors. Small teams have had to be flown in to some areas by helicopter because the roads have been blocked by dozens of fallen trees. In other areas, rescuers don't know what
30 they will find as they search through the debris. 'We're guessing that there are some people who

may have been pinned down under their own ceilings,' says Greg Hayden, a firefighter from Atlanta. 'Sometimes we can't tell the houses
35 from the stables or the garages. It's a mess. Dozens of people and animals could have been buried in there.'

One by one, the miracles and the tragedies are coming to light. Jim Clinton, having been
40 warned of the approaching storm on his radio, drove his wife and daughter to his local church. He thought it would be safer there than staying in his small house. Two of the church walls collapsed, but after being trapped inside for four
45 hours, the Clintons were found alive by rescuers this morning. Not far away, an old couple had retreated to the basement of their home as the storm approached. Tragically, they were both killed when part of a wall crashed through the
50 floor on top of them. The names of all victims are being withheld until their families can be notified.

At least 38 people have died and many more are missing. About 100 people have been
55 seriously injured and more than 1,000 have been left homeless. The search for the missing may last for days, but the effects of this one storm are going to be felt for many years. 'It's like someone dropped a bomb,' said one shocked
60 woman as she searched through the remains of what used to be her home.

B 从上面的新闻报道中选择合适的动词完成以下摘要，注意应使用动词的恰当形式。

At least 38 people have died, about 100 [1]＿＿＿＿＿＿＿＿ seriously ＿＿＿＿＿＿＿＿, and more than 1,000 [2]＿＿＿＿＿＿＿＿ homeless in northern Alabama after the area [3]＿＿＿＿＿＿＿＿ by a powerful storm last night. Farms, schools and churches [4]＿＿＿＿＿＿＿＿, and some people [5]＿＿＿＿＿＿＿＿ in the ruins of their own homes. Fallen trees [6]＿＿＿＿＿＿＿＿ roads in some areas, so rescue teams [7]＿＿＿＿＿＿＿＿ by helicopter. The effects of this storm [8]＿＿＿＿＿＿＿＿ for years.

主动（active）和被动

动词的主动式用于表示主语执行的动作（1），被动式用于表示主语承受的动作（2）。

1 *After the accident, someone **called** the police and they **arrested** the drunk driver.*

2 *After the accident, the police **were called** and the drunk driver **was arrested**.*

主动式动词的宾语被用作被动式动词的主语（3）。不能用不及物动词构成被动式（4）。

3 *We **clear** the table and **wash** the dishes.* → *The table **is cleared** and the dishes **are washed**.*

4 *We **swam** every day.* • *Richard **came** later.* （不说 ~~Richard was come later.~~）

动词的被动式由两部分构成，即动词 **be** 的某种形式 + 过去分词。

5 *You have to rewrite the first paragraph.* → *The first paragraph **has to be rewritten**.*

可以在被动式之后用 **by** 引出执行或引发动作的人或事物。

6 *My car **was repaired** by Andrew.* • *Some roads **are blocked** by fallen trees.*

C 下表列出了各种时态的被动式。再读一读第 **56** 页的新闻报道，就每种时态的被动式找出一个例子。

一般现在时的被动式: am / is / are + 过去分词

主动: *You place an order one day and they deliver your groceries the next.*

被动: *An order **is placed** one day and your groceries **are delivered** the next.*

1 ....

现在进行时的被动式: am / is / are + being + 过去分词

主动: *They are building a new school and creating two new roads for access.*

被动: *A new school **is being built** and two new roads **are being created** for access.*

2 ....

现在完成时的被动式: have / has + been + 过去分词

主动: *I've prepared the turkey and peeled the potatoes.*

被动: *The turkey **has been prepared** and the potatoes **have been peeled**.*

3 ....

一般过去时的被动式: was / were + 过去分词

主动: *Air Canada cancelled our flight and stranded us in Vancouver.*

被动: *Our flight **was cancelled** and we **were stranded** in Vancouver.*

4 ....

过去进行时的被动式: was / were + being + 过去分词

主动: *They were cleaning the floor and washing the windows earlier today.*

被动: *The floor **was being cleaned** and the windows **were being washed** earlier today.*

5 ....

过去完成时的被动式: had + been + 过去分词

主动: *Everyone had warned me about the weather before I went to Scotland.*

被动: *I **had been warned** about the weather before I went to Scotland.*

6 ....

→ 带有 by 短语的被动式 64　过去分词 17　及物动词和不及物动词 6　被动式的用法 62

情态动词、动词不定式和动名词的被动式

➊ 情态动词的被动式

情态动词被动式的一般形式为：情态动词（**can, may, will** 等）+ **be** + 过去分词（1）。若须使用过去时，用 **could, might, would** + **be** + 过去分词（2）。

1 *The police will arrest violent demonstrators. So, if you are violent, you will be arrested.*
You can be kept in custody for 24 hours and you may be questioned about your activities.

2 *'The police can't stop us!' The demonstrators claimed that they couldn't be stopped.*
They boasted that although they might be arrested, they wouldn't be silenced.

情态动词的被动完成式由情态动词 + **have been** + 过去分词构成。

3 *Anthony didn't study for the test. His answers must have been copied from someone else.*
If he had been caught cheating, he would have been expelled from school.

情态动词的被动进行式由情态动词 + **be being** + 过去分词构成（4）。这种结构很少使用。一般使用不带情态动词的主动式或被动进行式（5）。

4 *I see that men are working on the roof today. I think it may be being repaired at last.*

5 *Perhaps they're repairing it at last. • I think it's being repaired at last.*

短语情态动词的被动式由短语情态动词（如 **have to, be going to**）的现在式（6）或过去式（7）与 **be** + 过去分词构成。可以连用两个短语情态动词（8）。

6 *Someone has to tell Chris to stop interrupting. → Chris has to be told to stop interrupting.*
Are you going to need this extra paper? → Is this extra paper going to be needed?

7 *I had to find a place for all the boxes. → A place had to be found for all the boxes.*
Someone was probably going to steal them. → They were probably going to be stolen.

8 *We're going to have to sell my old car. → My old car is going to have to be sold.*

➋ 动词不定式和动名词的被动式

动词不定式的被动式一般由 **to be** + 过去分词构成（9）。动词不定式的被动完成式由 **to have been** + 过去分词构成（10）.

9 *He's trying to finish the work soon. He expects most of it to be finished before the weekend.*

10 *They have chosen Emily Watson to play the part. She's really excited to have been chosen.*

动名词的被动式一般由 **being** + 过去分词构成（11）。动名词的被动完成式由 **having been** + 过去分词构成（12）。

11 *He was asking about a lot of personal things. I didn't like being asked about my private life.*

12 *I think they've promoted Tom, but he didn't mention having been promoted when we talked.*

将 **not** 置于动词不定式的被动式（13）或动名词的被动式（14）之前，构成否定式。

13 *They didn't invite us. It was strange not to be invited.* （不说 *… to be not invited.*）

14 *No one had informed me about that. I resented not having been informed.*

D 根据第 **56** 页新闻报道中的信息，用 be, to be, being 或 been 补全下列句子，再选出每个句子对应的被动式类型。

◆ After _being_ trapped for hours, they were found alive. (_c_) a 情态动词被动式的一般形式

1 Herds of cattle are nowhere _____ seen. (___) b 情态动词的被动完成式

2 Small teams have had to _____ flown in to some areas. (___) c 动名词被动式的一般形式

3 Other buildings seem to have _____ blown away. (___) d 短语情态动词的被动式

4 If the wind returns, more trees may _____ knocked over. (___) e 动词不定式被动式的一般形式

5 Dozens of people could have _____ buried in there. (___) f 动词不定式的被动完成式

→ 动词不定式和动名词 139　情态动词和短语情态动词 29

E 选择合适的动词，用其被动式填空，补全下面的新闻报道。

block	close	~~destroy~~	expect	flood	injure	knock	leave	report	rescue

Many homes on the island of Jamaica ◆ _were destroyed_ by a hurricane yesterday. Today, high winds ¹ _____ to bring more rain and problems for the island's residents. Some parts of the island ² _____ without electricity last night and many roads ³ _____ by fallen trees that ⁴ _____ down during the storm. The area around Savanna-La-Mar on the south coast ⁵ _____ and some residents have had ⁶ _____ from the roofs of their houses. Most businesses and schools in Kingston ⁷ _____ today as people emerge from their battered homes to survey the damage. More than 100 people ⁸ _____, but no deaths ⁹ _____.

F 完成下列句子，使其与所给句子的意思尽可能接近，须用上动词的被动式。

1 You can't see the house from the street.
The house _____.

2 'They won't correct your papers before Friday.'
He said our papers _____.

3 Someone must have taken the towels out of the dryer.
The towels _____.

4 Nobody's going to steal your books from this room.
Your books _____.

5 People were telling me what to do all the time and I didn't enjoy it.
I didn't enjoy _____.

G 选择合适的被动动词短语填空。文本来自一篇关于警方使用 DNA 检测的报告。

is also called	has also been used	had been sentenced
is believed	have been shown	may have been convicted
was released	~~can be used~~	would never have been solved

DNA is the chemical in the cells of plants and animals which carries inherited characteristics, or genetic information. DNA testing ◆ _can be used_ to identify each person as a unique individual on the basis of that genetic information. It ¹ _____ 'genetic fingerprinting'. The results of DNA testing are now being accepted as evidence in cases where it ² _____ that the wrong person ³ _____ of a crime.

In recent years, more than 70 people ⁴ _____ to be innocent through DNA testing. Many of those people ⁵ _____ to life in prison. In one case, a man ⁶ _____ after 19 years in prison. DNA testing ⁷ _____ in some murder cases that ⁸ _____ without it.

动词的被动式

3 **接宾语的动词和不接宾语的动词**

只有后面可以接宾语的动词（及物动词）有被动式（1），后面不接宾语的动词（不及物动词）没有被动式（2）。

1　He repaired the bike. Then he painted it. → *The bike was repaired. Then it was painted.*
2　*Nothing happened.* • *We arrived early.*（不说 *We were arrived early.*）

通常用描述行为（3）而非描述状态（4）的动词来构成被动式。

3　They scored a goal in the last five minutes. → *A goal was scored in the last five minutes.*
4　*My sister has two sons.* • *That belongs to me.*（不说 *That is belonged to me.*）

有一些动词，其被动式比主动式更为常用。

5　*Her parents were married in 1997 and she was born two years later.*

及物的短语动词有被动式（6），不及物的短语动词没有被动式（7）。

6　She locked her house up. They broke into it. → *Her house was locked up. It was broken into.*
7　*Friends came over later.* • *My cold went away.*（不说 *My cold was gone away.*）

4 **接双宾语的动词**

有些动词后面可以接两个宾语：一个间接宾语（如 Maria）和一个直接宾语（如 first prize）。这类动词可构成两种被动结构。

8　They awarded Maria first prize. → *Maria was awarded first prize.*
9　They awarded first prize to Maria. → *First prize was awarded to Maria.*

此类动词还有：**give, hand, lend, pass, sell, send, show, teach, throw, write**。

选用哪种被动结构，取决于说话者想要谈论的对象是哪个人或事物。

10　No one taught us English. → *English wasn't taught there.* 或 *We weren't taught English.*

在被动句中，可把间接宾语用作主语，或置于介词 to 而不是动词之后。

11　He handed Cecilia a note. → *Cecilia was handed a note.* 或 *A note was handed to Cecilia.*（不说 *A note was handed Cecilia.*）

如果带双宾语的动词只能用于一种主动结构，那么其被动结构也只有一种。如果间接宾语可紧跟在主动动词之后，那么它就可以作被动句的主语。

12　The judge fined him £250.（不说 *The judge fined £250 to him.*）→ *He was fined £250.*（不说 *£250 was fined to him.*）

如果间接宾语不能紧跟在主动动词之后，就不能把它用作被动句的主语。

13　Then we explained our solutions to him.（不说 *We explained him our solutions.*）→ *Then our solutions were explained to him.*（不说 *He was explained our solutions.*）

这种用法的动词还有：**demonstrate, describe, mention, present, report, suggest**。

注意形式相似的结构"动词 + 宾语 + 对宾语加以分类的名词"。对宾语加以分类的名词不用于构成被动句的主语。

14　Many people considered John Nash a genius. → *John Nash was considered a genius.*
15　They elected Obama President twice. → *Obama was elected President twice.*
　　（不说 *President was elected Obama twice.*）

　　　　　→ 间接宾语 8　短语动词 134　及物动词和不及物动词 6

H 改写下列句子，在可以使用动词被动式的地方使用动词被动式。

1 Someone saw Erin outside the theatre as she was waiting to go in. She had a new hairstyle.

_____

2 Karen feels sad because they didn't promote her and she has to carry on as if nothing happened.

_____

3 He throws the ball to Evans. Evans tries to go past Jennings, but Jennings stops him. It's a foul.

_____

I 选择合适的形容词填空，并从 a、b 两个选项中选出正确的句子（两者可能都正确）。如有必要请查词典。

illegible	inaudible	knowledgeable	reusable
impossible	inexplicable	~~returnable~~	unspeakable

♦ It says here that your deposit isn't _returnable_____.
   a It won't be given back. ✓_____   **b** You won't be given back. _____

1 He doesn't think it's _____ to sell ice to the Inuit.
   a He thinks they can be sold ice. _____   **b** He thinks ice can be sold them. _____

2 His sudden disappearance remains _____. We have no idea what happened.
   a We can't be explained. _____   **b** It can't be explained. _____

3 They think Ted Green is more _____ about orchids than anyone else.
   a An expert is considered Ted Green. _____   **b** Ted Green is considered an expert. _____

4 She couldn't read us the note because of his _____ handwriting.
   a We couldn't be read. _____   **b** It couldn't be read. _____

5 His first two or three sentences were _____, but he soon got more confident.
   a He spoke up. _____   **b** He was spoken up. _____

6 None of us will ever understand the _____ suffering of the refugees.
   a We can never be described. _____   **b** It can never be described. _____

7 You can have one of these _____ envelopes to send Marta the magazine.
   a Marta can be sent the magazine. _____   **b** The magazine can be sent to Marta. _____

J 改正下文中的错误。

The Christmas I remember best from my childhood ~~was~~ happened when I was about five, just after my younger sister born. Lots of people were come to our house with presents for us. I gave the job of taking the gifts and saying 'Thank you'. As each guest was arrived, I handed boxes or bags which filled with things that wrapped in Christmas paper. I told which ones were for me and which ones had to be place in a pile for my new sister. So many presents brought for us. I will never forget the experience of given so much. It really was a very special Christmas.

被动式的用法

K 在本页和下一页的方格中填入对应的示例序号。

5 重点是行为和受影响的对象

使用被动式时，说话者意在通过谈论行为来描述一个过程，而不关注这一行为的施动者☐；或者是在陈述事件时并不知道是谁实施了这些行为，或认为该信息不重要☐。

1   *Wine is made from grapes. • Oranges are grown in Spain. • Oil has to be imported.*
2   *My bag was stolen. • Some trees have been cut down. • I think the old road has been repaired.*

被动式用于谈论在句中作主语的受某行为影响的人或事物☐。这类主语常常是两个或更多个句子谈论的主题☐。在一个句子中，可以用被动式表达对同一个主语造成影响的多个行为☐。

3   *Two old people were attacked in the park. • A tourist was robbed. • I wasn't badly injured.*
4   *After registration, courses cannot be added, dropped or changed without permission.*
5   *The house is still for sale. It was built in 1928. It was completely renovated in 2012.*

同一个主语之后的动词被动式可以用不同的时态：*It was built in 1928 and is being renovated.*

在非正式语言中，更常用不定代词（如 **someone**）或泛指代词（如 **they, you**）加主动动词，较少使用被动式。

6   *Someone stole my bag. • They make wine from grapes. • You should wash fresh fruit.*
也可以用 **one** 作主语，但这种表达非常正式：*One should always wash fresh fruit.*

6 语言风格客观

被动式常用于以一种客观的方式来给出一般信息（并不针对特定的某个人）。例如，被动式常用于表述规则和警告☐；用来描述步骤，特别是用于研究报告☐；以及用在其他类型的一般会避免提及个人（如 **I, we**）的正式书面报告中☐。

7   *20 students were given a test in which they were asked to answer 100 questions.*
8   *In the past year, two new computers were purchased and some old furniture was replaced.*
9   *Parking is prohibited. • Cars will be towed away. • Trespassers will be prosecuted.*

如果想要避免提出针对个人的命令☐，或不想表明所说之事只与说话者自身或个人行为有关☐，可以使用被动式。

10   *I can't do all this work in one day. → All this work can't be done in one day.*
11   *You must remove your shoes before entering. → Shoes must be removed before entering.*

L 改写下面的图书馆规定，将被动结构改为主动结构，用 you 作主语。

Reference books can only be consulted in the library. Special permission must be obtained to use them outside the library. All books should be returned on time or a fine will have to be paid. If the fine is not paid, borrowing rights will be lost. Library books may not be borrowed for others or given to others. If a book is lost, the cost of replacement must be paid.

→ 泛指代词 97 不定代词 98 主语和动词 4

7 用被动式进行转述

在转述由他人作出的陈述、提出的问题 ☐，或以不定式形式表达他人给出的命令和要求 ☐ 时，如果不知道或不想提及说话者，可使用转述动词的被动式。

12 *We were instructed to wait here.* • *I was asked to work late on several occasions.*

13 *I was told that everyone had passed.* • *Some students were asked if they were communists.*

说话者可以在形式主语 **it** 之后使用转述动词的被动式，从而撇清自己和所述信息的关系 ☐。如果不确定所述信息是否可靠，可以将 **claim** 或 **imply** 等动词用在这种结构中 ☐。

14 *It is often said that children can learn foreign languages more easily than adults.*

15 *It was claimed that Andy had stolen something. It was also implied that he was lazy.*

注意，这些转述动词的被动式之后跟的是 **that** 从句。（不说 ~~*It was reported a problem.*~~ ）
可用于这种结构的动词还有：**allege, assert, hint, report, state, suggest, suspect**。

可以将形式主语 **it** 用在 **mention** 之类的转述动词的被动式之前。

16 *Someone mentioned (to me) that he was Irish.* （不说 ~~*Someone mentioned me that he was Irish.*~~ ）→ *It was mentioned (to me) that he was Irish.* （不说 ~~*I was mentioned that he was Irish.*~~ ）

可以用现在时态的转述动词被动式 + 动词不定式来表明自己并不清楚所述的当前事件真实与否 ☐。如果是过去的事，可以用过去时态的转述动词被动式 + 动词不定式的完成式 ☐。

17 'The rebels are near the capital.' → *The rebels are reported to be near the capital.*

18 'She inherited a lot of money.' → *She was rumoured to have inherited a lot of money.*

可以在 **there** 和 **to be** 之间使用转述动词的被动式来转述关于存在某事物的说法。

19 'There are lots of problems.' → *There are said to be lots of problems.* （不说 ~~*There said to be …*~~ ）

20 *There were reported to be thousands of refugees in camps all along the border.*

注意，**tell** 没有这种用法。（不说 ~~*There were told to be thousands of refugees …*~~ ）

M 为每句选择一组合适的动词，用其恰当形式构成短语，将句子补全。

> not mention / receive   report / die   ~~request / keep~~   say / be   tell / not use

♦ Dog owners *are requested to keep* their dogs on a lead in the park.

1 There _____ more sheep than people in some parts of Scotland.

2 The students _____ their computers yesterday because of a virus.

3 Mr Harman's first wife _____ in a boating accident two years ago.

4 It _____ earlier, but six more applications _____ last week.

N 将下面这段话中可以使用动词被动式的地方改写为被动式。

People have claimed that they cannot use tasks successfully with beginner-level students. I designed the following study so that I could investigate that claim. I created two groups of students, each with different proficiency levels. I gave them a task in which I showed them a set of pictures and I asked them to tell a story. I recorded them as they spoke and then I examined their stories.

_____
_____
_____
_____

→ 形式主语 it 102   转述动词 152   that 从句 161

带有 by 短语的被动式与作格动词 (ergative)

8 带有 by 短语的被动式

施动者（agent）指实施或引起某行为的人或物。在主动句中，施动者作主语（1）。在被动句中，通常不提及施动者。如果句子因没有施动者而意思不完整（2），或者为了进行强调和对比（3），可以在动词之后用一个由 by 引导的短语说明施动者。通常不在 by 短语中使用具泛指意义的代词或名词，如 people（4）。

1 *Shakespeare wrote* Hamlet. *Many famous actors have played the title role.*
2 Hamlet *was written by Shakespeare.* （不说 Hamlet ~~was written.~~） *The title role has been played by many famous actors.* （不说 ~~The title role has been played.~~）
3 *Was the* Mona Lisa *painted by Michelangelo or (by) Leonardo da Vinci?*
4 *We / People store equipment in the basement.* → *Equipment is stored in the basement.*

可用 by 短语说明原因（5）或实现某事的方法（6）。

5 *The girl was bitten by a snake. • Flu is caused by a virus and can't be cured by antibiotics.*
6 *The temperature can be controlled by adjusting the thermostat.*

可用 by 短语引出一个行为的施动者，可用 with 短语引出实行此行为所用的事物（7）。在描述句中，有些动词（如 cover, decorate）的被动式后通常用 with 短语而不用 by 短语（8）。

7 *The rescue was filmed by a man* <u>with a video camera</u>. • *The box was locked* <u>with a gold key</u>.
8 *The Christmas tree was covered* <u>with ornaments</u> *and decorated* <u>with lights</u>. （不说 ~~The tree was decorated by lights.~~）

在使用被动式时后面常跟 with 短语的动词还有：**align, associate, crowd, fill**。

O 选择合适的动词并用其恰当形式填空（文本摘自一篇关于莎士比亚的文章），在必要的地方补充 by 或 with。

consider	establish	experience	fill	perform	not write

The Globe

1 Shakespeare was born in 1564 and ＿＿＿＿＿＿＿ many to be the greatest English writer.
2 His early reputation ＿＿＿＿＿＿＿ writing and appearing in his own plays.
3 His plays ＿＿＿＿＿＿＿ interesting characters and memorable speeches.
4 Today, at the new Globe Theatre, the plays ＿＿＿＿＿＿＿ in conditions similar to those which ＿＿＿＿＿＿＿ audiences in Shakespeare's time.
5 Some people have claimed that many of the plays ＿＿＿＿＿＿＿ Shakespeare.

9 作格动词

作格动词是不带宾语（9）但有相应（词形、词义相同）及物动词（10）的动词。

9 *The park closes at six o'clock. • The door suddenly opened.*
10 *A guard closes the park at six o'clock. • Someone suddenly opened the door.*

许多语法书将作格动词与那些只有不及物用法的动词一同视为不及物动词。

有时，使用作格动词而不使用下面这样的被动式。

11 *The park is closed (by the guard) at six o'clock. • The door was suddenly opened.*

作格动词可用于描述自然界中的过程和变化（12），或描述动态但不谈原因（13）

12 *The snow is melting. • This material won't shrink. • The river has dried up this summer.*
13 *Exchange rates stabilized yesterday. • I don't know how it happened, but the string broke.*

作格动词不与反身代词连用。（不说 ~~The string broke itself.~~）
此类动词还有：**burst, crack, crash, grow, increase, shake, start**。

→ by 和 with 132　反身代词 100　及物动词和不及物动词 6

含有 get 的被动式

通常在非正式表达中，可把 **get** + 过去分词（1）用作被动式，代替 **be** + 过去分词（2）。

1 *I'll get paid on Friday. • My books got damaged when the basement got flooded last year.*
2 *I'll be paid on Friday. • My books were damaged when the basement was flooded last year.*

在构成疑问句或否定句时，将助动词 **do** 与含有 **get** 的被动式连用。

3 *Why does Lucy get asked to go to all the parties? We don't get invited to any of them!*

含有 **get** 的被动式常用于表述意想不到的事件（4）和艰难或糟糕的经历（5）。

4 *Professor Brown got stuck in traffic so her lecture got moved till later in the afternoon.*
5 *Did anyone get injured? Some people got hurt. They were lucky they didn't get killed.*

此类短语还有：**get arrested, get broken, get caught, get divorced, get smashed**。

P 为左侧的句子和分句（1—4）选择合适的下文（a—d），再选择合适的词或短语填空。

| get beaten up | reacted | were reported | were stolen |
| get caught | were defeated | were smashed | were treated |

1 After their team _____
   2–0 by a local rival on Wednesday
   night,   (.....)

2 Several shop windows _____
   _____   (.....)

3 'Did any of the thieves
   _____?' asked
   one shop owner in frustration.   (.....)

4 Some people _____
   in hospital for minor cuts and bruises, (.....)

a but no serious injuries _____,
   according to the police.

b 'Of course not,' he explained. 'Because
   nobody wants to _____ by
   those hooligans.'

c and items such as televisions, laptops and
   cameras _____.

d angry football fans _____
   violently.

Q 选择合适的动词并用其恰当形式填空。

| carry | crash | explode | hand | injure | knock |
| open | run | shake | stop | ~~tell~~ | |

When I was in Ireland, people often *▸ told* _____ me that I was lucky. I remember one time, years ago, when I was sitting with friends in the Emerald Arms, Belfast. The door suddenly [1] _____ and a voice called out, 'Bomb! Get out!' Conversations [2] _____ instantly as everyone and everything suddenly moved. Glasses and bottles [3] _____ to the floor. As I started to get up from my seat, I [4] _____ down. I struggled to my feet and then I [5] _____ along by the surging crowd towards the back door. I was pushed out of the door backwards by the force of the people behind me. Then I just [6] _____ like everyone else until I reached a crowd at the end of the street. As I stood there waiting, an old woman told me that there was blood on my cheek. We waited, but no bomb [7] _____, no walls [8] _____ and no windows shattered into a thousand pieces. I wiped the blood from my cheek with a piece of cloth that [9] _____ to me by the old woman. I thanked her. 'It's just a scratch,' she said. 'You're lucky you didn't [10] _____ seriously _____.'

在上文中找出所填动词的施动者（如果有）。

施动者：*people,* _____
_____

测验

A 选出最恰当的词或短语完成下列句子。

1 We were told to put it where it was usually ....
   a belonged   **b** fit   **c** had   **d** stored

2 It wasn't the first time they had been .... how it worked.
   a taught   **b** reported   **c** explained   **d** described

3 DNA tests .... accepted in court cases.
   a are known   **b** were used   **c** have been   **d** will have

4 Something .... happened or they would be here by now.
   a must   **b** must be   **c** must have   **d** must have been

5 There .... to be serious flaws in the design.
   a claimed   **b** reported   **c** were said   **d** were told

B 从每句标有下划线的部分（A，B，C，D）中选出错误的一项。

1 When he said they weren't going to <u>get engaged</u> because they were <u>getting married</u> right away, I
   assumed he wasn't already <u>got married</u>, but I didn't know he had just <u>got divorced</u> that day.

2 No one <u>died</u>, but four people <u>were injured</u> and had <u>to be taken</u> to hospital after a small plane
   <u>was crashed</u> near Dublin last night.

3 The main door <u>couldn't be opened</u>. It <u>had been locked by a special key</u> that the caretaker
   <u>didn't have</u>. He <u>had been given</u> a large set of keys, but none of them fitted the main door.

4 The sign said parking <u>was prohibited</u>, but my car <u>wasn't left</u> there more than five minutes while
   I ran to pick up the shoes <u>were repaired</u> at Mendems, but I <u>was given</u> a parking ticket anyway.

5 A new company has <u>taken</u> over the office which <u>located</u> next to yours and it's going to be
   <u>redecorated</u> after it's been <u>cleaned up</u> a bit.

C 选择合适的动词并用其恰当的被动形式填空，在必要的地方补充 by。

| believe | bite | consider | can cure | experience | recommend | may say |

A hangover is the unpleasant physical feeling which [1] .... the day after
drinking too much alcohol. The expression 'a hair of the dog that bit you' refers to
another drink of alcohol that you might have to help you recover from a hangover.
In the past, it [2] .... that, if you [3] .... a mad dog, you
[4] .... placing a hair from that dog on the wound. This treatment
[5] .... widely .... doctors up to the middle of the
18th century, but it [6] .... no longer .... effective. The
same [7] .... about trying to use more alcohol as a cure for a hangover.

D 完成下列句子，使其与所给句子的意思尽可能接近。

1 'They didn't build Rome in a day.'
  There's a saying that Rome ....

2 They have collected the tests and checked the answers.
  The tests ....

3 A bee sting is more likely to cause death these days than a snake bite.
  Death ....

4 It was reported that there were serious problems with the new design.
  There ....

5 No one gave us instructions or showed us what to do.
  We ....

E 从每对动词（短语）中选择恰当的一个填空。

a are feeding	c are being caused	e being hit	g brought
b are being fed	d have caused	f having hit	h was brought

i died	k frightened	m have driven	o to take
j was died	l was frightened	n have been driven	p to be taken

Thailand has a problem with unemployed elephants which [1] .... on to
the streets by the country's economic crisis and a loss of traditional employment. Many
of them [2] .... by tourists who like [3] .... photographs of
them. Major traffic problems [4] .... by homeless elephants wandering
the streets. Traffic [5] .... to a standstill one day by a raging bull elephant
which [6] .... by the sounds of motorcycles and cars. Another elephant
[7] .... after [8] .... by a car in Bangkok last month.

6 冠词 (article) 和名词 (noun)

名词可分为首字母须大写的专有名词 (proper noun)（如 **Shakespeare**）和首字母不用大写的普通名词 (common noun)（如 **poet**）。一些普通名词是可数的，有单数形式（如 **woman, poet**）和复数形式（如 **women, poets**）。其他一些普通名词是不可数的，没有复数形式（如 **poetry, weather**）。

名词之前可以使用不定冠词 (indefinite article)（*a poet, an old woman*），定冠词 (definite article)（*the weather, the women*），或零冠词（即不使用冠词）（*We're studying _ poetry written by _ women.*）。

A 阅读以下表述，选择你认为最佳的答案。

1	A person is more likely to die in a car accident than an aircraft accident.	True / False
2	It is safer to fly in a newer plane than in an older plane.	True / False
3	A smaller plane is much safer than a larger plane.	True / False
4	The chance of being killed in a major airline crash is close to one in	8 / 18 / 80 million
5	Airplane accidents rarely occur during the take-off and landing.	True / False
6	The more stops in a flight, the more dangerous it will be.	True / False
7	The likelihood of surviving an aircraft accident is about	8 / 18 / 80 per cent
8	Natural materials are safer than synthetic materials if there is a fire.	True / False

B 阅读下面这篇文章，并找出：

1 一个使用不定冠词 an 的例子；　　2 一个和定冠词连用的专有名词。

Flying in modern jets is one of the safest forms of transportation. It has been estimated that travelling by air is 25 times safer than travelling by car. This means that you are much more likely
5 to get killed driving to or from the airport than during the flight.

The safest planes are the large modern jets of the major commercial airlines of Europe and the United States. One study showed that the
10 chance of being killed in a commercial airline crash was only one in eight million. Smaller planes, commuter planes and older planes are far more likely to be involved in accidents.

Most airplane accidents occur during the take-
15 off and landing parts of a flight. It follows that a non-stop flight will be safer than a flight with one or more stops. The duration of the flight doesn't seem to be a factor.

It is estimated that 80 per cent of the people
20 involved in an aircraft accident survive. You can increase your chances of survival by knowing what to do before an accident occurs. Keep your seat belt fastened at all times. Identify the nearest emergency exit and count the number
25 of seats between you and the exit. You may have to feel your way to the exit in the dark. Learn how to open the emergency door in case you are the first person to reach it. Wear clothes made from natural fibres such as cotton and
30 wool rather than synthetic materials which may burn or melt on the skin. Think about carrying a smoke hood with you on the plane. If there is a fire, the hood can help protect you against smoke and toxic gases. Above all, don't panic.

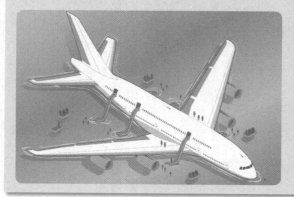

冠词和名词的类型

1 冠词

定冠词 **the** 既可与单数名词连用，也可与复数名词连用。

1　*The names of the authors of the books on the top shelf begin with the letter 'A'.*

不定冠词 **a / an** 与单数名词连用。用 **a** 还是 **an** 取决于紧跟在它后面的单词读音的第一个音，而不是首字母。辅音前用 **a**（2），元音前用 **an**（3）。

2　*Have a banana! • Is this a one-way street? • I need a holiday. • Write a 'U', then a 'P'.*

3　*Have an apple! • Is this an old Rolls Royce? • He has an honest face. • Write an 'N', then an 'O'.*

有时，名词前可以不加冠词。

4　*Do you take milk or sugar? • I like fish, but not chips. • Cheetahs are quicker than ostriches.*

冠词 **a / an** 和 **the** 都属于限定词（参见第 83 页）。可以用其他限定词（**this, those, my, your** 等）代替冠词，但不可把它们与冠词连用。

5　*These books belong on that shelf. • Nora wiped her cheek.*（不说 ~~Nora wiped her the cheek.~~）

2 名词

专有名词以大写字母开头，用来表示人、地点、组织机构、一周中的某天、月份和特殊时节的名称。大多数专有名词前不用冠词（6）；但是，有些专有名词前要用定冠词，这些专有名词有的是复数形式的（7），有的是单数形式的（8）。

6　*Elvis Presley, Shakespeare, Denmark, Rome, NATO, Microsoft, Monday, July, Christmas*

7　*the Robertsons, the Arabs, the Alps, the Netherlands, the United Nations, the Middle Ages*

8　*the Queen, the United Kingdom, the BBC, the Eiffel Tower, the White House, the Gulf War*

普通名词用于对人和事物进行分类或标记。普通名词分为可数名词（countable noun）和不可数名词（uncountable noun）。可数普通名词的单数形式前可以用 **a / an** 或 **each**（9），复数形式前可以用数字或 **many**（10）。

9　*Do you have a black pen or a pencil? • Each child should have a book.*

10　*We don't sell pens or pencils. • There are 20 children. • How many books will you need?*

不可数的普通名词常用于表示一个抽象概念、一项活动、一种物质或一种材料。不可数名词不和 **a / an** 连用，也没有复数形式。不可数名词前可用零冠词（11），也可用 **much**（12）。

11　*Her poem is about flying, freedom and bad luck.*（不说 ~~… a bad luck.~~）

12　*They have food and clothing, but they don't have much water.*（不说 ~~… waters.~~）

不可数名词在英文中又称 non-count noun 或 mass noun。

C 从第 **68** 页关于乘飞机旅行的文章中找出恰当的例子，填入下面的表格。

	不定冠词	定冠词	零冠词
专有名词	*a Rolls-Royce* *an Audi*	*the United Kingdom* *the United States*	*Shakespeare* 1 ....
普通名词 可数名词：单数	*an accident* 2	*the shelf* 3	*(by) bus* 4 ....
可数名词：复数		*the books* 5	*children* 6 ....
不可数名词		*the food* 7	*clothing* 8 ....

冠词: a / an 或 the

D 将恰当例句的序号填入对应的方格中。

3 a / an 或 the

当第一次提到某人或某物时，通常用 **a / an** 来表达它们所属的类别 ☐。如果认为某人或某物已经为他人所知，要用 **the** 来明确地指出该对象 ☐。

1 *We read a story about a man, a young Irish girl and a priceless diamond ring.*

2 *Do you remember the story about the man who tried to steal the ring from the Irish girl?*

4 a / an：用于分类

a / an 可用于将所谈论的事物分类 ☐，即说明该事物所属的类别，也可用于谈论某类事物中的任意一例 ☐。

3 *What's that? ~ It's a mouse. • His first film was a comedy.* （不说 *His first film was comedy.*）

4 *Do you have a ruler? • I'm looking for a knife.* （不说 *I'm looking for knife.*）

a / an 可用于通过人们从事的工作 ☐ 或拥有的信仰 ☐ 对人加以分类。

5 *I'm a socialist, not a communist. • Isn't your friend Voltra a vegetarian?*

6 *Sheila's an architect. • Marcus talks like an engineer. • I'm a student.* （不说 *I'm student.*）

a / an 可用于按定义对事物进行分类 ☐，或用于描述某种特征 ☐，或用在专有名词前来表示该类事物中的一例 ☐。

7 *That painting is a Picasso. • Have you driven a Mercedes? • Is your watch a Swatch?*

8 *The professor had a big nose, a small mouth and an enormous moustache.*

9 *Is a tomato a fruit or a vegetable? • A dolphin isn't a fish, it's a mammal.*

5 the：用于确指

当说话者明确地指出某事物时，是在把它当作听者或读者已了解的事物。如果认为他人像自己一样熟悉某样寻常事物，可以用 **the**。该事物可能是日常生活中的 ☐ 或自然界中的 ☐。

10 *Please don't mention the sun, the sky, the earth, the weather or the environment today.*

11 *Where's the phone? I left it beside the vase on the table in the corner near the window.*

the 可用于通过职业 ☐ 或某种独一无二的社会角色 ☐ 来指明某人。**the** 也用在表示专业机构的名词前 ☐。

12 *Will you wait for the plumber? ~ I can't. I have to go to the dentist. • Ask the caretaker.*

13 *He's thinking about joining the police or the army. • His brother works for the government.*

14 *Would you recognize the Pope, the Emperor of Japan or the Queen?*

the 可用于谈论某个一般概念而不指具体的个例。这种表达方法适用于发明物、乐器 ☐，也适用于泛指某类人、事物或动物 ☐。

15 *The horse was a symbol of freedom to the Apache. • The customer isn't always right.* （泛指任何顾客）

16 *What was life like before the computer? • Can anyone here play the piano or the organ?*

有些表示某人、某事物或某事物一部分的名词后面跟有描述性的短语，特别是含 of 的介词短语 ☐ 或关系从句 ☐。在指明这样的对象时，用 **the**。**the** 也可用在形容词最高级和强调形容词（如 **main, first**）之前 ☐。

17 *The best part was being the first person to get in. That was the main reason for going early.*

18 *Can I see the book that you bought? • The person who called yesterday said you owed him £20.*

19 *It's the middle of June already and I haven't finished painting the front of my house.*

→ a / an, one, the 或零冠词 72   强调形容词 111   形容词最高级 120

E 用 a, an, the 或零冠词（–）填空，补全下面的描述。

◆ *The* Channel Islands are ◆ *a* group of ◆ *–* islands in [1] _____ English Channel near [2] _____ north-western coast of [3] _____ France. They have belonged to [4] _____ Britain since [5] _____ Normans arrived in [6] _____ 11th century, although they are not part of [7] _____ United Kingdom.

Charlie Chaplin was [8] _____ English film actor. He was also [9] _____ director. He did most of his work in [10] _____ USA. Many people consider him [11] _____ greatest comic actor of [12] _____ silent cinema. He appeared in many films as [13] _____ poor man with [14] _____ small round hat, [15] _____ small moustache and [16] _____ trousers and [17] _____ shoes that were too big for him, causing him to walk in [18] _____ funny way.

F 为问题（1—6）选择合适的答语（a—f），并在横线处补充 a 或 the。

1 How often have you done this?　　　（　）　a It's on _____ bottom shelf of my bookcase.
2 What exactly is an olive?　　　　　（　）　b I think he's in _____ navy.
3 Where's your dictionary?　　　　　（　）　c She'd like to be _____ journalist.
4 Why is it so bright outside tonight?（　）　d I'm sure it's _____ fruit.
5 What kind of career does Sally want?（　）　e It must be _____ moon.
6 What does Mrs Reynolds' son do?　　（　）　f Yesterday was actually _____ first time.

G 用 a, an, the 或零冠词（–）填空，补全下面这则新闻。

Lonesome George was [1] _____ giant tortoise in [2] _____ Galapagos Islands who had never found [3] _____ mate and was believed to be [4] _____ last known individual of his species. Scientific studies suggested that [5] _____ lonely tortoise, who was living on [6] _____ Pinto Island, actually belonged to [7] _____ species from [8] _____ island of [9] _____ Española. George was eventually relocated to [10] _____ special breeding centre on [11] _____ Santa Cruz Island where [12] _____ female tortoises from [13] _____ different parts of [14] _____ islands were living. Although he never did become [15] _____ father, George certainly wasn't lonesome any more.

H 改正下文中冠词用法有误的地方。

I remember /really embarrassing moment when I was starting to learn the English. My teacher's name was Trevor Jones. He was from Cardiff in the Wales. He was always making the jokes. One day he wrote words 'English Gramer' on blackboard. He asked us if that was correct. Immediately I offered to answer question. I told him the E should be changed to the A. Trevor said that was good answer and he changed letter. Then he asked me if I was happy with new spelling. With the absolute confidence, I said that it was now correct. Suddenly, the other students started laughing. I looked around in the confusion. My friend whispered that it needed second M. 'Oh, it should have the M too!' I shouted out and Trevor nodded with the smile. It was correct. But I still remember terrible feeling of the embarrassment from that moment.

a / an 或 one，a / an 或零冠词，the 或零冠词

6 a / an 或 one

a / an 和 one 均用在名词之前，表示单个的事物或人。

1　*In some places, there are graves that are used again after one / a year and one / a day.*

one 用于强调数目（表示"只有一个"或"只是一个"）（2）；或谈论一个特定的但未具体说明的时间，通常用于叙事（3）。

2　*We only have room for one passenger. • He tried to balance on one leg, but he fell over.*

3　*One day there was a terrible storm. • One time we almost had an accident.*

one 用于表示确切的数字，特别是在表示较大数字的短语中（4）。a / an 用于表示大致数量和分数（5）。

4　*Our first car cost one thousand, one hundred and twenty pounds. • Add one cup of flour.*

5　*That trip cost almost a hundred pounds. • It took about a day and a half to complete.*

7 a / an 或零冠词

a / an 用于表示被视作单一单位的事物（6）。如果某事物不是单个的或是不可数的，则前面可以不用冠词（7）。

6　*Would you like a coffee? • We have started a new research project. • Look! I caught a fish!*

7　*Do you prefer coffee or tea? • He's doing research on fish or shellfish.*（不说 *He's doing a research …*）

把 a / an 用在名词前，可谈论某类一般事物中的一个个例（8）。当谈论一般概念时不使用冠词（9）。

8　*We bought a cheap wine. • I have a terrible fear of heights. • The old man had a good life.*

9　*I hate cheap wine. • Fear of death can affect anyone. • Life is beautiful, so enjoy it!*

8 the 或零冠词

在复数形式的名词（如 dogs）和不可数名词（如 money）前用 the 表示特指（10），用零冠词表示泛指（11）。

10　*The dogs next door are friendly. • The children have already spent the money we gave them.*

11　*My sister is afraid of dogs. • Michelle's boyfriend is always talking about money.*

对于 poetry, history 等某些名词，如果后面跟有 of 短语，则前面要用 the（12），在其他一些情况中则不用冠词（13）。

12　*The poetry of Philip Larkin is unusual. • We studied the history of Scotland.*

13　*Poetry isn't their favourite subject. • He taught us Scottish history.*（不说 *He taught us the Scottish history.*）

the 加名词可用于表示一个具体的时间（14）或地点（15）。但如果同样的名词跟在介词 in 或 at 之后表示更笼统的概念，则不用冠词（16）。

14　*That was the Christmas before you were born. • Did you hear that noise during the night?*

15　*After you pass the school, you'll see the church. • The prison is a big red building.*

16　*Most people would rather be in school or in church than in prison. • I can never study at night.*
此类介词短语还有：at Christmas, at university, in town, in winter。

在许多表示普遍概念的介词短语中不用冠词。例如，在 going by bus 这个短语中，bus 并不是某辆要被归类或特别指出的公共汽车（17）。在谈论运动项目时也不用冠词（18）。

17　*They came by bus. • Let's go to bed. • Send it by email.*（不说 *Send it by the email.*）

18　*Anwar loves cricket. • Tennis is her favourite sport. • I don't play golf.*（不说 *I don't play the golf.*）

→ a / an 或 the 70　at Christmas 等 126　by bus 等 132　可数名词和不可数名词 74

I 用 a, an, one 或零冠词（-）填空。

One time I went out for *a* meal with [1]_____ group of people from work. That was [2]_____ big mistake! We went to [3]_____ Japanese restaurant. There was only [4]_____ big table and we all sat around it. [5]_____ of my colleagues asked if I'd ever tried [6]_____ dish called shabu-shabu. I hadn't, but I'd eaten sushi before and I assumed it was something similar. I'm [7]_____ vegetarian but I eat [8]_____ fish. So I was horrified when they brought [9]_____ plate of [10]_____ raw beef. Each person takes [11]_____ piece of meat and holds it in [12]_____ dish of boiling water in the middle of the table to cook it, then dips it in a dish of [13]_____ sauce. It was too late to tell them that I didn't eat [14]_____ meat. I began wondering whether I could just leave. How could I make [15]_____ exit without having to eat the meat?

J 用 a, an, the 或零冠词（-）填空，补全下面的释义。如有必要请查词典。

* *A* Christmas tree is [1]_____ evergreen or artificial tree decorated with [2]_____ lights and [3]_____ coloured ornaments in [4]_____ people's homes at [5]_____ Christmas.

* *An* Easter egg is [6]_____ egg made of [7]_____ chocolate or [8]_____ hen's egg with [9]_____ painted shell, given as [10]_____ present to [11]_____ children at [12]_____ Easter.

* _ Passover is [13]_____ Jewish religious festival in [14]_____ memory of [15]_____ freeing of [16]_____ Jews from [17]_____ slavery in [18]_____ Egypt.

* _ Ramadan is [19]_____ ninth month of [20]_____ Muslim year, when [21]_____ Muslims do not eat or drink anything between [22]_____ sunrise and [23]_____ sunset.

* _ Thanksgiving (Day) is [24]_____ public holiday in [25]_____ USA, on [26]_____ fourth Thursday in [27]_____ November, and in [28]_____ Canada, on [29]_____ second Monday in [30]_____ October.

K 用 a, an, one, the 或零冠词（-）填空，补全下面这则新闻。

John Millar, who lives near [1]_____ Stirling in [2]_____ central Scotland, thought he had found [3]_____ bargain when he bought [4]_____ Volkswagen for just [5]_____ thousand, [6]_____ hundred and sixty-five pounds at [7]_____ auction in [8]_____ April this year. Everything was fine for about [9]_____ month, then [10]_____ day, [11]_____ car just stopped. John took it to [12]_____ local garage where [13]_____ mechanic thought there was [14]_____ problem with [15]_____ petrol supply. He was really surprised when he discovered [16]_____ source of [17]_____ problem. He had to remove [18]_____ large, tightly-sealed plastic bag from [19]_____ petrol tank. Inside [20]_____ bag was [21]_____ wad of [22]_____ hundred pound notes. It amounted to fifteen thousand pounds. Suddenly, [23]_____ Volkswagen was [24]_____ even bigger bargain than John had imagined. But John is [25]_____ honest Scot and he reported his discovery to [26]_____ police. They are now trying to find [27]_____ car's previous owner because they want to know where [28]_____ money came from and why it was hidden. John is waiting patiently and hoping that it will eventually be his. When that happens, he won't have to worry about [29]_____ money for [30]_____ petrol for quite some time.

可数名词和不可数名词

L 将恰当示例的序号填入对应的方格中。

9 可数名词

可数名词既有单数形式也有复数形式，通常用来指称可以被视为单独个体的人、生物、物体□或行为、事件□。

1 *actor, bird, car, child, dog, ladder, man, monkey, mountain, telephone*
2 *arrival, crash, goal, lesson, mistake, party, punch, problem, riot, theft*

10 不可数名词

不可数名词与单数动词连用，但并不指称单个事物。它们通常不与 **a / an** 连用。不可数名词用于表示物质和材料□，抽象的概念、品性和状态□，或活动□。

3 *camping, chess, jogging, photography, research, shopping, tennis, training, work*
4 *anger, bravery, education, evidence, freedom, honesty, ignorance, love, poverty, safety*
5 *alcohol, chocolate, cotton, fur, ink, meat, paint, petrol, rice, salt, shampoo, soil, wool*

英语中的一些不可数名词，如 **advice** 和 **information**，在其他语言中的对应词可能是可数的。

6 *advice, applause, assistance, cash, equipment, evidence, furniture, health, homework, information, laughter, leisure, luck, machinery, money, permission, pollution, progress, rubbish, traffic, violence*（不说 *an advice, a homework, equipments, informations*）

11 可数用法和不可数用法

一些名词既可作可数名词，也可作不可数名词。这取决于想用这个名词指单个事物□，还是指一种物质或笼统概念□。

7 *She owns a business. • I saw a chicken. • There's a hair in my tea. • Did you hear a noise?*
8 *Business is booming. • Do you eat chicken? • He has long hair. • There's too much noise.*

一些名词，如 **piece** 和 **drop**，可以与不可数名词□连用，构成可数的名词短语□，来表示不可数名词的独立单位或独立部分。

9 *Nobody likes having to move furniture. • She had blood on her sleeve.*（不说 *She had a blood on her sleeve.*）
10 *There wasn't a piece of furniture left in the house. • I could see drops of blood on the floor.*

此类短语还有：**an act of bravery, a bit of cheese, a bottle of water, a carton of milk, a chunk of concrete, items of information, sheets of paper, two slices of bread**（不说 *two breads*）。

M 为每条释义选择一组合适的名词，搭配 a, an 或零冠词（–），将释义补全（不一定按单词的原顺序填空）。如有必要请查词典。

> bread / piece / soup / toast　　　breakfast / cereal / fruit / milk / mixture / nuts
> country / government / ~~system~~

Democracy is ◆ *a system* of [1]_____ in which everyone in
[2]_____ can vote.

A crouton is [3]_____ small square _____ of
[4]_____ or [5]_____ fried _____, usually served
with [6]_____ .

Muesli is [7]_____ of [8]_____ , [9]_____ , and
[10]_____ dried _____ , usually eaten with [11]_____
at [12]_____ .

泛指名词（generic noun），双数概念的名词（pair noun），集体名词（group noun），复数名词和词尾为 -s 的单数名词

12 泛指名词

名词的泛指用法用于就人或事物的任意个例（前面用 a / an）、一般概念（前面用 the）或大多数例子（复数名词，不用冠词）作笼统表述（1），而非针对真实具体或特定的例子（2）。

1 *An orange has lots of vitamin C.* • *The smartphone rules my life.* • *Women live longer than men.*
2 *I just ate an orange.* • *Camila's new phone is pink.* • *I can see about ten women and two men.*

13 双数概念的名词

双数概念的名词（如 **scissors, trousers**）用于指称供人使用或穿戴的、由两个相配部分构成的物体。通常与复数动词连用（3）。这类名词前有短语 **a pair of** 时，与单数动词连用，用复数代词（**them, they**）代指（4）。

3 *These scissors aren't very sharp.* • *White trousers don't go very well with black shoes.*
4 *A good pair of scissors is hard to find.* • *There's a nice pair of trousers on sale. You should get them because they're really cheap. In fact, you should buy two pairs!* （不说 ~~two trousers~~）

此类名词还有：**binoculars, clippers, jeans, pants, pliers, pyjamas, shoes, sunglasses, tights**。

14 集体名词

集体名词用于指称一群人。把他们视为一个整体时，用单数动词和单数代词（5），视为多个个体时，用复数动词和复数代词（6）。集体名词在英文中也称 collective noun。

5 *The public isn't really interested in what the government is doing unless it increases taxes.*
6 *The public are more likely to complain if they have to pay more taxes.*

此类名词还有：**audience, band, club, committee, family, jury, majority, parliament, team**。在美式英语中，集体名词通常与单数动词连用。

一些专有名词可用作集体名词，表示团队和组织，与复数动词连用。

7 *England are ready to play France.* • *National Rail have announced new plans.*

15 复数名词和词尾为 -s 的单数名词

有些复数名词具有明确含义而且在表达该含义时没有单数用法。

8 *He said thanks for looking after his belongings.* • *Good manners are important.*

此类名词还有：**clothes, congratulations, groceries, outskirts, remains, surroundings, troops**。
词尾不是 -s 的复数名词有：**cattle, clergy, people, police, poultry**。

一些词尾为 -s 的名词看似是复数的，但与单数动词连用，多表示学科、活动或疾病。

9 *Statistics was a difficult course.* • *Aerobics is hard work.* • *Rabies has become a deadly disease.*

此类名词还有：**athletics, billiards, cards, diabetes, electronics, measles, physics, politics**。

一些含复数名词且表示数量的短语也与单数动词连用。

10 *Five miles is a long walk.* • *Twenty pounds is too much!* • *Two weeks isn't enough time.*

N 为句子的前半句（1—5）选择合适的后半句（a—e），再选择合适的名词并搭配 is 或 are 填空。如有必要请查词典。

binoculars	fortnight	mathematics	outskirts	press

1 The _____ of a town _____ (___)   a   to see things far away.
2 The _____ a general term (___)   b   the science of numbers.
3 _____ described as (___)   c   called a _____ in Britain.
4 _____ used (___)   d   for newspapers and journalists.
5 Two weeks _____ sometimes (___)   e   the parts that are far from the centre.

→ 专有名词 69　主谓一致 4

名词所有格（possessive noun）和复合名词（compound noun）

O 将恰当示例的序号填入对应的方格中。

16 使用名词所有格还是复合名词？

名词所有格通常用于表示某事物为某个特定的人或物所有☐，而复合名词通常表示事物的常见结合体，不表示所有关系☐。

1　*Each student's office has a PC.* • *That red thing on a chicken's head is called 'a comb'.*
2　*You have to take these forms to the student office.* • *Do you like chicken soup?*

17 名词所有格

大多数名词通过后加 **'s** 构成名词所有格，以 -s 结尾的名词后一般只加撇号（**'**）。

3　*one man's story, Lee's birthday, children's books, girls' stories, Burns' poems*

注意，Dickens' novels 和 Dickens's novels 这两种写法都是正确的。

名词所有格短语用于表示存在于第一个名词和第二个名词之间广义上的"所有"关系。通常，第一个名词指人或其他生物☐、团体或机构☐、时间☐或地点☐。

4　*London's night life, China's economic policy, Europe's currency, the world's population*
5　*my mother's sister, the Beatles' music, the killer's mistake, a dog's life, birds' nests*
6　*the company's change of plan, the committee's decision, the BBC's news programmes*
7　*yesterday's meeting, next week's schedule, a week's pay, Monday's news*

名词所有格也用于拟人化（personification）表达，也就是将抽象的概念当作人来看待☐，或将一个物体描述为某事物的"所有者"☐。

8　*death's cold hand, love's passionate embrace, jealousy's dark thoughts*
9　*the car's previous owner, the computer's faulty design, the newspaper's circulation*

如果认为他人知道某名词所有格后面的名词是什么☐，或该名词以多数之一而非某特定个体的形式出现☐，可单独使用名词所有格，省略后面的名词。

10　*It's a film of Hitchcock's.* • *She's a friend of Maddie's.*（Maddie 的许多朋友之一）
11　*She's at the doctor's.* • *He has Alzheimer's.* • *We stayed at Tom's.* • *It's bigger than Paul's.*

也可以在名词之后使用 **of** 短语来表示"所有"关系，特别是当某事物是另一事物的一部分时☐，正在描述过程、想法或行为时☐，或者当所有者以一个长短语表示时☐。

12　*the development of industry, the concerns of students, the withdrawal of NATO forces*
13　*the arm of the chair, pages of a book, the roof of the building, the cost of repairs*
14　*What was the name of that girl in Amsterdam?* • *He's the son of the woman we met in Bonn.*

18 复合名词

复合名词由两个（或更多的）单词构成，用于更具体地指称人或事物，说明其应用对象☐、构成材料☐、具体工作☐、所属类型☐，或者发生或应用的地点或时间☐。有时在拼写复合名词时使用连字符（-）☐。

15　*bus driver, car mechanic, history teacher, production manager, airline safety inspector*
16　*application form, can opener, fire extinguisher, swimming pool, emergency exit door*
17　*detective story, horror movie, junk food, health food magazine*
18　*chicken soup, feather pillows, glass bottle, paper plates, vegetable curry filling*
19　*birthday party, morning sickness, street lights, winter coat, dining room table*
20　*a house-husband, a get-together, a do-it-yourself store, a live-and-let-live approach*

→ of 短语 132　物主代词 97　引导关系从句的物主词 178

P 从括号内的每对短语中选择正确的一个填空，完成下面母亲节贺卡上的祝福语。

1 (Life's troubles / Troubles of life)
.... can sometimes leave us with a frown,

2 (each day's worries / worries of each day)
And the .... can get us down;

3 (morning special of news / morning's special news)
But this .... is here

4 (world's problems / worlds of the problems)
To make all the .... disappear;

5 (love's woman / woman's love)
Because of one ...., we can say

6 (Mother Day / Mother's Day)
Thanks and best wishes to you on this ....!

Q 第一部分。选择合适的名词（短语）填空。

sense of responsibility	consumer groups	credit rating	college student
interest rates	buy-now-pay-later world	money matters	give-aways
application forms	bottom line	high-risk borrowers	~~credit card users~~
credit cards	credit card offers	T-shirts	

Is your child starting school soon? Does he or she have a credit card yet? This isn't as strange as it sounds. According to Cathy Yuen, director of College Marketing Services in Los Angeles, ♦ _credit card users_ are getting younger and younger. You may be surprised to learn that teenagers have become one of the most important
¹ .... In the USA, those teens spend over $150 billion a year and an increasing amount of that spending is done with ² .... For credit card companies, it has become crucial to establish a credit relationship with consumers as early as possible. That first credit card is the one that people are likely to keep using for the longest time. As a result, the typical ³ .... receives over 40 ⁴ .... every year. Some lenders are now sending credit card ⁵ .... to high school students with offers of ⁶ .... such as free ⁷ .... Younger teens used to have to wait until they were 18 to sign a contract to get a card, but now their parents are co-signing. Credit card companies lose less money with teenagers than with adults, mainly because of parents willingness to help pay off their childrens credit card debt. Yuen says that, in terms of the ⁸ ...., teens are not ⁹ .... There is also an advantage to getting an early start in the world of credit. If you establish a good ¹⁰ .... early on, you can get better ¹¹ .... when you want to borrow money later for a car or a house. Teenagers may not be famous for their ¹² .... when it comes to ¹³ ...., but in this ¹⁴ ...., they are learning at an early age how to get what they want by using plastic.

第二部分。在第一部分的文章中找出两个错误的名词所有格短语，写出其正确形式。

1 ....

2 ....

语篇中的冠词和名词

19 新信息、旧信息和重述信息

以不同的方式使用冠词和名词来帮助读者和听者理解语篇中的信息。用 **a / an** 引入新信息，用 **the** 再次表述旧信息。

1 *A gunman tried to use a female employee as a hostage after a failed attempt to rob a bank this morning. The hostage was released unharmed and the gunman surrendered.*

2 *There was once a king of a far-away country who had a beautiful daughter. The king had searched the whole country to find a young prince to marry his daughter.*

3 *We read a report in a medical journal about a new treatment for asthma. The report said that the treatment had been effective, but was still experimental.*

可以用 **the** 加一个意思更笼统的名词来重述旧信息。

4 *After police surrounded the bank, the woman was released and the situation ended peacefully.*

5 *The beautiful girl was known throughout the land as 'the lonely princess'.*

6 *Soon after the report was released, the news of the breakthrough brought a barrage of phone calls from asthma sufferers.*

作家有时会在故事的开篇用 **the** 来表述开场白性的信息，仿佛这是旧信息且对故事的叙述在之前就已经开始了。

7 *The boy with fair hair lowered himself down the last few feet of rock and began to pick his way toward the lagoon.*

20 相关信息和简缩信息

可用 **the** 加另一个名词来引入与前面提到的名词相关的信息。在大多数情况下，这两个名词之间存在基于常识的联系。

8 *We were thinking of buying a house in Wimbledon, but the kitchen was too small.*
（一所房屋通常有一间厨房）

9 *Luckily there was a taxi available and the driver spoke English.*

10 *She's written a new book. I can't remember the title. The cover is red with gold letters.*

在一些情况下，这种联系存在于动词和名词之间。

11 *I really liked it, but didn't buy it because the price was too high.*

12 *He asked me about you. There was something odd about the tone of the question.*

13 *We were driving through heavy rain when the windscreen wipers stopped working.*

14 *I worked there for a while, but the pay was terrible.*

也可以用 **the** 加一个复合名词来压缩并重述前面的信息。该复合名词可以由前面一个或多个句子中的信息要素组合而成。

15 *The curve that indicates supply can shift in response to many factors that can't be measured. However, the supply curve shift can be measured.*

16 *You have to fill out a form to apply for a credit card. The credit card application form actually represents a contract.*

R 选择合适的名词并搭配 a, an 或 the 填空。

bicycle	board	film	job	owner	pay	price	restaurant	shop	teacher

1 Lucy got ＿＿＿＿＿ part-time ＿＿＿＿＿ in ＿＿＿＿＿ Italian ＿＿＿＿＿, but ＿＿＿＿＿ was really low.

2 I found ＿＿＿＿＿ old ＿＿＿＿＿ in a repair shop. ＿＿＿＿＿ said it had been his son's.

3 In class, ＿＿＿＿＿ always writes things on ＿＿＿＿＿.

4 According to Allied Cinemas, it will cost you more to see ＿＿＿＿＿ this summer. ＿＿＿＿＿ increase will take effect on 1ˢᵗ June.

→ a / an 或 the 70　复合名词 76

S 用 a, the 或零冠词（–）填空，完成下面这段短篇小说的开头。

Inside [♦] _the_ station café it was warm and light. ¹_____ wood of ²_____ tables shone from wiping and there were ³_____ baskets of ⁴_____ pretzels in glazed paper sacks. ⁵_____ chairs were carved, but ⁶_____ seats were worn and comfortable. There was ⁷_____ carved wooden clock on ⁸_____ wall and ⁹_____ bar at ¹⁰_____ far end of ¹¹_____ room. Outside ¹²_____ window, it was snowing.

T 为左侧的句子和分句（1—10）选择合适的下文（a—j），并在横线处补充 a, one, the 或零冠词（–）。

1　There was _____ dog looking lost outside (____)

2　She's spending _____ Christmas in hospital. (____)

3　I can't understand _____ finance report (____)

4　There was only _____ toilet roll left (____)

5　There's _____ girl pounding the grand piano. (____)

6　We're going to buy _____ new lawnmower. (____)

7　_____ young boy had gone missing. (____)

8　She has _____ terrible cough. (____)

9　He spent his teenage years indoors, worrying about _____ pimples. (____)

10　As I told you, _____ my computer keeps crashing. (____)

a　She's really banging the instrument.

b　Youth is really wasted on the young!

c　They needed people to help with the search.

d　so Mary stopped to help _____ poor animal.

e　I'll get rid of the thing and get _____ new one.

f　because the language is too technical.

g　so the stuff was treated like _____ gold.

h　The old machine was always breaking down.

i　The problem won't go away without _____ medical treatment.

j　It isn't _____ happiest time of her life, I'm sure.

U 下列句子是对一起撞车事故的描述，但句子的顺序不正确。将句子排成最恰当的顺序来描述车祸的发生经过，把序号写在横线上。

_4_ _____

1　There was a small white van behind the tour bus.

2　I saw a tour bus coming down the main road towards me.

3　The bus signalled that it was turning left into the side street,

4　When I was waiting to cross King street,

5　There was also a Mercedes waiting to come out of a side street and turn right.

6　but it couldn't complete the turn because of the Mercedes.

7　and it crashed right into the Mercedes.

8　But the white van had already started to pass the bus

9　So the Mercedes started to come out and turn right.

测验

A 选出最恰当的词或短语完成下列句子。

1 A demonstration is an act of showing by giving proof or _____ evidence.
a a **b** an **c** the **d** –

2 What's in this book? Look at the _____ page.
a content **b** contents **c** content's **d** contents'

3 Dessert is any sweet food eaten at _____ end of a meal.
a a **b** an **c** the **d** –

4 She worked here for a while then _____ afternoon she just quit and left.
a an **b** one **c** the **d** –

5 The police have a new _____ in their search for the bank robbers.
a assistance **b** clue **c** progress **d** information

B 从每句标有下划线的部分（A，B，C，D）中选出错误的一项。

1 Two metres are about the size of most doorways.
 A   B   C   D

2 I take the bus to the university and meet Tom at the sports complex so we can play the tennis.
      A   B   C   D

3 In one class we had to do a research on the language used in business.
   A   B   C   D

4 He took one pair of shoes, two shirts and two trousers, but he forgot to take socks.
                    A   B   C   D

5 Teenagers with credit cards like to buy device's and clothing.
   A   B   C   D

C 用 a, an, the 或零冠词（–）填空。

In ¹_____ morning, Sam listened to ²_____ performance by ³_____ Royal Philharmonic Orchestra on ⁴_____ radio. Then he took ⁵_____ children to ⁶_____ school and went on to ⁷_____ hospital where he works. Two new patients were in hospital with ⁸_____ virus, and ⁹_____ elderly lady with ¹⁰_____ pneumonia.

Around ¹¹_____ midday, he met his wife Clara who teaches ¹²_____ physics at ¹³_____ university. They ate ¹⁴_____ lunch with ¹⁵_____ Hamptons, a couple who work for ¹⁶_____ BBC.

D 将下面的标题改写成句子，补充恰当的冠词并作出其他必要改动。

1 Masked Man Robs Woman Outside Post Office
   Yesterday, _____.

2 Bank of England Raising Interest Rates by 1.5%
   In business news, _____.

3 Murder of Priest in Kent Shocks Community
   Yesterday's news of _____.

4 New Account of Scottish History by English Writer Criticized
   Reviewers have criticized _____.

E 用所给名词组成正确的短语，填入下文中的横线处，并在必要的地方补充冠词。

authors / report	earth / health	group / latest report
century / middle	~~environmental disaster / threat~~	organization / Sims
challenges / urgency	destruction / environment	population / world

The Earthguard Institute has issued a report warning of ◆ *the threat of environmental disaster*
by ¹ _____ unless we do something soon.

'² _____ facing us requires action now,' said
Dennis Sims, one of ³ _____ .

⁴ _____ is a watchdog group that regularly issues
reports on ⁵ _____ and its people. According
to ⁶ _____, rising temperatures, falling
water supplies and shrinking forests are problems that will only get worse as
⁷ _____ increases to 9 billion by 2050.

'People's optimism about the future is blinding them to the potential for worldwide
disaster,' Sims warned. 'We must try to reduce global warming by replacing coal
and oil with renewable energy sources such as wind and solar power. If we continue
⁸ _____, our grandchildren will inherit a wasteland.'

7　限定词（determiner）和数量词（quantifier）

限定词指冠词（**a / an, the**）、指示词（demonstrative）（**this, that, these, those**）和某些物主词（possessive）（**my, your, her, his, its, our, their**）这类可以和名词搭配以进一步明确名词所指人或事物的词（*That man with the beard is my uncle.*）。

数量词是用于谈论可数（**a few, many, ten** 等）或不可数（**a little, much** 等）的数量的词或短语。数量词可以用在名词之前（*I ate a few biscuits and drank some milk.*），可以代替名词（*Did you want any? There wasn't much left.*），或与 **of** 短语连用（*I left most of the biscuits for you. I couldn't eat all of them.*）。

A 阅读下面这则故事，并找出：

1　一个将 all 和限定词连用的例子；
2　一个使用了 all 但没用限定词的例子。

A My grandfather always drove the car and my grandmother sat beside him. I sat in the back seat, my eyes just below the level of the window, seeing the world through their voices.

5 **B** My grandfather had learned to drive in the country where there were few people or vehicles on the road. My grandmother sometimes mentioned that there were a lot of other cars on the road now and he should 10 take a little more care. In reply to this, my grandfather liked to say, 'All cars have brakes.' He would slow down to turn a corner and we would hear the sound of screeching tyres behind us, followed by the loud blast of a car 15 horn. 'George, you have to signal sooner,' she would suggest. 'Oh, what's all the fuss about?' he'd ask. She'd say, 'That car could have hit us,' and he'd reply, 'Oh, all cars have brakes.'

C Both of my grandparents had grown up on 20 farms in this area, but during their lifetimes the whole area had changed a lot. They said it was strange that there were no farms now. In place of those old farms were lots of new houses, new streets and a big new shopping centre. There 25 were still a few old houses with large gardens and my grandparents lived in one of them.

D The advantage of all these changes, my grand-

mother tried to point out, was the convenience of shopping. Everything was close now, even 30 a new supermarket. My grandfather enjoyed the advantages, but he complained about some of the problems that came, he said, from 'too many people in too little space trying to do too much at once!' But he really liked the 35 new coffee house that sold fresh pastries. We seemed to end up there each Saturday.

E It was on our return from one of those Saturday trips that we had our accident. We had eaten some strawberry tarts and my grandfather was 40 telling me how lucky I was that I didn't have to get up every morning and pick strawberries on the farm as he had to. We reached our driveway and turned in. Perhaps his thoughts were back on the farm. Perhaps he didn't expect anyone to 45 be there. He just kept driving up our driveway and straight into the back of another car. There was a terrible crunching sound and we jolted to a stop. A woman appeared beside his window. 'Are you okay?' she asked. 'Of course not! What 50 are you doing in my driveway?' he demanded. 'I was hoping to persuade you to sell your house. Couldn't you stop?' she asked. 'You were in the way!' he almost shouted. 'Well, all cars have brakes, you know,' she said in a very matter-of- 55 fact way.

B 选择合适的句子作为上文各段（A—E）的结尾句，将对应段落的字母序号填入括号。

1　There was always someone trying to get them to sell it.　(......)
2　As my grandmother turned to see if I was okay, her worried look changed to a smile.　(......)
3　He always winked and said it was a special treat for me.　(......)
4　I think they sometimes forgot I was there.　(......)
5　The circumstances would change, but this answer seemed to cover every situation.　(......)

限定词

1 冠词

冠词（**a / an**, **the**）是最常见的限定词（参见第 **70** 页）。

    1 *I'm sure I read an essay or a story by Theroux, but I can't remember the title.*

2 指示词

用在单数名词前的指示词（**this**, **that**）不同于用在复数名词前的指示词（**these**, **those**）。这类指示词也叫"指示限定词"。

    2 *I love this chair. • That car was speeding. • These people were here first. • I forgot those papers.*

指示词也可以用作代词：*Here are the files. Those are older. These are new.*

this / these 用于谈论距离说话者较近的某物，或与此地、此时紧密相关的某物。**that / those** 用于谈论距离此地、此时较远的某物。这种区别也适用于描述时间和事件（**3**）、地点（**4**）、人物（**5**）时。

    3 *I'm free this afternoon. • I'm busy these days. • That party was great! • I hated those meetings.*

    4 *This classroom is better than that awful place we had before with those tiny windows.*

    5 *Look at these people in this photo – they're crazy. • Do you remember that weird teacher we had?*

指示词还可用于清楚区别已发生的事（**that / those**）（**6**）和将发生的事（**this / these**）（**7**）。

    6 *We discussed the economy last week. In that class, we were concerned with money.*

    7 *In this class, we will shift our focus to politics and the use of power.*

that / those 可用在表达消极的情感时，增加些许"疏远"的表达效果。

    8 *Those idiots in Parliament do nothing but talk. • I never liked that old grey carpet.*

3 物主词

被用作限定词的物主词，即物主限定词（possessive determiner），有 **my, your, his, her, its, our** 和 **their**。它们被用在名词前（如 **my seat**），不同于 **mine** 等物主代词，后者用于替代名词或名词短语。

    9 *Are these our seats? ~ I think 12A is your seat and 12B is my seat.*（不说 ~~mine seat~~）

注意，物主限定词 **its** 不同于 **it's**（= it is 或 it has）。

物主限定词可用于表达某人与所拥有物的关系（**10**），某物或某人的一部分（**11**），感觉或想法（**12**），家庭成员或朋友（**13**），以及事件（**14**）。

    10 *I don't know where I left my bag. Can I borrow your dictionary for a minute?*

    11 *The guard put his hand on my shoulder. The guard dog just stood there, wagging its tail.*

    12 *Tasha tried not to show her disappointment. She just thanked the teacher for his advice.*

    13 *My wife has invited her parents and a couple of their friends to our son's birthday party.*

    14 *When is your birthday? • In our last conversation, he told me about his holiday in Spain.*

用介词短语谈论已指明的某个人的身体一部分时，通常使用 **the**，而不是物主词。该身体部位被视为一个地点，而不是某人的所有物。

    15 *One man was shot in the leg. • Robin leaned forward and kissed me on the cheek.*

注意，应说：*He kissed my cheek.*（不说 ~~He kissed the cheek.~~）

C 在第 **82** 页的故事中，找出以下限定词与名词连用的例子。

    1 四个不同的指示词：............... ....

    2 四个不同的物主词：............... ....

数量词

4 • 数量词和名词

数量词指诸如 **both, most, several, two** 之类的单词和 **a little, a lot** 之类的短语，用于谈论数（*How many?*）或量（*How much?*）。数量词可以像限定词一样用在名词前（1），也可以像代词一样替代名词（2）。

1 *There were two pies left.* • *Can I have a little sugar, please?* • *We've had several complaints.*
2 *'Let's get both,' she said.* • *I don't need a lot.* • *Most were about the loud music.*

有些数量词（如 **a few, many**）只和复数名词连用（3），有些（如 **each, every**）只与可数名词的单数形式连用（4），而另一些（如 **a little, much**）则只与不可数名词连用（5）。

3 *There are many occasions when seat belts save lives, yet a few drivers still won't wear them.*
4 *Each person has to take a card. Every card has a different number.* （不说 *Every cards …*）
5 *I think the soup needs a little salt.* • *I hope there isn't too much traffic.* （不说 *too much cars*）

数量词 **all, every, no** 用在名词之前时，可以和数字连用。

6 *All nine players were tired.* • *We get a bill every three months.* • *No two people are the same.*

D 根据给出的用法说明，将下列数量词填入合适的位置。

| ~~all~~ | a few | a little | both | each | every | many | much | one | several | ten |

1 *all,* _____ 用在不可数名词（如 money）之前。
2 _____ 用在单数可数名词（如 book）之前。
3 *all,* _____ 用在复数名词（如 books）之前。

5 • 数量词与 of 短语连用

数量词可以和 **of** 搭配，用在限定词（7）或代词（8）之前。

7 *Two of the students were late.* • *Take any of these chairs.* • *Some of my friends got ill.*
8 *Two of them were absent.* • *You can't take any of those.* • *Some of us felt really tired.*

在这类结构中，名词之前一定要有 **of** + 限定词，代词之前要有 **of**。
（不说 *Two of students*; *Take any these chairs*; *Some my friends*; *Two them*; *Some us*）

数量词加 **of** 也可以用在表示地点名称的专有名词前。

9 *Most of Europe will have sunny weather tomorrow.* （不说 *Most Europe*; *Most of the Europe*）

数量词和限定词之间通常有 **of**，但 **all, both, half** 之后的 **of** 可以省略。

10 *All of these books are old.* • *Both of his sons play rugby.* • *I spent half of the morning in bed.* •
All these books are old. • *Both his sons play rugby.* • *I spent half the morning in bed.*

every one（不是 **every**）和 **none** 可以用在 **of** 短语之前（11），或单独用作代词（12）。

11 *Every one of my friends had a phone, but none of them called me.*
12 *Is there no sugar? ~ There's none.* • *Did you check every container? ~ I checked every one.*

E 从第 82 页的故事中找出四个由数量词与 of 短语构成的表达。

1 _____ 3 _____
2 _____ 4 _____

→ 可数名词和不可数名词 74　限定词 83

F 为每个段落选择一组合适的词或短语，将段落补全（不一定按词语的原顺序填空）。

> a / both / each / half　　　his / my / these / those　　his / much / some / the
> a little / most / some / 30　　a few / our / that / this

A　I got ¹＿＿＿＿＿＿ earrings, the small ones I'm wearing, from ²＿＿＿＿＿＿ grandmother. I really didn't like ³＿＿＿＿＿＿ green earrings that Andy brought back from ⁴＿＿＿＿＿＿ trip to Sri Lanka.

B　Look at ⁵＿＿＿＿＿＿ photograph here in the newspaper. Doesn't it remind you of ⁶＿＿＿＿＿＿ strange woman who came to teach ⁷＿＿＿＿＿＿ French class for ⁸＿＿＿＿＿＿ weeks last year?

C　Peter wasn't paying ⁹＿＿＿＿＿＿ attention to the lecture when Angela leaned over and tapped him on ¹⁰＿＿＿＿＿＿ shoulder. As he turned, she pointed to ¹¹＿＿＿＿＿＿ notepad and whispered, 'Can I borrow ¹²＿＿＿＿＿＿ paper?'

D　Although there are ¹³＿＿＿＿＿＿ mountain peaks that receive over ¹⁴＿＿＿＿＿＿ inches of rain annually, ¹⁵＿＿＿＿＿＿ of Arizona has a warm, dry climate with only ¹⁶＿＿＿＿＿＿ rain in winter.

E　When two horses in ¹⁷＿＿＿＿＿＿ race finish together at exactly the same time, it's called a dead heat. It means that ¹⁸＿＿＿＿＿＿ of them win and ¹⁹＿＿＿＿＿＿ of them receives ²⁰＿＿＿＿＿＿ the prize money.

G 选择合适的数量词或其他词填空。如有必要请查词典。

> a few　every　most　lottery　maximum　quota
> any　many　much　majority　minority　unanimous

◆ A *minority* is the smaller part of a group, sometimes consisting of only *a few* people.

1　The ＿＿＿＿＿＿ weight allowed per passenger is a restriction on how ＿＿＿＿＿＿ luggage each passenger is permitted to put on board an aircraft.

2　A ＿＿＿＿＿＿ system is one that sets a limit on how ＿＿＿＿＿＿ people are permitted to do something.

3　A ＿＿＿＿＿＿ choice is one that ＿＿＿＿＿＿ person agrees with.

4　In a ＿＿＿＿＿＿, people can usually choose ＿＿＿＿＿＿ number that they think will win.

5　A ＿＿＿＿＿＿ decision is one that is based on what ＿＿＿＿＿＿ people want.

H 改正下文中限定词和数量词用法有误的地方。

I read a newspaper article about some ~~of~~ Spanish boys who got lost while they were hiking in Scotland. One of boys fell and twisted the ankle badly so he couldn't move. Unfortunately, there was no phone or GPS signal there. Most them stayed with injured boy while two the older boys left to find help. However, this two boys didn't know where to go and, after walking round in big circle for a few hour, ended up back with his friends. Luckily, each boys had brought some water and food with him, so all them managed to survive a cold wet night out of doors. They were rescued the next day.

some 和 any, no 和 none

I 将恰当例句的序号填入对应的方格中。

6 some 和 any

some 和 any 与复数名词和不可数名词连用 ☐，或用作代词 ☐，表示不明确的数量。some 和 any 可与 of 短语连用，谈论具体的人或物 ☐。

1 *Some students don't get any homework.* • *I wish I had some money.* • *Do you have any matches?*
2 *I love seashells. I was hoping to find some on the beach, but I didn't see any.*
3 *Some of the new teachers have already arrived. Have you met any of them yet?*

some 用在肯定句 ☐ 以及期望得到肯定回答的提问或主动提议 ☐ 中。

4 *Did you get some new furniture?* • *Can I borrow some paper?* • *Would you like some tea?*
5 *Some trees stay green all year.* • *We have some friends in Rome.* • *Let's get some blueberries.*

any 用于含有否定意思的句子 ☐。any 也用于不期望得到具体回答的问句 ☐、if 从句 ☐，以及表达"任何一个，无论哪个" ☐。

6 *Do Mr and Mrs Young have any children?* • *Is there any food left?* • *Are there any questions?*
7 *Anna can't eat any milk products.* • *We never have any free time.* • *He denied any wrongdoing.*
8 *Any piece of paper will do.* • *Any doctor knows that.* • *Call any time after eight o'clock.*
9 *If there are any problems, give me a call.* • *I asked her if she had any money.*

some 可用于粗略地谈论一个相当大的数量 ☐，一个大约的数字或百分比 ☐，以及某个身份或名称不详的人、地点或事物 ☐。

10 *It will take some time to recover.* • *They have known about the problem for some years now.*
11 *He now lives in some village in Wales.* • *There was some woman here asking about you.*
12 *That was some 20 years ago.* • *In one survey, some 70 per cent of Americans described themselves as middle class.*

7 no 和 none

no 和 none 可用于强调 "not any" ☐。在作主语的名词之前用 no，不用 not any ☐。

13 *There aren't any farms left in that area.* → *There are no farms left.* • *There are none left.*
14 *No explanation was given.* • *No dogs are allowed.* （不说 ~~Not any dogs are allowed.~~）

no 用在单数形式或复数形式的名词之前 ☐。none 用作代词，且可与 of 短语连用 ☐。

15 *I had six phone messages, but none from Mr Blake. None of them seemed very urgent.*
16 *When my parents were young, they had no television and no Internet so they read books.*

J 为左侧的句子（1—6）选择合适的下文（a—f），并在横线处补充 any, some 或 no。

1 I don't know what Joseph does with all his money. (___)
2 I hope you'll be careful when you're using the paint. (___)
3 Do you mind having black coffee today? (___)
4 You have to pick a number between one and ten. (___)
5 I think we'll probably need paper plates and napkins. (___)
6 The concert was good, but I couldn't stay to the end. (___)

a I'll bring _____.
b I'm afraid there's _____ milk.
c He never has _____.
d So I missed _____ of it.
e Choose _____ of them.
f Don't spill _____.

→ 可数名词和不可数名词 74　no, none 等 48　some, any 104

K 改写下列句子，在句中加入 some 和 any，并作出其他必要改动。

♦ Have you had news from your family in Prague? I heard that areas were badly flooded.
*Have you had **any** news from your family in Prague? I heard that **some** areas were badly flooded.*

1 There was woman here yesterday asking if we had old clothes, but I told her we had not them.

2 Information in that newspaper article was incorrect. There isn't wolf or bears in Scotland.

3 I've managed to find dry paper to start a fire, but I can't light it. Don't you have match?

4 I'm sure I made mistake when I was typing. If you find mistake, please correct them.

L 下列句子选自一篇关于学生生活的文章，用 any, no 或 some 填空。

Did you know that ♦ *some* thirty percent of students have to leave university, not because they can't cope with their studies, but because they simply can't afford it?

In one survey, researchers found that students cited [1] money' more often than [2] other reason, such as 'courses too difficult', for ending their studies.

During interviews with the researchers, [3] of these former students said that they had tried to do part-time jobs after classes, but they had discovered that they didn't have [4] time or they had [5] energy left for study when they finished their jobs at night.

When the researchers asked these students if they had received financial support from their parents, [6] said they had, but the majority said they hadn't received [7] .

Most of those interviewed said they had [8] plans to return to university [9] time soon.

M 选择合适的数量词或形容词填空。如有必要请查词典。

| any | some (×2) | no (×2) | none (×2) | dead |
| empty | extinct | scoreless | uninhabited | |

1 I went to get those _____ boxes from the back of the bookshop, but someone else had taken the whole stack. There were _____ left.

2 Morgan Island is _____ now. At one time there were _____ 20 fishing families who lived on the rocky island during the summer months, but nowadays there are _____ .

3 There may still be _____ red squirrels in the forests of Scotland, but there aren't _____ left in England. They are certainly _____ in the southern parts of England.

4 The last England–Sweden game had a lot of great football, but _____ goals, ending in a _____ draw.

5 Latin is considered a _____ language in the sense that there is _____ population of speakers who learn it as their first language.

all 和 both, half 和 whole

8 all 和 both

all 用在复数名词和不可数名词之前，用于作出非常笼统的陈述（1）；**all (of)** 用在限定词加名词之前，用于作出更具体的陈述（2）。

1 *All cars have brakes.* • *All students must wear uniforms.* • *All information is confidential.*
2 *All (of) these cars are for sale.* • *All (of) the information you asked for is on our website.*

all of（不是 ~~all~~）可用在代词前（3）。一般不单独使用 **all**，而使用 **everyone / everything**（4）。

3 *Did you write down their names? ~ No, not all of them.* （不说 ~~all them~~）
4 *Everyone laughed at his jokes.* • *Everything was a mess.* （不说 ~~All was a mess.~~）

在谈论两个物或人时，用 **both** 而不用 **all**，用 **both of** 而不用 **all of**。

5 *Use both hands to hold it.* • *Both (of) my brothers are older than me.* • *Both of them live in London.*

可把 **all** 和 **both** 用在主语或宾格代词后（6），或者助动词或动词 **be** 后（7），表示强调。

6 *The men all agreed to wait.* • *Tim explained it all.* • *We both need a holiday.* • *I like them both.*
7 *We had all heard about the two Williams sisters. They were both very talented.*

9 half 和 whole

half 用在限定词之前（8），或限定词和名词之间（9），表示测定的量。有时用 **half (of)** 表示大约一半（10）。

8 *A pint is more than half a litre.* • *We'll be there in half an hour.* （不说 ~~half of an hour~~）
9 *Get a half litre if you can.* • *A half hour should be long enough.* （不说 ~~a half of hour~~）
10 *I've only answered half (of) the questions.* • *I lost half (of) my money.* • *Take half (of) this pie.*

代词前要用 **half of**：*I can't eat half of it.* （不说 ~~I can't eat half it.~~）

可把 **whole** 用在限定词和单数名词之间（11），把 **the whole of** 用在限定词、代词或表示地点的专有名词之前（12），强调 "全部" 或 "整个"。

11 *The whole area had changed.* • *I can't eat a whole pie!* • *The woman told us her whole life story.*
12 *I spent the whole of this past weekend in bed.* • *The strike is affecting the whole of France.*

N 为问题（1—4）选择合适的答语（a—d），并在横线处补充 all, both, half 或 whole。

1 How much longer will the rain last? ( )   a You can have _____ of them for £10.
2 How much is 16 ounces? ( )   b It might go on like this for the _____ week.
3 How much are those two books? ( )   c _____ of it, so he's penniless now.
4 How much money did he lose? ( )   d I think it's almost _____ a kilo.

O 选择合适的限定词填空，在必要的地方补充 of。

> all   both (×2)   half   no   none   one (×2)   whole

Nowadays, ♦*all* _____ young girls can play football if they want to. When I was young, I really wanted to play football, but [1] _____ girls were allowed to in my school. In fact, [2] _____ the girls was allowed to play any ' boys' sports'. It was just [3] _____ the rules. I learned about the game from my father and my uncle. [4] _____ them had been football players and they often watched games on TV. I knew that [5] _____ teams in a match started with 11 players and [6] _____ them had special positions. I learned that that there was a break after 45 minutes, when [7] _____ the game was over and that 'full time' meant the [8] _____ game was finished. It was fun to watch, but I would rather have been [9] _____ the players.

→ 可数名词和不可数名词 74   限定词 83   everyone / everything 98   分数 93

each 和 every, either 和 neither

0 each 和 every

each 和 every 用于单数可数名词之前。如果把两个或更多的人或物分开看待，用 each（1）。如果把三个或更多的人或物合在一起看待，用 every（2）。

1 *Each day is better than the last.* • *He came in with a cup in each hand.* （不说 *… in every hand.* ）

2 *Every window was broken.* • *The Browns go to Paris every year.* （不说 *… every years.* ）

可把 each of （不是 every of）用在带限定词的复数名词前（3），或用在复数代词前（4）。each（不是 every）可用在句中的不同位置（5）。

3 *Each of her toenails was a different colour.* （不说 *Each her toenails …* ）

4 *Each of you must work alone.* • *Give a pen to each of them.* （不说 *… every (of) them.* ）

5 *We each got one piece.* • *We were each given one piece.* • *We were given one piece each.*

every （不是 each）可用于强调 "尽可能多的"（6），或谈论每隔一段固定时间就发生的事（7），可用在 almost 和 nearly 之后（8）。

6 *He had every opportunity to complete the work.* • *We wish you every success in your new job.*

7 *There's a bus every ten minutes.* • *Take two tablets every four hours.* （不说 *… each four hours.* ）

8 *His team lost almost every game.* • *We run nearly every day.* （不说 *We run nearly each day.* ）

11 either 和 neither

想表示两个人或物中的 "任何一个" 时，把 either 用在单数可数名词之前（9），或把 either of 用在带限定词的复数名词之前或代词之前（10）。

9 *Either parent can sign the form.* • *Left or right?* ~ *You can go either way.* （不说 *… either ways.* ）

10 *Either of the parents can sign.* • *Tea or coffee?* ~ *I'd be happy with either of them, thanks.*

用 neither / neither of 而不用 either / either of 来表达 "两者都不"。以 neither of 开头的主语在正式语言中用单数动词（11），在非正式语言中有时用复数动词（12）。

11 *Neither parent has signed it.* • *Neither of the boxes was big enough.* • *Neither of us likes coffee.*

12 *I'm sorry, but neither of my kids are up yet.* ~ *So, do neither of them want to go with us?*

P 选择合适的词填空。如有必要请查词典。

| choice | couple | doubles | ~~pair~~ | quarterly |
| twins | each | either | every | neither (x2) |

◆ Behind the nun came four young white-faced boys, dressed in grey uniforms, walking in pairs, _each pair_ _____ holding hands.

1 Simon Weston and Joe Barnes were actually _____ who had been adopted by different families when they were born and _____ of them knew about the other until they were almost 40 years old.

2 The _____ was between a boat trip or a bus tour round the island and _____ would have been fine with me, but Sian wasn't feeling well and didn't want to leave the hotel.

3 James and Lyndsay are a young _____ who have been together for about three years, but _____ of them wants to get married.

4 Next year you'll have to send £400 in _____ payments, which is £100 _____ three months.

5 In a mixed _____ match in tennis, _____ team consists of a man and a woman.

many, much 和 a lot (of); more 和 most

12 many, much 和 a lot (of)

含糊地表达"许多个；大量"的意思时，可以在复数名词前用 **many**（1），在不可数名词前用 **much**（2），两种情况下都可以使用 **a lot of**（3）。

1　*Many people believe in life after death.* • *There are **many** ways to improve your health.*
2　*How **much** money did you bring?* • *Please hurry, because there isn't **much** time left.*
3　*I used to smoke **a lot of** cigarettes when I studied. I drank **a lot of** coffee too.*（不说 ~~a lot coffee~~）

通常在正式语言中用 **many / much**，在非正式语言中用 **a lot of** 或 **lots of**。

具体谈论某群体中的个体或某事物的部分时，可以将 **many of** 用在限定词加复数名词之前，或复数代词前（4）；将 **much of** 用在限定词加不可数名词之前，或单数代词前（5）。可将 **much of**（不是 ~~many of~~）与单数可数名词或表示地点的专有名词连用，表示"……的一大部分"（6）。

4　*Many of their customers have complained.* • *Many of them have started going to other shops.*
5　*How **much of** your time is devoted to research? ~ Not **much of** it, I'm afraid.*
6　*Cats spend **much of** the day asleep.* • *It will be a dry sunny day over **much of** Britain.*

many 和 **much** 可以不与名词搭配，单独使用。

7　*People still use butter in cooking, but **many** say they don't use as **much** as before.*

在非正式语言中，**a lot**（不是 ~~a lot of~~）也可以单独使用：*We don't need **a lot**.*

many 和 **much** 通常用在疑问句和否定句中（8），也可用在肯定陈述句中的 **as, so** 和 **too** 之后（9）。通常在正式的肯定陈述句中，可用短语 **a good / great deal (of)** 而不用 **much (of)**，用 **a large number (of)** 而不用 **many (of)**（10）。

8　*How **many** do you want?* • *How **much** do they cost?* • *There aren't **many** left.* • *I don't have **much** cash.*
9　*Take as **much** time as you need.* • *I have so **much** work to do!* • *You bought too **many** things.*
10　*It requires **a great deal of** money and **a large number of** dedicated people to run a school.*

在非正式表达中，可把 **many**（不是 ~~much~~）用在限定词之后（11），或用在 **a / an** 之前（12）。

11　*I'm just one of her **many** admirers.* • *He explained **the many** rules and regulations they had.*
12　*He had spent **many an** uncomfortable night in cheap hotel rooms with thin walls.*

much（不是 ~~many~~）可用作副词，位于否定式的动词之后，或比较级之前。

13　*I didn't sleep **much** last night because I was so worried.* • *I'm feeling **much** better now.*

可以在肯定式和否定式的动词之后把 **a lot** 用作副词：*The area had changed **a lot**.*

13 more 和 most

表达比较含义时用 **more** 和 **most**，不用 **much** 或 **many**。**more** 表示"（数量）更多的"（14），**most** 表示"（数量）最多的；大多数，大部分"（15）。

14　*More children are being educated at home. They are spending **more** time with their parents.*
15　*Most American teenagers say they have **most** fun when they are shopping at the mall.*

也可把 **more** 和 **most** 用在形容词和副词之前：**more quickly, the most expensive**。

more of 和 **most of** 可用在限定词（16）、代词（17）和专有名词（18）之前。

16　*I've already eaten **more of** the cake than I should.* • *Most of those bananas were rotten.*
17　*I really liked it, but I can't eat any **more of** it.* • *I had to throw **most of** them away.*
18　*I hope to see **more of** Spain during my next trip.* • *Most of Venice is under water.*

more（不是 ~~most~~）表示"另外的"时，前面可用其他数量词修饰。

19　*I don't need **much more** time, just **two more** hours.* • *Is there any **more** tea?* • *There's **no more**.*

→ 可数名词和不可数名词 74　限定词 83　more / most 与形容词 / 副词连用 120

Q 改写下列句子，在句中加入 many 或 much，并作出其他必要改动。

- ♦ There wasn't food left, but we weren't very hungry so we didn't need.
  *There wasn't **much** food left, but we weren't very hungry so we didn't need **much**.*

1 There hasn't been discussion of the new road, but older village residents are against it.

2 Did you ask how these postcards cost? How them are you going to buy?

3 I'll be later today because I have so different places to go to and there's so traffic in town.

4 I asked my classmates if they did homework and said they didn't do unless there was a test.

R 用 many, many of, much 或 much of 填空。这些句子选自一篇关于英国酒吧的文章。

- ♦ Pubs are important in the social life of *many* British people.
1 _____ village pubs are very old and are the centre of village life.
2 For _____ the year they rely on local customers.
3 In the summer they get _____ their customers from nearby towns or cities.
4 _____ old pubs are quite small and don't have _____ room inside.
5 In recent years, _____ them have added garden areas, with tables outside.

S 为句子的前半句（1—6）选择合适的后半句（a—f），并在横线处补充 more, more of, most 或 most of。

1 Saudi Arabia is very hot   (_) a so I have _____ to spend.
2 I liked those pens so much   (_) b I am not very good at making speeches.
3 I earn a lot _____ than you (_) c but I don't like _____ vegetables.
4 I can eat _____ types of fruit, (_) d and _____ it is desert.
5 As _____ you know, (_) e but I can't eat any _____ it.
6 The pie is really good,   (_) f that I bought six _____ them.

T 用 many, more 或 much 填空，补全下面的天气预报。

There's not ♦ *much* _____ sunshine in the forecast for this weekend and
¹ _____ areas will see ² _____ rain than usual for this
time of the year. Saturday will start with some bright spells and scattered showers,
³ _____ of them heavy, giving way to ⁴ _____ persistent
rain later in the afternoon. Southwest winds will bring ⁵ _____ unsettled
weather and rain to ⁶ _____ of England and Wales on Sunday.

(a) few 和 (a) little, fewer / fewest 和 less / least

14 ▶ a few 和 a little

含糊地表达"几个；少量"的意思时，可以在复数名词前用 a few（1），在不可数名词前用 a little（2）。a few 和 a little 也可以不与名词搭配，单独使用（3）。

1. *There may be a few minutes left at the end.* • *I brought a few pieces of paper.*
2. *There may be a little time left at the end.* • *If you add a little salt, the soup will taste better.*
3. *Do you want milk? ~ Just a little.* • *Did you see any stars? ~ There were a few.* （不说 ~~There was a few.~~）

具体谈论某群体中的个体或某事物的部分时，将 a few of 用在限定词或复数代词之前（4），将 a little of 用在限定词或单数代词之前（5）。

4. *I've seen a few of those cartoons that Gary Larson drew. Mary has a few of them on her wall.*
5. *I use a little of this moisturizing cream when my skin feels dry. You only need a little of it.*

a little 可用作副词，位于动词之后，或位于分词形容词或比较级之前。

6. *I only slept a little.* • *We were a little annoyed at first.* • *My mother is feeling a little better now.*

15 ▶ few 和 little

通常在正式语言中，用 few（不是 ~~a few~~）和 little（不是 ~~a little~~）来表达"不多的"（7）。常用 not (very) many（代替 few）和 not (very) much（代替 little）来强调数量很少（8）。

7. *The refugees have few possessions and little hope of returning home soon.* （不说 ~~a little hope~~）
8. *They don't have (very) many possessions. They don't have (very) much hope.*

通常在正式语言中，若想强调某物的总数或总量少，将 few / little 用在限定词和名词之间。

9. *I quickly packed my few belongings and spent the little money I had on a one-way ticket home.*

16 ▶ fewer / fewest 和 less / least

表达比较含义时用 fewer 和 less，而不用 few 或 little。fewer 用在复数名词之前（表示"数目更少的"），less 用在不可数名词之前（表示"更少量的"）。

10. *I've been trying to eat fewer snacks and less junk food as part of my diet.*

在非正式语言中，less 也可以和复数名词连用：*There were less questions than last time.*

fewer of 和 less of 可用在限定词（11）和代词（12）之前。

11. *There are fewer of those small shops now.* • *I'd like to spend less of my time in meetings.*
12. *The swans are back, but there are fewer of them this year.* • *Sugar isn't good for you. Eat less of it!*

可用 the fewest（13）和 the least（14）表示"（数量）最少的"。

13. *Ali made the fewest mistakes. Nick is the most cheerful and seems to have the fewest worries.*
14. *You complain that you make the least money here, but that's because you do the least work.*

也可把 least 和 less 用在形容词和副词之前：less quickly, the least expensive。

U 为句子的前半句（1—5）选择合适的后半句（a—e）。在横线处补充 a few, few, a little 或 little，并在必要的地方添加 of。

1	We had very _____ problems living here ( )	a	and the _____ water that was left.
2	The teacher seemed _____ disappointed ( )	b	so I only ate _____ it.
3	The home-made soup was very salty ( )	c	and we've had _____ sunny days too.
4	We shared the _____ pieces of fruit ( )	d	until our car was stolen _____ days ago.
5	It's been _____ warmer recently ( )	e	that only _____ us had done the work.

→ 比较级，less / least 120　可数名词和不可数名词 74　限定词 83

乘数(multiplier), 分数(fraction)和百分比(percentage)

17 乘数

乘数是 **once, twice, three times** 之类的单词和短语,可用在限定词之前来说明某事发生的频率(1),或倍数关系(2)。乘数还可以与含 **many / much** 或形容词 / 副词的 **as … as** 结构连用(3)。

1 *I play tennis once a week.* • *I see my sister about four times a year.* • *We eat three times a day.*

2 *He sold it for twice the original price.* • *Those tomatoes are two or three times the average size.*

3 *We have twice as many saucers as cups left.* • *She's paid three times as much as I am.*
   • *He can run twice as fast as me.* • *Some of the essays were twice as long as mine.*

18 分数和百分比

分数(如 **a quarter, two-thirds**)可与 **of** 连用,后接限定词或代词。

4 *It takes a quarter of an hour.* • *I only used two-thirds of the oil, so there's a third of it left.*

half 用在限定词之前时可以省略 **of**:*Half (of) my answers were wrong.*

百分比(如 **5%, five per cent**)可用在名词前,或与 **of** 搭配,用在限定词或代词之前。

5 *There was a 10% increase.* • *They take 30% of my pay. I get 70% of it.*

per cent 有时写作一个单词(**percent**),尤其在美式英语中。

分数和百分比与单数可数名词或不可数名词连用时,搭配单数动词;与复数名词连用时,搭配复数动词。

6 *Two-thirds of the report is written.* • *About 20% of the students are Asian.*

V 选择合适的词或短语填空,在必要的地方补充 of, as, a 或 the。如有必要请查词典。

~~eighth~~	four times	once	quarter	twenty per cent	twice	two-fifths

◆ A furlong is *an eighth of a* _____ mile.

1 The money was divided equally among the four brothers, so each received _____ it.

2 _____ year we have our annual family gathering at my grandparents' house.

3 A centimetre is about _____ inch, or 0.394 inches to be exact.

4 A litre bottle holds almost _____ much as a pint.

5 Did you know that at least _____ adult population can't read?

6 At £600,000, the selling price is almost _____ price (£151,000) that Dan and Ginny Swisher paid for their house just six years ago.

W 选择合适的词或短语填空。

a few	fewer	fewest	fifty per cent	little

Although the world's population is still increasing, the rate of growth has slowed down over recent decades. There is [1] _____ chance that population growth will level off before 2050 at the earliest, but there are [2] _____ indications that the growth rate will probably keep declining. Women in the wealthiest countries continue to have the [3] _____ children. However, partly because of better education and employment opportunities, many women in poorer countries are choosing to have [4] _____ babies. In some places, the birth rate is now [5] _____ lower than just 30 years ago.

测验

A 选出最恰当的词或短语完成下列句子。

1 When Mary said to the dog, 'Stop wagging your tail', _____ tail started wagging faster.
a your **b** hers **c** its **d** their

2 The new job provided money for expensive toys, but not very _____ time to play with them.
a little **b** few **c** much **d** a lot

3 They said on the news that _____ of Scotland was covered in snow.
a each **b** half **c** whole **d** any

4 Cars were parked on _____ side of the street.
a all **b** both **c** each **d** every

5 She liked to say that she was just one of his _____ happy customers.
a all **b** lots of **c** many **d** some

B 从每句标有下划线的部分（A，B，C，D）中选出错误的一项。

1 All their neighbours each gave a little money and some their friends helped too.

2 A third of them had blue triangles and two-thirds had green squares or circles, but I didn't like either colours or any of the designs.

3 We spent a great deal of time looking through a large number of books to help him find a few information about Bermuda, but he knew most of it already.

4 I talked to the students and all think that both Mike and I have lots of money, but we really don't have very much.

5 Claire and Charlie said that they'd seen most of the Europe on their trip and they both mentioned that every city centre was starting to look the same, with only a few exceptions.

C 从每对词或短语中选择更恰当的一个填空。

| all / both | any / some | many / a lot of | ~~my / mine~~ |
| a few / a little | either / neither | that / the | |

When we were young, * *my* _____ sister and I spent ¹ _____ time together on our own. Our parents ² _____ worked and they always seemed to be busy with ³ _____ big project. One of them was usually there when we came home from school, but sometimes ⁴ _____ of them could make it home before dark and they would ask our neighbour, Mrs Green, to check if we were okay. I remember one time when we were playing basketball. My sister got annoyed and threw the ball at me. I turned my back and it bounced off and hit her straight in ⁵ _____ face. As her nose started to bleed, Mrs Green arrived and let out a terrible shriek. We all got a fright, but there was only ⁶ _____ blood. It wasn't serious. We decided not to tell our parents about it.

D 完成下列句子，使其与所给句子的意思尽可能接近。

1 There aren't a lot of people who are willing to help others.
Not many ....

2 We've written fifty per cent of the report already.
Half ....

3 We weren't given any explanation for the delay.
No ....

4 We all want to live forever.
All ....

E 选择合适的词或短语填空，在必要的地方补充 of。

| no | many | more | most (x2) | little |
| twice | a great deal | 88 per cent | 51 per cent | |

A recent article on "Injuries in Extreme Sports" in the *Journal of Orthopaedic Surgery and Research* presented a summary of the findings of medical research in that area, as well as advocating for more doctors with relevant professional expertise.

Extreme sports are activities involving high speed, real or perceived danger, [1] .... physical exertion, specialized equipment and spectacular stunts. Participation in these activities is associated with [2] .... [3] .... injuries and deaths than regular sports. One major reason is that they often take place in remote locations with [4] .... or [5] .... access to medical care. [6] .... the injuries reported are fairly predictable.

Since skydiving involves jumping from a plane and waiting as long as possible before opening a parachute, the majority of injuries, around [7] ...., occur during landing, with [8] .... them involving the lower extremities.

The risk of serious injury from snowboarding is estimated at about [9] .... that of traditional downhill skiing, with bone fractures the [10] .... common type of injury.

The number of people participating in extreme sports continues to increase with the inevitable result that more medical professionals will be needed with specializations in orthopaedic surgery.

8 代词（pronoun），代替（substitution）和省略（ellipsis）

代词是一种用来代替名词或名词短语的语言形式，例如：it, someone, these, they, them, theirs, themselves 和 each other。（*There was a £5 note on the floor of the cafeteria. Someone must have dropped it. The boys looked at each other.*）

代替指用 one, ones, so 和 do so 等语言形式来代替名词短语、动词短语或分句。（*'Is it a real one?' asked Barney. 'I think so,' said Max.*）

省略指略去某些词或短语，不再重复。（*Max looked round quickly, then _ reached down, _ grabbed the money and _ hurried out of the room.*）

A 阅读下面几篇短文，并找出：

1　一个使用 it 的例子；
2　一个含有 she 并运用省略手法的句子。

A I was born in 1939. The other big event of that year was the outbreak of the Second World War, but for the moment that did not affect me. Sydney in those days had
5　all of its present attractions and few of the drawbacks. You can see it glittering in the background of the few photographs in which my father and I are together. Stocky was the word for me.

B In the 1940s, a couple of American
10　scientists tried to raise a chimpanzee named Viki in their own home, treating her as a human child. They spent five years trying to get Viki to say English words by
15　shaping her mouth as she made sounds.

C They always say that boys are better at maths than girls. When we actually look at the test results, we find that girls generally do better than boys during the primary
20　school years, but the advantage shifts to boys in high school. That shift occurs when students are given more freedom to select the subjects they will study and girls tend not to go for more maths.

25　**D** You know the feeling. You meet someone for the first time, and it's as if you've known each other all your lives. Everything goes smoothly. You know just what she means; she knows just what you mean. You laugh
30　at the same time. Your sentences and hers have a perfect rhythm. You feel terrific. You're doing everything right.

E She took his right hand and placed it against hers, palms touching. He didn't get
35　the point at first. Then he realized that she was comparing the size of their hands. The difference made her laugh.
'What's funny?'
She told him his hand was funny.
40　'Why mine? Why not yours?' he said. 'If the difference is great, maybe you're the funny one, not me.'
'You're the funny one,' Lu Wan said.
She matched left hands now and fell
45　sideways to the bed laughing. Maybe she thought they were two different species.

B 选择合适的句子作为各篇短文（A—E）的结尾句，将对应短文的字母序号填入括号。

1　And you think she's terrific too.　(......)
2　They are more likely to choose something else.　(......)
3　One of them was exotic and it wasn't her.　(......)
4　Handsome was the word for him.　(......)
5　Despite their efforts, she never did speak.　(......)

人称代词（personal pronoun），泛指代词（generic pronoun）和物主代词（possessive pronoun）

1 人称代词：**I, me, they, them** 等

人称代词中作为主格代词，用在动词之前的有：**I, you, he, she, it, we, they**。作为宾格代词，用在动词和介词之后的有：**me, you, him, her, it, us, them**。

1　*We like her.* • *She loves him.* • *He hates you.* • *You told them about me.* • *I hope they'll listen to us.*

在简短回答中不使用动词而只使用人称代词时，人称代词用宾格形式（2）。在比较结构中，通常在 **as** 和 **than** 之后使用代词的宾格形式（3）。

2　*I'm feeling hungry. ~ Me too.* • *Who was making all that noise? ~ Them, not us.*

3　*We don't have as much as them.* • *Both of my brothers are older than me.*

有时也使用主格代词，但这种表达听起来非常正式：*They are older than I.*

通常用 **it** 代指动物。如果认为某个动物，例如宠物或故事中的角色，具备人的特质或特殊的性格，可以使用 **he** 和 **she** 来代指。

4　*Pooh is a friendly bear. He enjoys eating, singing and playing with his friends.*

如果所指之人男女都有可能，可以使用词组 **he or she**（而不是只用 **he**）（5）。经常用复数名词和 **they** 代替 **he or she**（6）。

5　*By the age of two, a child can understand five times as many words as he or she can say.*

6　*By the age of two, children can understand five times as many words as they can say.*

2 泛指代词：**you, we, one, they**

泛指代词包括：**you, we, one** 和 **they**。**you** 用于泛指包括说话者在内的"人们"（7）。**we**（不是 I）用来陈述一种把读者或听者也涵盖进来的更普遍的看法（8）。用 **one** 来泛指"人们"是很正式的表达，在现代英语中很少这样用（9）。

7　*If you are 'self-absorbed', it means that you are only concerned about yourself and your own interests.*

8　*When we think of cheese, we don't usually think of sheep, but as we saw in the last chapter, …*

9　*If one wishes to be a good parent, one should never lose one's temper with a young child.*

在非正式语言中，可以用 **they** 来泛指除了说话者以外的"人们"，或代指"权威人士"（10），从而代替被动语态（11）。

10　*They say that an apple a day keeps the doctor away.* • *They should rehabilitate criminals.*

11　*It is said that an apple a day keeps the doctor away.* • *Criminals should be rehabilitated.*

3 物主代词：**mine, theirs** 等

物主代词包括：**mine, yours, his, hers, ours** 和 **theirs**。它们可以代替名词所有格短语（12），或回答以 **whose** 开头的问题（13）。

12　*I couldn't work in Mary's room. Hers* (= Mary's room) *is even smaller than yours or mine.* • *Mary's parents have a hot tub too, but I think theirs is different from ours.*

13　*Whose bag is this? ~ I thought it was yours. It isn't mine.*（不说 *It isn't ~~the mine~~.*）

可以将物主代词置于 **of** 短语中（如 of mine），用在以限定词或数量词（**a, some** 等）开头的名词短语之后（14）。这种结构可用于谈论非特定的实例（如 a painting of his），而不是特定的或独一无二的实例（如 his painting）（15）。

14　*Was Erica a roommate of yours?* • *I went hiking with some friends of mine.*

15　*Sam Piper is a successful artist. I read that a painting of his recently sold for over £10,000.*

C 在第 96 页的短文中找出符合下列描述的代词。

1　在同一篇短文中出现的两个不同的泛指代词：_____

2　在同一篇短文中出现的三个不同的物主代词：_____

→ 限定词 83　of 短语 132　名词所有格 76　数量词 84

指示代词 (demonstrative pronoun) 和不定代词 (indefinite pronoun)

4 指示代词：**this, these, that, those**

指示代词，或指示词，包括 **this, that, these** 和 **those**。**this / these** 用于代指距离说话者较近的或与说话者关系密切的某物（1），**that / those** 用于代指距离说话者较远的某物（2）。

1 （在正门旁边拿起一个盒子和一些信件）*This is quite heavy.* • *These look like bills.*

2 （从房间另一头指着正门这里的盒子和信件）*That must have books in it.* • *Those are just bills.*

介绍某人时可用 **this / these**（3），指出某人身份时可用 **that / those**（4）。

3 （介绍某人）*This is Anna Thomas and these are her two sons, Nick and Jason.*

4 （指出远处某人的身份）*That's Mrs Parker and those are her two grandchildren.*

指示词也可以作为限定词用在名词之前：**that woman, those children**。

可以用指示代词来区别在时间上距离现在较近的事（用 **this, these**）（5）和较远的事（用 **that, those**）（6）。

5 *The next question is this: who will pay for it?* • *These are the best days of your life, so enjoy them.*

6 *Jack and Amber got married? ~ When did that happen?* • *Those were the happiest days of my childhood.*

5 不定代词：**someone, something** 等

someone 和 **something** 是不定代词。不定代词还有：**anyone / anything, everyone / everything, no one / nothing**。它们用于泛泛地谈论人（7）和事物（8），通常用在说话者无法或不想更具体地指明这些人和物的情况下。

7 *Someone must have taken my book. Has anyone seen it? ~ No one took it. It's over there.*

8 *The fire destroyed everything. We couldn't find anything afterwards. There was nothing left.*

可以用 **somebody, nobody** 等代替 **someone, no one** 等，表达的意思不变。

不定代词作主语时，后面通常使用单数动词和复数代词。

9 *Someone has been calling and saying they have to talk to you about their schedule.* • *If anyone calls, just take their number and say I'll call them back as soon as possible.*

someone / something 通常用在肯定句或期望得到肯定回答的疑问句中（10）。**anyone / anything** 用在含否定意义的句子或开放性问题中（11），或用于表达"任何人 / 事物，无论哪个人 / 什么事物"（12）。

10 *I was looking for someone who spoke Arabic.* • *Can I ask you something about the homework?*

11 *Can you see anyone outside?* • *I didn't say anything.* （不说 ~~I didn't say something.~~）

12 *It isn't difficult, anyone can do it.* • *Isaac is really helpful, he'll do anything you ask him to.*

somewhere, anywhere 等是不定副词 (indefinite adverb)，用于泛泛地谈论地点。

13 *Let's go somewhere different for lunch. ~ But there's nowhere within walking distance.* • *I've looked everywhere for my glasses, but I can't find them anywhere.*

不定代词和不定副词之后可以使用形容词（14）和 **else**（15）。

14 *Do you have anything smaller?* • *I think he's someone important.* • *There's nothing new here.*

15 *Do you want anything else?* • *It wasn't me, it was someone else.* • *There's nowhere else nearby.*

D 在第 **96** 页的短文中找出两个含不定代词的句子。

1 ....

2 ....

→ 代词后的形容词 112　指示限定词 83　every 89　some, any, no 86

E 选择合适的代词填空。

| him | his | that | this | they | it | yours |

1 Excuse me, Graham. Is this bag _____?
2 I think _____ should cut government spending rather than raise our taxes again.
3 We read a story about Winnie the Pooh and a friend of _____ called Christopher Robin.
4 John volunteered to take Anna and William's mail, so I gave _____ to _____.
5 I know we allowed you to go away for a whole month before and now we're asking you to take only a fortnight, but _____ was last year and _____ is now. Things have changed.

F 使用 you, we 和 they 将下列句子改写为不那么正式的语言。

♦ It is said that one cannot teach an old dog new tricks.
They say you can't teach an old dog new tricks.

1 A person should not use a phone while he or she is driving.
You know that _____
2 This old factory is going to be demolished so that a new school can be built.
I heard that _____
3 People who are self-indulgent allow themselves to do or have too much of what they like.
If _____
4 One should not criticize when one is not sure of one's facts.
I think that _____

G 选择合适的名词（短语）或代词填空，补全下列释义。如有必要请查词典。

| camouflage | a disguise | a mirage | everything | no one | nothing | something (×3) |

1 _____ is _____ you use to change your appearance so that _____ can recognize you.
2 _____ is a way of hiding _____ by making it look the same as _____ around it.
3 _____ is an effect caused by hot air on roads or in deserts which makes you think you see _____ such as water when _____ is there.

H 改正下文中的错误。

I studied English in my first school, but I don't remember learning ~~something~~ *anything* there. We had one teacher who always brought songs and she played it for we to learn the words. I think they were hers favourite songs, but in our class no really understood the words. She put us in groups to discuss the music, but every talked about different something in his groups. And no ones were trying to practise his English very much. I only remember the words of one song that went like that: 'You can't always get what your want, but if you try sometimes you get what your need.' That was interesting words and obviously I did learn somethings from that teacher.

反身代词（reflexive pronoun）和相互代词（reciprocal pronoun）

6 反身代词：**myself, themselves** 等

反身代词（也称作 reflexive）包括：**myself, yourself, himself, herself, itself, ourselves, yourselves** 和 **themselves**。当宾语和主语为同一个人或物时，使用反身代词代替宾格代词。

  1 *Be careful or you'll hurt yourself.* • *I'm afraid I might cut myself.*（不说 *I'm afraid I might cut me.*）
     • *Isn't it amazing how the human body heals itself after an injury?*（不说 *... the body heals it ...*）

反身代词没有所有格形式。可以在名词前使用 **my own** 等：*He has his own ideas.*

当介词的宾语与句子主语相同时，在大多数介词之后可以使用反身代词（2）。在 **above, below, beside, near** 等地点介词之后，或与 **bring, take** 等动词搭配的 **with** 之后，使用宾格代词（不用反身代词）（3）。

  2 *Alice never buys anything for herself.* • *Carlos only thinks about himself.*
  3 *Amy put the bag down beside her.* • *You should take an umbrella with you.*（不说 *... with yourself.*）

反身代词也可用来表示强调。可把反身代词用在名词短语或代词之后，强调正是某个人或物本身（4）；也可用反身代词描述行为，强调没有他人帮忙，"亲自"做某事（5）。

  4 *This book was signed by the writer herself!* • *You yourself said that she was a great writer.*
  5 *I repaired the flat tyre myself.* • *Isaac and Maddie painted the whole house themselves.*

by + 反身代词强调"独自，单独"：*She lives by herself.* • *I'll do it by myself.*

描述某些动作，如刮胡子（**shave**）和洗淋浴（**shower**），通常不使用反身代词（6）。但是，如果想特别强调，如强调完成这一行为很艰难，可以使用反身代词（7）。

  6 *Their father used to get up, shave, shower, get dressed and make breakfast for all of them.*
  7 *But since his accident, he can't shave himself or even dress himself without their help.*

I 为句子的前半句（1—4）选择合适的后半句（a—d），并在横线处补充恰当的代词。

1	He got a hammer and some nails	( )	a	and take care of _____.
2	Remember to eat well, exercise regularly	( )	b	and they saw the city below _____.
3	Thanks for offering to help,	( )	c	and repaired it _____.
4	The plane started to descend	( )	d	but I can do it _____.

7 相互代词：**each other** 和 **one another**

相互代词 **each other** 和 **one another** 在意思上没有差别。

  8 *The cat and the dog hate each other / one another.* • *They always avoid one another / each other.*

如果同样的行为或情感双向发生在两个或更多个人或事物之间，使用相互代词（9），而不用反身代词（10）。

  9 *The candidates described each other.*（所有人相互描述）
  10 *The candidates described themselves.*（每个人描述了自己）

相互代词可用在介词之后（11），也可以使用所有格形式（12）。

  11 *The two girls never argued with one other. They were always chatting to each other.*
  12 *They even wore each other's / one another's clothes sometimes.*

如果动词表示的行为是双向发生的，可以用 **each** 作主语，**the other(s)** 作宾语（13）。如果某一行为由一方做出，作用于另一方，用 **one** 作主语，**the other(s)** 作宾语（14）。

  13 *I asked the boys if they had broken the window and each blamed the other.*
  14 *There are two buses at five-thirty and one always follows the other in case the first one gets full.*

→ 宾格代词 97　地点介词 129

J 用代词 it, they, we, you 或恰当的反身代词填空。

They say that if you want something done right, ◆ *you* _____ have to do it
1 _____. And we all know that if something is broken, 2 _____
certainly won't fix 3 _____. As a result, there are many more DIY ('Do
It Yourself') shops in Britain these days. It seems that 4 _____ have all
suddenly decided to do our home repairs 5 _____. So, are all the real
builders and plumbers out of work now? Apparently not. They're even busier now, trying
to fix the mess left by those who discovered that 6 _____ really couldn't do
it 7 _____ and had to call for professional help.

K 用介词 about, by, for, near, with 与恰当代词组成的短语填空。

1 Erica York was a self-taught mathematician who liked to spend hours _____ in
the library.

2 The man seemed very self-centred and only wanted to talk _____.

3 People who are self-employed work _____, not a company.

4 I took a small knife _____, hoping I would only have to use it in self-defence.

5 Test your self-restraint by placing something you really like to eat _____, but
don't eat it.

L 为每段描述选择一组合适的词语，将描述补全（不必按词语的原顺序填空）。如有必要请查
词典。

> another / each / one / the other   another's / each / one / other's
> each / other / you / yourself

Mutual respect is a feeling of admiration that people have for 1
2 _____ equally, and self-respect is a feeling of pride in 3 _____
and the belief that what 4 _____ do or say is right and good.

An exchange is an arrangement through which two people or groups from
different countries visit 5 _____ 6 _____ homes or do
7 _____ 8 _____ jobs for a short time.

Wrestling is a sport in which two people fight by holding onto 9 _____
10 _____ while 11 _____ tries to throw or force
12 _____ to the ground.

M 用下列动词（短语）的恰当形式与反身代词或相互代词组成短语，补全句子。

> agree with   blame   express   hurt   meet

1 All students are required to give a presentation on their projects and to _____ as
clearly as possible.

2 The boy said that his sister had slipped on the wet floor and _____.

3 Both drivers said it wasn't their fault. They _____ for the accident.

4 My aunt and uncle always seem to have different opinions about things and they almost never
_____.

5 Before they got married, Gavin and Gwen visited his parents in England and then her parents
in California, so they could _____ families.

形式主语（empty subject）it

在表达时间、距离或天气的句子中，可把 **it** 用作形式主语，与动词 **be** 搭配。

1　*It's ten o'clock. • It's two miles to town. • Is it raining?*（不说 ~~Is raining?~~）

it 作主格人称代词时，代指某事物或动物（2）。**it + be** 之后可以跟形容词或名词，再接名词性从句（3）。

2　*Where's the breadknife? ~ It's in the drawer. • We saw their new puppy. It was really cute.*

3　*It's sad that she's leaving so soon. • It was just a coincidence that we were both in London.*

it + be 之后可以跟形容词或名词，再接动名词（4）或动词不定式（5）。

4　*It was nice talking to you. • It's an advantage having a rich father.*

5　*It's not wise to hike in the mountains by yourself. • It might be an exaggeration to say he's rich.*

在正式语言中，可以用名词性从句（6）、动名词（7）或动词不定式（8）作主语，代替 **it**。但是，不能用名词性从句、动名词或动词不定式代替 **there**（9）。

6　*It was obvious that Brazil was going to win.* → *That Brazil was going to win was obvious.*

7　*It's often a problem for Henry being so tall.* → *Being so tall is often a problem for Henry.*

8　*It's a real pleasure to meet you at last.* → *To meet you at last is a real pleasure.*

9　*There will be someone to meet you at the airport.*（不说 ~~To meet you at the airport will be someone.~~）

在 **it** 之后，通常使用某种形式的动词 **be**，但也可以使用 **surprise** 和 **frighten** 等动词及宾语来描述某种反应（10），还可使用 **seem** 和 **appear** 等动词表达某个结论（11）。

10　*It surprised everyone that Maria won. • It really frightened me to see the horse and rider fall.*

11　*It seems that he was unhappy in London. • It appears that he has been neglecting his studies.*

it 也可以作形式宾语，用在表示"喜欢"（或"不喜欢"）的动词之后，后跟名词性从句（12）；或用在 **find, make, think** 等动词之后，后跟形容词，再接从句或动词不定式（13）。**it** 位于 **regard, see, view** 等某些用于表达观点的动词之后时，后面要跟 **as**（14）。

12　*I hate it when the alarm suddenly goes off. • My parents love it that we live closer now.*

13　*I find it surprising that you waited so long. • The loud music made it difficult to talk. • We thought it strange that he was still in his pyjamas.*（不说 ~~We thought strange that he was …~~）

14　*They regard it as encouraging that both sides are willing to continue negotiations.*

N　将下列句子改写为以 it 开头的正式程度较低的句子。

1　That Anthony never helps with the cleaning really annoys everyone.

_____

2　Not having a car can be a big disadvantage.

_____

3　To see potential problems in advance is very important in my job.

_____

4　Why she left so suddenly was a complete mystery.

_____

5　To discover that your passport was missing must have been a shock.

_____

6　That people can eat such unhealthy food and live so long always amazes me.

_____

→ 动词不定式和动名词 139　名词性从句 162　人称代词 97

形式主语 there

there 作形式主语与动词 be 搭配，用在名词短语之前。名词短语决定动词用单数还是复数形式。名词短语之后常跟状语，例如表示所在处（如 in *Travel* magazine）或时间（如 on Friday）的介词短语。

1   *There was an article in* Travel *magazine about Munich.* • *There are two meetings on Friday.*

在非正式语言中，**there's** 常与复数名词搭配：*Don't forget there's two meetings.*

there + be 用来陈述（2）或询问（3）某人或某事物是否存在于某地或者客观存在。

2   *There was an old man in the waiting room.* • *There are no snakes in Ireland.*

3   *Are there any questions?* • *Is there a bathroom upstairs?* （不说 *Is a bathroom upstairs?*）
不用 **it** 陈述或询问某物是否在某地或客观存在。（不说 *Is it a bathroom upstairs?*）

可用 **there**（不是 **it**）**+ be** 搭配数量词，表述关于数量的信息。

4   *There's a lot of crime now in the city centre.* • *There wasn't much room inside his car.*
     （不说 *A lot of crime is now in the city centre.* • *It wasn't much room inside his car.*）

如果想表达关于某地存在某物或某物客观存在的看法，可以在 **there** 和 **be** 之间加情态动词和 / 或 **certainly, probably** 这类副词（5）。还可以在 **there** 和 **to be** 之间加 **seem** 或 **appear**（6）。

5   *There should be a guard rail here.* • *There certainly are problems.* • *There will probably be a fight.*

6   *There seem to be a lot of unanswered questions.* • *There didn't appear to be anyone in charge.*

there + be 之后也可以跟 **likely** 和 **sure** 这类形容词，再接 **to be** 和名词短语，表达对于所述信息的确定程度。

7   *There isn't likely to be peace for many years.* • *There are sure to be protests about the decision.*

可以在 **there** 和 **to be** 之间使用 **report, say** 和 **think** 这类动词的被动式来转达信息，不过 **there** 之后通常不使用动词的被动式。

8   *There were thought to be some problems in the original design and indeed a number of flaws were found.* （不说 *… and indeed there were found a number of flaws.*）

在 **there + be** 之后，通常用 **a / an** 或不定代词来引入新信息（9）；但如果把某信息视为对方熟悉或已知的信息，可以用 **the** 或指示词（10）。

9   *Is there a problem? ~ Yes, I think there's something wrong because there's a long queue.*

10 *I think we should go early. There's the problem of parking and when we go later there's always that long queue to get into the car park.*

O 改正下列句子中 there 和 it 用法有误的地方。

♦   I'm sure ~~it~~ *there* will be someone to help you with your luggage.

1   It was such a nice day in the valley that it was a surprise to hear there was snowing in the mountains.

2   It isn't much time left to prepare for the meeting if it's first thing tomorrow morning.

3   There certain to be questions about Ireland in the history test.

4   It was said to be hundreds of people stranded by the floods.

5   A lot of fat and sugar is in pies and cakes.

6   Everyone found very amusing that I'd started taking karate lessons.

7   They viewed it offensive that he just slumped in the chair and put his feet up on the coffee table.

8   It really wasn't surprising that there were found no survivors in the wreckage of the plane.

→ 指示词 83, 98   不定代词 98   被动 57   数量词 84

代替: one 和 ones

可以在句中用 **one** 和 **ones** 来避免重复可数名词（1）。**one** 用于代替单数可数名词（如 banana）或名词短语（如 a small ripe banana）（2）。**ones** 用于代替复数名词（如 bananas），但不能代替复数名词短语（如 these small bananas）（3）。

1   *We bought bananas at the local market. Would you like one? ~ Oh, I love the small ones.*
2   *I'm not sure if there's a small one that's ripe. ~ Oh, yes, there's one in this bunch.*
3   *I've never seen these small ones in the supermarket.*（不说 ~~I've never seen ones …~~ ）

可以通过使用 **some** 或 **any** 来避免重复复数名词短语（4）或不可数名词（5）。

4   *I love these small bananas, but I've never seen any in the supermarket. I must get some.*
5   *I'm going to buy more fruit. Do you need any? I'll get some for the picnic.*（不说 ~~some ones~~ ）

泛泛地谈论某样物品时，用 **one** 代指（6）；谈论某类物品中具体的一例时，用 **it** 代指（7）。

6   *Do you have a French dictionary? I'm looking for one.*（并非特定的某本法语词典）
7   *Do you have the French dictionary? I'm looking for it.*（特定的某本法语词典）

a / an 通常不与 **one** 连用（8），数量词通常不与 **ones** 连用（9），除非中间有形容词。

8   *I need a pen, preferably a red one. Do you have one?*（不说 ~~Do you have a one?~~ ）
9   *Most of the tomatoes were still green, but I picked out three ripe ones.*（不说 ~~three ones~~ ）

each / every 可以和 **one** 连用：*I examined each / every one.*

the 通常不与 **one** 或 **ones** 连用，除非在 **one** 或 **ones** 之前有形容词（10），或在后面有描述性的短语或从句（11）。

10   *We bought a new table, so you can have the old one.*（不说 ~~… you can have the one.~~ ）
11   *Do you mean the one in the kitchen or the one that used to have the TV on it?*

通常直接用指示代词或物主代词（而不是限定词与 **one / ones** 的搭配）（12），除非要用形容词进行修饰（13）。

12   *I put our books in two piles. These are mine and those are yours.*（不说 ~~… those ones are your ones.~~ ）

13   *Computers have changed a lot. My new one is so much faster than that other one I used to have.*
在非正式语言中，有时会使用 **my one**, **your one** 等表达和 **that one**, **this one** 等表达。

P 为左侧的句子和分句（1—4）选择合适的下文（a—d），再选择合适的词填空。

> any   it   one   ones (×2)   some   them

1   **Sian**: I need six large brown envelopes.   (___)   a   but _____ wasn't large enough.
2   **Rachel**: We have a lot of small _____,   (___)   b   but he may have used _____ already.
3   Ask Jack, he had _____ earlier,   (___)   c   but no large _____, I'm afraid.
4   **Sian**: I got _____ from him,   (___)   d   Do you have _____?

Q 改正下文中的错误。

My grandma told me this story about her first fridge. After my grandparents got married, they
rented a flat. She said it was a very small ᵒⁿᵉ‸ with an oven, but no fridge, so they started looking

for it in the newspaper. She said that fridges weren't as common then and some ones were really

expensive. But she kept looking for it. She eventually found a second-hand that wasn't too

expensive and the man said he would deliver it for free, so she bought right away. She was really

happy. She waited a week, then two weeks, but she never saw the man or the fridge again. Later,

she heard about some other people who had gone to see that man and his fridge and every had

fallen for the same trick.

→ 可数名词和不可数名词 74   指示代词 98   物主代词 97   some, any 86

代替：so 和 do so

在某些表达看法或期待的动词之后，可以使用 **so** 来避免重复一个分句。

1 *The rain will stop soon. ~ I hope so.* （= *I hope the rain will stop soon.*）（不说 ~~I hope it.~~）

可以这样用的动词（短语）还有：**be afraid, believe, expect, guess, think**。

不把 **so** 用在 **be sure** 和 **know** 之后：*It's getting late. ~ I know.*（不说 ~~I know so.~~）

表达否定意义时，将 **so** 用在 **believe, expect** 和 **think** 的否定式之后（2），或将 **not** 用在 **be afraid, guess** 和 **hope** 的肯定式之后（3）。

2 *Perhaps it will be nice and sunny. ~ I don't think so.* （不说 ~~I don't think. / I don't think it.~~）

3 *The weather may actually get worse. ~ I hope not.* （不说 ~~I don't hope so. / I don't hope it.~~）

也可在 **say** 之后或 **tell (someone)** 之后使用 **so**，不再重复前面说过的话。

4 *Jones was fired. They said so on the news.* （= *They said that Jones was fired on the news.*）
   I thought it was a mistake to fire him and I told them so. （不说 ~~… I told them it.~~）

在条件句中，可使用 **if so** 来避免重复某个分句。

5 *Landa says you took her book. If so, you must return it.* （= *If you took her book, …*）

可以通过在 **less** 和 **more** 之后使用 **so** 来避免重复某个形容词（6）或副词（7）。

6 *He used to be really serious. He's less so now.* （= *He's less serious now.*）

7 *They're working hard, even more so than usual.* （= *… even harder than usual.*）

可以将不同形式的 **do** 和 **so** 连用，而不再重复前面出现过的动词和宾语。

8 *They asked me to revise the first paragraph and I did so.* （= *… I revised the first paragraph.*）•
   Anne Elliot refused Wentworth's offer of marriage, then regretted doing so.

通常在正式语言中使用 **do so**。在非正式语言中可以用 **do it** 或 **do that**（9）。动作重复但主语不同时，用 **do it**（不是 ~~do so~~）（10）。

9 *Jump across the stream. Come on. Just do it! ~ Oh, no. It's too far. I can't do that.*

10 *Brandon forgot to take the rubbish out and I can't do it. Can you do it?* （不说 ~~Can you do so?~~）

R 用 so 或 it 填空，并在必要的地方补充恰当形式的 do。

◆ Adam likes to drive fast, even more *so* ＿＿＿＿＿＿＿ since he got that new sports car.

1 Did we miss the bus? ~ I'm afraid ＿＿＿＿＿＿. Will there be another one? ~ I certainly hope ＿＿＿＿＿!

2 Can you complete the work today? ~ I don't think ＿＿＿＿＿. I'm sure I can't ＿＿＿＿＿ before Friday.

3 **WARNING.** Dangerous currents. Anyone who swims here ＿＿＿＿＿ at their own risk.

4 One of my friends has asked me to go snowboarding, but I've never ＿＿＿＿＿ before.

5 Many teenagers want to earn money in part-time jobs and are encouraged ＿＿＿＿＿ by their parents.

S 用 one, ones 或 so 填空，补全下面的对话，有的地方不用填（–）。

A: 'Would you like to hear a joke? Have you heard the ◆*one* ＿＿＿＿＿ about the five flies?'

B: 'I don't think [1] ＿＿＿＿＿.'

A: 'Okay. If there are five flies on the table and I kill one, how many will be left?'

B: 'I'm not sure [2] ＿＿＿＿＿. Will there be four [3] ＿＿＿＿＿ left?'

A: 'Wrong! There'll only be the dead [4] ＿＿＿＿＿.'

B: 'What about the other [5] ＿＿＿＿＿?'

A: 'Well, they'll fly away, of course!'

B: 'Ha! I should have known [6] ＿＿＿＿＿.'

→ if so 192   否定句 45

省略

T 将恰当例句的序号填入对应的方格中。

8 **词的省略**

省略即略去句子中的某些词。为了避免重复某个名词短语（如 the guard），可以使用代词，也可以省略该代词 **1**。为避免重复某个动词短语（如 take the money），可以使用代替结构，也可以把该代替结构省略 **2**。

    1   *The guard looked over and he smiled. / The guard looked over and _ smiled.*
    2   *She could take the money, but she won't do it. / She could take the money, but she won't _.*

在由 and, but, or 连接的短语中，通常省略名词前的某些词，以避免重复。

    3   *You'll need a pen or _ pencil. • Ashley's aunt and _ uncle own property in France and _ Italy.*
在列举事物时，也可以在逗号之后用省略：*I'm afraid of bees, _ wasps and _ spiders.*

9 **省略主语和宾语**

在并列复合句中的 **and, but, or** 或逗号之后，通常省略与前面重复的主语☐，重复的主语和助动词☐，或重复的主语和动词☐。

    4   *She was shouting and _ throwing things. • Should we bring our bags or _ leave them here?*
    5   *We sat and _ talked. • He came, but _ left early. • They ran or _ walked the rest of the way.*
    6   *He looked okay, but _ tired. • I enjoy films, _ going to the theatre, and _ walks in the park.*

在 **then** 和 **yet** 后面的分句中，也可以省略重复的主语☐。从属连词之后的主语（和助动词等）通常不省略☐。

    7   *We tidied up before we left. • He's tired because he's ill.* （不说 *He's tired because ill.*）
    8   *The bird looked up, then _ suddenly flew away. • Nella liked England, yet _ longed for Italy.*

并列复合句中的宾语☐或介词短语☐重复时，通常省略前面分句中的重复部分。可在第二个或后面的分句中使用宾格代词而不是省略宾语☐。

    9   *We gave food _ and water to everyone. • I lived _ and studied in Rome for a year.*
   10 *She makes _ and sells jewellery. • We usually boil _ or poach some eggs for breakfast.*
   11 *She makes jewellery and sells it.* （不说 *She makes jewellery and sells.*）

10 **省略动词短语**

在第二个或后面的分句中，通常省略助动词之后重复的动词短语☐。系动词 **be** 后重复的形容词和介词短语也可以省略☐。

   12 *We thought they would be late, but they weren't _ . • I'm afraid he's in love and she isn't _ .*
   13 *I've seen the film, but Mike hasn't _ • The boys weren't feeling cold, but I was _ • We would help you if we could _ • Sarah will eat broccoli, but Jessica won't _ .*

可以省略动词不定式的 **to** ☐或 **not to** ☐之后重复的动词（短语）。在 **agree** 和 **want** 等某些动词之后，还可以省略 **to** ☐。

   14 *She'll leave unless he begs her not to _. • Some boys kept talking after I told them not to _.*
   15 *I don't smoke now, but I used to _ . • We haven't applied for a grant, but we plan to _ soon.*
   16 *They asked us to do this and you agreed (to) _ . • You can stay here if you want (to) _ .*
在否定式之后要保留 **to**：*He'd like me to stay, but I don't want to.* （不说 *... but I don't want.*）

在非正式语言中，当前后两个分句结构相同时，第二个分句中重复的动词可以省略☐。但当第二个分句的主语是代词时，通常保留重复的动词☐。

   17 *The girls go first and the boys _ after them. • Alex chose Oxford and Alice _ Cambridge.*
   18 *We go first and they go after us.* （不说 *We go first and they after us.*）

提出问题☐或转述问题☐时，可以省略疑问词之后重复的词语。

   19 *I have to leave now. ~ Why _? • It will cost a lot of money to repair the damage. ~ How much _?*
   20 *Dr Foster has said he's planning to go on holiday, but he hasn't told us where _ or when _ yet.*

→ 助动词 17   并列复合句 12   从属连词 12   代替 105

U 用所给名词以及 they, them 填空，补全下列释义，有的地方不用填（–）。

> litter   pollution   rubbish   waste

1 _____ : small pieces of paper or containers that people leave, 2 _____ drop or 3 _____ throw away in a public place.

4 _____ : the act of using things in a careless way, causing 5 _____ to be lost or 6 _____ destroyed 7 _____ unnecessarily.

8 _____ : the substances that make air, water or soil dirty and 9 _____ make 10 _____ unsuitable for people to use.

11 _____ : things that people throw away because 12 _____ no longer want or 13 _____ need 14 _____ .

V 为下列句子的前半句选择合适的后半句，将其改为恰当的省略形式并填入横线处。

> ~~we are hoping to leave soon~~   she didn't want to come with us
> he didn't help us move it   we can go by train
> she's working in Boston   no one was caught
> I sat in the back   she wouldn't tell us what she found
> the others hadn't been there

◆ We're packing our bags and *hoping to leave soon* _____.
1 We can go to Edinburgh by bus or _____.
2 Elizabeth is working in New York or _____.
3 I didn't think anyone would be caught and _____.
4 Lucy found something, but _____.
5 We had already been to Athens, but _____.
6 Chris could have helped us move the table, but _____.
7 My grandparents sat in front and _____.
8 I invited Malia to come with us, but _____.

W 划去每个句子中可以被省略的重复词语，使篇幅尽可能精简。

He put the money on the table and ~~he~~ sat down. He sat in his hot clothes and he felt heavy. The woman looked over at him and she smiled. Her smile said she was in charge and she could take his money if she wanted to take his money. Of course she could take his money, he thought, but obviously she didn't want to take his money yet. The smile lingered for a moment or two longer, then it disappeared and it was replaced by a dark stare.

'I asked you to pay me a thousand and you agreed to pay me a thousand. This is only five hundred.'

'You'll get your thousand. I'll give you half of your thousand now and I'll give you the other half of your thousand later when I get the orchid.'

'I could get the orchid and I could find someone else who'd want to buy it.'

'You won't find someone else who'd want to buy it. Nobody else is even looking for this orchid.'

The dark stare wanted to stay, but it was slowly replaced by half a smile. It said she would give him half of the smile now and the other half of the smile later.

测验

A 选出最恰当的词或短语完成下列句子。

1 .... a phone in here?
   a Is   **b** Is it   **c** Is it's   **d** Is there

2 Billy's shoes look really dirty. Didn't he bring clean ....?
   a one   **b** ones   **c** any   **d** some

3 You can't carry all those boxes. I'll get someone else to .... for you.
   a do   **b** do it   **c** do so   **d** do these

4 He came with his parents and two friends of ....
   a them   **b** their   **c** theirs   **d** themselves

5 I asked Megan earlier if she thought it would rain and she said, 'I ....'
   a hope   **b** hope it   **c** hope not   **d** don't hope so

B 从每句标有下划线的部分（A，B，C，D）中选出错误的一项。

1 She didn't bring a jacket or anything like that with herself, so I gave her one of mine.
   A   B   C   D

2 There were two men arguing with each other in the car park when suddenly one punched other
   A   B   C
   and knocked him to the ground.
                D

3 After fresh tea is made, she puts milk in the tea cup, then pours the tea and adds a little sugar
                          A   B   C
   before she tastes.
          D

4 The couple who bought the old pub in Torbrex regarded as an opportunity to make money and
                A   B   C
   enjoy themselves too.
   D

5 I'm not sure why it was necessary to evacuate the whole airport, but there was discovered a
                    A   B
   knife in someone's bag after they had gone through an electronic security check without being
                              C   D
   stopped.

C 为每处空格选择两个合适的词，将文章补全。

| do (×2)   else   it   myself   someone   something   them |

I'm not sure exactly why I became a regular blood donor. Perhaps it was because a few
years ago I started feeling a need to do something positive instead of just feeling helpless
in a world full of disasters. It's sort of the same feeling I would have if I saw someone
drowning. It wouldn't make any difference whether I knew them or not. I would have to
¹ .... to help. If I didn't think I could save ² ...., I would
try to find ³ .... who could ⁴ .... It's the same thing for
me when I give blood or when I can get other people to come with me and give blood. It's
just a good thing to do.

D 完成下列句子，使其与所给句子的意思尽可能接近。

1 Having wealthy parents should have been useful, but they didn't actually support her.
It ....

2 He doesn't like her and she doesn't like him.
They ....

3 Someone will be at the airport to meet you, I'm sure.
I'm sure there ....

4 To go swimming out in the ocean by yourself would not be a good idea.
It ....

5 Thousands of people were said to be affected by the rail strike.
There ....

E 选择合适的词填空。

anyone	anywhere	him	himself	it	me	myself	one	ours	she	that

My mum and I got a guard dog because ¹ .... sometimes has to go
away on business trips and didn't want to leave ² .... at home by
³ .... We called ⁴ .... Rufus. When Rufus was about four
months old, he started barking if ⁵ .... came near the cottage, especially
the postman. When friends of ⁶ .... came to visit, Rufus would go to the
front door and growl even before we knew they were outside. We didn't train him to do
⁷ .... , he just seemed to train ⁸ .... to be our watchdog.
However, when he was about seven months old, he started growling at people in the
street and barking ferociously if ⁹ .... of them came near our car in a car
park. It has become really embarrassing and now we can't take him ¹⁰ ....
with us. We like ¹¹ .... that he's protective, but we are now afraid that he
might become really dangerous and even attack someone. We're not sure what to do.

9 形容词 (adjective) 和副词 (adverb)

形容词是用于修饰名词的单个词（如 **new, exciting, thorough**）和复合词（如 **hard-working, well-organized**）。可将形容词用在名词之前（*The new teacher has exciting ideas.*）或用在 **be** 和 **seem** 等系动词之后（*She's hard-working and her classes seem thorough and well-organized.*）。

副词（如 **always, really, thoroughly, totally**）是用于修饰动词、形容词、其他副词和句子的词（*She always does everything really thoroughly and seems totally dedicated to her job.*）。

A 阅读下面这篇杂志文章，并找出：

1 一个用副词修饰形容词的例子；

2 一个在名词之前连用三个形容词的例子。

---

* The ancient Chinese art of Feng Shui has been adopted by modern designers as a way of creating environments which feel comfortable and harmonious. Originally developed as a
5 means of planning the perfect agricultural system in harmony with the forces of nature, Feng Shui has been used for centuries to improve the physical surroundings in which people live and to maintain balance in their lives.

10 Those principles of Feng Shui that are beneficial in the organization of outdoor environments can also be used in the design of areas inside the house such as the bedroom, which is considered to be the most important room in the house.

15 Finding the best position for the bed is very important. The main rule of bed positioning is never to have the foot of the bed directly facing the door. That is what is known as the 'death position'. Traditionally, the dead were laid out
20 with their feet pointing towards the door to give them better access to heaven. (It also made it easier for the living to carry them out.)

Ideally, you should position the bed diagonally opposite the door, with the head against a wall,
25 not a window. Avoid putting the bed directly under a horizontal beam that seems to cut across the sleeper. Such a position is believed to cause headaches and even illness.

Small tables on both sides (not just one side) at
30 the head of the bed help maintain balance, but it is best to avoid cluttering the room with a lot of furniture. Let air flow easily through the space. Those large heavy wooden wardrobes, often with boxes or suitcases stored on top, are a really bad
35 idea.

As they tower over the bed, they can make the sleeper feel vulnerable and cause a restless sleep. Do not position tables or other furniture with pointed edges facing the sleeper as their negative
40 energy will cause health problems.

The bedroom should be kept as a relaxing space and should not be used for work or as an office. There should be a feeling of lightness, not seriousness, in the air. Blue curtains and
45 bedcovers are more soothing than brown ones. Soft natural materials are recommended. With Feng Shui in your bedroom, you can create a peaceful sanctuary from the stresses of contemporary living.

* 注：本文旨在展示、训练语法，不代表编者观点。

B 从上面有关风水的文章中选择合适的形容词和副词，补全下面这篇概述。

You can use Feng Shui to make your bedroom a sanctuary. Finding the * *best* position for the bed is ¹_____ ²_____. It should be ³_____ opposite the door, not ⁴_____ under a ⁵_____ beam, and with the head against a wall. You can have ⁶_____ tables on both sides of the head of the bed, but avoid ⁷_____ wardrobes or furniture with ⁸_____ edges facing the sleeper. ⁹_____ curtains and bedcovers made from ¹⁰_____ ¹¹_____ materials are also recommended.

110

表示强调 / 描述 / 类属的形容词

1 强调形容词（emphasizing adjective）

强调形容词起限定（restrictive）或强化（intensifying）作用。限定形容词用于谈论某个特殊的或独一无二的事物（1）。强化形容词用于加强名词所表达的意思（2）。限定形容词通常位于强化形容词之前（3）。

1 *Safety is my chief concern.* • *Our main problems are financial.* • *Try to give a specific reason.*
2 *I haven't played before, I'm an absolute beginner.* • *The meeting was a complete waste of time.*
3 *The boy was the only real hero in the story.* • *Maria got 100%, which was the first perfect score.*

C 从第 110 页的文章中找出两个强调形容词，填入以下示例列表。（一个词在第一段，另一个词在第三段。）

限定	强化
chief, exact, first, major, only, principal, sole, specific, ...	*absolute, complete, entire, extreme, real, sheer, total, utter,* ....

2 描述形容词（describing adjective）

使用不止一个形容词描述人或事物时，通常按照下表给出的顺序排列这些形容词。例如，表示存在时间的形容词（如 old）位于表示颜色的形容词（如 **green**）之前。但要注意，这是一般的顺序，不是唯一的顺序。

4 *I loved that old green sofa with the lovely round seats and the big soft cushions.*

可以根据不同的语境使用同一个描述形容词的不同意思。

5 *The Smiths live in a modest home near Canterbury.*（"不太大的；不很贵的"）
Charlotte is a very modest young woman.（"谦虚的"）

D 从第 110 页的文章中为下列每种描述形容词分别找出一个例子，填入下表。

看法	大小	物理特性	年龄、存在时间或所处时间	形状	颜色
excellent, lovely, ugly,	*big, huge, long, tiny,*	*dry, hard, hot, light,*	*new, old, recent, young,*	*circular, round, spiky, square,*	*green, pink, red, yellow,*

3 类属形容词（classifying adjective）

使用多个形容词来表示某人或某事物所属的类别时，通常按照下表给出的顺序排列这些形容词。例如，表示材料的形容词（如 **nylon**）位于表示用途的形容词（如 **running**）之前。但要注意，这是一般的顺序，不是唯一的顺序。

6 *I hate nylon running shorts.* • *It's southern French style.* • *We found a Victorian medical text.*

E 从第 110 页的文章中为下列每种类属形容词分别找出一个例子，填入下表。

所在位置	起源或来源	材料	类型	用途
distant, indoor, southern, west,	*African, French, Muslim, Victorian,*	*leather, metal, nylon, plastic,*	*economic, medical, scientific,*	*camping, running, swimming,*

→ 形容词的位置 112　形容词与动词不定式连用 144　形容词与名词性从句连用 166

形容词的位置和相关的标点符号用法

4 位置

形容词通常位于名词之前（1）或 **be** 和 **seem** 等系动词之后（2）。

   1 *I had an amusing experience.* • *They faced enormous challenges.* • *He has a kind, honest face.*

   2 *Don't be silly.* • *She became ill.* • *They felt angry.* • *It got cold.* • *He seemed anxious and upset.*

注意，用在名词之前的形容词被称作"定语形容词"（attributive adjective），用在系动词之后的形容词被称作"表语形容词"（predicative adjective）。

名词前使用不止一个形容词时，要遵循一定的顺序。强调形容词一般位于描述形容词之前（3），这两类词一般位于类属形容词之前（4）。

   3 *The weather has been our principal recent concern.* • *Her necklace had real red rubies in it.*

   4 *Kenya was the sole African representative.* • *The recent economic news isn't encouraging.*

有些形容词一般只用在系动词之后，不用在名词之前。

   5 *The old man is asleep. The girl seemed glad.* （不说 ~~the asleep man~~ • ~~the glad girl~~）

此类形容词还有：**afraid, alike, alive, alone, ashamed, awake, ill, well**。

在一些表达中，形容词位于名词之后（6）或不定代词之后（7）。

   6 *six feet tall, two metres deep, two years old, notary public, the time available*

   7 *someone nice, anything unusual, everything necessary, nothing new* （不说 ~~new nothing~~）

F 从第 **110** 页的文章中找出两个把描述形容词与类属形容词连用的例子。

   1 ....   2 ....

5 标点符号

名词前的两类或更多类形容词之间通常没有标点符号（8）。两个或更多个同一类型的描述形容词连用时，之间一般加逗号，尤其是描述看法的形容词，它们的词序可轻易改变（9）。

   8 *Anderson works in a lovely old Victorian building. His office has big black leather chairs.*

   9 *She likes wild, vivid, flashy designs.* • *He was just a normal, quiet, rather shy teenager.*

两个颜色形容词（10）或两个同一类型的类属形容词（11）用 **and** 连接。

   10 *I lost my blue and white scarf.* • *He wore a red and black cap.* （不说 ~~a small and black cap~~）

   11 *She likes Greek and Lebanese food.* • *We discussed financial and educational topics.*

系动词之后的形容词用 **and** 连接：*It's small and black.* （不说 ~~It's small black.~~）

三个颜色形容词（12）或三个同一类型的类属形容词（13）连用时，一般在前两个形容词之间使用逗号，在后两个形容词之间使用 **and**。

   12 *The flag had black, green and yellow stripes. The tulips were yellow, orange and red.*

   13 *In recent years, the island has experienced social, political and economic problems.*

G 在下列句子的适当位置添加逗号或单词 and。

1 The flags of Britain and the USA both have red white blue designs.

2 He described the wonderful friendly outgoing people who worked in the little Italian café.

3 You immediately notice the large plastic vases with pink purple flowers on every table.

4 There are many industrial agricultural applications of the new chemical compounds.

5 What are the cultural religious historic origins of these current regional conflicts?

→ 名词前的形容词顺序 111   不定代词 98   系动词 10

H 下列部分句子中形容词的位置有误。如果有误，请改正。如果无误，在横线处打 ✓。

- ♦ I was looking for a plastic little spoon.   *I was looking for a little plastic spoon.*
- ♦ There are excellent indoor facilities here.   ✓
1 The German entire team played well.   ....
2 The wine made a red small stain.   ....
3 There's new nothing in the Christian main values.   ....
4 You'll need hiking leather comfortable boots.   ....
5 It has a pointed long stem with tiny pink flowers.   ....
6 The windows are in circular wooden huge frames.   ....
7 They are the northern industrial major nations.   ....
8 I love those marvellous new Italian designs.   ....
9 They found a rocking beautiful antique chair.   ....
10 Her alone mother was in the chaos total.   ....
11 The old public swimming pool is closed.   ....
12 We don't understand economic recent American policies.   ....

I 为每条释义选择一组合适的形容词，以最恰当的词序将释义补全。如有必要请查词典。

> northern / sharp / cool / thin   prickly / juicy / large / tropical / yellow
> similar / white / rare / large / black   bluish-grey / great / hard / shiny white / small

panda: a ^1 .... ^2 .... ^3 .... and
^4 .... animal ^5 .... to a bear.

pearl: a ^6 .... ^7 .... ^8 .... or
^9 .... ball that forms inside some oysters and is of ^10 ....
value as a jewel.

pine: a tree that produces cones and has ^11 .... ^12 ....
leaves throughout the year. Pines grow in ^13 .... ^14 ....
regions.

pineapple: a ^15 .... ^16 .... fruit with ^17 ....
^18 .... flesh and a ^19 .... skin.

J 将各组形容词按最恰当的顺序填入横线处。在必要的地方添加 and 或标点符号。

> English older   ~~Italian Greek~~   big plastic square   great little outdoor
> European southern   Spanish cheap   carefree crazy happy   sour twisted

Some people like to talk a lot about food and restaurants they go to. I have a friend called
Lee who lectures on ♦ *Italian and Greek* history at the university. He gets very excited
when he describes a ^1 .... café in Rome and 'all the ^2 ....
people' who work there. I also remember listening to an ^3 ....
woman, who is a professor of ^4 .... literature, complaining about
how Spanish dishes are served in some places with ^5 .... wine
from ^6 .... boxes. When she speaks about it, her mouth becomes
^7 ...., as if she were reliving the terrible experience.

分词形容词（participle adjective），复合形容词（compound adjective）和形容词作名词的情况

6 分词形容词

一些现在分词可用作形容词（如 **surprising**），描述对象是某行为或情感的来源或起因（1）。一些过去分词也可用作形容词（如 **surprised**），描述的是受某行为或情感影响的对象（2）。

1 *The news was surprising.* • *The teacher drew a very confusing diagram on the board.*
2 *My parents were surprised.* • *The confused students said that they couldn't understand it.*

人和其他生物既可以被视为某种情感的来源（如 **He's boring**），也可以被视为受某种情感影响的对象（如 **I'm bored**）（3）。非生物只能被视为某种情感的来源（如 **It's boring**）（4）。

3 *Darwin was a fascinating person.* • *I was disappointed.* • *Why is the dog getting so excited?*
4 *Mars is a fascinating planet.* • *The news was disappointing.* （不说 ~~The news was disappointed.~~）

K 为句子的前半句（1—4）选择合适的后半句（a—d），再将所给动词转换成分词形容词，填入横线处。

> astonish   exhaust   irritate   worry

1 I think it's very _____ (....)   a are revealed in a new book.
2 Mrs Barnett seemed _____ (....)   b after they had walked ten miles.
3 They were really _____ (....)   c that she might not have enough money.
4 The _____ tricks of magicians (....) d when students come in late.

7 复合形容词

复合形容词可以由形容词、副词或名词搭配现在分词或过去分词构成（5）。含现在分词的复合形容词的意义常基于动词的主动用法（6）。含过去分词的复合形容词的意义常基于动词的被动用法（7）。

5 *I'm in slow-moving traffic.* • *Was it a well-planned trip?* （不说 *... a planned-well trip?*）
6 *'Modern Maids' is the name of a house-cleaning service.* （= ... *a service which cleans houses.*）
7 *I'd really like a home-cooked meal for a change.* （= ... *a meal which is cooked at home ...*）

此类复合形容词还有：**energy-saving, life-threatening, low-paid, urgently-needed, well-trained**。

一些复合形容词由形容词和名词（8）或副词和形容词（9）构成。

8 *He likes fast-food restaurants.* • *Let's try to get front-row seats.* • *Do you have a full-time job?*
9 *Abortion is a highly-sensitive issue.* • *There are a lot of politically-independent voters.*

8 形容词用作名词

可以将某些形容词放在 **the** 之后，用作名词，表示社会中特定的某一类人。这些名词短语相当于复数名词，但词尾不加 -s。

10 *The rich aren't happier than the poor.* • *The disadvantaged should be cared for by the wealthy.*
注意，也可以说 **poor people** 或 **a poor person**。（不说 *the poors / a poor*）

表示国籍的形容词（如 **Italian, French**）也可用在 **the** 之后，表示某国人、某国政府、某国家队等。这些名词短语是复数的，词尾加 -s，但以 -ch, -sh, -se, -ss 结尾的不加 -s。

11 *The Italians are here and the French have also agreed to send a peace-keeping force.* • *The United Nations proposal has support from the Spanish, the Japanese and the Swiss.*

在 **the** 之后使用某些形容词，可以表示抽象概念。这些名词短语相当于单数名词。

12 *The unknown isn't the same as the impossible.* • *In sports, the unpredictable often happens.*

→ 动词的主动式和被动式 57   过去分词 17

L 选择合适的形容词填空。

> amazed　　amazing　　annoyed　　annoying　　~~bored~~　　boring　　interested　　interesting

Monday was a school holiday and, unfortunately, it rained all day, so the children kept telling me they were ◆ _bored_ and there was nothing ¹ _____ to do at home. I was trying to write up some of my reports, but they kept interrupting me every five minutes and just became very ² _____. I'm ³ _____ that their teachers can keep them busy and ⁴ _____ in their lessons every day. After only one morning with them, I was extremely ⁵ _____ because of the constant noise and squabbling. I was ready to throw them out in the rain. Instead, I decided to take them to the cinema. It's really ⁶ _____ to see how calm they can become in a dark cinema. The film seemed rather ⁷ _____, but at least it kept them quiet.

M 用每对词构成的复合形容词填空。

> distance / long　　end / never　　~~grow / fast~~　　keep / peace
> educate / well　　funny / look　　home / make　　wash / white

◆ Ghana had to increase food imports to meet the needs of a _fast-growing_ _____ population.

1　Mrs Baxter offered us scones with cream and her _____ jam.

2　Please don't use this phone to make any _____ calls.

3　Soldiers have to learn to talk rather than fight when they are sent on _____ missions.

4　The president's wife seemed to have a _____ supply of new shoes and handbags.

5　We have to invest more in schools and teachers if we want to have a _____ population.

6　That _____ piece of cloth at the end of each sleeve is called a frill.

7　We rented a small cottage in Devon, with a red-tiled roof and _____ walls.

N 改正下文中的错误。

Sometimes I wonder what people in other countries think about us. We are no longer among the rich and powerful of Europe. In a very short period, we seem to have turned into the poor and /weaks. The situation is appalled. You cannot walk down a street in our cities without seeing a homeless. The unemployeds stand around on our street corners. The old and sick receives no help. Why are we no longer shocking that this is going on? Is it like this everywhere? Does the Japanese and the Canadian have the same problems? I doubt it. The unthinkable have happened here and we must do something about it.

副词的位置；地点副词，时间副词，频次副词，与预期相关的副词（expectation adverb），焦点副词（focus adverb）

9 副词的位置

副词通常位于它们所修饰的形容词或副词之前，紧挨着被修饰词。

1 *It's nearly complete.* • *Is it politically correct?* • *She did it fairly easily.* • *He spoke very quietly.*

用副词修饰动词或句子时，可放在分句或整个句子的开头或结尾（2）。副词还可以位于句子中间，在动词 **be** 或助动词之后（3），在主要动词之前（4）。

2 *Usually I have a piece of toast and orange juice in the morning. I might have a snack later.*
3 *Some people are always hungry when they wake up.* • *I've never wanted to eat breakfast in bed.*
4 *I really prefer to wait a while before eating.* • *I sometimes drink coffee.*

注意，副词不能位于动词和它的宾语之间。（不说 ~~I drink sometimes coffee.~~）

10 地点副词和时间副词：nearby, tomorrow 等

地点副词，如 **nearby** 和 **upstairs**，用于补充关于地点或方向的信息（5），通常位于句末，且位于 **recently, tomorrow** 等时间副词之前（6）。

5 *He waited nearby while she took the money and went upstairs.* • *I slipped and fell backwards.*
6 *You must leave here immediately.* • *I'll be there tomorrow.* • *I haven't been abroad recently.*

11 频次副词：annually, usually 等

表示确切频次的副词，如 **annually, daily** 和 **twice**，通常位于句末（7）；表示非确切频次的副词，如 **ever, often** 和 **usually**，通常位于句子中间（8）。

7 *The contract is renewed annually.* • *Rooms are cleaned daily.* • *I've seen that film twice.*
8 *We often have to work late.* • *It usually rains in the evening.* • *Doesn't he ever study?*

12 与预期相关的副词：already, still 等

与预期相关的副词用于表达事件的实际进展与预期情况之间的关系。**already** 用于表明某件事发生的时间比预期早，通常位于句子的中间或末尾。

9 *His plane has already arrived.* • *Mrs Black had left already.* （不说 ~~Already Mrs Black had left.~~）

still 用于表明某事持续的时间比预期长，通常位于句子中间的某个位置。

10 *We are still waiting.* • *I still bite my nails when I'm nervous.* • *Ford still avoids crowds.*

可用 **no longer** 和 **not ... any longer / more** 表示曾经预期某事将持续存在或不断发生，但事实并非如此。它们通常位于句子的中间或末尾（11）。**no longer** 位于句首时（12），句子必须使用倒装结构（助动词在主语之前）。

11 *It no longer works.* • *We could not stay there any longer.* • *She doesn't live here any more.*
12 *No longer do the fishing boats come in large groups to Loch Fyne for the herring season.*

yet（含"到目前为止"之意）用于表示预期或曾经预期某件事发生。**yet** 通常位于疑问句、否定句以及表达"不确定"之意的句子的末尾。

13 *Have you read it yet?* • *Classes haven't started yet.* • *I'm not sure if he's finished yet.*

13 焦点副词：even, just, only

焦点副词 **even, just** 和 **only** 用于使读者或听者的注意力集中于句子的某个部分。

14 *She was only joking.* • *He can't even swim.* • *Her research isn't just about English.*

改变焦点副词在句中的位置，可以改变句子的重点和意思。

15 *Mark only works here on Fridays.* （只在星期五，而不在其他日子）
Only Mark works here on Fridays. （只有 Mark，而没有其他人）

→ 形容词 111　助动词 17　倒装 216　否定句和疑问句 45

O 改写下列句子，将副词置于更恰当的位置。

1 We thought we had started early our hike, but already other people had left the campsite.

....

2 The workers get paid usually weekly, but they haven't been yet paid for last week.

....

3 Still the students hadn't completed all their work when they had to leave yesterday here.

....

4 Alice lived recently here, but she doesn't here any more live.

....

5 We used to hear hardly ever them, but they've become lately noisy really.

....

P 选择合适的副词填空。

~~always~~ ever no longer only outside recently sometimes today twice yet

Actress and model Viviane Tavenard is ◆ _always_ the centre of attention wherever she goes and her appearance in a London boutique this morning was no exception.

But her big smile isn't [1] .... for the crowd of photographers waiting [2] .... [3] ....

She's enjoying her life these days and is [4] .... concerned about old romances or bad reviews.

Tavenard has won the Best Actress award [5] .... , but that hasn't stopped her from working on new and [6] .... unusual films.

'This is an excellent time,' she said [7] .... in an interview with *Celebrity Life* magazine. 'I think that my life is the best it's [8] .... been.'

The good news for all you Viviane Tavenard fans is that you may not have seen her best work [9] ....

Q 改写下列句子，选择合适的副词替换 just，并作出其他必要改动。如有必要请查词典。

almost exactly now only (×2) ~~simply~~ very recently

◆ They just weren't paying attention. *They simply weren't paying attention.*

1 The couple had just got married. ....

2 The baby looks just like her mother. ....

3 He isn't just an athlete, he's a scholar too! ....

4 Wait for us, we're just coming. ....

5 Lunch is just about ready. ....

6 Wear this silly hat. It's just for fun. ....

表示程度 / 方式 / 观点 / 评价的副词

14 程度副词（degree adverb）：**really, very** 等

程度副词用于说明行为、感受等的程度。一些程度副词可以用在句中或句尾，如 **really** 和 **completely**。

1 *He totally forgot.* • *She really hates fish.* • *We failed completely.* • *Prices increased moderately.*

某些程度副词，如 **pretty, quite** 和 **rather**，通常用在形容词和副词之前（2）。短语 **a bit** 和 **a little** 也可以用作程度副词，位于形容词和副词之前（3），但不与名词前的形容词连用。

2 *They're pretty good.* • *It's quite tasty.* • *Isn't it rather cold in here?* • *We listened very carefully.*
3 *She's feeling a little tired.* • *The music is a bit loud.* （不说 ~~It's a bit loud music.~~ ）

不将 **very** 用在动词之前：*I'm not enjoying it very much.*（不说 ~~I'm not very enjoying it.~~ ）

more / less 和 **most / least** 可以在比较级和最高级中作程度副词。

4 *Going by train can be more convenient than flying in Europe and it's usually less expensive.*

还可以把 **too** 用在形容词和副词之前，把 **enough** 用在形容词和副词之后。

5 *It's too difficult.* • *He spoke too quietly.* • *Is this box big enough?* • *You didn't leave early enough.*

15 方式副词（manner adverb）：**carefully, quickly** 等

方式副词用于描述做某事的方式，通常位于句子末尾。

6 *I'll read it carefully.* • *He writes clearly.* • *They searched the room quickly and thoroughly.*
注意，方式副词位于表示时间的词之前：*She works hard now.*（不说 ~~She works now hard.~~ ）

有时，用方式副词描述说话的方式，这种用法在小说中尤为常见。

7 *'I have a torch, just follow me,' she said nervously.*
   'I would follow you to the end of the world,' he whispered hoarsely in reply.
此类副词还有：**angrily, anxiously, cheerfully, gloomily, impatiently, passionately, seriously**。

16 观点副词（viewpoint adverb）：**commercially, socially** 等

观点副词用于表述考虑事情的角度，通常位于句子末尾（8），或位于开头，后面跟一个逗号（9）。

8 *It did well commercially.* • *They're working individually.* • *It was not done scientifically.*
9 *Financially, the project makes sense. Psychologically and socially, it's a terrible idea.*

17 评语副词（comment adverb）：**probably, surprisingly** 等

评语副词用于表达对所说或所写内容的意见或看法。有些评语副词，如 **probably**，可用在句子的中间；但评语副词，如 **surprisingly, of course** 等，通常位于句首或句尾，且与逗号连用。

10 *It was probably a misunderstanding.* • *Surprisingly, he failed.* • *I'll refund the cost, of course.*

definitely 和 **obviously** 等评语副词可用于表达说话者对某事的确定程度（11）。**fortunately** 和 **seriously** 等评语副词可用于表达说话者的感受（12）。

11 *I'll definitely call you tonight.* • *Obviously, someone forgot to lock the door.*
12 *Fortunately, no one was injured in the crash.* • *Seriously though, we're thinking about moving to the country.*
此类副词还有：**actually, apparently, certainly, frankly, honestly, no doubt, presumably, sadly**。

→ 形容词 111　副词作连接词语 209　比较级和最高级 120　too 和 enough 144

R 改写下列句子，为每句选择一对合适的副词，添加到句中的恰当位置。

carefully / tomorrow   completely / yesterday   enough / really   too / very much

1 I forgot my brother's birthday.

2 The piano is large and our doorway isn't wide.

3 We enjoyed the trip, but it was expensive.

4 I'll read the report.

S 为句子的前半句（1—6）选择合适的后半句（a—f），再选择适合的副词填空。

angrily   casually   enough   extremely   of course   traditionally
carelessly   completely   even   individually   only   very

1 _____, marriages were arranged,   (___)   a and everyone wanted it, _____.
2 There was _____ one ticket left   (___)   b he wasn't _____ relaxed.
3 He did the test so _____,   (___)   c but that's _____ changed now.
4 _____, each player is good,   (___)   d he started complaining _____.
5 Although he was dressed _____,   (___)   e he didn't _____ finish part of it.
6 Because he was _____ annoyed,   (___)   f but they don't play well _____ as a team.

T 选择合适的副词填空。

actually   certainly   nervously   probably   still   uncontrollably
apparently   completely   of course   seriously   very   unfortunately

'You've seen the ghost?' I asked.

'More than once,' the old man replied. '[1] _____, I have a photograph. Want to see it?'

This is absurd, I thought, but asked, 'You took a photo of the ghost?'

'No, not me. It's a photo of Lady Barnett from an old newspaper report of her death. She's wearing a long white gown, almost [2] _____ the same one she wears when she appears at night.'

He said all this [3] _____ [4] _____ as if it was solid evidence for the truth of his ghostly tale. 'She was rich and, [5] _____ for her, she was murdered for her money. It all happened about ten years ago. The police thought it was her husband who did it. He disappeared soon after. They found him later, locked in a small basement room. His hair had turned [6] _____ white and his eyes were wide open. He was dead, [7] _____. He was clutching the key to Lady Barnett's safe deposit box in the bank. I think her ghost had [8] _____ found him and had scared him to death.'

'Oh, my goodness! And she-she-she's still here?' I found myself stuttering [9] _____.

'Oh, yes. I think she [10] _____ walks through the house in search of his mistress. She only appears when there's a new woman in the house. [11] _____ her husband was in love with another woman and he just wanted Lady Barnett's money so he could run away with her.'

'What happened to the mistress?' I asked rather [12] _____, looking round the dark room.

'Nobody knows,' he answered. 'But if I was her, I would stay far away from this house.'

同级（equative），比较级（comparative）和最高级（superlative）

18 同级

as ... as 和 **not as ... as** 是同级比较结构的标志。形容词和副词的同级形式用于说明一个人（1）、事物（2）或行为（3）在某方面与比较对象一样（或不一样）。

1　*She's as tall as her father.* • *I'm as hungry as a horse.* • *He's not as young as he looks.*
2　*The van was as big as a house.* • *His new book is not as interesting as his other one.*
3　*I came as soon as possible.* • *Write as fast as you can.* • *It didn't do as well as we had hoped.*
　（不说 *She's as tall her father.* • *Write fast as you can.* • *It didn't do well we had hoped.*）

在同级比较结构前可使用焦点副词，如 **just** 和 **only**（4）。在否定句中有时也用 **not so ... as**（5）。

4　*Our plan is just as good as theirs.* • *You're only as old as you feel.* • *He's not even as tall as her.*
5　*This year's harvest wasn't so bad as last year's.* • *He's not so arrogant as he used to be.*

注意同级比较结构和单数名词连用时的句子结构：*He's not as good a teacher as Mrs Marshall.*
（不说 *He's not as good teacher as Mrs Marshall. / He's not as a good teacher as her.*）

19 比较级

通过改变形容词和副词的形式，可说明一个人（6）、事物（7）或行为（8）在某方面超过或不如另一方。通过在较长的形容词和副词之前加 **more** 或 **less**，在较短的形容词和副词词尾加 **-er**，构成其比较级形式。

6　*She's more intelligent than him. She's also more interesting.* • *He's slower than a snail.*
7　*Some ideas are less practical than others.* • *His flat is smaller and cheaper than ours.*
8　*I should practise more often.* • *She always finishes her work faster than me.*

有时在 **than** 之后使用主格代词（如 faster than I），但这种表达听起来很正式。

有些形容词，如 **friendly** 和 **quiet**，可被视作较长的词（9），也可被视作较短的词（10）。

9　*Our neighbours have become more friendly recently.* • *The boys seem more quiet than usual.*
10　*Everyone was friendlier this time.* • *My new office is quieter than the old one.*

此类形容词还有：**clever, common, crazy, likely, lonely, narrow, simple, untidy, yellow**。

good / well 和 **bad / badly** 有特殊的比较级形式（11）。**further**（原级为 **far**）既可用于谈论距离，也可用于表达"更多的；附加的"（12），而 **farther** 只用来谈论距离。

11　*I thought the weather would be better in July, but it actually got worse.*
12　*How much further / farther do we have to walk?* • *We hope to get further details of the plan soon.*

重复使用比较级形式并用 **and** 连接，可强调某情况正在不断增强或减弱（13）。**the** + 比较级 ... **the** + 比较级这一结构可用于描述某情况的发展与另一情况的进展相关联（14）。

13　*We meet more and more frequently.* • *It's less and less common.* • *Alice got taller and taller.*
14　*The sooner we leave, the faster we'll get there.* • *The older I get, the crazier everything seems.*

20 最高级

可以使用形容词和副词的最高级来谈论一个人（15）或事物、行为（16）在某方面程度最高或最低。通过在较长的形容词和副词之前用 **the most** 或 **the least**，在较短的形容词和副词词尾加 **-est**，构成其最高级形式。

15　*He's the most likely to succeed.* • *She's one of the cleverest students.*
16　*Where's the most beautiful beach in the world?* • *That's the simplest question of all.* • *It's the least dangerous.* • *The least popular subject is algebra.* • *I was sure my golf ball had landed nearest to the hole.*

注意特殊的最高级形式：**good / well (best), bad / badly (worst)** 和 **far (farthest / furthest)**。

在最高级之后，用 **in** 或 **on**（不用 ~~of~~）引导表示群体（17）或地点（18）的单数名词。

17　*Oliver is the youngest student in the class.* • *I'm the tallest in my family.*
18　*I think we stayed in the worst hotel on the island.* • *He's the best player in the world.*
　（不说 *He's the best player of the world.*）

→ 形容词 111　副词 116, 118　焦点副词 116　主格代词 97

U 为每句选择一组合适的词，用其最恰当的形式将句子补全。

bad / skilled / well	early / new / well-behaved	easy / short / well-known
beautiful / different / quick	fast / old / tall	good / likely / long

1 The _____ you wait, the _____ you are to miss the _____ bargains in the sale.

2 Our _____ son is _____ than his dad, but our other two haven't grown as _____.

3 The _____ group of students is _____ than that other group who stayed here _____.

4 His _____ book is _____ and _____ to read than all the others.

5 There are several _____ ways to get to the _____ beach on the other side of the island, but the _____ way is by boat.

6 I can't play as _____ as most of the others, but I'm not the _____ player or the _____ of all those who want to participate.

V 选择合适的形容词（短语）或副词（短语）填空。该段落是一篇与快餐有关的论说文的首段。

better	puzzled	as quickly as	more easily	the best
faster	smaller	less beneficial	more wasteful	the most important

When did we decide that 'more convenient' is [1] _____ way to choose between two different things to eat? Why do people now want food [2] _____ possible, in containers that are [3] _____ thrown away? How did '[4] _____ is [5] _____' become our slogan? Don't we see that this is [6] _____ and much [7] _____ than making our own food? Is it because we want food to have a much [8] _____ place in our lives? But isn't food one of [9] _____ things? Am I the only one who is [10] _____ by this?

W 改正下文中的错误。

In one experiment, students were asked to look at photographs of people and choose the *best* ~~good~~ words and phrases to describe them. The students didn't know that the researchers had chosen the photographs to represent two groups. In Group A, they put the good-looking of all the people whose photographs were used. For Group B, they chose people who (they decided) were not attractive as those in Group A. According to the students, the people in Group A were warm, kind, exciting and sensitive than those in Group B. Also, Group A would find high-paid jobs, have successful marriages and lead happy lives than Group B. The women in Group A were considered to have appealing personalities and to be socially skilled than the Group B women, but also to be vain, materialistic, snobbish and likely to get divorced than them. Interestingly, the students decided that Group A would be bad parents than Group B.

测验

A 选出最恰当的词或短语完成下列句子。

1 I'm .... a swimmer as my sister.
   a better   **b** good as   **c** not as good   **d** so good

2 Is St Paul's the oldest cathedral .... Britain?
   a from   **b** in   **c** of   **d** to

3 When we heard the good news, we were ....
   a delight   **b** delighted   **c** delighting   **d** delightful

4 I'm waiting up here with Anthony, but Amber has .... gone.
   a already   **b** downstairs   **c** once   **d** yet

5 I left the book on the table. ...., someone else has borrowed it.
   a Perfectly   **b** Personally   **c** Presumably   **d** Properly

B 从每句标有下划线的部分（A，B，C，D）中选出错误的一项。

1 I stared into the long rectangular black hole, six deep feet, and shuddered.

2 After the first real attack started, some afraid soldiers didn't want to fight any more so they just
   surrendered.

3 I get up early, shower first, then I drink usually some tea and get dressed as fast as I can.

4 We all very agree that some tests are not difficult enough and others are just too hard.

5 The Dutch are playing the Italian first, and then the Spanish and the Portuguese play.

C 为每句选择一组合适的形容词和／或副词，将句子补全。

| already / never | black / round | easier / eventually |
| further / just | longer / reading | short / suddenly |

1 I know I'm .... in my 40s, but I .... imagined that I would
   need glasses.
2 I .... kept trying to read the newspaper by holding it .... away.
3 I really had to decide whether to get .... arms or a pair of ....
   glasses.
4 ...., I chose the .... solution.
5 ...., with my new glasses, those .... wiggly lines at the top of
   the page turned into words.
6 And the .... spots that seemed to dance on the floor became ants.

D 完成下列句子，使其与所给句子的意思尽可能接近。

1 We all thought they organized the event well and we were all excited by it.
   Everyone thought the event ....

2 You will get there quicker if you leave here earlier.
   The earlier ....

3 Mark is a good cook, but David is a better cook.
   Mark is not as ....

4 Do you have any scarves? I'm looking for one that's woollen, green and fairly long.
   I'm looking for a scarf. ....

E 从每对词中选择更恰当的一个填空。

acute / acutely	colour / coloured	far / further	just / only
pleased / pleasing	certain / certainly	early / earlier	Japan / Japanese
now / yet	young / youngest		

One evening in the spring of 1936, when I was a boy of 14, my father took me to a dance performance in Kyoto. I remember only two things about it. The first is that he and I were the [1] .... Westerners in the audience; we had come from our home in the Netherlands only a few weeks [2] ...., so I had not [3] .... adjusted to the cultural isolation and still felt it [4] .... The second is how [5] .... I was, after months of intensive study of the Japanese language, to find that I could now understand fragments of the conversations I overheard. As for the [6] .... [7] .... women dancing on the stage before me, I remember nothing of them except a vague impression of brightly [8] .... kimono. I [9] .... had no way of knowing that in a time and place as [10] .... away as New York City nearly 50 years in the future, one among them would become my good friend and would dictate her extraordinary memoirs to me.

10 介词（preposition）

介词可以是单个单词，如 **at, from, in, of** 和 **on** 等，也可以是短语，如 **in front of, next to** 和 **out of** 等。可以把介词和名词（短语）连用，描述人（*a group of Italian students*）或物（*the train from London*），或者补充关于某行动或某场景的信息，如时间或地点（*Their train arrives at four-thirty in the afternoon. I told them that, if I'm not on the platform, they should just walk out of the station and wait in front of the news stand next to the main entrance and I'll meet them there.*）。

A 阅读下面这篇有关学生兼职工作的研究报告，找出四个描述时间的介词短语。

Contrary to popular belief, students do work

According to one National Union of Students survey, many students attending universities in the UK had a job during term-time. With more tuition fees and other additional costs,
5 it seems reasonable to assume that this figure is increasing. The students we talked to confirmed that this is the case.

For many of the students we interviewed, the idea of a part-time job on top of their
10 full-time studies is no longer an option, but a necessity. At the same time, some of them said universities offer little help regarding employment or simply advise students against having a job. They expect students
15 to be working on their degrees and nothing else. One medical student reported: 'When I told my director of studies that I had a job in the Christmas break, he frowned. He clearly didn't think it was a good idea.'

20 Most students are employed in part-time or temporary jobs and, as a result of this, have no job security and don't qualify for sick leave or holiday pay. Many students are hired in place of regular workers, but are generally paid less than
25 them. Some students don't actually work for pay, but do jobs in exchange for lower rent and / or meals. These are usually caretaker jobs.

With the exception of those able to find work inside their universities and colleges, the
30 majority of students have jobs at night or during the weekend. One student reported that, apart from working, her weekends were spent sleeping: 'I work as a security guard until 3 a.m. on Friday and Saturday nights,
35 so I end up sleeping all day Saturday and Sunday.' Another student said she works 22 hours a week in addition to her 20 weekly hours of lectures: 'I wouldn't say it has had any effect academically, but it means that I
40 can't go out much.'

According to the NUS employment study, more than 10 per cent of students had missed lectures or failed to submit work because of job commitments. For those with term-time
45 jobs, 30 per cent had missed lectures, while 20 per cent had not handed in assignments. It seems almost inevitable that, due to financial pressures, the university experience will change. Increased costs in education together
50 with pressures to succeed in a competitive world are defining the circumstances in which today's students struggle to complete their degrees. Student life really does involve a lot more work these days.

B 从以上报告中找出恰当的介词补全下面的概述。

Although universities often advise them ♦ *against*_____ having a job, many students now work [1]_____ term-time. Some students do jobs [2]_____ lower rent, but most of them work [3]_____ part-time jobs, [4]_____ less pay [5]_____ regular workers and usually [6]_____ night or [7]_____ the weekend. Students [8]_____ term-time jobs are a lot more likely to miss lectures and assignments, [9]_____ a National Union [10]_____ Students study.

124

介词和介词短语（prepositional phrase）

1 简单介词（simple preposition）

简单介词指由一个单词构成的介词。常见的简单介词包括 at, in, of, to 和 with 等，这些词的含义非常广泛（1）。另一些简单介词，如 behind, during 和 past，含义就相对有限（2）。还有少量动词的现在分词可以被用作简单介词，如 following 和 including（3）。

  1 *At Easter I went with a friend of mine to a special ceremony in Westminster Abbey.*

此类介词还有：as, by, for, from, off, on。

  2 *During the ceremony, we had to sit behind a huge pillar. We couldn't see anything past it.*

此类介词还有：above, across, against, before, between, inside, over, through, until, without。

  3 *Following the ceremony, we went to lunch. Including lunch, the whole trip took three hours.*

此类介词还有：considering, excluding, regarding。

2 复杂介词（complex preposition）

复杂介词指由两个或更多单词构成的介词，例如：next to 和 instead of（4），as well as 和 in front of（5）。复杂介词的最后一个单词为简单介词。

  4 *Come and sit next to me. • Could I have coffee instead of tea?*（不说 *… coffee instead tea?*）

此类介词还有：according to, apart from, because of, due to, out of, together with。

  5 *There were two or three men as well as a group of girls in front of me waiting to buy tickets.*

此类介词还有：as a result of, in addition to, in place of, on top of, with regard to。

3 介词短语

介词短语由介词和介词宾语构成。这里的介词宾语可以是名词（短语）（6）或宾格代词（7），名词也包括动名词（8）。

  6 *The boy cut the rope with a penknife. • I gave the keys to the woman who works in your office.*

  7 *Apart from us, it was empty. • Let's keep this between you and me.*（不说 *… between you and I.*）

  8 *Some people left without paying. • Besides swimming, I also like hockey and basketball.*

通常介词后紧跟着它的宾语，但是在疑问句（9）和关系从句（10）中，介词常位于句末。在正式用法中，有时把介词放在疑问句的句首或关系代词前（11）。

  9 He cut it with something. → *What did he cut it with?*

  10 Jess is the woman. I gave the keys to her. → *Jess is the woman (that / who) I gave the keys to.*

  11 *With what did he cut it? • Jess is the woman to whom I gave the keys.*（不说 *… to who …*）

有些介词只能用在疑问句和关系从句的句首，不能用在句末。

  12 *After which war was the Treaty of Versailles signed?*（不说 *Which war was it signed after?*）

此类介词还有：above, because of, before, below, besides, during。

C 用第 124 页的报告中的信息补全下列句子，并分析其中介词的用法，从 a，b，c，d 四个选项中选出对应的一项，将字母填入括号。

a	与宾格代词连用	c	位于关系从句句首
b	与动名词连用	d	位于关系从句句末

1 The students _____ confirmed that this is correct. (....)

2 Students need jobs, but some _____ said universities don't help with employment. (....)

3 One student said that, _____, she spent her weekends sleeping. (....)

4 Higher costs are defining the circumstances _____ students try to finish their degrees. (....)

→ 连接词语和介词 210   疑问词与介词连用 50   关系从句中的介词 179

时间介词：at, in, on 等

at 后接准确的时间点。

1   *The morning session begins at 8.30 and ends at noon. • At that time I was still a student.*

at 后面可以接表示就餐时间或泛指某节日的词（2）。把某人的年龄作为时间点来谈论时，也用 **at**（3）。

2   *I'll see you at breakfast. • What does your family do at Christmas?*（不说 ~~at Christmas Day~~）

3   *Both my parents left school at 16. • At your age, I was already married and had a baby.*

in 后接一段时间。

4   *We usually listen to music in the evening. • They did all the repairs in one day.*

注意，**in the night**（用于谈论在具体某个夜晚期间发生的事，把夜晚看作时间段）和 **at night**（用于谈论在夜间常发生的情况，把夜晚笼统地看作一个时间点）用法不同。

in 后可接月份、季节或年份（5），也可接表示世纪或历史时期的短语（6）。

5   *Summer time begins in March. • It's very dry here in summer. • Dickens died in 1870.*

6   *The house was built in the 19ᵗʰ century. • Jazz first became popular in the 1920s.*

in 后接一段时间，可表示距某事发生或完成还有多久。

7   *I'll be back in an hour. • They said they'd finish the work in two or three days.*

on 后接特定的一天或特定一天的一部分，也可接具体日期。

8   *I'll see you on Sunday. • The meeting is on Monday morning. • The exam is on 30ᵗʰ May.*

在非正式用法中，特别是在美国英语中，**on** 通常可以省略：*I'll see you Sunday.*

on 后可接特别的日子。

9   *I'll be there on your birthday. • What do you do on Christmas Day?*（不说 ~~on Christmas~~）

在以 **each, every, last, next** 开头的时间短语之前，通常不用 **at, in** 或 **on**。

10   *We had meetings every day last week. • I'm leaving next Friday.*（不说 ~~on next Friday~~）

可用 **from** 和 **to** 引导一段时间的起止点（11）。**past**（"晚于，在……之后"）后可接时间点（12）。

11   *The class meets from 2.30 to 4.30. • We lived in Athens from 2008 to 2012.*

12   *What time is it? ~ It's past eight o'clock. Actually, it's already twenty past eight.*

D 选择一对合适的词或短语填空，在必要的地方补充 at, in 或 on。

Christmas Day / the past	her birthday / next Saturday	six / the morning
four o'clock / Friday afternoon	~~midnight / New Year's Eve~~	65 / 2015
the 4ᵗʰ of July / 1776	night / winter	September / every year

♦ We all held hands and sang together *at midnight on New Year's Eve* ....

1 I hated the early shift at the factory because I had to start work ....

2 We're going to have a big party for Rachel ....

3 They harvest the grapes ....

4 Because it was so cold in the bedroom, I often didn't sleep very well ....

5 It wasn't as common for people to get a holiday from work ....

6 I can't leave work early because I have a meeting ....

7 Although he didn't think of himself as old, Frank Jones had to retire ....

8 The American Declaration of Independence was signed ....

→ at, in, on（地点）128   from, to, past（移动或地点）130

时间介词：during, for, since 等

4 during, for, since

during 和 **in** 均可用于表示某事发生在一段特定时间内的某个或某些时间（1）。通常用 **during**（不用 **in**）来描述某事发生在整个时间段内（2）。

1 *We'll be on holiday during / in July.* • *The old road is sometimes closed during / in winter.*
2 *We need fewer workers during long weekends.* • *There were no classes during the whole of May.*

可以用 **during**（不用 **for**）谈论某事发生于何时，用 **for**（不用 **during**）谈论某事持续了多久。

3 *During April, I'm hoping to go to New York for a few days.* （不说 *… during a few days.*）

谈论一段持续到现在的时间时，用 **for** 引导持续的时长（4），用 **since** 引导时间的起点（5）。

4 *We've been waiting for hours.* • *I've been a student here for two years.*（不说 *… since two years.*）
5 *We've been waiting since eight o'clock.* • *I've been a student here since 2016.*

since 通常与完成时一起用，不与现在时一起用。（不说 *I'm here since 2016.*）

5 before, by, until

before 通常用于泛泛地描述某事发生的时间早于某个特定时间（6）。**by** 用于更精确地描述在某个特定时间或早于某个特定时间（7）。**until** 用于描述一直持续到某个特定时间为止（8）。**not … until** 用于描述不早于某个时间（9）。

6 Charlotte: *Didn't Rob say he would be here before 6.00?*（在早于 6 点的某个时间）
7 Sophie: *I think he said he hoped to be here by 6.00.*（在 6 点或 6 点之前，但不晚于 6 点）
8 Charlotte: *I guess we should wait for him until 6.15.*（直到 6 点 15 分为止）
9 Sophie: *I bet he won't get here until 6.30.*（不会早于 6 点 30 分）

在非正式用法中，有时用 **till** 代替 **until**：*He won't get here till 6.30.*

通常不会接连使用两个介词，不过有时会使用 **since before …**（"从……之前开始"）和 **until after …**（"直到……之后"）这两种表达。

10 *They've lived here since before the war.* • *Don't say 'Happy New Year' until after midnight.*

E 选择合适的名词（短语）或介词填空，补全下列释义。如有必要请查词典。

curfew	deadline	expiry date	after	at	by	during	in (×2)	until

1 _____ : the end of a period of time 2 _____ which something can be used.

3 _____ : a point 4 _____ time 5 _____ which something must be done or completed.

6 _____ : a law prohibiting people from going outside 7 _____ a particular time 8 _____ night 9 _____ a particular time 10 _____ the morning.

F 改正下列句子中的错误。

1 I've been waiting since an hour to have a minute with the boss till his next meeting.
2 My sister works as a teacher in Athens since after 2013.
3 Your application form must be received in this office until 9 a.m. in the first of March.
4 I have appointments in every morning this week, but I can see you on next Monday morning.

→ after, before, until, since 引导的时间状语从句 199　while 198　完成时 18, 20

地点介词：at, in, on

6 用 at, in, on 描述位置

at 可表示某物在离某处很近但没有接触的位置（1）。**at** 也可用于谈论衡量标度的某个数值或旅途中的某站（2）。

1 *We'll meet you at the bus stop. • I think I heard someone at the door.*

2 *Bake the pie in the oven at 170°. • I'm sure we stopped at York during our trip north.*

in 可表示某物在某空间内部（3）。**in** 也可用于谈论一个大致的区域，例如地区或国家（4）。

3 *The money was in a box in a drawer in the desk in my office. • What's in the envelope?*

4 *Lily is going to spend a week in Tuscany this summer. ~ Is that in France or Italy?*

注意，应该说：*Who is the small boy in the picture?*（不说 *… on the picture?*）

on 可表示某物在某表面上，与该物体有接触（5）。**on** 也可用于谈论与道路、河流等线状地点相关的位置（6）。

5 *I left the keys on the table. • She reached over and put her hand on his.*

6 *You'll pass Stratford on the way to Birmingham. It's just a small town on the river Avon.*

7 与 at, in, on 连用的动词和名词

shout 和 **smile** 这类动词可与 **at** 连用，后接表示施动对象的宾语。

7 *Why is that man shouting at us? • She smiled at me.*（不说 ~~She smiled me.~~）

此类动词还有：**bark, glance, laugh, look, scream, stare, swear, yell**。

believe 和 **include** 这类动词可与 **in** 连用，后接描述观念或事物的宾语，类似于后接地点。

8 *I don't believe in life after death. • The tip is included in the bill.*（不说 ~~It's included the bill.~~）

此类动词还有：**indulge, interfere, invest, join, meddle, result, specialize, wallow**。

在 **comment** 和 **concentrate** 这类动词后，常用 **on** 来引出宾语。

9 *We can't comment on the test results yet. • I can't concentrate on my work.*（不说 ~~I can't concentrate my work.~~）

此类动词还有：**depend, focus, insist, lecture, plan, rely, remark, report**。

ban 和 **restriction** 这类名词可与 **on** 连用，后接另一个名词。

10 *Isn't there a ban on pesticides? • They have restrictions on the amount of money you can send.*

此类名词还有：**attack, constraint, effect, emphasis, imposition, limit, perspective, sanctions**。

G 为句子的前半句（1—4）选择适合的后半句（a—d），并在横线处补充介词 at, in 或 on。

1 There are restrictions ___ travel （___）　a rather than shouting ___ each other.
2 Jess kept staring ___ the goldfish （___）　b of counting the money ___ his wallet.
3 They believe ___ negotiating quietly （___）　c as it swam round ___ its small glass bowl.
4 He was concentrating ___ the task （___）　d ___ some parts of the country.

H 在下列句子中必要的地方补充介词 at, in 或 on。

◆ Craft shops ᵢₙ many small villages rely ₒₙ tour buses to bring them customers.

1 The meeting focused economic problems developing countries South-East Asia.

2 You can either stand the bar or sit a table most pubs Britain.

3 We were depending my brother to meet us the exit door after the concert.

4 The children were laughing something they had seen a cartoon.

→ at, in, on（时间）126

地点介词：above, below, between 等

8 above 和 over

above 和 over 均可用于表示某物处在比另一物更高的位置。

1　*There's a full moon above / over the mountain.* • *He has a small scar above / over his left eye.*

描述某物的水平高度或谈论其他有纵向尺度的情况时，用 above（不用 ~~over~~）（2）。表示某物以某种方式遮盖、覆盖在另一物上面时，用 over（不用 ~~above~~）（3）。在更抽象的层面，可用 above 表示"超过，胜过"，可用 over 表示"多于"（4）。

2　*It's always colder above the snowline.* • *Her name is above mine on the waiting list.*

3　*There are thick clouds over most of Scotland.* • *I had to wear a scarf over my head.*

4　*His work is above average.* • *Are you over 21?*（不说 ~~Are you above 21?~~）

9 below 和 under

below 和 under 均可用于表示某物处在比另一物更低的位置。

5　*Their flat is below / under ours.* • *I keep the bleach below / under the sink in the kitchen.*

描述某物的水平高度或谈论其他有纵向尺度的情况时，用 below（不用 ~~under~~）（6）。表示某物被以某种方式遮盖、覆盖在另一物下面时，用 under（不用 ~~below~~）（7）。在更抽象的层面，可用 under 表示"少于，小于"（8）。

6　*Most of New Orleans is below sea level.* • *I'm sure the temperature is below zero tonight.*

7　*The puppy likes to hide under the sofa.* • *Do you always wear a vest under your shirt?*

8　*If you're under 21, you can't get into the club.* • *The total cost of the trip was under £50.*

强调"被（某物）掩盖"时可用 underneath：*I keep my money underneath my mattress.*

10 between 和 among

可用 between 谈论处在两个或更多个单独的人或物之间的位置（9），用 among 表示处在由多于两个的人或物组成的群体之中（10）。

9　*Find Luxembourg on the map. It's between Belgium, France and Germany.*

10　*Find Luxembourg on the map. It's among the countries of Western Europe.*

在更抽象的层面，可用 between（而不是 ~~among~~）描述事物之间的关联（11），可用 among（而不是 ~~between~~）表达"在……中，……之一"（12）。

11　*In the study, they investigated the relationship between education, diet and health.*

12　*Among the advantages of private schools are small classes and more individual attention.*

I 为每句选择一个形容词 / 名词和一个介词，将句子补全。如有必要请查词典。

overalls	overflow	overlap	above	below	over
~~overcoat~~	overhead	overpopulation	among	between	~~under~~

◆　I'm wearing a woollen pullover and a jacket <u>under</u> this <u>overcoat</u>, but I still feel cold.

1　High birth rates combined with better health care for children have created serious problems with _____ some of the world's poorest nations.

2　There does seem to be quite an _____ the subject areas of maths and physics.

3　The work is really dirty so you'd better wear _____ your clean clothes.

4　The number of young children starting school this year is well _____ normal and we don't have enough room for them all, so we're having to use temporary buildings for the _____ .

5　A number of people who live near or _____ those massive power lines say that they have suffered health problems because of them.

表示移动（movement）或地点的介词：**from, across, along** 等

11 from, to, towards

from 用于表示移动的初始位置或起点，**to** 用于表示移动的目的地或终点（1）。在更抽象的层面，**from** 和 **to** 可用于表示变化的起止状态（2）。

  1 *We flew straight from London to San Francisco. • I can walk from my flat to work.*
  2 *He translated the book from Russian to English. • It went from quite cool to very hot in an hour.*

towards（"朝，向"）可用于强调移动的方向（3）。在更抽象的层面，**towards** 可用于表示发展或变化的方向（4）。

  3 *I suddenly saw a car coming towards me. • If you get lost, try to walk towards the south.*
  4 *The trend is towards much larger farms. • This agreement is an important step towards peace.*
注意，也可以用 **toward**，特别是在美国英语中：*It's a step toward peace.*

12 into 和 onto

可用 **into** 强调移动到某物里面（5），用 **onto**（或 **on to**）强调移动到某物的表面上（6）。

  5 *We took a bus into the city centre. • The waiter poured some wine into each glass.*
  6 *Let's move the small books onto the top shelf. • Paint was dripping from his brush onto the floor.*

13 across, over, through

across, over 和 **through** 可用于表示从某物的一边移动到另一边。

  7 *The early explorers had to get across / over / through the Rocky Mountains to reach the coast.*

通常，**across** 用于描述从某表面或地区的一边移动到另一边（8），**over** 用于表示从较高的物体或状似一条线的物体的一侧移动到另一侧（9），**through** 用于表示从某空间内部穿过（10）。

  8 *We spent a month travelling across America. • She pushed a note across the table to him.*
  9 *The gate was locked so I climbed over the wall. • It was a good shot, but it went over the bar.*
  10 *You have to go through the kitchen to get to the bathroom. • The Thames flows through London.*
across 和 **over** 也可用于表示地点（"在……对面"）：*There's a café across / over the street.*

14 along 和 past

along 可用于表示沿着某个方向移动，或描述某物在该方向上的某处（11）。**past** 可用于表示移动时经过了某点，或描述某物在越过某点的某个位置上（12）。

  11 *I like walking along country lanes. • There's a café along the street.*
  12 *We drove past Stratford, but didn't stop there. • There's a café just past the church.*

15 off 和 out of

off 可用于表示从某表面上移开，或描述某物与某表面的相对位置（13）。**out of** 可用于表示从某物的里面出来，或描述某物已不在某空间内部（14）。

  13 *Could you take that box off the table? • The platform was about two feet off the ground.*
  14 *I lifted the kitten out of the box. As soon as it was out of the box, it started crying.*
注意，**out**（不加 **of**）不能单独用作介词。（不说 *It was out the box.*）

在更抽象的层面，**off** 可表示"不相关的；不相连的"（15），**out of** 可表示"用尽；缺少"（16）。

  15 *This part of your essay is completely off the main topic. • Skye is an island off the west coast.*
  16 *We're out of milk, so I have to go to the shop. • A lot of people are out of work now.*

→ from, to, past（时间）126   over（地点）129

J 根据下面的地图，选择合适的介词填空，补全下面对话中的行路指引。

> across　　along　　from　　out of　　past　　to　　towards

Anthony (talking on the phone): Hi, Annie, it's me again. I'm sorry to bother you, but I'm in the shoe shop and I can't remember how to get ♦ *to* the Red Lion [1] _____ here.

Annie: That's okay. The Red Lion is on King Street, so when you're [2] _____ the shoe shop, you should turn right and walk [3] _____ the cathedral. Go [4] _____ Port Street and turn left when you reach Baker Street. Walk [5] _____ Baker Street [6] _____ King Street and turn right. The Red Lion will be on your right just [7] _____ the library.

K 选择一对合适的介词填空，如有必要请查词典。

> along / towards　　out of / from　　through / to

1　When you go via a particular place, you go _____ that place on your way _____ another place.
2　When you're going up or down a road, you're going _____ it _____ one end of it.
3　When you're asked to wait outside a room, you have to be _____ the room, but you mustn't move too far _____ it.

L 以下段落是一部小说的开头，选择合适的介词填空。

> along　　from　　into　　on　　over　　through　　towards

She stands up in the garden where she has been working and looks into the distance. She has sensed a shift in the weather. There is another gust of wind, a buckle of noise in the air, and the tall cypresses sway. She turns and moves uphill ♦ *towards* the house, climbing [1] _____ a low wall, feeling the first drops of rain [2] _____ her bare arms. She crosses the loggia and quickly enters the house.

In the kitchen she doesn't pause but goes [3] _____ it and climbs the stairs which are in darkness and then continues [4] _____ the long hall, at the end of which is a wedge of light [5] _____ an open door.

She turns [6] _____ the room which is another garden – this one made up of trees and bowers painted over its walls and ceiling. The man lies on the bed, his body exposed to the breeze, and he turns his head slowly [7] _____ her as she enters.

表示关联（connection）的介词：of, with, by

16 of 和 with

of 和 with 可用于谈论有关联的人／事物。将 of 放在两个名词短语之间，可表示前者属于后者或是后者的一部分（1）。将 with 放在两个名词短语之间则可表示后者是前者的特征（2）。

1 *The roof of their house is bright red.* • *The sleeves of this shirt are too long.*
2 *Theirs is the house with the bright red roof.* • *I'm looking for a white shirt with short sleeves.*

of 可用于表示人与人之间的关系（3），with 可用于表示和某人（或物）在一起（4）。

3 *Is Briony the daughter of Alice Hawthorn? ~ Yes, she's a good friend of mine.*
4 *I think Lea went shopping with her friends.* • *Would you like some wine with your meal?*

一些形容词后接 of（5），一些形容词后接 with（6）。

5 *Millie is afraid of dogs.* • *The report was full of mistakes.* （不说 ~~It was full with mistakes.~~）
Are you aware of the risks involved? • *I was fond of my old car, but it had too many problems.*
6 *We were faced with a difficult choice.* • *I wasn't familiar with that software.* •
There are side effects associated with most medicines. • *He wasn't satisfied with my work.*

17 with 和 by

可使用 with + 限定词 + 名词表示用特定的某物完成某行为（7）。通常用 by + 名词（不加限定词）或动名词更为笼统地描述一个行为（8）。

7 *I paid with my credit card.* • *The thief broke the lock with a knife.* （不说 ~~by a knife~~）
8 *I paid by credit card.* • *He opened the door by breaking the lock.* （不说 ~~by break the lock~~）
此类表达笼统含义的 by 短语还有：**by air, by bus, by email, by phone**。

M 选择一对合适的词语填空（不一定按词语的原顺序填空），在必要处补充 by, of 或 with。

a cheque / the yellow lampshade	the door / a screwdriver	the match / scoring
American history / reading	her / taxi	ours / some friends
~~any problems / the way~~		

◆ We weren't aware *of any problems* _____ until we started getting complaints from people who clearly weren't satisfied *with the way* _____ their new computers were working.

1 He tried to remove the old broken handle _____ .

2 I'm becoming more familiar _____ about the Civil War.

3 We went out to dinner _____ .

4 Robertson celebrated his return to the Scottish team _____ the best goal _____ against England yesterday.

5 They don't allow dogs on the buses so Bethany always goes _____ whenever she wants to take her dog _____ .

6 I wanted to buy that lamp _____ but I didn't have enough cash and they wouldn't let me pay for it _____ .

→ by（时间）127　与被动式连用的 by 和 with 64　限定词 83　of 和名词所有格 76

表示例外（exception）的介词：except (for), besides, without 等

8 **except (for), besides, apart from**

except 和 except for（"除……之外"）用于表示所述的一般情况不包括某人或某物，通常前面会出现 every 之类的数量词（1）。except for（而不是 ~~except~~）通常用于对某种具体情况提供细节上的修正，说明前面所述情况不完全符合事实（2）。

1   *It's open every day except (for) Sunday. • Everyone liked the film except me.* （不说 ~~except I~~ ）
2   *She says she's stopped smoking except for an occasional cigarette at a party.*

except（而不是 ~~except for~~ ）之后可接介词短语（3）和从句（4）。

3   *I work here all day except on Friday. • It will be sunny everywhere except in the north.*
4   *I've never heard their baby cry except when it gets tired.*

在否定句中，可用 besides 表达与 except (for) 相同的含义（5）。在其他句型中，besides 通常意为"除……之外（还）"（6）。

5   *I didn't know anyone in London besides / except (for) my uncle Henry.*
6   *Besides football, what other sports do you like? • I've talked to a lot of people besides Henry.*

apart from 既可表达与 except (for) 相同的含义（"除……之外"），又可表达与 besides 相同的含义（"除……之外（还）"）。

7   *It's open every day apart from Sunday. • Apart from football, what other sports do you like?*
注意，aside from 与 apart from 用法相同，特别是在美国英语中。

9 **without 和 minus**

except (for) 用于说明某事物不包含在一般情况之内；without 则表示更宽泛的"没有"（8）或"不（做某事）"的含义（9）。想强调缺少了某事物时可使用 minus（10）。

8   *I prefer tea without milk, don't you? • Romeo chose death rather than life without Juliet.*
9   *William changed his travel plans without any explanation. Then he left without saying goodbye.*
10 *They eventually published the report, without / minus several important sections.*

N 为每句选择一个名词和一个介词，将句子补全。如有必要请查词典。

bread	fruit	meal	pizza	besides	except for	with
fish	ice cream	omelettes	~~rice~~	except	minus	without (×2)

♦   We don't usually eat much *rice except* ＿＿＿＿＿ when we have Indian food.

1   My grandfather liked to say that you can't make ＿＿＿＿＿ breaking eggs.

2   I first learned how to cook salmon and now I cook a lot of other ＿＿＿＿＿ that.

3   They usually drink wine with their evening ＿＿＿＿＿ during Lent.

4   My children don't eat a lot of ＿＿＿＿＿ bananas at breakfast sometimes.

5   Would you like some ＿＿＿＿＿ your strawberries?

6   We won't be able to make ＿＿＿＿＿ flour.

7   It was obvious that someone had already decided it was time to start eating because on the table was our ＿＿＿＿＿, ＿＿＿＿＿ one very large slice.

→ besides 作连接词语 212   数量词 84   unless 192

短语动词 (phrasal verb)

in, on 之类的词常用在名词短语前作介词（1）；但是，它们也可跟在动词后面，形成固定用法，此时通常被称为小品词（particle）（2）。其他一些词，如 **away, back, out** 等，也可作小品词（3）。这种动词 + 小品词的结构（**sleep in, go out** 等）被称为双词动词或短语动词。

1 *I usually drink coffee in the morning.* • *He said he left the keys on the table.*
2 *I slept in this morning and missed my bus.* • *He put on his boots and overcoat.*
3 *I tried to catch the dog, but it ran away.* • *When will she come back?* • *Did you go out last night?*

其他短语动词例如：**fall over, get through, go ahead, sit down, stand up, take off**。

有的短语动词后面不跟宾语（4），有的跟宾语。当宾语是名词短语时，通常可以将它放在小品词之后（5）或之前（6）。当宾语是代词时，要将它放在小品词之前（7）。

4 *It's time to get up.* • *I wish these flies would go away.* • *Watch out!* （不说 *Watch out that!*）
5 *Don't turn on the light. You'll wake up the baby.* • *He took off his shoes.*
6 *Don't turn the light on. You'll wake the baby up.* • *He took his shoes off.*
7 *Don't turn it on. You'll wake him up.* • *He took them off.* （不说 *He took off them.*）

短语动词之后可以接动名词（8）或从句（9）。通常不把从句或非常长的短语放在动词和小品词之间。

8 *Have you given up smoking?* • *They told us to carry on working.* （不说 *… to carry on work.*）
9 *Andy pointed out that we didn't have enough time.* • *You should read over what you've written.* （不说 *You should read what you've written over.*）

短语动词之后可以接介词。动词 + 小品词 + 介词的组合有时被称为三词动词。多数三词动词只在最后跟有介词的宾语，宾语是代词时也跟在介词后。

10 *This book is valuable and you should hold on to it.* （不说 *… hold on it to. / … hold it on to.*）• *Go ahead and I'll catch up with you later.* （不说 *… I'll catch up you with. / … I'll catch you up with.*）

常见的三词动词还有：**face up to, get round to, go along with, look forward to, watch out for**。

在非正式语言中，常常会使用 **put off, leave out** 等短语动词（11），而不用 **postpone, omit** 等具有相似含义但可能听起来较正式的动词（12）。

11 *Let's put the meeting off till next week.* • *Don't leave out the author's name.*
12 *We should postpone the meeting until next week.* • *You must not omit the author's name.*

O 用所给短语动词改写下列句子，使句子听起来不那么正式。注意应使用短语动词的恰当形式。如有必要请查词典。

cut back on	fill in	give up	go in	send back
do away with	find out	go along with	go up	take off

1 You should complete this form and return it with your payment.
   You have to _____

2 My father has abandoned his attempt to get the university to abolish tuition fees.
   My dad _____

3 It was necessary to reduce our spending after we discovered that our rent was increasing.
   We had to _____

4 Please observe local customs at the temple and remove your shoes before entering.
   Please _____

→ 动名词 139 动词和宾语 6

P 用所给动词和小品词组成恰当的短语动词，补全下文。

bend	breathe (×2)	go	lift	~~push~~	raise	stand
~~away~~	back	down	in	out	up (×3)	

When you have to spend a lot of time sitting at a desk, it is important to take short breaks and stretch your neck and back. You can use this exercise to help you stretch.

◆ *Push* your chair *away* to the side and stand up, making sure there is some space in front of you. [1]_____ straight, with your arms hanging loosely by your side.

Breathe in deeply as you [2]_____ your arms _____ over your head. Pause a moment.

Then [3]_____ slowly as you swing your arms forward, letting them fall as you [4]_____ your whole body _____ until your hands are near your feet. Pause a moment.

Then, [5]_____ as you [6]_____ your body _____ very slowly, beginning with your hips, then your upper body, followed by your head and arms.

Repeat the exercise at least once before you [7]_____ to your desk again.

Q 选择正确的选项完成对话。有时两个选项均正确。

Ani: What's the meaning of 'reimburse'?

1 **Raz:** I don't know. (**A**) Let's look up it in the dictionary. (**B**) Let's look it up in the dictionary.

2 **Ani:** (**A**) Hand over the dictionary and I'll do it. (**B**) Hand it over the dictionary and I'll do it.

3 **Raz:** (**A**) I left behind it at home this morning. (**B**) I left it behind at home this morning.

4 (**A**) I think I put down beside my computer. (**B**) I think I put it down beside my computer. Okay, so we can't use a dictionary. What's the context?

Ani: It says, 'They reimbursed his tuition fees.'

5 **Raz:** (**A**) Maybe it means they worked out what his tuition was.
(**B**) Maybe it means they worked what his tuition was out.

6 **Ani:** (**A**) But then it says he paid off some debts. (**B**) But then it says he paid off some.

7 **Raz:** (**A**) Maybe it means to pay back money to someone.
(**B**) Maybe it means to pay money back to someone.

8 **Ani:** (**A**) So, they gave back him the money for his tuition.
(**B**) So, they gave him back the money for his tuition.

Raz: Sounds good to me.

测验

A 选出最恰当的词或短语完成下列句子。

1 I know I don't look like everyone else, but I don't like it when people stare _____ me.
   a at **b** on **c** to **d** –

2 Please don't call me until _____ eight o'clock on Saturday morning.
   a after **b** at **c** by **d** to

3 I _____ waiting here for you since 8.30.
   a am **b** was **c** have been **d** will be

4 The United Nations is drawing up an economic plan aimed at _____ Timor-Leste with a stronger economy based on coffee.
   a provide **b** provides **c** to provide **d** providing

5 If you borrow something from someone, make sure you give _____.
   a them back to it **b** back it to them **c** it back to them **d** it to them back

B 从每句标有下划线的部分（A，B，C，D）中选出错误的一项。

1 <u>According</u> to a recent report, more students are choosing to work <u>in</u> part-time jobs <u>instead</u> using their weekends to study <u>during</u> term-time.

2 <u>For</u> a whole week Loretta came to class <u>on</u> every day <u>with</u> her hair a different colour.

3 <u>Between</u> 1850 and 1900, coal production <u>off</u> the US rose <u>from</u> 14 million tons <u>to</u> 100 million.

4 The ball went <u>between</u> the legs of another player, <u>past</u> me <u>towards</u> the goal, and rolled <u>through</u> the goal line.

5 The children were laughing <u>at</u> a cartoon <u>in</u> which a cat <u>on</u> a wobbly ladder kept trying to get a small bird <u>out</u> its cage.

C 从每对介词中选择恰当的一个填空。

at / in	away / up	during / for
from / of	off / out of	to / towards

Does the new 'global economy' simply mean that well-paid jobs will be taken

1 _____ 2 _____ people in rich countries and changed

3 _____ low-paid jobs for people 4 _____ poorer countries?

Is this a bad thing? It may actually mean that some poor people who have been

5 _____ work 6 _____ a long time can start to have a better life

and other people will have to work a bit harder to maintain their comfortable lifestyle.

D 完成下列句子，使其与所给句子的意思尽可能接近。

1　This building will be closed for renovation from the beginning to the end of August.
　　During ....

2　What else did you do in addition to shopping when you were in Rome?
　　Besides ....

3　Haven't you eaten anything else today besides the apple I gave you earlier?
　　Apart ....

4　We won't be able to do much unless we get more financial support.
　　Without ....

E 选择合适的介词填空。

| across | along | at | by | into | of | past | towards | under | with |

Whenever I see a newspaper lying on the ground beside a door, I think of Jacob. A few years ago, Jacob had to travel to a meeting and his flight was delayed for several hours because of bad weather. [1] .... the time he got to his hotel it was [2] .... midnight. Once in his room, he felt really tired so he just undressed and got into bed. [3] .... some point during the night, he had to get up and go to the bathroom. He wasn't really awake and it was very dark, but he could see a light [4] .... the bathroom door, so he walked [5] .... the light. He opened the bathroom door and went in. The bright light blinded him for a moment. As the door closed behind him, he vaguely wondered why there was a doormat on the bathroom floor. Facing him was another door [6] .... a number on it. It was number 325. That was strange. Then he realized he wasn't in the bathroom. He was in the corridor. He turned to go back [7] .... his room, but the door was locked. And he was naked. He heard voices coming from the far end of the corridor. What was he going to do? Then he noticed a newspaper on the floor beside the door [8] .... number 325. He quickly grabbed the newspaper and held it in front of him as a man and a woman in dark uniforms came [9] .... the corridor towards him. The man said, 'Good morning, sir. Having a bit of trouble?' They were security guards. Jacob explained his embarrassing situation and they unlocked the door for him. He thanked them as if they had just saved his life. After they left, he opened his door, made sure it wouldn't close again, stepped [10] .... the corridor and put the newspaper back on the floor outside number 325. Someone else might need that newspaper.

动词不定式主要由动词原形构成。**to** 加动词原形为常见的带 **to** 的不定式（*I didn't really want to read when I was younger.*），在有些结构中则要使用不带 **to** 的不定式（*I thought it was torture when the teacher made us read aloud in class.*）。

动名词通常由动词原形加 **-ing** 构成（*Now I enjoy reading more than anything else.*）。动名词虽然与动词的现在分词形式相同，但用法类似于名词（*Reading is the key to knowledge.*）。

A 以下文章选自一本杂志的咨询栏。阅读文章，找出 avoid 和 smoke 各自被用作不定式和动名词的地方。

My best friend smokes a lot. I tell her she should quit, but she says she can't. What can I do to help her?

Quitting is hard but not impossible – as long as
5 your friend really wants to kick the habit. 'She has a good chance of stopping successfully if she thinks about quitting as a three-part process: she has to deal with her social habit, her psychological dependence and then her
10 physical addiction,' says Lowell Kleinman, MD, a doctor who has helped hundreds of people to stop smoking for good.

Let's start with the habit: when does your friend smoke – on her way to college, after
15 a meal, when she's with friends? Help her break the pattern. 'Try going a different way to college, eating at a different place and avoiding social situations that will make her want to smoke,' says Dr Kleinman. As for psychological
20 dependence: does your friend smoke when she's bored or stressed? Nicotine can have a calming effect, which is why many people continue

smoking even though they know it's bad for their heart, lungs, skin and teeth. Encourage her to
25 avoid stressful situations and to find healthier ways of coping with stress – doing yoga, keeping a journal or just talking to you.

Finally, physical addiction: when your friend doesn't have a cigarette at regular intervals,
30 does she experience withdrawal symptoms – restlessness, anxiety, irritability and strong cigarette cravings? If so, her body is addicted. And traditional techniques, like going cold turkey or cutting back gradually, often aren't
35 successful in beating an addiction. Instead, Dr Kleinman recommends Nicotine Replacement Therapy (NRT) – the patch, gum or an inhaler – which helps wean your body off nicotine by supplying decreasing doses. The inhaler used
40 to be available only by prescription, but now they can all be purchased over the counter.

You can also point out that there are real advantages to becoming a non-smoker. She'll not only have better health, but also fresher
45 breath, clearer skin and whiter teeth.

B 从上面的文章中找出符合下列定义的四个短语。

1 .... : to stop doing something harmful that you have done for a long time.
2 .... : performing a system of exercises for your body and for controlling your breathing, used by people who want to become fitter or more relaxed.
3 .... : the unpleasant state that drug addicts experience when they suddenly stop taking a drug; also a way of treating addicts that makes them experience this state.
4 .... : without needing a prescription (written permission from a doctor).

动词不定式和动名词的一般形式

1 **动词不定式**

不定式（**to** + 动词原形）和不定式的否定式（**negative infinitive**）（**not to** + 动词原形）常用在动词、形容词或名词之后（1）。它们也可以用在不定代词或 **wh-** 疑问词之后（2）。

　　1　*We agreed to meet on Friday. • I'm happy to be here. • You made a promise not to tell anyone.*
　　2　*I was looking for someone to help me. • I wasn't sure about what to do and what not to do here.*
不定式还可用于表示目的（= in order to）：*He only did it to get attention.*

不定式后面可以接宾语、介词短语和副词。除非表示强调，否则通常不将副词置于不定式的 **to** 和动词之间（分裂不定式 [split infinitive]）。

　　3　*We're planning to take the children to the zoo later. • I want to (really) understand Shakespeare.*

当两个不定式由 **and** 或 **or** 连接时，通常省略第二个不定式的 **to**（4）。如果意思清楚的话，可以用 **to** 代替整个动词不定式短语（5）。

　　4　*Noah just wants to sit and _ watch videos all day. • Do they intend to buy a flat or _ rent one?*
　　5　*Would you like to play? ~ I'd love to _. • I was hoping to go with you, but I've decided not to _.*
但是，**to be** 中的 **be** 不可省略：*Was Michael happy? ~ He seemed to be.*（不说 ~~He seemed to.~~）

2 **不带 to 的动词不定式**

在情态动词之后（6），**hear** 和 **see** 等感官动词所接的宾语之后（7），以及 **let** 和 **make** 所接的宾语之后（8），要用不带 **to** 的不定式（即动词原形）。

　　6　*I can't stay long. • What will we do if they tell us we must pay more?*（不说 ~~… we must to pay more?~~）
　　7　*I didn't hear Tom come in. • I've never seen anyone eat as much as your friend can.*
　　8　*Please make her stop! • They won't let us leave.*（不说 ~~They won't let us to leave.~~）
动词 **help** 之后可以接带 **to** 或不带 **to** 的不定式：*Annie helped me (to) clean up.*

3 **动名词**

动名词和动名词的否定式（**negative gerund**）（**not** + 动名词）可用在动词或介词之后（9）。动名词也可以作主语（10）。

　　9　*I don't mind waiting. • Paul enjoys not having a job. • She watches TV instead of working.*
　　10　*Studying makes me sleepy. • My doctor says that swimming is the best kind of exercise.*
动名词也被称作 "-ing 形式"。在标牌上，动名词常用在 **No** 之后：*No Parking*。

动名词后面可以接宾语、副词和介词短语（11）。在动名词之前可以使用名词（如 **Tom**）和宾格代词（如 **them**），也可以用名词所有格和物主限定词（如 **Tom's, their**），后者更常见于正式语言中（12）。

　　11　*He denied taking the money. • They recommend washing silk shirts gently in cold water.*
　　12　*I can't recall Tom / Tom's visiting us. • We listened to them / their arguing all night.*

4 **是动名词还是现在分词？**

动名词的用法类似名词，可以作主语或宾语（13）。现在分词通常用作动词，与不同形式的动词 **be** 连用（14）。在简化的关系从句或状语从句中使用的是现在分词，而非动名词（15）。

　　13　*Talking and action are two quite different things. • Have they finished (the) cleaning yet?*
　　14　*We were talking about money. • I have been cleaning my room all morning.*
　　15　*The man (who is) talking to Liz is her dad. • While (I'm) cleaning, I listen to music.*

C 阅读第 **138** 页底部练习 B 的四条英文定义，就下列描述各找出一个例子。

　1　在动词后使用带 to 的不定式 ＿＿＿＿＿＿　　2　在动词后使用不带 to 的不定式 ＿＿＿＿＿＿
　3　在不定式后使用动名词 ＿＿＿＿＿＿　　4　在介词后使用动名词 ＿＿＿＿＿＿

→ 形容词与动词不定式 / 动名词连用 144　名词 / 代词与动词不定式 / 动名词连用 145

动词不定式和动名词的复杂形式

5 动词不定式的复杂形式

如果想要明确表达所谈论的事情是先前发生的，或某行为已经完成，不用不定式的一般形式（1），而要用不定式的完成式（**to have** + 过去分词）（2）。

    1 *Ali seems to be ill a lot. • I'm hoping to read the guidebook before we get to Berlin.*

    2 *Ali seems to have been ill a lot. • I'm hoping to have read the guidebook before we get to Berlin.*

谈论先前的事情时，可以在 **would** + **like** / **hate** / **love** / **prefer** 后使用不定式的完成式（3）。还可以在 **would have liked** 等短语后使用不定式的一般形式，表达相似的含义（4）。有时在非正式语言中，两处都使用完成式（5）。

    3 *I would like to have been there. • You would hate to have seen all the destruction.*

    4 *I would have liked to be there. • You would have hated to see all the destruction.*

    5 *I would have liked to have been there. • You would have hated to have seen it.*

不定式的进行式（**to be** + 现在分词）可用于描述正在进行的行为（6），不定式的完成进行式（**to have been** + 现在分词）可用于描述在更早时正在进行的行为（7）。

    6 *The children will pretend to be sleeping. • The girl seemed to be waiting for someone.*

    7 *They'll pretend to have been sleeping. • She seemed to have been waiting there for hours.*

可用不定式的被动式（**to be** + 过去分词）表示主语现在或将来承受的动作（8），用不定式的被动完成式（**to have been** + 过去分词）表示主语先前承受的动作（9）。

    8 *My car is supposed to be repaired today. • The workers want to be paid in cash.*

    9 *It was supposed to have been repaired last week. • They were hoping to have been paid already.*

6 动名词的复杂形式

如果想要明确表达所谈论的行为发生在过去，不用动名词的一般形式（10），而要用动名词的完成式（**having** + 过去分词）（11）。

    10 *Kirsten regretted telling us about the money. • We thanked them for supporting us.*

    11 *She regretted having told us about the money. • We thanked them for having supported us.*

可用动名词的被动式（**being** + 过去分词）表示主语承受的动作（12），用动名词的被动完成式（**having been** + 过去分词）强调动作发生在过去（13）。

    12 *In her book, Annie O'Neill wrote about being punished as a child for speaking Irish.*

    13 *She still has nightmares from having been locked up in a small dark cupboard for hours.*

D 用 to be, being, to have 或 having 填空。

◆ I didn't mind *being* _____ the youngest in a family of ten, but I knew I really wanted *to have* _____ a large living space all to myself when I got older.

1 I'm supposed _____ studying today, but I'm too tired from not _____ slept at all last night.

2 You wouldn't like _____ been living here during the war, with bombs falling and people _____ killed every day.

3 The original tower is believed _____ been constructed in 1810. It has always had structural problems from not _____ been built on more solid ground.

4 The cleaners want _____ finished their work in this room before they leave today because there are another two rooms on the second floor that have _____ done tomorrow.

→ 动词不定式和动名词的一般形式 139   过去分词 17   被动式 57

E 动词不定式和动名词。从第 140 页练习 D 中补全后的句子里找出合适的例子填写下表。

> ◆ 动词不定式的一般形式：to + 动词原形（如 to play）*to have*
>
> 1 动词不定式的完成式：to have + 过去分词（如 to have played）
>
> 2 动词不定式的进行式：to be + 现在分词（如 to be playing）
>
> 3 动词不定式的完成进行式：to have been + 现在分词（如 to have been playing）
>
> 4 动词不定式的被动式：to be + 过去分词（如 to be played）
>
> 5 动词不定式的被动完成式：to have been + 过去分词（如 to have been played）

> ◆ 动名词的一般形式：动词原形 + -ing（如 playing）*being*
>
> 6 动名词的完成式：having + 过去分词（如 having played）
>
> 7 动名词的被动式：being + 过去分词（如 being played）
>
> 8 动名词的被动完成式：having been + 过去分词（如 having been played）

F 完成下列句子，使其与所给句子的意思尽可能接近，须用上动词不定式或动名词。

1 You were supposed to do your homework before you went out.
  Your homework ....

2 She had taken the time to help me and I wanted to thank her for that.
  I wanted ....

3 They hadn't been told about the changes and complained about it.
  They complained about ....

G 选择合适的动词不定式或动名词填空。

to be burning	being held	to have visited	to have been based	to be using
meeting	not to have seen	to have been built	travelling	to have been doing

Did Marco Polo tell the truth when he wrote about [1] .... to China and
[2] .... the emperor Kublai Khan? Or did the 13th-century Italian explorer
just make up stories about places he would like [3] .... and things he would
like [4] .... instead of [5] .... captive in prison? According
to some experts, his stories appear [6] .... on things he had heard
about rather than things he had seen himself. In his account, the Chinese were said
[7] .... paper money and [8] .... 'large black stones' (coal)
for heat long before Europeans. However, the Great Wall is known [9] ....
before his travels, yet he appears [10] .... it.

动词与动词不定式／动名词连用

7 可与不定式连用而不与动名词连用的动词

在 hope 和 offer 等动词之后用不定式，不用动名词（1）。invite 和 tell 等动词后须接一个名词或宾格代词，指明不定式的主语（2）。ask 和 want 等动词与不定式连用时，有时后面须接不定式的主语；如果不定式的主语就是 ask 和 want 等动词的主语，则可省略（3）。

1　*I'm hoping to get a day off soon.* • *We offered to pay for the damage.* （不说 *offered paying*）
2　*They told me not to wait for them.* • *David invited us to go with him.* （不说 *invited to go*）
3　*I asked Sam to stay. I wanted him to wait, but he wanted to leave right away.*

8 可与动名词连用而不与不定式连用的动词

在 avoid 和 enjoy 等动词之后用动名词，不用不定式（4）。在 imagine 和 mind 等动词后可以先接一个名词或宾格代词，再接动名词（5）。在 concentrate on 等带介词的动词以及 give up 之类的短语动词之后用动名词（6）。

4　*Avoid eating cakes and sweets.* • *We enjoy travelling by train.* （不说 *enjoy to travel*）
5　*I imagined Jenny walking on a sunny beach.* • *Would you mind us waiting outside?*
6　*He should concentrate on studying, not singing.* • *Have you given up exercising already?*

9 可与不定式或动名词连用的动词

在 begin, continue, intend 和 start 后，通常既可用不定式也可用动名词，含义几乎一样。

7　*Josh started to drink / drinking the soup, but it was very spicy. He began to cough / coughing.*
在现在分词之后要用不定式：*Is it starting to rain?*（不说 *Is it starting raining?*）

在 hate, like, love 和 prefer 之后，通常既可用不定式也可用动名词，两者意思几乎一样（8）。笼统地谈论某种活动（并非由主语执行的）时，用动名词（9）。在 would hate / like / love / prefer 之后用不定式（10）。

8　*Katy loves to play / playing the piano.* • *Don't you prefer to study / studying at home?*
9　*I hate wrestling because it's so violent. It shouldn't be on TV. I don't like boxing either.*
10　*Would you like to come with us?* • *I'd love to see you tonight.* （不说 *I'd love seeing you tonight.*）
注意 would rather + 动词原形的用法：*I'd rather stay here.*（不说 *I'd rather to stay here.*）

在 advise, allow, encourage 和 permit 后面，可以加一个名词或宾格代词作为不定式的主语。若是笼统地谈论某行为，没有主语，此时用动名词。

11　*They don't allow us to smoke.* • *They don't allow smoking.* （不说 *They don't allow us smoking.*）

在 feel, hear, see 和 watch 后，可用一个名词或宾格代词作后面动作的主语，之后或用不带 to 的不定式表示一次性或已完成的动作，或用动名词表示反复发生或持续进行的动作。

12　*When I rang the doorbell, I heard a dog bark.* • *Did you hear that dog barking last night?*
这类动词后面没有主语时，用动名词：*I also heard shouting.*（不说 *I also heard shout.*）

在 forget, regret, remember 和 stop 之后，用不定式谈论以后将发生的动作（13），用动名词谈论已经发生的动作（14）。

13　*Remember to take an umbrella.*（稍后当你外出时）• *I regret to say this.*（我将要说出来）
14　*Don't you remember taking it?*（之前在你离开时）• *I regret saying that.*（我之前说了那话）

need 之后常跟不定式，但是也可以使用动名词，表达的意思与使用不定式的被动式时相同（15）。mean 之后可以用不定式（= intend），也可以用动名词（= result in）（16）。try 之后可以用不定式（= make an effort），也可以用动名词（= experiment with）（17）。

15　*I need to do some laundry.* • *These towels need washing.* （= *These towels need to be washed.*）
16　*I meant to ask you about your new job. Will it mean spending more time away from home?*
17　*I must try to get to work on time tomorrow. I think I'll try setting my alarm a bit earlier.*

→ 动词不定式和动名词的一般形式 139　转述动词与动词不定式或动名词连用 152　need 38

H 为每句选择一组合适的动词，将句子补全，第一个动词要采用恰当形式，第二个动词要使用不定式或动名词形式。

> enjoy / take   hope / visit   imagine / make   invite / stay   love / be   want / spend

1 **动词 + 不定式：** I _____ Japan next summer.
   其他可用于该结构的动词：*agree, aim, apply, decide, demand, fail, offer, plan, refuse, vote*

2 **动词 + 名词 / 宾格代词 + 不定式：** My friend Ryoko has _____ me _____ with her.
   其他可用于该结构的动词：*command, convince, force, instruct, order, persuade, remind, tell, tempt, urge*

3 **动词 (+ 名词 / 宾格代词) + 不定式：** She _____ me _____ a whole month there.
   其他可用于该结构的动词：*ask, beg, expect, wish*

4 **动词 + 动名词：** She says she'll _____ me to all her favourite places.
   其他可用于该结构的动词：*admit, avoid, consider, deny, finish, give up, mention, practise, recommend, suggest*

5 **动词 (+ 名词 / 宾格代词) + 动名词：** I can _____ her _____ plans already.
   其他可用于该结构的动词：*celebrate, detest, dislike, involve, keep, mind, miss, prevent, recall, resent*

6 **动词 + 不定式 / 动名词：** I would _____ able to go sooner.
   其他可用于该结构的动词：*begin, continue, forget, hate, like, learn, mean, regret, remember, try*

I 为每句选择一组合适的动词，用其恰当形式将句子补全。

> allow / take   avoid / try / drive   force / stop / play   forget / send   mean / tidy   prefer / not talk

1 My teachers would never _____ students _____ the exams home.
2 Don't _____ me a postcard when you go to Japan.
3 I'm sorry about the mess. I _____ up before you came back.
4 Most people _____ about how much money they have or earn.
5 We usually _____ through the centre of town during rush hour.
6 Bad weather _____ us _____ tennis earlier today.

J 改正下文中不定式和动名词用法有误的地方。

I have never forgotten/~~work~~ *working* as a cleaner at a hotel one summer when I was a teenager.
My aunt was an assistant manager at the hotel and she encouraged me take the summer
job. She had been a housekeeper at one time and she advised me remember clean
the bathrooms really well. Nobody likes clean bathrooms, but I didn't mind do it as
part of my summer job. That's when I was first starting learn English. Some of the
visitors were really nice and I could practise speak English with them. I enjoyed try
improve my English and it helped me when I went to college later. I also learned that
I didn't want work as a hotel cleaner forever, but I don't regret do it for one summer.
I decided study harder at school so I could go to college and try get a different job.

形容词与动词不定式 / 动名词连用

10 可与不定式连用而不与动名词连用的形容词

有些形容词可用于谈论确定会做某事（如 **sure**）或想要做某事（如 **eager**）（1），或者谈论感受或反应（如 **glad** 和 **delighted**）（2），在这类形容词后可使用不定式，不用动名词。

  1 *The children are sure to get up early tomorrow. They're eager to go to the beach.*
  2 *I'm glad to meet you. • I was delighted to hear the good news about your scholarship.*

此类形容词还有：**disappointed, happy, pleased, sad, sorry, surprised**。

在一些形容词之后，可以用 **for** 引导一个名词短语或代词，来指明不定式的主语（3）。如果是就某人的行为作出评价，则可以用 **of**（不用 **for**）（4）。

  3 *It was good for the children to visit their grandparents.* （孩子们探望祖父母的经历是愉快的）
  4 *It was good of the children to visit their grandparents.* （孩子们探望祖父母的行为是好的）

此类形容词还有：**bad, nice, silly, stupid, wrong**。

too + 形容词和形容词 + **enough** 后常跟不定式。

  5 *Is the tea still too hot (for you) to drink? • The small bags are light enough (for us) to carry.*

11 可与不定式或动名词连用的形容词

形式主语 **it** + **be** + **nice, difficult** 之类的形容词后，可用不定式（6）或动名词（7），两者含义几乎一样。如果想突出动作对象，将其作为句子主语，则在这些形容词后用不定式（8）。

  6 *It was really nice to talk to Mrs Anderson. • Was it very difficult to learn Arabic?*
  7 *It was really nice talking to Mrs Anderson. • Was it very difficult learning Arabic?*
  8 *Mrs Anderson was really nice to talk to. • Was Arabic very difficult to learn?*

此类形容词还有：**easy, exciting, great, hard, impossible, interesting**。

动名词可以作主语，后面使用 **be** + **important, necessary** 之类的形容词（9）。但是在形式主语 **it** + **be** + 此类形容词之后，要使用不定式（10）。

  9 *Listening carefully is important, but writing everything down isn't necessary.*
  10 *It's important to listen carefully, but it isn't necessary to write everything down.*

此类形容词还有：**crucial, essential, unnecessary, vital**。

在 **anxious** 之类的形容词之后，可以用不定式，或者用介词加动名词，但两者含义不同（11）。在很多形容词后面，只可用介词加动名词（12）。

  11 *I was anxious to leave.* （我急于离开） • *I was anxious about leaving.* （我为此感到焦虑）
  12 *Percy is famous for inventing microwave popcorn.* （不说 ~~He's famous to invent it.~~） • *Isn't Lucia capable of doing it by herself?* （不说 ~~Isn't Lucia capable to do it by herself?~~）

K 完成下列句子，使其与所给句子的意思尽可能接近，须用上动词不定式或动名词。

1 Planning ahead is essential in my kind of job.
   It's ....

2 Jessica didn't see any of her friends at the shopping centre and she was disappointed.
   Jessica was disappointed ....

3 Christopher was so good to come to our rescue when our car broke down.
   It was so good ....

4 It isn't easy driving those huge buses along narrow winding roads.
   Those huge buses ....

名词 / 代词与动词不定式 / 动名词连用

🔟 可与不定式连用而不与动名词连用的名词和代词

有些名词与第 **143** 页练习 H 中列出的那些与不定式连用的动词含义相似（如 **agree** 和 **agreement**），这些名词后也可接不定式（1）。可将这些名词用作主语，后接 **be** 和不定式；或者用在形式主语 **it + be** 后面，之后再接不定式（2）。还可以将 **ambition** 和 **goal** 之类的名词用在这两种句式中，与不定式连用，谈论未来的行为（3）。

1 *We agreed to share the cost.* • *We had an agreement to share the cost.*
2 *The agreement was to share the cost.* • *It was our agreement to share the cost.*
3 *Our goal is to save £500 by next summer.* • *It's his ambition to become an astronomer.*

此类名词还有：**aim, decision, desire, expectation, hope, offer, plan, wish**。

不定式可用在 **person** 或 **place** 等笼统地指人或物的名词后（4），以及不定代词和不定副词，如 **someone** 和 **nowhere** 后（5）。这种情况下，不定式用于说明该人或物可实现的目的或具备的作用。在名词和不定代词后，可加 **for + 名词短语 / 宾格代词**来表明不定式的主语（6）。

4 *Rob's the person to ask about graphics.* • *Iceland is a great place to visit.* • *I brought a book to read.*
5 *He needs someone to love.* • *Is there anything to eat?* • *They have nowhere to go at night.*
6 *It's time for the kids to go to bed.* • *There's nothing for us to do.* • *I brought a book for you to read.*

🔟 可与不定式或动名词连用的名词和代词

动名词通常不会紧跟在名词后面，只有 **have a problem, it's no use** 等少数短语是例外（7）。**interest** 和 **talent** 之类的名词后可接介词 + 动名词（8）。**the + 名词 + of + 动名词**这一结构（如 **the cost of living**）十分常见（9）。

7 *Did you have a problem finding the place?* • *It was no use complaining because no one cared.*
8 *Julia had a talent for acting.* • *I had no interest in studying.* （不说 ~~I had no interest to study.~~）
9 *The cost of living in London is very high.* • *The thought of eating eggs makes me feel queasy.* • *He stressed the importance of being on time.* • *I don't like the idea of (you) going alone.*

在 **attempt** 和 **intention** 之类的名词后面，可以用不定式，也可以用介词 + 动名词，两者含义几乎一样（10）。当谈论某物的用途或可实现的目的时，可以在名词或不定代词后使用不定式（11），也可以使用 **for + 动名词**（12），两者含义并无不同。

10 *His attempt to break / at breaking the record failed.* • *I have no intention to leave / of leaving.*
11 *They have a machine to clean carpets.* • *I need to find something to remove stains.*
12 *They have a machine for cleaning carpets.* • *I need to find something for removing stains.*

🇱 选择合适的单词组合（一个名词 / 代词和一个动词）填空，动词要用不定式或动名词形式。

cost / rent	information / reserve	plan / take	someone / ask
~~idea / study~~	place / stay	problem / keep	task / call

Leila was both excited and nervous about the ♦ *idea* of *studying* in Edinburgh during the summer. Her [1] .... was only two courses at the university because she didn't want to have a [2] .... up with the lectures and assignments. She had heard that the most convenient [3] .... was in the student halls of residence, but they hadn't sent her any [4] .... about .... a room there. So, her next [5] .... was .... and find [6] .... about the kind of accommodation they had and the [7] .... of .... one of their rooms during the summer months.

→ 不定代词和不定副词 98　可与动词不定式连用的动词 142

测验

A 选出最恰当的词或短语完成下列句子。

1 You know they don't allow _____ in here.
  a eat and drink **b** you eat and drink **c** to eat and drink **d** eating and drinking

2 He never _____ doing that.
  a agreed **b** concentrated **c** mentioned **d** persuaded

3 Flights kept _____ because of bad weather.
  a delaying **b** being delayed **c** having delayed **d** having been delayed

4 In my dream, Batman offered me a ride on his motorbike and I told him I'd rather _____.
  a walk **b** walking **c** walked **d** to walk

5 Mrs Jacobson reminded us of the importance _____ our passports in a safe place.
  a keep **b** keeping **c** to keep **d** of keeping

B 从每句标有下划线的部分（A，B，C，D）中选出错误的一项。

1 I really do regret not to learn to play the piano when I had so many opportunities to learn and
  practise in school.

2 When I asked the students to help me move the chairs, some girls volunteered to carry one each
  for me and some boys offered to take the others, but Mark refused me to help at all.

3 When we're ready to leave the house, my mother always tells us wait while she checks in the
  kitchen because she's afraid to go out without making sure everything is turned off.

4 I will never forget to visit Egypt as a child. It was so exciting to stand beside the pyramids.
  When it was time for us to go home, my parents say I cried and begged them not to leave.

5 It really is better to ask for help instead of pretending to know how to do something when you
  are probably not capable to do it at all.

C 将下列各组动词填入文本，第一个动词要采用恰当形式，第二个动词要使用不定式或动名词形式。

allow / go   assume / be   hear / sneeze   remember / tell   smell / burn

I had just arrived at the International Adventure Camp in Florida. They had spent the
afternoon assigning us to our cabins and telling us all the rules. The evening meal
was pizza. Now it was after ten o'clock and we were all ¹ _____ in
bed asleep. I was still awake, stretched out on the uncomfortable camp bed, when I
² _____ someone _____ outside the cabin window. Just
once, then silence. I ³ _____ the camp leader _____ us
that we weren't ⁴ _____ outside after dark. Someone was breaking that
rule. Then I thought I could ⁵ _____ a cigarette _____.
There was another rule against that.

146

D 完成下列句子，使其与所给句子的意思尽可能接近，须用上动词不定式或动名词。

1 It's sometimes hard finding a place to park.

A place to park _____.

2 Is keeping all these old files really necessary?

Is it really necessary _____?

3 He shouldn't buy a new car now.

It would be a mistake for _____.

4 Amy was bitten by a dog when she was very young and she still remembers it.

Amy still remembers _____.

5 The boy said that he hadn't done anything wrong.

The boy denied _____.

E 选择合适的动词，用其不定式或动名词形式填空。

go　look　put　start　regain　do　keep　lose　stop　try

If it's so hard to lose weight, why do people keep [1] _____? Because they want [2] _____ better is the usual answer. The problem is that going on a diet is likely [3] _____ more harm than good, according to health experts. There is a strong tendency [4] _____ all the weight lost within one year of [5] _____ the diet. Only three per cent of those who take off weight have been found [6] _____ it off for at least three years. Moreover, the 'yo-yo' pattern of [7] _____ a diet, [8] _____ some weight and then [9] _____ it back on may be more harmful to an individual than not [10] _____ on a diet in the first place.

12 转述（reporting）

转述某人说的话时，可以重复说话者的原话（*He said, 'I'm sorry.'*），这就是直接引语（direct speech）。如果不需要或者不想重复原话，可以使用间接引语（indirect speech）（*He said that he was sorry.*）或总结性转述（summary report）（*He apologized.*）。

A 阅读下面的故事，找出两个包含动词 say 的句子，其中一句使用了直接引语，另一句使用了间接引语。

A On Sunday afternoons my grandmother used to take me with her to visit Mr Calum Mackenzie. My grandmother and Mrs Mackenzie, his wife, had been good friends
5 and had gone to church together every Sunday. When Mrs Mackenzie died, my grandmother was one of the women who helped Mr Mackenzie and she still liked to visit him, even on the coldest winter days.

10 **B** Mr Mackenzie was, as my grandmother put it, 'a man of few words'. This probably wasn't obvious to everyone because, when we arrived, he would always call out, 'Well, hello there!' and give us a big smile like a friendly
15 neighbour ready to stop and chat. But I never saw him talking to any of the neighbours. I remember one time my grandmother commented that maybe he didn't speak much because he didn't hear as well as he used to.
20 Mr Mackenzie turned in his chair. 'Maybe I don't hear anything worth talking about,' he grumbled.

C My grandmother would tell him about everything that had been going on in the
25 church as she walked round the house picking things up and putting them away. The news would be served with the tea and cakes we always had on Sundays with him. From the outside, it would have sounded as if we were
30 all having a lively conversation, punctuated by the sound of teaspoons clinking on saucers.

D When we cleared the tea things away and my grandmother disappeared into the kitchen, a silence would fall over the living room. I
35 would sit quietly with Mr Mackenzie and stare into the glowing embers of the open fire. He would cut up chunks of black tobacco and put them in his pipe and light it. He'd puff away with his eyes almost closed as the sweet smell
40 filled the warm room.

E In my English class we had read a story about the poets Wordsworth and Coleridge. One time Wordsworth went to visit Coleridge at his cottage. He walked in, greeted his friend,
45 and sat down. He didn't say another word for three hours. Nor did Coleridge. Then Wordsworth got up and, as he was leaving, thanked Coleridge for a perfect evening. The teacher asked us what we thought about the
50 story and those who had opinions mostly said that it was a strange story or impossible or that poets must be weird people. I didn't say anything.

F When we eventually got ready to leave, my
55 grandmother would give Mr Mackenzie advice about eating and his health. He would just nod and say, 'Thanks for coming round,' in a voice that told us he had had a perfect afternoon.

B 选择合适的句子作为上文各段（A—F）的结尾句，将对应段落的字母序号填入括号。

1 But it was really only my grandmother who was talking. (.....)
2 We could easily spend an hour like that. (.....)
3 He didn't say much, but he obviously wasn't deaf. (.....)
4 It always felt so much colder when we left. (.....)
5 She said we were going 'just to see how Calum is doing'. (.....)
6 It didn't seem strange to me and I knew it wasn't impossible. (.....)

直接引语

直接引语通常要加引号（quotation marks），跟在 **reply, say** 等转述动词（reporting verb）后。

　　1　*Mark said, 'I need you here.' Rose replied, 'I can't come before next weekend.'*
在美国英语中，用双引号：*He said, "I need you."*

主语和转述动词还可以放在直接引语之后（2），也可以放在直接引语的两部分之间（3）。

　　2　*'That's too late,' he said. 'Well, that's just too bad,' she told him and hung up.*
　　3　*'Hi,' he began. 'It's me again. I was wondering,' he continued, 'if we could start over.'*

用在直接引语之后时，有时把转述动词放在主语之前（4）；但是当主语是代词时，转述动词只能放在主语之后（5）。

　　4　*'We will never give up,' shouted one of the demonstrators as he was dragged away.*
　　5　*'Where's Tim?' he asks impatiently. 'Not here yet,' she replies.*（不说 ~~… replies she.~~）

直接引语有时也被置于括号内（6）或跟在冒号后（7），在这些情况下不使用转述动词。还可以用直接引语来表达内心的想法和反应，就像这些是已经说出来的话（8）。

　　6　*Blythe Danner didn't want her daughter to be an actor ('I thought she was too bright').*
　　7　*She never had any doubts: 'I always knew what I wanted to do.'*
　　8　*I suddenly realized 'I hate him!' Then I thought 'Oh, no!' when I remembered that kiss.*

在准确转述特定的单词、短语或标题时，要用引号（9）。在英国英语中，如果在直接引语中还有引用，就在单引号内使用双引号（10）。

　　9　*There was a sign with 'No Entry' printed in big red letters. • Have you read 'War and Peace'?*
　　10　*She said, 'I heard someone whisper "Jess" and I turned, but no one was there.'*

在美国英语中，如果在直接引语中还有引用，则是在双引号内使用单引号：*"I heard someone whisper 'Jess' and I turned, but no one was there."*

C　再读一读第 **148** 页的故事，就下列描述各找出一个例子：

1　位于直接引语前的转述动词（除了 say 以外）：...
2　位于直接引语后的转述动词：...

D　参考上面的例子 1—3，用 comma 或 quotation mark 填写下面关于标点符号使用规则的描述。

After the reporting verb, before direct speech, we put the [1].................... before the
[2].................... . After direct speech, before the reporting verb plus subject, we put
the [3].................... before the [4].................... . When the reporting verb plus
subject is in the middle of two parts of direct speech, we use a [5].................... to
close the first part and a [6].................... to open the second part.

E　给下文加上合适的标点符号。

Susanna Mrs Alder called out I'd like you to come and meet Michael a girl
appeared in the doorway how do you do she said nice to meet you he mumbled
please don't call him Michelle or Mikey or any other silly names warned Mrs
Alder as she swept out of the room have you read Harry Potter Susanna suddenly
said what one he asked oh no you little Mickey Mouse she said as she came into
the room you must say which one not what one if you're going to survive here

→ 间接引语 150　转述动词 152

间接引语

间接引语转述的是他人话语的含义而非确切词语。可用由 **that**（1）或 **wh-** 疑问词（**what, where, when** 等）（2）引导的名词性从句来表述间接引语。在非正式语言中，常省略 **that**。

1 'It's a strange story.' → *They said (that) it was a strange story.*
2 'What do you think about the story?' → *The teacher asked us what we thought about the story.*

1 间接引语中表示地点、时间和人物的词

在间接引语中，要把从说话者角度出发谈论自身情况的词（**I, my, this** 等）改为转述者视角下的用词（**she, her, that** 等）。

3 'I don't like my hair in this style.' → *She said she didn't like her hair in that style.*

通常须调整说话者提到的表示所处地点（4）和时间（5）的词语，使之符合转述者的视角。

4 'Wordsworth lived here, but not in this particular cottage.' → *The tour guide explained that Wordsworth had lived there, but not in that particular cottage.*
5 'It rained yesterday and most of last week.' → *The workman pointed out that it had rained the day before and most of the previous week.*

注意以下变化：'**now**' → **then**，'**tomorrow**' → **the next day**，'**two days ago**' → **two days earlier**。

各类代词、物主限定词均应反映转述者的视角。

6 'We fixed it ourselves.' → *The boys claimed that they had fixed it themselves.*
7 Tom said to Anna, 'I'll give you my book.' → *Tom said that he would give her his book.*
8 Amber said to me, 'I'll give you my book.' → *Amber said that she would give me her book.*

2 间接引语中的时态

通常，当转述动词是一般过去式时，原话语中的一般现在时要变为一般过去时（9），现在完成时要变为过去完成时（10）。

9 'It is late and I have a headache.' → *She complained that it was late and she had a headache.*
10 'I've heard that they have been arguing.' → *He said he'd heard that they had been arguing.*

如果原话语的时态为一般过去时，在转述时可以用一般过去时，也可以改为过去完成时来强调事情发生在说话之前。

11 'I didn't see Mark.' → *He said he didn't see Mark.* 或 *He said he hadn't seen Mark.*

当转述动词是一般现在式（偶尔也会用现在进行式）时，间接引语中的动词时态通常与原话语中的相同（12，13，14）；当转述动词是过去式时，间接引语有时用现在时，表示情况没有发生改变（15）。

12 'Business is good and profits are up.' → *Delco reports that business is good and profits are up.*
13 'It is going to be very cold.' → *The forecast says that it is going to be very cold.*
14 'My parents live in Monaco.' → *She likes to tell everyone that her parents live in Monaco.*
15 'I love you.' → *He said he loves me.*

3 间接引语中的情态动词

在变为间接引语时，这些情态动词通常要变：**can** → **could**，**may** → **might**，**will** → **would**。

16 'You can go.' → *He said we could go.* • 'I'll wait.' → *She said that she would wait.*

在变为间接引语时，**could, might, ought to** 和 **should** 不变。

用 **shall** 表示将来会发生某事时，在间接引语中要改为 **would**（17）；主动提出要为他人做某事或提建议时，在间接引语中要改为 **should**（18）。

17 'I shall do it right away.' → *I remember she said that she would do it right away.*
18 'Shall I close the door?' → *The new student asked if he should close the door.*

在转述中表示有必要去做某事时，可以用 **must** 也可以用 **had to**。

19 'You must do more.' → *He said we must do more.* 或 *He said we had to do more.*

→ 情态动词 29　名词性从句 161—162　转述动词 152　时态 17

F 完成下列句子，使其与所给句子的意思尽可能接近。

1 'I left my jacket here yesterday.'
He said that _____.

2 'Carlin's new book is the funniest thing I've ever read.'
The reviewer wrote that _____.

3 'We won't eat it now, but we may have it for lunch tomorrow.'
She said that _____.

4 'You should take as much water as you can carry.'
He advised us that _____.

5 'I must get something to eat or I'll faint.'
You told me that _____.

6 'Demand for new PCs in the UK is declining.'
CompCo is reporting that _____.

7 'Shall I get rid of these old boxes in the cupboard?'
She asked if _____.

G 选择合适的词填空。

are	is	has	live	can	can't	will
were	~~was~~	had	lived	could	won't	would

When she died at the age of 122, Jeanne Calment was the oldest person on record. This amazing woman, from Arles in France, had not exactly lived what might be described as 'a healthy lifestyle'. Family and friends reported that she * _was_____ fond of cheese, wine and chocolate. She had also smoked cigarettes until she was 117. We asked several experts how a person, especially a cigarette smoker, 1 _____ live so long. They offered more than one answer. 'The average life expectancy 2 _____ now about 80 for women and 75 for men,' observed Dr Elizabeth Jones, director of the Centre for Studies on Ageing. She says that there 3 _____ been a steady rise in the maximum age of death throughout Europe during the past century and a major reason for this is improved medical care. Another researcher, Dr Michael Glass, says, 'There 4 _____ no theoretical reasons why we 5 _____ have a life span of 200 years.' Better medical care 6 _____ be the only factor, according to Dr Glass. He explained that genetic engineering 7 _____ soon allow us to repair or replace damaged cells, the real cause of ageing. He believes that we 8 _____ be able to stop the ageing process. Other researchers have noted that attitude is also an important factor in longer life. Dr John Park is the author of *Living Beyond 100*. 'Those who 9 _____ to a ripe old age,' he says, 'are those who 10 _____ cope with stress and other difficulties in life.' He wrote in his best-selling book that people who 11 _____ past 100 12 _____ almost always optimistic and 13 _____ a great attitude to life.

转述动词

4 转述动词与 **that** 从句（*that*-clause）连用

mention, say 等词可以作为转述动词，后接表述间接引语的 **that** 从句。

    1 'I've been ill.' → *She mentioned that she'd been ill.* • 'It's cold.' → *Kara said that it was cold.*

在 tell, assure 之类的转述动词后，必须先接表示听者的宾语，再接 **that** 从句。

    2 'She has gone home.' → *He told me that she had gone home.* （不说 ~~He told that she had gone home.~~ ）
    3 'You will be paid.' → *I assured them that they would be paid.* （不说 ~~I assured that they …~~ ）
此类动词还有：convince, inform, notify, persuade, remind。

在 say 之类的转述动词之后、that 从句之前，可以加入 to + 宾语（4）；在 agree 之类的转述动词之后、that 从句之前，可以加入 with + 宾语（5）。

    4 'I'm not ready.' → *He said (to me) that he wasn't ready.* （不说 ~~He said me that he wasn't ready.~~ ）
此类动词还有：admit, confess, mention, propose, report。

    5 'You're right. There is a mistake.' → *He agreed (with me) that there was a mistake.*
      （不说 ~~He agreed me that there was a mistake.~~ ）
此类动词还有：argue, check, confirm, disagree。

5 转述动词与动词不定式或动名词连用

在 invite, encourage 之类的转述动词后，先加宾语，再加不定式。

    6 'You can go with me.' → *He invited us to go with him.* （不说 ~~He invited us that we could go.~~ ）
    7 'You shouldn't quit.' → *She encouraged me not to quit.* （不说 ~~She encouraged not to quit.~~ ）
可使用该结构的动词还有：ask, expect, order, remind, urge, warn。

在 offer 之类的转述动词后，不加宾语，直接加不定式。

    8 'I'll help you later.' → *He offered to help us later.* （不说 ~~He offered us to help us later.~~ ）
可使用该结构的动词还有：apply, decide, decline, demand, refuse, volunteer。

在 promise 之类的转述动词后，可以用不定式也可以用 **that** 从句。

    9 'I'll fix it.' → *He promised to fix it.* 或 *He promised that he would fix it.*
此类动词还有：agree, claim, hope, propose, threaten, vow。

在 deny 和 suggest 之类的转述动词后，可以用动名词也可以用 **that** 从句。

    10 'I didn't take it.' → *She denied taking it.* 或 *She denied that she had taken it.*
    11 'You should leave.' → *He suggested leaving.* 或 *He suggested that they should leave.*
      （不说 ~~He suggested them leaving. / He suggested them to leave. / He suggested to leave.~~ ）
此类动词还有：admit, mention, propose, recommend, report。

6 总结性转述中的转述动词

一些转述动词可用于概括他人所说的话（12）。某些动词，如 speak, talk 和 thank，只能用于总结性转述，不能用于直接引语或间接引语（13）。

    12 'Don't come back – or else!' → *They threatened us.* • 'It was me. I did it.' → *He confessed.*
    13 *He talked to Nathan about the problem.* • *She spoke briefly to reporters.* • *I thanked them.*
      （不说 ~~He talked to me, 'Hi, how are you?'~~ • ~~She spoke to us that she liked it.~~ ）

boast, lie 之类的转述动词可与 **about** 搭配，用于总结性转述。

    14 'I beat everyone. I'm the best!' → *He boasted about his win.* • *He lied about how he did it.*
此类动词还有：complain, explain, inquire, joke, protest, speak, write。

→ 间接引语 150   动词不定式和动名词 139   用被动式进行转述 63   that 从句 161

H 完成下列句子，使其与所给句子的意思尽可能接近。

1 'Mr Brody, there's something wrong with the lights.'
 I mentioned ....

2 'Julia, you and your friends have to tidy up after the party.'
 I reminded ....

3 'Don't touch any of the wires.'
 He warned ....

4 'I didn't do anything wrong.'
 He denied ....

I 选择合适的转述动词填空，注意应使用动词的恰当形式。

ask beg claim explain mention ~~shout~~ talk tell think wonder

I was in the Arctic last summer to photograph foxes, but I had been having no luck.
I was on my way home one day when I saw a construction engineer called Malcolm
Davidson waving and *shouting* .... to me as I drove by. We had met the previous
weekend and he [1] .... some areas further north where I might find foxes.
I [2] .... why he was trying to stop me there. I pulled over and got out to
[3] .... to him. He [4] .... if I was still looking for foxes.

We walked over to what was left of some old rusted cars by the side of the road. I looked
down and saw three little foxes asleep beside a broken car door. He [5] ....
me that he would have to catch them all and move them away from there. It was his next
construction site, he [6] .... 'I'm afraid that when we [7] ....
that we are "developing" or "improving" an area, we don't always make things better for
wild animals.'

'Let me get my camera and take some photos before you do anything,' I
[8] .... him. I ran to get my camera. I do hope they'll survive, I
[9] .... to myself.

That afternoon I used up all the film I had while the young foxes played among the old
cars.

J 改正下文中的错误。

The word 'biker' is used for people who ride motorcycles. They sometimes ride around
in gangs. Some people say ~~me~~ that bikers are dangerous criminals, but I can't agree them
that all bikers are like that. One time I had a flat tyre on the motorway and two bikers
in black leather jackets stopped and offered me to help. I explained them that I can't get
the wheel off. One of them told that it was 'no problem' and assured that it wouldn't take
long. He even suggested me to stand behind the car for safety and warned me watch out
for broken glass on the ground. They fixed it really quickly and joked the small wheels on
my little car. I spoke them thanks. They refused take any money when I offered pay them.
They were like angels. Actually, it said on their jackets that they were 'Hell's Angels'.

转述陈述句和疑问句

7 **转述陈述句**

在正式用法中，转述陈述句时通常要在转述动词后加 **that**（1）；但是在非正式用法中，常常省略 **that**（2）。

> 1 *The prime minister said that she would consider it.* • *The police report that crime is down.*
> 2 *She said _ she'd think about it.* • *I told him _ I was leaving.* • *He agreed _ it was a good idea.*

如果 **that** 从句跟在描述说话者意图的动词（**complain, deny** 等）（3）、表示说话方式的动词（4）或短语动词（5）后，或者转述动词和 **that** 从句之间有其他信息，通常不省略 **that**。

> 3 *They complained that they had been left out.* • *He denied that he was responsible.*
> 4 *She whispered that she had to go.* • *The poor man shouted that he was innocent.*
> 5 *One student pointed out that the date was wrong.* • *She called out that dinner was ready.*
> 6 *He said in last week's meeting that we were wrong.* • *We agree with the critics that it's old.*

转述陈述句时，可把 **announcement, response** 等名词放在包含间接引语的 **that** 从句之前。这些名词之后的 **that** 通常不省略。

> 7 *'Classes are cancelled.'* → *Did you hear the announcement that classes were cancelled?*
> 8 *'I worked hard.'* → *His response that he worked hard isn't true.*（不说 ~~His response he worked …~~ ）

此类名词还有：**argument, claim, comment, explanation, report, statement**。

名词 + **be** + 包含间接引语的 **that** 从句也可用于转述陈述句。

> 9 *'It'll cost a lot.'* → *Her only comment was that it would cost a lot.*

8 **转述疑问句**

转述的疑问句（也称"间接疑问句"）以 **wh-** 疑问词（10）或者 **if / whether**（11）开头。

> 10 *'Who is she?'* → *He asked who she was.* • *'What does she do?'* → *He asked what she did.*
> 11 *'Is she a doctor or a nurse?'* → *He wanted to know if / whether she was a doctor or a nurse.*

在转述疑问句时，要把主语放在动词前，并且不使用问号（12）。当问句的主语就是 **wh-** 疑问词时，不改变语序（13）。

> 12 *'Where are the keys?'* → *I asked where the keys were.*（不说 ~~I asked where were the keys?~~ ）
> 13 *'Who has the keys?'* → *I asked who had the keys.*（不说 ~~I asked who the keys had.~~ ）

可以用动词不定式来转述含有 **should** 的 **wh-** 疑问句（询问该做什么、该怎么做等）。

> 14 *'When should I come and what should I do?'* → *I asked them when to come and what to do.*

注意，不能这么使用 **why**：*I asked them why I should do it.*（不说 ~~… why to do it.~~ ）

转述 **yes / no** 疑问句时，用 **if** 或 **whether** 开头。

> 15 *'Are you a nurse?'* → *I asked if / whether she was a nurse.*（不说 ~~I asked if was she a nurse?~~ ）

在介词之后（16），或不定式之前（17），或动词 **question** 之后（18），要用 **whether** 而不用 **if**。可以使用短语 **whether or not**，但不能说 ~~if or not~~（19）。

> 16 *'Is it okay to use a dictionary?'* → *Someone inquired about whether it was okay to use a dictionary.*
> （不说 ~~Someone inquired about if it was okay to use a dictionary.~~ ）
> 17 *'Should I wait for him?'* → *She's wondering whether to wait for him.*（不说 ~~… if to wait for him.~~ ）
> 18 *'Are they really terrorists?'* → *The reporter questioned whether they were really terrorists.*
> 19 *'Did he win or not?'* → *I asked whether or not he won.*（或 *I asked whether / if he won or not.* ）

→ 间接引语 150　疑问句的语序 45　that 从句 161　whether 和 if 161, 192

K 完成下列句子，使其与所给句子的意思尽可能接近，须用上间接引语。

1 'I'm not guilty!' called out one of the defendants.
One _____.

2 It really surprised us when she said she'd been adopted.
Her statement _____.

3 The students' argument is that the cost of tuition has increased too much and I agree.
I agree _____.

4 He claimed, 'I'm not a thief!', but no one believed him.
No one believed his _____.

L 为句子的前半句（1—4）选择合适的后半句（a—d），并在横线处补充 that, where, whether 或 who。

1 Some of them were arguing about　(......)　a _____ isn't here.
2 The teacher is trying to find out　(......)　b _____ the weather was going to be bad.
3 I asked another student　(......)　c _____ to leave or stay there for another day.
4 We heard one report　(......)　d _____ to find the library.

M 改正下列句子中的错误，把正确的句子写在横线上。

1 One of the visitors asked about if will there be a fridge in the hotel room?

_____

2 He asked me why to do that and I pointed out it was part of my job.

_____

3 She asked me what do next and my response that she gets some more chairs.

_____

4 Her explanation no one asked her if or not she has a degree was incredible.

_____

N 将所给陈述句和疑问句改为间接引语，填入下文合适的位置。

'There is a "moster" under my bed.'	'Why aren't you sleeping?'
'Have you seen the monster?'	'I haven't, but I know it has big teeth.'
'What is a "moster"?'	'Where did it come from?'

One time when I was babysitting for some friends, their five-year-old daughter got out of bed and came into the living room. I asked her ¹ _____.

She climbed on to the sofa beside me and whispered ² _____.
I started to ask her ³ _____, then I realized that she meant 'monster'. I asked her ⁴ _____.

She said ⁵ _____.

I asked her ⁶ _____. She didn't know, but it had really big eyes and sharp teeth. We eventually both fell asleep on the sofa and, luckily for us, the monster stayed in the bedroom.

转述命令、请求、建议和观点

9 转述命令和请求

转述命令时，**tell** 后接宾语和不定式的结构十分常用。

1 'Don't touch it.' → *He told us not to touch it.* • 'Be quiet!' → *She told everyone to be quiet.*

其他不那么常见但也可用于转述命令的动词包括：**command, direct, instruct, order**。

还可以用含短语情态动词 **have to** 或情态动词 **must** 的 **that** 从句来转述命令（2）。有时在较正式的语言中，**demand** 和 **insist** 等动词后要用虚拟语气（3）。

2 'Stop arguing!' → *Their mother told them that they had to / must stop arguing.*

3 'Do it yourself!' → *He insisted that I had to do it myself.* 或 *He insisted that I do it myself.*

转述请求时，**ask** 后接宾语和不定式的结构十分常用（4）。如果转述的请求谈论的是说话者本人的行动，不定式前面不加宾语（5）。

4 'Please don't smoke.' → *I asked him not to smoke.* • 'Come in.' → *He asked me to come in.*

5 'May I leave?' → *She asked to leave.* • 'Can I go?' → *He asked to go.*（不是 ~~He asked me to go.~~）

其他用于转述请求的动词和短语包括：**beg, plead with, request**。

还可以用含情态动词 **could** 或 **would** 的 **if** 从句来转述请求。

6 'Please help me.' → *The old man asked (us) if we could / would help him.*

10 转述建议

转述建议时，可将 **recommend** 或 **suggest** 等动词与含 **should** 的 **that** 从句连用（7）；在较正式的语言中，从句可用虚拟语气（8）。如果不想提及由谁实施建议的行为，可使用动名词（9）。

7 'You should go by train.' → *He recommended that we should go by train.*

8 'You should take the express train.' → *He suggested that we take the express train.*

9 'You should drive.' → *He recommended driving.*（不说 ~~He recommended us driving.~~）

还可以用动词 **advise**，后接宾语和不定式（10），或接 **that** 从句或动名词（11）。

10 'Wait a few days.' → *She advised him to wait a few days.*（不说 ~~She suggested him to wait.~~）

11 *She advised (him) that he (should) wait a few days.* • *She advised waiting a few days.*

可用不同的转述动词，如 **remind** 和 **warn**，引导 **that** 从句，从而转述不同类型的建议。

12 'A taxi will be much faster.' → *She reminded him that a taxi would be much faster.*

13 'You must be careful.' → *She warned them that they must / had to be careful.*

转述警告时还可以用不定式：*She warned them to be careful.*

11 转述观点

转述观点时，在表示"想""认为"等含义的动词后使用 **that** 从句。

14 'Oh, it's nice!' → *She thought that it was nice.* • 'I'll win.' → *He believes that he'll win.*

此类动词还有：**expect, feel, imagine, reckon, suppose, suspect**。

在非正式语言中，可以用 **say** 或 **tell** 的进行式转述普遍观点。

15 *The students were saying that the test was unfair.* • *Teachers are telling us there's a problem.*

还可以在名词（16）和形容词（17）后使用 **that** 从句，转述观点和感受。

16 'Girls mature earlier than boys.' → *It is her view that girls mature earlier than boys.*

此类名词还有：**belief, conclusion, diagnosis, hypothesis, opinion, theory**。

17 'It's a mistake.' → *I was sure that it was a mistake.* 或 *She is certain that it is a mistake.*

此类形容词还有：**aware, convinced, doubtful, positive, sorry, worried**。

O 完成下列句子，使其与所给句子的意思尽可能接近。

1 Professor to her students: 'Please do not eat or drink during lectures.'
   The professor asked ....

2 Guard to the prisoner: 'Stand up when the judge comes in.'
   The guard ordered ....

3 Worker to his boss: 'Can I leave early on Friday?'
   The worker asked ....

4 Scott's mother to Scott: 'You should apply to several universities.'
   Scott's mother recommended ....

P 将所给直接引语改为恰当的间接引语并填入下文合适的位置。

'Place your napkin in your lap.'	'Don't put a lot of food on your plate all at once.'
'Don't rest your elbows on the table.'	'Don't take more food until it is offered.'
'Chew your food with your mouth closed.'	'Ask somebody.'
'Don't talk with your mouth full.'	'Please pass the salt.'

My friend Karen Currie and I were huddled beside the small heater in her room, eating slices of pizza from a cardboard container. She was telling me about an old book she had been reading, called *Table Manners for Young Ladies*. It instructed the reader, when she is sitting at the table before the meal, [1] .... and [2] .... It told her, while she is eating, [3] .... and [4] .... Certain things were bad manners and the book advised her [5] .... and [6] .... It also said that, when she needed something, such as salt, she [7] .... [8] .... rather than reach across the table for it.

'Ah, the good old days,' she sighed as she reached into the box for another slice.

Q 选择一个合适的形容词或名词，搭配一个改写自所给直接引语的 that 从句，补全下列各句。

aware	diagnosis	'I lost my temper.'	'Take the early flight to Glasgow.'
positive	belief	'Dogs aren't allowed here.'	'You will all pass the exam.'
sorry	recommendation	'You have an ear infection.'	'A perfect life can be achieved.'

1 It was the travel site's ....
2 Idealism is the ....
3 My doctor's .... was ....
4 Sarah has quietened down and she's very ....
5 Our teacher was ....
6 The visitor obviously wasn't ....

测验

A 选出最恰当的词或短语完成下列句子。

1 They recommended that the windows _____ opened.
   a had to **b** not be **c** ought not to **d** should not

2 He _____ to take part.
   a advised not them **b** invited not them **c** offered them not **d** ordered them not

3 She _____ that she liked cold coffee.
   a described **b** replied **c** spoke **d** talked

4 The teachers were talking about a trip to see castles and the students were wondering _____
   a why to go. **b** where they go? **c** when it was. **d** what were they?

5 Her father _____ that Ellen had been to Prague before.
   a mentioned **b** persuaded **c** reminded **d** told

B 从每句标有下划线的部分（A，B，C，D）中选出错误的一项。

1 We thought flying would be faster, but when Thomas suggested she go by train Marla realized she had enough time and she will be able to see all the small towns along the way.

2 Because I suspected that our bill was too high, I asked our waiter if he would check it again and he agreed me that there had been a mistake.

3 Jessica was complaining to the coach that she felt tired and told him she had to rest, but he encouraged not to quit and said she didn't have much farther to go.

4 One student inquired about if it was okay to ask what was going to be in the test and the teacher's only comment was that he had already told them what would be tested.

5 We've invited Josh to come and he's offered us to bring extra food, but Linda has warned us that he sometimes promises to do things then forgets completely.

C 选择合适的动词并使用其恰当形式填空。

ask   explain   point out   reply   not say   not speak   talk   tell

In her best-selling book *You Just Don't Understand*, Deborah Tannen recalled a joke that her father liked to [1] _____ people. In the joke, a woman went to court to get a divorce from her husband. When the judge [2] _____ her why she wanted a divorce, she [3] _____ that her husband [4] _____ anything to her in two years. The judge turned to the husband and asked him why he [5] _____ to his wife in two years. The husband [6] _____ , 'I didn't want to interrupt her.' Tannen [7] _____ that the joke was based on an old-fashioned stereotype of women: that they [8] _____ all the time. Her research had shown that it was, in fact, a false stereotype.

D 完成下列句子，使其与所给句子的意思尽可能接近，须用上间接引语。

1 'I will buy the flowers myself.'
   Mrs Dalloway said ....

2 'Henry, did you leave your keys in the door?'
   She asked ....

3 An announcement was made that the strike was over.
   There was ....

4 'I shall return tomorrow.'
   His only comment ....

5 It surprised us that he said, 'I won't do it.'
   His statement that ....

6 I remember one time when my aunt said to me, 'Don't talk with your mouth full.'
   I remember one time when my aunt told ....

7 They said, 'You can stay at our house.'
   They invited ....

E 将所给直接引语改为间接引语或总结性转述，填入下文合适的位置。

> 'Do you know where Rob is?'   'I'm sorry.'
> 'I'll be there by eight o'clock.'   'I think he went out about half an hour ago.'
> 'I forgot that I promised to take my mother into town this morning.'

I was sitting in my living room, surrounded by my luggage, waiting for Rob to come and drive me to the airport. It was already twenty past eight and there was still no sign of him. He had said [1] .... I had already tried to call him at home. His younger sister answered, so I asked her [2] .... She sounded sleepy, but said [3] .... Normally it would only take about five minutes to drive from his place to mine, so something had gone wrong. Suddenly the phone rang. It was Rob. He [4] .... for being late and explained [5] .... It wasn't the first time his forgetfulness had made me nervous and his mother had made me take second place in his plans.

13 名词性从句 (noun clause)

名词性从句是用法类似于名词或名词短语的从句，可用作主语、宾语等。名词性从句可以由 that（*I'm hoping that the weather is going to be nice this weekend.*）、wh- 疑问词（*Do you know what the forecast is?*）、if 或 whether（*I was wondering if / whether we might be able to have a picnic on Sunday.*）引导。

A 阅读下面这篇杂志文章，找出符合下列要求的句子（各找一句即可）：

1 包含两个以 that 开头的名词性从句；
2 包含一个以 if 或 whether 开头的名词性从句。

According to one old song, love and marriage go together like a horse and carriage. These days, however, a long-lasting marriage may be almost as hard to find as a horse and carriage on our
5 busy streets. Statistically, it is now more likely that a marriage will end in divorce than continue in a loving relationship. It makes you wonder if getting married is worth the effort.

Is it simply the case that marriage has become a
10 gamble with less than a 50% chance of success? Not really, say researchers at the Newport Institute, who have discovered that there are clear clues to what makes a successful marriage. The Newport researchers have been conducting
15 a study of married couples for the past ten years. They started with 50 pairs of newly-weds and interviewed them every six months. During that time, 11 of the couples dropped out of the study, 15 couples split up and 24 couples stayed
20 married. The researchers were delighted that so many of their couples stayed together, but they don't think that it was simply a matter of luck.

One clear sign of a happy relationship is the frequent use of 'we' by a couple. This is one
25 indication that the couple speaks with a single voice about their experiences. Another clue is how past experiences are described. The happily married couples tend to focus on their experiences together, even when describing
30 difficulties. As an example, two different couples described holidays in which their suitcases were lost. One couple (still married) reported that it was one of their best memories because

they went out and bought some really different
35 clothing and had a crazy time. Another couple (no longer married) ended up blaming each other for everything going wrong during the holiday.

Researchers have also noticed that individuals in successful marriages tend to talk about their
40 spouses in much more positive ways. They focus on accomplishments. They often mention something new they enjoy doing now because of their partner. They also seem to be willing to change in ways that allow the couple to do things together. In
45 marriages that aren't working, there is more focus on self. One of the individuals typically insists that he or she will not stop doing something despite the fact that it is a source of conflict. Sometimes one of them will say that he or she actually prefers
50 it that the other has separate interests.

When the researchers asked couples what advice they would give to younger people thinking about getting married, they got some revealing answers. Among those who eventually got
55 divorced, the man would often give a response that was quite different from the woman's. It was obvious that these individuals had really different views about marriage. Among those who remained married, the answers were
60 more similar and often referred to the ideas of friendship, support and 'being on the same team'. On the basis of their study, the researchers have concluded that a modern marriage may begin with passionate love, but its survival depends a
65 lot on 'companionate love', a feeling that includes affection, caring and friendship.

B 根据以上杂志文章，判断下列表述是正确的（T）还是错误的（F）。

1　In this article, the author claims that more than half of all marriages end in divorce. 　　　　　T / F
2　In the Newport study, more than 20 couples were interviewed twice a year for ten years. 　　T / F
3　After ten years, the researchers found that three-quarters of the couples were still married. 　T / F
4　Couples who get divorced frequently speak with a single voice about their experiences. 　　　T / F
5　The researchers reported that happily married couples typically had separate interests. 　　　T / F
6　The researchers concluded that passionate love was the crucial factor in a long-term marriage. 　T / F

that 从句(*that*-clause)和 wh- 从句(*wh*-clause)

1 that 从句

由 **that** 引导的名词性从句(**that** 从句)可跟在用于表述想法(1)或感受(2)的动词后,还可以用于转述陈述(3)。

1   *People used to believe that the earth was flat. • I didn't realize that you were waiting for me.*
2   *Do you ever feel that you might be in danger? • I always worry that something could go wrong.*
3   *He mentioned that he had seen the report. • She whispered that she would have to leave early.*

that 从句还可以跟在名词和形容词后面。

4   *I was faced with the problem that I had no money. • Were you surprised that he passed the test?*

在非正式语言中,常常会省略引导名词性从句的 **that**,特别是当该从句跟在动词 **know, say, think** 之后时。

5   *I knew (that) you'd finish first. • Dan said (that) he had a cold. • Do you think (that) it's OK?*

在正式语言中,通常不省略 **that**(6)。如果从句跟在名词后(7),或者有短语(8)或从句(9)夹在动词和 **that** 从句之间,通常也不省略 **that**。

6   *A recent government study has concluded that drug use among adolescents is declining.*
7   *A contract is a written agreement that you and / or others will do something.*
8   *They discovered during the investigation that some money was missing.*
9   *Michelle forgot when the meeting was and that she was supposed to unlock the door for us.*

用 **that** 从句作主语时,**that**(= the fact that)不可省略。

10 *That Juliet loved him was never in doubt. • That he said nothing doesn't surprise me.*

2 wh- 从句

由 **what, where, how** 等 wh- 疑问词引导的名词性从句(wh- 从句)可跟在用于表述想法或疑问的动词后(11)。与间接疑问句相同,wh- 从句中的主语位于动词前,并且句末不用问号(12)。

11 *I wonder what it means. • They don't know where he went. • He asked how often we studied.*
12 *I can't understand what she is saying.*(不说 ~~I can't understand what is she saying?~~)

在介词后面可以用 wh- 从句,不用 **that** 从句。

13 *He disagreed with what we said. • I read about how he did it.*(不说 ~~I read about that he did it.~~)

以 **if** 或 **whether** 开头的名词性从句可以用在表达"不知道"的动词后面,还可用于转述 yes /
no 疑问句(14)。不确定名词性从句所表达的信息时,用 **if** 或 **whether**(15);可以确定名
词性从句所表达的信息时,用 **that**(16)。

14 *I can't remember if / whether I locked the door. • He asked us if / whether we were students.*
15 Was he married? Mary didn't know. → *Mary didn't know if / whether he was married.*
16 He was married. But Mary didn't know. → *Mary didn't know that he was married.*

C 再读一读第 **160** 页的杂志文章,就下列描述各找出一个例子。

1   用于转述陈述的 that 从句: ....
2   跟在名词后的 that 从句: ....
3   跟在形容词后的 that 从句: ....
4   用于转述问题的 wh- 从句: ....
5   跟在介词后的 wh- 从句: ....

→ 间接引语 150   间接疑问句 154   wh- 疑问词 45

名词性从句作主语和宾语

3 名词性从句作主语或与形式主语（empty subject）it 连用

以 that（= the fact that）（1）或 wh- 疑问词（2）开头的名词性从句可放在动词之前，作动词的主语。不过，这种结构通常仅用于正式文体。

1 *That we won the match surprised everyone.* • *That the other team played badly really helped us.*
2 *How the thieves broke in is obvious, but why they only took one old computer is a mystery.*

通常，不把名词性从句直接放在句首的主语位置，而是把 it 用作形式主语，把 that 从句（3）或 wh- 从句（4）放在句末。

3 *It surprised everyone that we won the match.* • *It really helped us that the other team played badly.*
4 *It's obvious how the thieves broke in, but it's a mystery why they only took one old computer.*

it 作形式主语时，可用 **whether** 或 **if** 引导名词性从句，放在句末（5）；但是，如果名词性从句位于句首作主语，则只能用 **whether**（6）。

5 *It doesn't really matter whether / if you go now or later.*
6 *Whether you go now or later doesn't really matter.* （不说 ~~If you go now or later doesn't matter.~~）

4 名词性从句作宾语或与形式宾语（empty object）it 连用

名词性从句可以作宾语，跟在动词之后，用于表述事实（7）或想法（8），或者用于转述话语（9）。

7 *We learned that pineapples don't grow on trees.* • *No one noticed that the keys were missing.*
8 *She could never anticipate what he might want.* • *Ewan suggested that we should leave early.*
9 *He screamed that he hated school.* • *She said that she felt that everyone was against her.*

在 **show, tell** 等某些动词后，在作直接宾语的名词性从句前，通常或必须有间接宾语（**you, me** 等）。

10 *I'll show you how it works.* • *He told me that he loved me.* （不说 ~~He told that he loved me.~~）
此类动词还有：**assure, convince, inform, notify, persuade, remind, warn**。

在表达"喜欢"（或"不喜欢"）的动词之后，可将 **it** 用作形式宾语，后接名词性从句。

11 *He doesn't like it that she still smokes.* • *I hate it that nobody ever cleans up after the meetings.*

在 **consider** 和 **think** 等用于表达想法的动词后，可将 **it** 用作形式宾语，后接名词（短语）（12）或形容词（13），再接名词性从句。在 **regard, see, view** 等动词后，用 **it + as** 接名词（短语）或形容词，再接名词性从句（14）。

12 *They consider it an offence when women go out in public without covering their heads.*
13 *We thought it odd that no one called us.* （不说 ~~We thought odd that no one called us.~~）
14 *Many people regard it as a really bad idea that the police have started carrying guns.*

D 下面列出了多种可与名词性从句连用的动词。再看一看上面的示例 7—14，在横线处各填一个相应的例子。

1 表达感觉的动词（如 fear, sense, worry）： *she felt that everyone was against her.* (9)
2 表达"得知；发现"的动词（如 discover, find, realize）： _____
3 表达"注意到；意识到"的动词（如 observe, perceive, recognize）： _____
4 谈论预期或希望的动词（如 expect, forecast, hope）： _____
5 表达"显示；展示"的动词（如 demonstrate, indicate, reveal）： _____
6 表达"说"的动词（如 explain, mention, whisper）： _____
7 表达"建议"的动词（如 advise, propose, recommend）： _____
8 表示思维活动的动词（如 believe, conclude, imagine）： _____

→ 形式主语 it 102　间接引语 150　转述动词 152　that 从句和 wh- 从句 161

E 改写下列句子，用 it 作为句首，使语言风格不那么正式。

1 That they don't have any money left doesn't surprise me at all.

2 That children would rather sit watching TV instead of playing outside just astonishes me.

3 Why the government didn't act immediately to stop the movement of all animals has never been explained.

4 Whether Nicole's father had been for or against her marriage wasn't clear, but he did participate in the wedding ceremony.

F 将三组词分别填入下列各句中，将句子补全（不一定按单词的原顺序填空）。

it / that / that	it / that / what	that / where / whether

A He wanted to know [1]＿＿＿＿＿ we were doing, but [2]＿＿＿＿＿ was obvious [3]＿＿＿＿＿ he didn't really seem very interested in our answer.

B Sometimes one of them will say [4]＿＿＿＿＿ he or she actually prefers [5]＿＿＿＿＿ [6]＿＿＿＿＿ the other has separate interests.

C [7]＿＿＿＿＿ Robert's new schedule will be an improvement remains to be seen, but no one liked it [8]＿＿＿＿＿ he just decided [9]＿＿＿＿＿ the changes would be made without consulting anyone.

G 改正下列句子中的错误，把正确的句子写在横线上。

1 Mr Baker complained about the noise was predictable, but we assured it wouldn't happen again.

2 The headmaster warned during our meeting some teachers wouldn't like their classrooms had suddenly been changed.

3 They told me about Sam had said in the meeting, but I thought strange he hadn't mentioned money.

4 The police regarded suspicious the dead woman's husband had recently taken out a life insurance policy in her name.

5 The prosecutor showed the jury how could the crime have been committed by Feldman, but he didn't convince that Feldman was guilty.

5 用在名词之后的名词性从句

名词性从句可以用在那些与第 **162** 页练习 D 所列动词相关的名词（**conclude – conclusion**，**indicate – indication**）后面。在这些名词之后通常不省略 **that**。

　　1　*Her conclusion that boys are faster is wrong.*
　　2　*There have been some recent indications that the economy is slowing down.*

此类名词还有：**belief, discovery, expectation, feeling, observation, proposal, realization**。

名词性从句还可以用在表示可能性的名词之后，且在非正式语言中常省略 **that**（3）。在 **issue** 和 **question** 等名词后，使用 **of** 加 **wh-** 从句这一结构（4）。

　　3　*There's a possibility (that) I'll be in town next week. Is there any chance (that) we can meet?*
　　4　*We considered the issue of what we mean by freedom. • It's a question of how we can survive.*

其他和 **of** 连用的名词：**consideration, discussion, example, knowledge, matter, problem, review**。

有时，还可以在名词后使用作插入语的名词性从句（**parenthetical noun clause**），起补充说明或提醒作用。用逗号（5）、破折号（6）或括号（7）将该从句隔出来。

　　5　*His excuse, that he had fallen asleep on the bus, was hard to believe.*
　　6　*One idea – that Elvis is still alive – kept coming up in interviews with fans.*
　　7　*They were questioning her about her first explanation (that there had been a burglar) when she suddenly changed her story completely.*

6 用在"名词 + 系动词 be, seem, appear"之后的名词性从句

可以用系动词 **be** 来连接名词和说明该名词具体内容的名词性从句（8）。在非正式用法中，常省略 **be** 后的 **that**（9）。

　　8　*One theory is that gravity travels at the speed of light. Our concern is how we can test the theory.*
　　9　*Matt's basic problem was (that) he had failed two tests. The truth is (that) he never studies.*

可以使用名词 + **seem / appear + to be +** 名词性从句（10）。还可以在形式主语 **it** 后使用 **seem** 或 **appear**（不接 **to be**），再接名词性从句（11）。

　　10　*The assumption seemed / appeared to be that we would all pay more for high-speed service.*
　　11　*It seems that it was too expensive. • It appears that they didn't do any real market research.*

7 the fact that …

可使用 **the fact that**（而不是单独的 **that**）引导名词性从句，作句子的主语或宾语（12）。在 **discuss** 等动词后面，必须用 **the fact that**（不单独用 ~~that~~）引导名词性从句（13）。

　　12　*The fact that he was married didn't bother her. She also ignored the fact that he had children.*
　　13　*We discussed the fact that he had been absent a lot.*（不说 ~~We discussed that he had been absent a lot.~~）

此类动词还有：**conceal, dispute, disregard, hide, overlook, support**。

the fact that 还可以跟在介词（14）或短语动词（15）后面（不单独用 ~~that~~）。在这类结构中，也可以将 **fact** 换为其他含义更具体的名词，例如 **idea** 或 **news**（16）。

　　14　*He pointed to the fact that Britain is an island.*（不说 ~~He pointed to that Britain is an island.~~）
　　　Despite the fact that she's small, she's very strong.（不说 ~~Despite that she's small, …~~）
　　15　*They covered up the fact that people had died.*（不说 ~~They covered up that people had died.~~）
　　16　*I don't agree with the idea that older is wiser. • They played down the news that prices had risen.*

8 that 从句：是名词性从句还是关系从句？

名词后面既可以接 **that** 引导的名词性从句（17），也可以接 **that** 引导的关系从句（18）。在关系从句（而非名词性从句）中，**that** 是代词，并且可以换为 **which** 或 **who**。

　　17　*The story that he was in a crash isn't true.*（不说 ~~The story which he was in a crash …~~）
　　18　*The story that / which he told us isn't true. • I saw a boy that / who looked just like Harry.*

→ 形式主语 it 102，162　系动词 10　短语动词 134　that 引导的关系从句 173

H 将以下每题的两个句子改写为一个包含名词性从句的句子，须使用一个与原句某动词对应的名词，句中可以有其他合理改动。

♦ I expected that the task would be simple. That was obviously too optimistic.
My *expectation that the task would be simple was obviously too optimistic* .

1 He explained that he had been stuck in traffic for over an hour. It didn't sound right.
His _____.

2 They discovered the boy suffered from asthma. It changed their attitude.
Their _____.

3 People believe there are aliens from outer space living among us. It's quite widespread.
The _____.

I 选择合适的词或短语填空，补全以下报告，在必要的地方补充 that。

belief	example of	against the idea	to the fact
conclusion was	in agreement	despite the fact	with the view

In our group we discussed the death penalty. Two people agreed ¹_____
the death penalty was necessary for serious crimes. They pointed ²_____
it was still used in the USA as punishment for murder and their ³_____
it acted as a deterrent, stopping people from committing crimes. One woman argued
⁴_____ the death penalty could stop or reduce crime. She said that the USA
provided an ⁵_____ what happens when a society is based on violence.
⁶_____ they had the death penalty, the USA continued to have the worst
and most violent crime rates. It was her ⁷_____ no government should be
allowed to kill its own people, even if they are criminals. The others in our group were
generally ⁸_____ there should not be a death penalty.

J 选择合适的名词填空，并补充 that（构成名词性从句）或 which（构成关系从句），将以下释义补全。如有必要请查词典。

déjà vu	premonition	scepticism	superstition

1 A _____ is a feeling _____ something is going to happen, often
something _____ is unpleasant.
2 _____ means having doubts _____ statements are true or
_____ something will happen.
3 A _____ is a belief _____ events happen in a way
_____ cannot be explained by reason.
4 _____ is the sense _____ you have already experienced something
_____ is happening now.

K 改正下文中用法有误的名词性从句。

According to one definition, the women's movement is a social and political

　　　　　　the idea that
movement promoting/men and women should have equal rights in society. It

tries to raise issues how equality can be accomplished by first getting people to

recognize the fact which women don't have equal opportunity. It is based on the

belief people's attitudes can be changed and the assumption other peaceful changes

can be made through the legal system, in spite of it is largely controlled by men.

形容词与名词性从句连用

形容词后面可以接 **that** 从句（1）和 **wh-** 从句（2）。在 **sorry, happy** 等某些形容词之后，如果使用 **wh-** 从句，则要先加一个介词；如果接 **that** 从句，则不加介词（3）。

1 *Mark was surprised that you asked about him.* • *It isn't surprising that the weather was bad.*
2 *We weren't certain when he would arrive.* • *Isn't it amazing how much teenagers can eat?*
3 *I'm sorry about what I said.* • *I'm sorry that I was late.*（不说 ~~I'm sorry about that I was late.~~）
   • *We're happy with how it looks.* • *We're happy that it looks OK.*（不说 ~~We're happy how it looks.~~）

可以使用形式主语 **it** + 系动词（如 **be, seem**）+ 形容词 + 名词性从句这个结构（4）。在正式语言中，有时把名词性从句放在句首作主语（5）。

4 *It's disgraceful that children can't spell their own names!* • *It seems odd that he didn't call.*
5 *That children can't spell their own names is disgraceful!* • *That he didn't call seems odd.*

在非正式语言中，常常省略形容词后面引导名词性从句的 **that**。

6 *I'm sure (that) it's a mistake.* • *We're glad (that) you're here.* • *He's lucky (that) he wasn't hurt.*

可在描述个人情感的形容词（如 **afraid, worried**）后面使用名词性从句，说明这些情感产生的原因（7）。还可在描述确定程度的形容词（如 **positive, sure**）后面使用名词性从句，说明某人或多或少确定或不确定的信息（8）。

7 *We were afraid (that) you wouldn't come.* • *Aren't you worried (that) Tess might get injured?*
此类形容词还有：**amazed, angry, disappointed, happy, proud, sad**。
8 *He was positive (that) he had chosen the right answer.* • *I'm not sure if I heard him correctly.*
此类形容词还有：**certain, confident, convinced, doubtful, unsure**。

L 将以下每题的两个句子改写为一个包含名词性从句的句子。

♦ He made such a mess. I was angry about it. *I was angry (that) he made such a mess*.

1 Our old car might break down. We were afraid of that.
   We ....

2 Karen suddenly decided to quit her job. I was completely surprised by that.
   I ....

3 The test would be easy. Sean was absolutely sure of it.
   Sean ....

M 选择合适的词或短语填空，在必要的地方补充 that, how, what 或 when。

> aware of   embarrassed by   glad   amazed   surprising   unlikely

Our teacher always encouraged us to try to guess what new words and phrases meant because it was ^1 .... we would always be able to use our dictionaries. It was good advice, but I was very ^2 .... wrong my guesses could be sometimes. For example, I had guessed that the phrase 'kick the bucket' must mean that you are very happy and you show that you are happy by kicking a bucket. You just give it a good kick. That made sense to me. So, it was rather ^3 .... I discovered that it meant the same as 'die'. I was really ^4 .... I hadn't tried to use the phrase. I would be so ^5 .... people would think if they had told me that they had good news and I had said, 'Great! Now you'll kick the bucket!' They would be totally ^6 .... I had said such an inappropriate thing.

→ 形容词 111—112，114 形式主语 it 102 系动词 10 that 从句和 wh- 从句 161

在名词性从句中使用虚拟语气（subjunctive）或 should

N 将恰当例句的序号填入对应的方格中。

在 **that** 从句中可使用以动词原形呈现的虚拟语气形式，即现在虚拟语气 ☐。在现在虚拟语气的否定形式中，应把 **not** 放在动词前 ☐。虚拟语气通常只用于正式语言。可以使用 **should** + 动词原形来代替现在虚拟语气 ☐。

1　*Dr Evans specifically requested that no one have access to patients' files unless authorized.*
2　*We have already recommended that young children not be left alone in parked cars.*
3　*The doctor requested that no one should have access to the files.* • *We have already recommended that children shouldn't be left alone.*

在 **wish** 后的名词性从句中，也可使用过去虚拟语气（动词 **be** 用 **were**）：*I wish (that) I were taller.*

在表示命令 ☐、规定 ☐ 或建议 ☐ 的动词后面的 **that** 从句中，可使用现在虚拟语气或 **should**。

4　*The committee has suggested that the cost of admission (should) be increased.*
5　*The job description stipulates that the applicant (should) have a degree in English.*
6　*The judge insisted that the boy (should) be punished and that he (should) pay for the damage.*

此类动词还有：**advise, ask, demand, order, propose, require**。

虚拟语气或 **should** 可用于转述命令、指示 ☐，但不能用于转述陈述 ☐。

7　*'He has to be over 18.'* → *They insist that he (should) be over 18.*
8　*'I am over 18!'* → *He insists that he is over 18.*

在表示命令 ☐、规定 ☐、建议 ☐ 的名词和表示必要性的形容词 ☐ 后面的 **that** 从句中，也可以使用现在虚拟语气或 **should**。

9　*It is our recommendation that he (should) not say anything until the investigation is over.*
10　*Isn't there a rule that safety equipment (should) be worn whenever machinery is running?*
11　*They gave instructions that all passengers (should) have passports ready for inspection.*
12　*It is essential that no one (should) feel excluded. It is vital that every voice (should) be heard.*

此类形容词还有：**crucial, imperative, important, necessary**。

b 为句子的前半句（1—6）选择合适的后半句（a—f），再选择合适的词填空，动词形式要使用恰当。在适当的地方使用虚拟语气或 should。

arrest	give	insist	recommend	spend	suggestion
crucial	have	not disturb	requirement	stipulate	wear

1　The nurse says it's _____ (__)
2　The advertisement _____ (__)
3　The travel agent _____ (__)
4　Someone offered the _____ (__)
5　The school had a _____ (__)
6　The prisoner _____ (__)

a　that the winner _____ a car as the prize.
b　that uniforms _____ at all times.
c　that the applicant _____ two years' experience.
d　that the patient _____ .
e　that they _____ the wrong person.
f　that we _____ a week in Paris.

→ 转述陈述句 154　should 41　条件句中的过去虚拟语气 186

名词性从句的用法

⑨ 用多个名词性从句表达复杂信息

可以使用一系列名词性从句来表达复杂信息。有时为避免歧义，要保留从句句首的 **that**（如在下面的例句中，第一个 **that** 避免了出现 We have seen researchers 这样的结构）；有时为避免过多地重复 **that**，可适当省略（如在下面的例句中，可以直接说 … people will believe they witnessed … ）。

1　*We have seen that researchers have been able to show that people will believe (that) they witnessed certain things because of information presented in police questions.*

还可以用一连串名词性从句表达一系列连贯的观点（2）或几种不同的可能情况（3）。

2　*Bleck has argued that the long human childhood is needed for learning complex skills, that it allows children time to grow into many tasks and that it is actually beneficial for parents.*

3　*It is clearly not true that students learn everything they are taught or that they know only what they are taught or that they can remember everything they are taught.*

在名词性从句中，可在 **that** 后插入一个用逗号隔出来的短语（4）或从句（5）。注意，第一个逗号在 **that** 之后，而非之前。如果 **that** 之后跟的是作主语的 **wh-** 从句，则该 **wh-** 从句的前后都不加逗号（6）。

4　*An important discovery was that, in both types of environments, the children's language developed at the same rate.*（不说 ~~An important discovery was, that in both types …~~ ）

5　*Some teachers believe that, if students see or hear errors, they will learn those errors.*

6　*The idea that <u>what you eat</u> affects your long-term health shouldn't really be a big surprise.*

⑩ 名词性从句的位置

通常把作宾语的名词性从句放在句尾，特别是当该从句很长且包含大量信息时。

7　*It's usually assumed that government officials speaking on important matters of national security are telling the truth.*

如果想更紧密地承接上文内容（8），或者想在给出新信息前复述一遍已给信息（9），可以把名词性从句放在句首。

8　*Five days after the earthquake, a woman was found alive under the ruins of her house. That she had survived was described as a miracle. How she did it no one knew.*

9　*Speakers continually design their linguistic messages on the basis of assumptions about what their hearers already know. What a speaker assumes is true or is known by the hearer can be described as a presupposition.*

如果想将某信息（包括新信息）作为既定事实来给出，可将 **the fact that** + 名词性从句置于句首。

10　*James's early years were spent with his deaf parents. His only contact with spoken language was through television. The fact that he couldn't speak English by the age of four is evidence that children need more than simple exposure to language.*

可在句子中间的某个地方使用名词性从句来详细说明某事实或观点（11）。也可以把名词性从句作为插入语，用逗号、破折号或括号隔出来，表明该信息是附加的（可以略去不看）（12）。

11　*It isn't hard to work out how the widespread assumption that women talk more than men came to be one of our social myths.*

12　*The idea behind 'Secret Santas' is for each person in a family or group to buy one present, ' from Santa', for only one other person. This solution (that you buy one present instead of ten or 20) helps to reduce the stress of Christmas as well as the cost.*

→ 形式主语 it 102，162　作插入语的名词性从句 164　the fact that 164

P 为每个段落选择一组合适的分句，将段落补全（不一定按分句的原顺序填空）。

> what happened that day / what they're thinking / who their best friends are
> if women and men talk equally / people think / the women talked more
> that men think / that they hear women / women talk a lot
> that men get the impression / that women are less likely than men / that women never tell jokes

A For women, the essence of friendship is talk, telling each other [1] ....
and feeling, and [2] .... When asked [3] ....,
most women name other women they regularly talk to.

B Women can and do tell jokes. However, it is true [4] ....
to tell jokes in large groups, especially groups including men, so it's not surprising
[5] .... [6] ....

C Studies have shown that, [7] .... in a group,
[8] .... [9] ....

D The finding [10] .... [11] .... may be due to the
fact [12] .... talking in social situations where men have little to say.

Q 选择合适的分句填空（文本选自一篇杂志文章），在适当的地方补充 that。

> Columbus wasn't the first European   there was another world
> Columbus reached Iceland   he could reach China
> Columbus's visit to Iceland gave him the confidence
> there would eventually be a place to land

Was it from the Vikings in Iceland that Christopher Columbus learned the crucial
information [1] .... further to the west?

Columbus's son described a voyage his father had made to the northern edge of Europe
in 1477.

Many scholars now believe [2] .... during that voyage.

Seven years later, in 1484, Columbus proposed to the king of Portugal that, by crossing
the Atlantic, [3] ....

The idea [4] .... to reach America may come
as a surprise to some, but scholars in northern Europe have always suspected
[5] .... to set sail across the Atlantic, knowing that,
if he kept going, [6] .... on the other side.

测验

A 选出最恰当的词或短语完成下列句子。

1 Can you understand .... ?
   a she is saying   **b** what is saying   **c** what she is saying   **d** what is she saying

2 .... you wait or come back later is up to you.
   a If   **b** That   **c** When   **d** Whether

3 They will recommend that she .... soon.
   a leave   **b** is leaving   **c** left   **d** will leave

4 Elizabeth explained during the meeting that it was a .... of what should have priority.
   a belief   **b** fact   **c** possibility   **d** question

5 The regulations .... that a lawyer always be present during any interrogations.
   a assure   **b** require   **c** seem   **d** state

B 从每句标有下划线的部分（A，B，C，D）中选出错误的一项。

1 Amber stayed with John wasn't surprising, but it was obvious to everyone that they had decided
   they were just friends and that marriage wasn't in their plans.

2 He didn't know who it was and couldn't imagine why they did it, but there must have been
   somebody that started the rumour which he was from London and very wealthy.

3 I heard about that the director said to them that he didn't think it necessary that he should have
   to agree with everything they proposed.

4 It became obvious that a lot of students didn't like that their new teacher considered it essential
   that they do homework every night.

5 Martin told me that he wanted to remind that what was important was not the cost, but
   how well the job was done.

C 下面这段文字中原本有六个引导名词性从句的连词（五个 that 和一个 how）。请仿照示例，
将其他五个词添加到合适的位置。

Categorization plays a crucial role in human cognition, yet we give little

that
thought to this process. Indeed, it seems/most of us have a very simple idea of

categorization works: we take it for granted categories have clear boundaries, and

all members of a given category must have something in common. If we consider

the purpose of categorization, we see it is not surprising we hold such a view.

D 完成下列句子，使其与所给句子的意思尽可能接近，须用上名词性从句。

1 His parents weren't English. He didn't conceal it.
He _____ .

2 Why anyone would want to jump out of a plane and put their trust in a parachute has always been a big mystery to me.
It _____ .

3 We expected that no one would be there.
Our _____ .

4 Her comments had upset Mark's mother. Bridget was sorry about that.
Bridget _____ .

5 These apples don't look very nice, but they're delicious.
Despite _____ .

E 选择合适的词或短语并使用其恰当形式填空，在必要的地方补充 that, if 或 when。

| argue | feel | notice | emotion | view | concede | know | rule out | reason to | unfair |

Kanzi is an adult bonobo, or pygmy chimp, kept at Georgia State University in Atlanta. He has grown up among humans, and is adept at communicating with symbols. He understands some spoken English, and can respond to phrases such as 'go out of the cage' and 'do you want a banana?'

Jared Taglialatela and Sue Savage-Rumbaugh, who work with Kanzi, [1] _____ he was making gentle noises during his interactions with them. 'We wanted to [2] _____ there was any rhyme or [3] _____ they were produced,' says Taglialatela.

So his team studied 100 hours of videotape showing Kanzi's day-to-day interactions and analyzed the sounds he made at various times. They picked situations in which the bonobo's actions were unambiguous: for example, while he was eating a banana, pointing to the symbol for 'grapes', or responding to a request to go outside the cage.

They identified four sounds Kanzi made in different contexts: banana, grapes, juice and yes. In each context, Kanzi made the same sound. 'We haven't taught him this,' says Taglialatela. 'He's doing it on his own.'

Some will [4] _____ the sounds are simply the result of differences in Kanzi's emotional state. Taglialatela [5] _____ emotions may play a part, but says they are not the whole story. For instance, Kanzi's sound for 'yes' stayed the same across very different emotional states.

Primatologist Frans de Waal of Emory University in Atlanta, Georgia, agrees. '[6] _____ is involved doesn't [7] _____ he's following rules that have some sort of cognitive component.'

Kanzi is just the latest primate to challenge the [8] _____ animals have no language ability. Language used to be popularly defined as symbolic communication until Washoe, a chimpanzee, stumped everyone by learning to communicate in American Sign Language. 'The linguists then came up with a definition that emphasized syntax much more than symbols,' says de Waal. 'Sometimes we [9] _____ it's a bit [10] _____ they move the goalposts as soon as we get near.'

14 关系从句（relative clause）

关系从句通常由 **that, who, which** 等关系代词（relative pronoun）引导，用于修饰刚提及的某人或某事物。（请查看第 267 页关于关系代词的术语解释，获取更完整的介绍。）关系从句可用于阐明某人身份（*I've just seen the woman who lives upstairs.*），描述某物（*She's climbing up a ladder that wobbles with every gust of wind.*），或给出额外的评论（*I think she's going to clean her windows, which seems rather dangerous in the circumstances.*）。有时，关系从句中的关系代词可省略（*With every step _ she takes, water splashes out of the bucket _ she's carrying.*）。

A 阅读短文，在每段中找出一个关系从句。

A The discovery of the wreck of an old ship on the ocean floor near the coast of North Carolina has revived interest in the colourful character who was the ship's last captain.
5 The ship is believed to be the 'Queen Anne's Revenge', which sank in 1718. Her captain, who was the most notorious pirate of his day, was called Blackbeard.

B Blackbeard, whose real name was Edward
10 Teach, had been a sailor on British ships in the Caribbean during Queen Anne's War (1702–1713). These ships were often involved in attacks on French and Spanish ships in the region and were allowed
15 to keep a percentage of whatever they captured from these enemies of the queen.

C All this changed in 1713 when the European powers declared peace and the war ended. Teach and hundreds of other sailors had to
20 choose between returning to unemployment in Britain or continuing to do what they knew best, only as pirates. They started as small bands in small boats, attacking and robbing merchant ships, and eventually took control
25 of larger ships which had the speed and power to dominate the trade routes in and

near the Caribbean. When they captured a large French ship, which they renamed
30 'Queen Anne's Revenge', Blackbeard and his crew finally had a true pirate ship, 80 foot long, with three masts and more than three dozen cannons.

D Blackbeard soon learned that a fearsome reputation, a pirate flag and some warning
35 shots from his cannons were all that he needed to stop most ships without a fight. In contemporary accounts, Blackbeard is described as a 'demon from hell', whose huge black beard was twisted into long
40 tails and who carried several guns and swords in belts slung across both shoulders. Sticking out from the sides of his cap were long smouldering fuses that he could use to ignite cannons during an attack.

45 **E** Blackbeard's reign of terror lasted until 1718 when he was killed in a sea battle with two British ships which had been sent to put an end to piracy in the region. After his death, Blackbeard became a romantic figure and
50 stories about his daring adventures and tales of secret buried treasure helped to create the popular image of pirates we still have today.

B 使用关系代词完成以下描述，适当时可省略关系代词。

Between 1713 and 1718, a pirate, * *whose* _____ real name was Edward Teach, but [1] _____ was known as Blackbeard, attacked ships [2] _____ sailed in and near the Caribbean. This pirate, [3] _____ some described as a 'demon from hell', had a large black beard [4] _____ was twisted into long tails. He wore belts across both shoulders in [5] _____ he carried guns and swords. His pirate days came to an end in 1718 [6] _____ he was killed in a sea battle, but the stories [7] _____ spread about his adventures helped to create the romantic image of pirates [8] _____ we have today.

关系从句和关系代词

1 关系从句

关系从句用于给前面的一个名词（短语）提供更多信息。可以用关系代词（如 **who** 和 **which**）代替主语，不必再重复前文。

1　I have a friend. The friend / He lives in London. → *I have a friend who lives in London.*
2　We found a shop. The shop / It sold old records. → *We found a shop which sold old records.*

使用关系代词代替作宾语的名词（短语）或代词时，把关系代词放在关系从句开头，从句的动词后不再重复该名词（短语）或代词。

3　I loved the card. You sent it. → *I loved the card that you sent.* （不说 … *the card that you sent it.* ）
4　He's one man. I admire him. → *He's one man whom I admire.* （不说 … *whom I admire him.* ）

关系从句通常紧跟在所描述的名词（短语）后（5），但名词（短语）和关系从句之间有时会夹有介词短语（6）。

5　The food came in plastic bags. We had to eat the food. → *The food that we had to eat came in plastic bags.* （不说 *The food came in plastic bags that we had to eat.* ）
6　*A pirate is a person on a ship who attacks and steals from other ships.*

2 关系代词 who, whom, which, that

谈论人时使用 **who** 和 **whom**。可用 **who** 作关系从句的主语（7），用 **whom** 作关系从句的宾语（8）。**whom** 用于正式语言，在非正式语言中可用 **who** 作宾语，更常见的做法则是省略作宾语的关系代词（9）。

7　Michael is a teacher. He works in Dublin. → *Michael is a teacher who works in Dublin.*
8　The person wasn't Michael. You met him. → *The person whom you met wasn't Michael.*
9　*The person who you met wasn't Michael.* 或 *The person _ you met wasn't Michael.*

如果关系代词是介词的宾语，在正式语言中，可将介词 + **whom** 用在关系从句句首。在非正式语言中，可在从句句首使用 **who**，将介词置于从句的动词后，而更常见的做法则是省略此处的关系代词。

10　The man is Joe Nash. You should talk to him. → *The man to whom you should talk is Joe Nash.* 或 *The man who you should talk to is Joe Nash.* 或 *The man _ you should talk to is Joe Nash.*

用 **which** 和 **that** 代指物品或动物（11）；当 **team** 等集体名词（group noun）所指的一群人被视为一个整体时，后面也用 **which** 或 **that**（12）。**which** 比 **that** 更正式。此外，在非正式语言中，有时也可以用 **that** 代替 **who** 和 **whom** 来代指人（13）。

11　*I found the keys which / that were missing.* • *They own a cat which / that doesn't have a tail.*
12　We were in the team. The team won the cup. → *We were in the team which / that won the cup.*
13　The woman is a nurse. She lives next door. → *The woman that lives next door is a nurse.*

在正式语言中，可将介词 + **which** 用在关系从句句首。在非正式语言中，可在从句句首使用 **that**，将介词置于从句的动词后，而更常见的做法则是省略此处的关系代词。

14　I can't remember the hotel. We stayed in the hotel. → *I can't remember the hotel in which we stayed.* 或 *I can't remember the hotel (that) we stayed in.* （不说 … *the hotel we stayed in it.* ）

C 在第 **172** 页的文章中找到两个以 **that** 开头但也可不使用关系代词的关系从句。

1　_____
2　_____

→ 集体名词 75　that 引导的名词性从句 164　介词 125　whose 178

限制性关系从句（defining relative clause）
与非限制性关系从句（non-defining relative clause）

3 限制性关系从句

限制性关系从句包含对人（1）或事物（2）作出辨认或加以分类的信息。如果没有该限制性关系从句，整个句子的意思不完整。

1 *Do you remember the woman who used to work in the bookshop? She's a teacher now.*

2 *Do you have a thing that measures temperature? ~ You mean a thermometer? Sorry, I don't.*

常把 **that** 放在限制性关系从句的开头，充当从句动词的宾语（3）或介词宾语（4）。含最高级（5）或数量词（6）的名词短语后通常使用 **that**。这些用法中的关系代词 **that** 均可省略。

3 *I brought the dictionary. Maria wanted it.* → *I brought the dictionary (that) Maria wanted.*

4 *The film is Twins. He's talking about it.* → *The film (that) he's talking about is Twins.*

5 *It's the best film (that) I've seen in years.* • *He was the worst teacher (that) I had at school.*

6 *There's a lot (that) I don't know about computers.* • *Every person (that) we met had a cold.*

限制性关系从句也可用 **who, whom** 或 **which** 开头。

7 *I don't know anyone who / whom I can trust.* • *There are two rules which you must always obey.*

4 非限制性关系从句

想要增加必要的信息时，使用限制性关系从句（8）。若仅仅是补充额外信息，使用非限制性关系从句（9）。通常在非限制性关系从句前后各加一个逗号，从句位于句尾时除外。

8 *The first entrant who can give the correct answer will win the prize.*

9 *The first entrant, who was from the London area, didn't give the correct answer.*

也可以使用括号或破折号：*The second entrant (who sounded Scottish) got it right.*

非限制性关系从句通常以 **who, whom** 或 **which** 开头（10），往往不以 **that** 开头，通常也不将关系代词省略（11）。

10 *Our new boss, who seems to be nice, has said nothing about Mr Bell, whom he replaced.*

11 *The Mini, which some people initially laughed at, soon became the most popular car.*（不说 ~~The Mini, (that) some people initially laughed at, soon became the most popular car.~~）

可用 **which** 引导的非限制性关系从句来就前面的陈述给出额外的评论（12）。在这类非限制性关系从句的开头，也可使用含 **which** 的介词短语，如 **in which case**（13）。

12 *They said Catherine had been in prison, which simply wasn't true.*

13 *There may be a strike, in which case the office will remain closed.*

在非限制性关系从句中，**of which** 和 **of whom** 可用在 **some** 之类的数量词之后（14），也可用在 **the most famous** 之类的最高级之后（15）。这些表达可用来补充关于已提及的某物的一部分或某群体中某个人的信息。

14 *The last lecture, some of which I just didn't understand, was about osmosis.*

15 *At the conference, there were several writers, the most famous of whom was Zadie Smith.*

也可把最高级放在关系代词之后：*… writers, of whom the most famous was …*

D 在第 172 页关于海盗"黑胡子"的文章中，找到四句以 **which** 开头的关系从句，判断它们是限制性的还是非限制性的。

限制性的：..

....

非限制性的：..

....

→ 关系从句和关系代词 173　数量词 84　最高级 120

E 为每段描述选择一组关系代词填空（不一定按单词的原顺序填空）。哪处关系代词可省略？

that / which / who (×2) / whom   that (×2) / which / who

Laurel and Hardy were a pair of comedy actors *who* made over 100 films from 1926 to 1940. Stan Laurel, [1] _____ was born in Britain, and Oliver Hardy, an American, were first successful in silent films and were famous for their slapstick style of comedy. In their films, Laurel often caused the many accidents [2] _____ happened to them both, after [3] _____ Hardy would get angry and say, 'This is another fine mess [4] _____ you've gotten me into.'

A Jekyll and Hyde is a person [5] _____ has two personalities, one of [6] _____ is bad and the other good. The expression comes from a novel about Dr Jekyll, [7] _____ investigates the good and evil parts of human nature and invents a drug [8] _____ can separate them. When he takes the drug, he becomes an evil version of himself, [9] _____ he calls Mr Hyde.

F 选择合适的分句填空。须用上关系代词并作出其他适当修改，且在必要的地方补充逗号。

he or she controls a sports game	most people know him as Mark Twain
some of them are poisonous	it uses exaggerated actions, often involving accidents
it consists of nine islands	the largest part of it is below the surface of the water
you rent a room or flat from him	each competitor takes part in three different sports in it
~~he has never been married~~	

♦ A bachelor is a man *who has never been married* _____ .
1 Slapstick is a type of comedy _____ .
2 A referee is an official _____ .
3 A triathlon is a sports event _____ .
4 A landlord is a person _____ .
5 An iceberg _____ is a solid mass of ice floating in the ocean.
6 Snakes _____ are long reptiles without legs.
7 Tuvalu _____ is a country in the south Pacific.
8 Samuel Clemens _____ was a major American writer.

G 改正下文中用法有误的关系从句。

        that

A strange thing/happened to me once was getting a letter said I had been 'terminated'. The letter, that came from the university, was an official notice of termination (means 'the end') of employment. It was like being fired from my job, which it felt really weird. I didn't have a job at the university that I could be fired from it! I was just a student didn't have a job. When I called the office, they said it was an error had been caused by a new computer system. I wasn't the only one had been terminated by that computer system. A lot of other people didn't have jobs at the university lost them that day.

简化的关系从句（reduced relative clause）

不含关系代词，由动词的分词构成的关系从句叫作简化的关系从句。用于构成简化的关系从句的分词包括现在分词（1）和过去分词（2）。

1 There are two students <u>who are waiting outside</u>. → *There are two students waiting outside.*

2 The strawberries, <u>which had been dipped in chocolate</u>, were really delicious! → *The strawberries dipped in chocolate were really delicious!*

用现在分词代替主动形式的动词（3），用过去分词代替被动形式的动词（4）。

3 There were teachers <u>who were shouting</u> and children <u>who were running</u> out of the building. → *There were teachers shouting and children running out of the building.*

4 Emily only drinks juice <u>that is made</u> from fresh fruit <u>that is grown</u> organically. → *Emily only drinks juice made from fresh fruit grown organically.*

可用分词代替描述过去、现在或将来的事的动词。

5 The winner is the person <u>who scored / scores / will score</u> the most points in the game. → *The winner is the person scoring the most points in the game.*

6 First prize is for the most points <u>which were scored / are scored / will be scored</u> in the game. → *First prize is for the most points scored in the game.*

可使用简化自一般被动式的分词来描述一般情况（7），使用简化自被动进行式的分词来强调一种情况仍在继续（8），使用简化自被动完成式的分词来强调一种情况从先前某一时间开始一直持续至今（9）。

7 *We are concerned about people held in prison without a trial.*（= who are held）

8 *We are concerned about people being held in prison without a trial.*（= who are being held）

9 *We are concerned about people having been held in prison for years.*（= who have been held）

分词短语还可用作非限制性定语从句，通常用在书面描述或记叙中。

10 *The old car, trailing black smoke, drove off towards town.*（= which was trailing black smoke）• *Robert Ball, nicknamed 'Big Bob', was my favourite teacher.*（= who was nicknamed 'Big Bob'）

在简化的关系从句的否定形式中，要把 **not** 放在分词前。

11 *My parents, not having much money, never went on holiday.*（= who didn't have much money）• *I'd prefer shirts not made with polyester if you have any.*（= which aren't made with polyester）

某些形容词和形容词短语可用在名词之后，这种用法与简化的关系从句相似。

12 *There was one seat available on the flight.*（= which was available）• *Mercury is a metal, silver in colour, often found in liquid form.*（= which is silver in colour）

此类形容词还有：**necessary, possible, present, ready, responsible, suitable**。

如果想描述单个的或突然发生的动作，不能用分词短语代替关系从句（13）；从句动词的主语并非关系代词所指对象时，也不能用分词短语代替关系从句（14）。

13 *There was a sudden bang that woke me up.*（不说 ~~There was a sudden bang waking me up.~~）

14 *There are several things that we need from the shop.*（不说 ~~There are several things needing …~~）• *This isn't the information that I was told before.*（不说 ~~This isn't the information told before.~~）

名词前有 **first, second** 之类的词时，后面通常用动词的不定式。

15 *Neil Armstrong was the first person to walk on the moon.*（= who walked）（不说 ~~Neil Armstrong was the first person walking on the moon.~~）

→ 主动和被动 57   非限制性关系从句 174   动词不定式 139   现在分词和过去分词 17

H 选择合适的名词或动词填空，补全下列释义。动词应变为恰当的形式以构成简化的关系从句。如有必要请查词典。

jigsaw	mermaid	cause	have	lacrosse	play
use	shadow	cut	print	stand	

1 _____ is a game _____ by two teams of ten players _____ sticks with curved nets on them to catch and throw a ball.

2 A _____ is an imaginary creature _____ the body of a woman but a fish's tail instead of legs.

3 A _____ is a picture _____ on cardboard or wood and _____ into various shapes that have to be fitted together again.

4 A _____ is a dark area on a surface _____ by an object _____ between direct light and that surface.

I 将所给分句改为简化的关系从句，填入下方句子中的横线处。

it was standing on the bed	they are sitting in it
it is based on a true story	they were accused of crimes
it is parked outside	they were committed during the war
it was covered with feathers	it starts at 8 p.m.

1 There's a black car _____ with two police officers _____.

2 I found the puppy _____ and _____ from one of the pillows that it had ripped open.

3 The film _____ is a drama _____.

4 Many people _____ had to be set free because no witnesses could be found to testify against them.

J 将下文中的关系从句尽量改为简化的关系从句，以缩短篇幅。

For all you food-lovers ~~who will be~~ sitting at home and who will be looking for something that is interesting on TV this afternoon, there's a fabulous new show which is called 'The Asian Kitchen', which has been created and which has been produced by Mary Sah, which begins at 4.30 this afternoon. Among the dishes which will be featured will be Saucy Tofu, which consists of tofu squares which have been dipped in a special batter, which have been deep-fried and which have been covered in a creamy peanut sauce, and Evil Shrimp, which is made with hot peppers which have been sautéed with other vegetables and which are served with shrimp which are sizzling in a shallow pool of red curry. It's the most delicious thing on TV today!

物主词、代词与关系从句

K 将恰当例句的序号填入对应的方格中。

5 引导关系从句的物主词

使用关系从句时，用物主关系代词 **whose** 代替 **his** 等物主限定词（possessive determiner），放在名词前。**whose** 通常用于指人 ☐，但也可以用在表示组织 ☐ 或地点 ☐ 的名词后。

1　*Is he the boy?* <u>His</u> *bag was stolen.* → *Is he the boy whose bag was stolen?*（不说 ~~who his bag~~）
2　*Napa is in a region whose wines are famous.* • *Come to Jamaica, whose people welcome you.*
3　*Delco is a company whose products are everywhere.* • *That's the club whose coach was fired.*

whose 还可用于谈论某物的一部分 ☐ 或属于某物的事物 ☐。

4　*Draw a circle. Its radius is one inch.* → *Draw a circle whose radius is one inch.*
5　*They live in a small town whose name I've forgotten.*（不说 ~~a small town which name~~）

谈论物时，可以不在名词前使用 **whose**，而是在名词后使用 **of which** ☐。在非正式用法中，可以将 **which** 或 **that** 放在从句开头，将名词加 **of** 放在从句末尾 ☐。

6　*They live in a small town which / that I've forgotten the name of.*
7　*It's a small town, the name of which I've forgotten.* • *Draw a circle, the radius of which is one inch.*

在正式用法中，**of which** 有时在名词前：*Draw a circle, of which the radius is …*

6 后接关系从句的代词

关系从句可用在人称代词 ☐ 和不定代词 ☐ 后。

8　*Do you know anyone who has a van?* • *There must be something (that) we can do about the cold.*
9　*She insists that it's you who must apologize.* ~ *But it wasn't me who broke the window.*

使用主格代词显得非常正式：*It wasn't I who broke the window.*

还可把代词 **those**（不是 ~~these~~）与 **who, which, that** 引导的关系从句或简化的关系从句连用。

10　*Those who know him well say he will fight.* • *Ask those (who are) waiting outside to come in.* • *His ideas are similar to those (which / that) we've heard before.*（不说 ~~similar to which~~）• *Organic vegetables are those (which / that have been) grown without the use of chemicals.*

数量词也可以用作代词，后面可接 **who** 或 **that** 引导的关系从句 ☐。在数量词后，也可以省略关系代词或使用简化的关系从句 ☐。

11　*We saw some (that) we liked in Italy.* • *I didn't find a lot (that was) written about Jeffreys.*
12　*There aren't many who like her.* • *There isn't much that he misses.*（不说 ~~much which~~）

L 将所给分句进行适当修改，填入下方句子中的横线处。

his or her parents are dead	they have completed their questionnaires
the wood of it is strong and durable	large flags were hanging from its upper windows
this person doesn't care about money	many of his paintings look like large comic strips

1　An orphan is a child _____ .
2　Have you ever met anyone _____ ?
3　The oak is a kind of tree _____ .
4　We passed an old palace _____ .
5　Those _____ should hand them in.
6　Roy Lichtenstein, _____ , helped establish pop art.

→ 不定代词 98　人称代词 97　物主限定词 83　数量词 84

关系从句中的介词

介词可以用在关系从句的开头或末尾。在非正式语言中，介词通常在末尾。

  1 This is the room. I work <u>in it</u>. → *This is the room in which I work / that I work in.*

将介词置于末尾时，从句开头通常用 **that**（2）或不使用关系代词（3）。在正式语言中，从句开头也可以使用 **which, who** 或 **whom**（4）。

  2 *Cook's was the shop that everybody went to for shoes.* • *There were bunk beds that we slept in.*

  3 *Your opponent is the person _ you play against.* • *The day _ I'd been waiting for soon arrived.*

  4 *Camden is the area (which) I grew up in.* • *Is he the boy (who / whom) you were telling us about?*

介词与短语动词连用时总是位于短语动词之后，关系从句的末尾。

  5 *There are things (which) he's had to cut back on.*（不说 …~~things on which he's had to cut back.~~）• *He is a person (who / whom) I've always looked up to.*（不说 …~~a person to whom I've always looked up.~~）

将介词放在关系从句的开头时，关系代词要用 **which**（不用 ~~that~~）（6）或 **whom**（不用 ~~who~~）（7）。

  6 *A clothes horse is a frame on which clothes are hung to dry.*（不说 …~~a frame on that clothes …~~）

  7 *A lot will be expected from people to whom a lot is given.*（不说 …~~people to who a lot is given.~~）

有一些介词只用在关系从句的开头（不用在末尾）。

  8 *The mid-19ᵗʰ century was a period during which many people left Ireland.*（不说 …~~a period which many people left Ireland during.~~）

此类介词还有：**after, because of, before, below, besides**。

将所给分句进行适当修改，填入下方句子中的横线处。

you look through it	you must complete something before it
you look up to him or her	you have promised to be responsible for his or her moral education

1 A deadline is a point in time ....

2 Your godchild is a child ....

3 A role model is a person ....

4 A telescope is a piece of equipment .... to see things that are far away.

改正下文中用法有误的关系从句。

           which

The saying for/~~that~~ I had to find the meaning was: 'People who live in glass houses

shouldn't throw stones'. My first guess was that it was about a situation which

those want to fight should first think about defending themselves from attack.

Obviously, a person who the house is made of glass, it's something is easily broken,

should be careful. If you throw a stone, the person you threw the stone at him

could throw it back and smash your house. However, this saying, the meaning

of it I looked up in the *Oxford Dictionary of English Idioms*, is not really about

fighting. It means that you should not criticize others for faults similar to you

have yourself. I think this is good advice for anyone is critical of other people.

---

where, what, whatever 等引导的从句

7 where, when, why 和 how 引导的从句

在表示地点的名词（1）和 **point, stage** 这类名词（2）后，可用 **where** 代替 **in which, at which** 等。**situation** 这类名词表达的内容更抽象但类似于地点，后面也可用 **where**（3）。

1 *There's a small box. I keep keys* <u>in it</u>. → *There's a small box where / in which I keep keys.*
2 *We have reached a stage where we now have more people applying than we have space for.*
3 *They show funny videos depicting situations where people get into all kinds of trouble.*

此类名词还有：**activity, case, example, experience, society**。

在表示时间的名词后可以用 **when** 代替 **at which, during which** 等。

4 *Do you have a moment when we can talk?* • *That was a period when everything was fine.*

each time 和 **every time** 后不使用 **when**：*That happens each / every time (that) it rains.*

在名词 **reason** 后可以使用 **why** 或不使用关系代词。

5 *There may be good reasons (why) he couldn't come.* • *There's no reason (why) you can't do it.*

可以用 **where, when, why** 或 **how** 代替名词加关系代词。

6 *That's where his car was parked.* • *He pointed to where he used to live.*（= the place where）•
That's when I start. • *They were talking about when they were children.*（= the time when）•
That's why I'm here! • *She never told anyone why she had to leave.*（= the reason why）•
That's how it's done. • *We showed him how we make rice pudding.*（= the way in which）

在 **the way** 之后不用 **how**：*the way (that) we make it*（不说 ~~the way how we make it~~）。

8 what 引导的从句

可以用 **what** 代替 the thing(s) that，将 wh- 从句用作宾语从句（7）或主语从句（8），代替~~
~~关系从句。

7 *She gave them* <u>the things that</u> *she had.* → *She gave them what she had.*
8 *What they're doing seems wrong.*（不说 ~~What they're doing it seems wrong.~~）

在数量词（9），以及名词或代词（10）后不使用 **what**。

9 *Some people lost all (that) they had invested.*（不说 ~~They lost all what they had invested.~~）
10 *We'll buy the food and everything (that) we need later.* 或 *We'll buy what we need later.*
（不说 ~~the food what we need; everything what we need~~）

9 whatever, whoever 等引导的从句

在充当宾语或主语的从句开头可以用 **whatever**，表示 "any thing(s) that"（11）；或使用~~
~~**whoever**，表示 "any person(s) that"（12）。若是在有限的数量或选择范围内谈论 "any~~
~~thing(s) that"，则使用 **whichever**（13）。

11 *If you take the big boxes, I'll take whatever is left.* • *Whatever she did made them happy.*
12 *We will work with whoever they send.* • *Whoever said those things is mistaken.*
13 *Write in pen or pencil, whichever you prefer.* • *I'll go by bus or train, whichever is cheaper.*

可用 **whatever, whoever** 和 **whichever** 来表达 "it doesn't matter what / who / which"。

14 *I'll always love you, whatever you do.* • *I'm not waiting all day for her, whoever she is.* • *He'll be in trouble, whichever he chooses.* • *Whichever way they go, we'll catch them.*

可用 **wherever, whenever** 和 **however** 来表达 "in or at any place / time / way that"（15），或 "it~~
~~doesn't matter where / when / how"（16）。

15 *Please sit wherever you like.* • *Call whenever you can.*
16 *He always keeps in touch wherever he is.* • *Whenever I see Chloe, she asks me about you.* • *Just buy it, however much it costs.*

→ 关系代词 173　非限制性关系从句 174　数量词 84　what 或 which 50

O 用 how, what, when, where 或 why 填空，补全以下电子邮件信息。

Do you have a minute or two this morning [1]_____ we can talk? I'm at a point [2]_____ I need to check with you about [3]_____ I should organize the report and [4]_____ I should include or leave out. If you agree with [5]_____ I'm planning to organize it, then there's no reason [6]_____ we can't have it finished by Friday.

P 选择合适的词填空，补全下列释义。如有必要请查词典。

crime	prison	revenge		that	when	which
motive	quarantine			what	where	why

1 _____ is a place _____ people are kept as punishment for crimes.
2 A _____ is an explanation of _____ someone acts in a particular way.
3 A _____ is an offence for _____ you may be punished by law.
4 _____ is deliberate punishment or injury _____ is inflicted in return for _____ someone has suffered.
5 _____ is a period _____ an animal or person is kept away from others in order to prevent the possible spread of disease.

Q 为句子的前半句（1—5）选择合适的后半句（a—e），再选择合适的词填空。

however	whatever	whenever	whichever	whoever

1 You can dress (....) a _____ they want to on Sunday morning.
2 We lived on potatoes (....) b _____ we think would enjoy the party.
3 The girls can get up (....) c and _____ else was available.
4 We'll go there (....) d _____ you like because it's really casual.
5 They said we could invite (....) e on Monday or Tuesday, _____ day you're free.

R 选择合适的词填空，补全以下电子邮件信息。

how	what	when	which	why
that	~~whatever~~	where	whichever	

Thanks for your email and the good news about the report. I've tried several times to think about the report, but then the phone rings and I have to pay attention to ♦ *whatever* is going on right at that moment. I can assure you that this won't happen every time [1]_____ we have to do one of these quarterly reports, but right now I'm in a position [2]_____ every problem in the office seems to land on my desk, [3]_____ is partly my own fault, I know. Anyway, that's not [4]_____ you wanted to hear about, I'm sure. I don't think there's a slot in my schedule this morning [5]_____ we can talk. How about late this afternoon around three or four, [6]_____ is best for you. If you already have some idea [7]_____ we should put the report together, then I agree with you that there shouldn't be any reason [8]_____ we can't complete it before the deadline. I'll talk to you later.

测验

A 选出最恰当的词或短语完成下列句子。

1 The house I grew up .... has been demolished and replaced by an office building.
   a in **b** in it **c** in that **d** in which

2 Fieldwork is practical work .... outside the school or office.
   a doing **b** done **c** which do **d** that does

3 A letterbox is a narrow opening in a door through .... mail is delivered.
   a it **b** that **c** which **d** where

4 I didn't recognize the man who she was talking to ....
   a him **b** her **c** his wife **d** –

5 Could you ask those .... outside to make less noise?
   a wait **b** waiting **c** waited **d** to wait

B 从每句标有下划线的部分（A，B，C，D）中选出错误的一项。

1 Her new boyfriend, who's from Denmark, seems nicer than Jordy, who was from Spain, or
   Toby, that had really long hair, and whom nobody really liked.

2 A slot is a narrow opening through which something can be put or a channel
   into which something fits or along something slides or a position for something in a timetable.

3 I have friends who had a baby a few years ago when we were neighbours in Wimbledon and,
   every time when I go back to visit them, their child, whose name is Sam, seems to have grown
   another ten centimetres.

4 We had about ten people helping us carry our belongings to a van parked outside when there
   was a sudden crash making us turn round to find the big mirror lying in pieces on the ground.

5 Everyone who was on the committee agreed that we should set aside some of the money
   we had collected to pay whoever still had to be paid for their work and then we should put
   all which was left into a savings account.

C 用合适的词引导从句，补全下文。

Genetic engineers, ¹ .... success stories include crops
² .... will grow in areas ³ .... they have never grown
before, have produced their first genetically engineered insect. ⁴ ....
is being called the 'biotech moth' is a modified version of a small moth known
to attack and destroy cotton plants. This new version will be sterile, so it will
produce no offspring. The Department of Agriculture is planning an experiment in
⁵ .... some 3,600 of these biotech moths will be set free under large
screened cages in a cotton field. The goal is to have a moth-free field in one generation.

完成下列句子，使其与所给句子的意思尽可能接近，须用上本单元学过的各类从句。

1 Betty is derived from the name Elizabeth.
   Elizabeth is the name ....

2 Her parents were born in India.
   India is ....

3 I liked Hemingway's short stories best.
   Hemingway is the author ....

4 Her parents will never like me, no matter what I do.
   Whatever ....

5 He talked about humanism during the first lecture.
   I was at the first lecture, ...

将所给分句改为恰当的关系从句，填入下文合适的位置。

it is called a beanstalk	they grow very quickly
he suspects something is wrong	he then cuts it down
he steals some things from him	his mother thinks they are worthless
it is often told to children	he is chasing him
he discovers a giant there	he sells a cow

Jack and the Beanstalk is a traditional tale or fairy story [1] ....

Jack is a boy [2] .... for three magic beans

[3] .... , but [4] .... into a really

tall plant [5] .... Jack climbs up the beanstalk into the

clouds [6] .... [7] .... The giant,

[8] .... , tries to find Jack and recites the famous lines:

'Fee, fi, fo, fum, I smell the blood of an Englishman.

Be he alive or be he dead, I'll grind his bones to make my bread.'

Jack escapes down the beanstalk, [9] .... , so that the

giant, [10] .... , falls to the ground and is killed.

条件句通常用以 **if** 开头的从句表述一件事（*if I don't leave the house before 7.30*），而这件事是主句所表述的另一件事（*I usually miss the bus to town*）发生的前提条件。真实条件句（real conditional）描述的事情在现在或过去是事实，或者有可能会发生（*If I miss the bus, I have to walk all the way to town.*）。非真实条件句（unreal conditional）描述的事情或者实际上没有发生过，或者不太可能发生，或者是想象（*If I lived in town, I wouldn't have this problem.*）。

A 阅读各段文字，找出两个含有一般过去式动词的 if 从句：

1 一个表达真实条件；

2 一个表达非真实条件。

Anna

She started when she was 14. She wanted to be just like the boys. In those days, if she had a cigarette in her hand, she was cool. That's
5 what they all thought back then. But it's easier to start than to stop. She is trying to quit, but it isn't simple. If she has a cup of coffee, she always wants to smoke a cigarette.

Bea

10 She had always known that she wasn't the fastest or the most talented. Her mother had once told her, 'If you are successful, it will be because of hard work.' And that was how she had approached her tennis.
15 Like going to work. She saw the other kids just hanging around while she ran to tennis practice. She had spent her whole life on tennis courts. Now she had won her first championship. She heard her mother's
20 words, 'If you don't have a struggle, you won't experience the triumph.'

Cathy

The teacher was describing a film about a farmer who had turned one of his fields
25 into a baseball park. The farmer had heard a voice telling him, 'If you build it, they will come.' She wanted us to write about that as our topic. I couldn't imagine that

happening where I live. I like swimming, but
30 if I put a huge swimming pool in front of my house, people would think I was crazy. Plus, I wouldn't want lots of people coming to my pool. If I went to all that trouble, I would put the pool at the back of my house.

35 ### Dave

'If I were you, I would sell it.' That was his sister's advice in response to his request for help. She was putting on her coat and getting ready to leave. If he had wanted to sell his car, he would
40 have done that already. But he didn't have a job, so he couldn't really afford to keep the car. It was his own fault, he knew that. If he had worked harder at school, he would have had some kind of career by now. That obviously
45 wasn't happening. 'If you were in my situation, I would help you out!' he called out to his sister.

Erin

When she was younger, she didn't care about anything. She thought she was really
50 tough. If she caught a cold, she didn't stop. Nothing could get her down or make her stay at home. But these days she gets sick really easily, so she has to pay more attention. If she catches a cold, she goes to bed immediately.
55 She doesn't try to be tough because she's not as strong as she used to be.

B 为上面每段（Anna—Erin）选择一句话作为结尾句，将对应段落开头的名字填入括号。

1 And I would build a high fence round it. (.......................................)

2 But she isn't complaining. (.......................................)

3 She has had to avoid one so that she can avoid the other. (.......................................)

4 But she had already left. (.......................................)

5 Now she knew what they meant. (.......................................)

真实条件句

① 事实条件句（factual conditional）

事实条件句也叫作"零条件句（zero conditional）"，用于表达两件事之间现有的或一直存在的固定关联（**if** + 现在时 + 现在时）。

> 1　*If I wash the dishes, he dries them.* • *If the fruit feels soft, it's ready to eat.*

事实条件句还可以用于表达过去存在的联系（**if** + 过去时 + 过去时）。

> 2　*If it rained, we went by bus.* • *If my uncle caught fish, he always gave us some.*

注意，只有在事实条件句中，**if** 的含义才类似于 **when**。

② 预测条件句（predictive conditional）

预测条件句也叫作"第一条件句（first conditional）"，用于表达一件事（**if** + 现在时）与另一件可能会发生的事（**will**）之间可能存在的关联。

> 3　*If your friends don't arrive by five, we'll leave without them.* • *If I see Eva, I'll tell her.*

主句中最常用的情态动词是 **will**，但也可以用其他情态动词和短语情态动词，如 **can** 和 **be going to**。

> 4　*If we get there early, we can sit at the front.* • *If he says that again, I'm going to scream!*

if 从句中通常不用 **will**。但是，可以用 **will** 的非缩约强调形式来表达"如果你坚持要这样"（5）；礼貌地提出邀请或请求时也可用 **will**（6）。

> 5　*If you will put off doing your homework, then of course you'll get bad marks.*
> 6　*If you'll just follow me, I'll take you to your room.* • *If you'll open the door, I'll bring these in.*

C 再读一读第 **184** 页的段落，就下列描述各找出一个例子。

1　一个采用现在时的事实条件句

_____

2　一个采用过去时的事实条件句

_____

3　一个预测条件句

_____

D 为句子的前半句（1—6）选择合适的后半句（a—f），再选出正确的动词。

1	If there is / was a lot to do,	(......)	a	she won't do well.
2	If the students come / came to us,	(......)	b	we can't make you do it.
3	If the test is / will be difficult,	(......)	c	she goes by bus.
4	If there is / was a lot to carry,	(......)	d	we can usually help them.
5	If you don't / didn't want to study,	(......)	e	we ask the porter to help us.
6	If it is / was cold and wet,	(......)	f	everyone helped.

→ 混合条件句 188　情态动词和短语情态动词 29　will 32—33

非真实条件句

3 假设条件句（hypothetical conditional）

假设条件句也叫作"第二条件句（second conditional）"，用于表达某种远离现实、不大可能发生的情况，即谈论一件假想的事（**if** + 过去时）和另一件假想的事（**would**）之间的联系。

> 1 *If I got the job, I'd move to London.* • *If you lived closer, we'd visit you more often.*

假设条件句中也可以使用过去虚拟语气（动词 **be** 用 **were**）：*If I were you, I'd go.*

主句中最常用的情态动词是 **would**，但也可以用其他情态动词，如 **could** 和 **might**。

> 2 *If you came in the summer, you could stay with us and you might even get your own room.*

if 从句中通常不用 **would**，但可以用 **would** 表达说话者期望的结果。

> 3 *If he would only behave himself, I'd take him with me.* • *If it would stop raining, we'd go.*

4 反事实条件句（counterfactual conditional）

反事实条件句也叫作"第三条件句（third conditional）"，用于表达一件未曾发生的事（**if** + 过去完成时）与另一件未曾发生的事（**would have** + 过去分词）之间的假想的联系。

> 4 *He didn't call me. I didn't help him.* → *If he had called me, I would have helped him.*

主句中最常用的情态动词是 **would**，但也可以用其他情态动词，如 **might** 和 **could**。

> 5 *If she had asked us, we might have known how to fix it, or we could have tried at least.*

缩约形式 **you'd** 既可以在 **if** 从句中代表 **you had**，也可以在主句中代表 **you would**。

> 6 *If you'd seen him, you'd have laughed.*（= *If you had seen him, you would have laughed.*）• *We'd have been really disappointed if they'd lost.*（= *We would have been … if they had lost.*）

E 再读一读第 **184** 页的段落，就下列描述各找出一个例子。

1 一个假设条件句

2 一个反事实条件句

F 利用所给句子的信息，用非真实条件句补全句子。

♦ I don't have extra pens. I won't give you one. → If *I had extra pens, I would give you one* .

1 I don't know Jason's phone number. I can't tell him what happened.
If

2 She didn't prepare for the test. She didn't pass.
If

3 You didn't warn us about the bad weather. I didn't bring a raincoat.
If

4 I'm not in your situation. I'll start looking for another job.
If

→ 情态动词 29　情态动词的完成式 30　虚拟语气 167　用 would 谈论偏好 33

G 选择合适的动词（短语）填空，补全下面这段关于为退休进行储蓄的短文。

£31 per month   £552 per month

| would have contributed | ~~were~~ | wanted | would start | would cost | could have paid |
| would contribute | started | decided | had started | could do | would end up |

How many times have you heard, 'If I * _were_ you, I [1] _____ saving now for retirement'? If you [2] _____ to have £100,000 at age 65, you [3] _____ it for as little as £31 per month. The earlier you start, the lower your monthly payments will be and the lower your total payment (the amount you contribute) will be.

Look at Amber. She's 24 now. Beginning next year, if she [4] _____ investing £31 every month, she [5] _____ only £14,880 in total over 40 years. So, she'd invest less than £15,000 in total and receive £100,000 from her investment.

Now look at David. He's 55. If he [6] _____ investing at 30, he [7] _____ only £46 every month and [8] _____ £19,320.

But if he [9] _____ to start investing now, it [10] _____ £552 every month and he [11] _____ paying a total of £66,240. Doesn't it make sense to start early?

H 改正下文中条件句用法有误的地方。

My mother keeps trying to give me a big old armchair that used to belong to my grandparents. I remember that, when I was a child, if my grandfather ~~sit~~ _sat_ in that chair after dinner, he always fall asleep. He snored too. If his feet are near the fire, his slippers start to smoke and my grandmother has to rush over and wake him up. I have also noticed recently that if my father sit in that chair, he immediately go to sleep and start snoring. My mother get really annoyed if that happen. It's like a chair with a curse. I am worried that if I take the chair, the same thing happen to me. I don't have this dilemma if my older brother didn't move away two years ago. If he stays, he is given the chair first and I am not faced with the problem. But it is a really nice-looking chair and maybe I could make room for it. If I move a small table, the chair fit in my living room next to the fire. Do I really have a problem if I settle into its comfortable embrace after dinner and give in to its seductive charms? But who wake me up if my slippers catch fire?

混合条件句（mixed conditional）

5 混合真实条件句（mixed real conditional）

在事实条件句中，两个分句的时态通常一致（1），但有时也会混合使用过去时和现在时（2）。

1. *If it snowed heavily, we didn't go to school. • If she works late, I wait for her.*
2. *If you saw the film, you know how it ends. • If they don't understand what to do, they probably weren't listening earlier.*

有些事实条件句用 **would**（**'d**）描述过去的习惯。此时，其含义与 **used to**（"过去经常"）相同。这样的用法让句子看起来像假设条件句，但其实不是。

3. *When we were kids, if it rained a lot, we'd stay indoors. But if it was sunny, we'd often go down to the lake.*

在预测条件句中，**if** 从句通常用一般现在时（4），但也可以用一般过去时（5）或现在完成时（6）。

4. *If we don't eat now, we'll get hungry later during the concert.*
5. *If you studied for the test, you won't have any problems.*
6. *If they've finished already, we'll give them something else to do.*

用预测条件句表达偏好时，可以在主句中将 **would** 与表达"喜欢"或"不喜欢"的动词连用（7）。如果就已有的多个选择表明偏好，也可以用 **would rather** + 动词原形（8）。

7. *If it isn't too late, we'd like to watch the news on TV.*
8. *If it's OK with you, I'd rather stay here.*（对方提出了去其他地方的建议）

6 混合非真实条件句（mixed unreal conditional）

在假设条件句中，除了用 **would** 将一件想象的事与现在或将来可能发生的事联系起来（9），还可以用 **would have** 将想象的事与过去可能发生的事联系起来（10）。

9. *If we were rich, we would offer to help those poor people who are suffering.*
10. *If we were rich, we would have offered to help those poor people who were suffering.*

在反事实条件句中，除了用 **would have** 将一件假想的在过去发生的事与另一件过去的事联系起来（11），还可以用 **would** 将对过去的假设与现在的事或情况联系起来（12）。

11. *If your parents hadn't met, you wouldn't have been born.*
12. *If your parents hadn't met, you wouldn't be sitting here now.*

I 用 he / he'd 和所给词填空，将 T. S. 艾略特的诗《罗腾塔格》（*The Rum Tum Tugger*）的选段补充完整。

chase	have	prefer	rather	wants

The Rum Tum Tugger is a Curious Cat.
If you offer him pheasant, [1] _____ would _____ have grouse.
If you put him in a house, [2] _____ would much _____ a flat,
If you put him in a flat, then [3] _____ rather _____ a house.
If you set him on a mouse, then [4] _____ only _____ a rat,
If you set him on a rat, then [5] _____ rather _____ a mouse.
Yes, the Rum Tum Tugger is a Curious Cat.

→ 真实条件句 185　非真实条件句 186　用 would 谈论过去的惯常行为 33

条件句中的语序与标点符号

可以把 **if** 从句放在主句之前或之后（1）。把 **if** 从句放在主句之前时，用逗号将两个分句隔开会让句子结构更清楚（2）。

1 *If you feel dizzy, you shouldn't go to work.* • *You shouldn't go to work if you feel dizzy.*

2 *If I had some eggs, I could make a cake.* ~ *If I go and get some eggs, will you make one?*

也可以通过在主句的开头使用 **then** 来强调主句是 **if** 从句的结果。

3 *The bus service is limited. If you hire a car, **then** you'll be able to go wherever you choose.* • *If the key isn't in the drawer, **then** Cathy must have taken it.*

注意，不要这样使用 **so**（不说 *~~If it isn't there, so Cathy must have taken it.~~*）。

用 **if** 从句表达附加看法，放在主句之后时，可以用逗号将 **if** 从句与主句的关系拉开。

4 *I'd like to get a ticket, if they still have some.* • *Kate always goes to work, even if she feels bad.*

J 在下文中添加四个 if，并补全遗漏的句号和逗号。

A number of idioms have come from the game of cricket something is described as *not cricket* it means that it is not fair or honourable someone is *on a sticky wicket* they are in a difficult situation this is because balls do not bounce very well the ground near the wicket is sticky (wet and muddy) it is said that someone had *a good innings* it means they had a long life or career.

K 第一部分。在每对动词（短语）中选择正确的一个填空，将下列分句补充完整。

completes / has completed	don't watch / didn't watch	isn't / wasn't
~~have paid~~ / are paying	wouldn't be / wouldn't have been	didn't eat / hadn't eaten
will stay / would stay	would arrive / would have arrived	take / took

♦ if you *have paid* _____ the men already

1 if I _____ so much at lunch

2 if it _____ going to be a problem

3 if you _____ television as a child

4 if they _____ the test earlier today

5 if Sarah _____ all her work already

6 I _____ so tired now

7 we _____ in bed until noon

8 it _____ by now, I'm sure

第二部分。用第一部分的分句（1—8）完成下列句子（a—h），并加上恰当的标点。

♦ *If you have paid the men already,* they probably won't come back to work after lunch.

a _____ they won't get the results until tomorrow.

b _____ I'd like to leave my bike in the hallway tonight.

c If William sent the parcel last week _____

d If it was a terribly cold day outside _____

e If the neighbour's dog hadn't started barking at 4 a.m. _____

f I wouldn't feel so full now _____

g _____ we can let her leave early today.

h _____ you probably won't know why some of these people from old TV programmes are famous.

→ even if 192   then 和 so 214

条件句的用法

L 将恰当例句的序号填入对应的方格中。

7 事实条件句：**What happens if … ? What happened if … ?**

事实条件句用于描述现在 ☐ 或过去 ☐ 事情发展的典型模式。

1　*What happens if there's a lot of demand? If demand increases, prices usually go up.*
2　*What happened if there was bad weather? If it was really bad, crops failed and people starved.*

可用事实条件句谈论规则 ☐、习惯 ☐ 和因果关系（如科学现象）☐。用来解释怎样做某事时，主句可以用祈使句 ☐。

3　*If people earn more, they spend more. • If the paper turns red, the solution is acid.*
4　*If it was a nice Sunday morning, we always walked to church.*
5　*If the ball touches the line, it's in, not out.*
6　*If you need customer service, press 1. If you want to place an order, press 2.*

8 预测条件句：**What will happen if … ?**

预测条件句用于描述可能性。

7　*What will happen if the situation gets worse? If things get worse, we'll leave the country.*

可用预测条件句表达计划 ☐ 和预测 ☐。还可以用主句为疑问句式的预测条件句来询问将来的事 ☐ 或提出请求 ☐。

8　*If we have time later, we'll go to the theatre and get tickets for the concert.*
9　*If Williams is mentally ready, she'll win easily.*
10　*If you have a moment, will you check this for me?*
11　*If the camps are closed, where will these people go?*

9 假设条件句：**What would happen if … ?**

假设条件句用于描述想象或虚构的情况。

12　*What would happen if a volcano erupted underneath the ocean? If a volcano erupted underneath the ocean, there would be a huge tidal wave.*

可用假设条件句谈论纯粹的想象 ☐，或描述某种做法可能产生的结果 ☐。还可以用假设条件句来表达做某事的意愿，虽然实际上并没有能力去做 ☐。

13　*If I were feeling better, I would help you move your boxes.*
14　*If England was a communist country, there wouldn't be a queen.*
15　*If they agreed to make classes smaller, we could give each student more attention.*

10 反事实条件句：**What would have happened if … ?**

反事实条件句用于设想与过去的事实不同的情况，以及由此产生的与事实不同的结果。

16　*What would have happened if she hadn't said 'Yes'? • If she had said 'No', I would have been devastated.*

可以用反事实条件句来表达懊悔 ☐ 或进行指责 ☐。

17　*If I had told her that I loved her more often, she might not have left me.*
18　*If you had listened to his advice, we wouldn't have lost all our money.*

→ 事实条件句与预测条件句 185　假设条件句与反事实条件句 186

M 下列每个问题都可以用第 **190** 页上的某个例句（1—18）来回答。先判断应该用哪种类型的条件句回答问题，再选出一个最恰当的句子。

◆ Can you remember your childhood? What happened if the weather was nice?
（*事实，4*　　　　　　）

1 What do you think will happen if there's a Carrera-Williams final? (　　　　　　　　　)

2 What happens in the economy if real wages rise? (　　　　　　　　　)

3 What would happen if your ideas about class size were adopted? (　　　　　　　　　)

4 Can you remember what the rule is if the ball hits the line? (　　　　　　　　　)

5 What would you have felt if Helen had given a negative answer? (　　　　　　　　　)

6 What do I do if I want to order something? (　　　　　　　　　)

7 What did he actually say would happen if he didn't have the flu? (　　　　　　　　　)

8 What would have happened if I had paid better attention to what your father said?
(　　　　　　　　　)

N 为句子的前半句（1—5）选择合适的后半句（a—e），再选择合适的动词（短语）填空。

don't want	had asked	hadn't forgotten	need	was

1 If you ＿＿＿＿＿＿ for directions　　(　) 　a would you lend it to other people?

2 If this ＿＿＿＿＿＿ your car,　　(　) 　b lunch would have been much better.

3 If I ＿＿＿＿＿＿ to order the book yet, (　) 　c we wouldn't have got lost.

4 If we ＿＿＿＿＿＿ the bread,　　(　) 　d press 3.

5 If you ＿＿＿＿＿＿ to talk to the operator, (　) 　e can I just examine one copy?

O 将 if 从句填入正确的位置，补全这篇题为 Public Enemy Number One 的短文。

if he hadn't spent	if his father hadn't told	if the times hadn't been so hard
if he had found a job	if FBI agents hadn't started	

The early 1930s were called the 'public enemy era' in the United States because there were so many robbers, murderers and outlaws on the roads. There probably wouldn't have been so many outlaws [1] ＿＿＿＿＿＿＿＿＿＿＿＿＿＿, but this was the period of the Great Depression when millions of Americans were poor and unemployed. [2] ＿＿＿＿＿＿＿＿＿＿＿, 21-year-old John Dillinger probably wouldn't have committed his first crime, the theft of $50 from a grocery store. Dillinger was sentenced to ten years in prison. [3] ＿＿＿＿＿＿＿＿＿＿＿＿＿＿ young John to admit to the crime, he probably wouldn't have gone to prison at all. By the time Dillinger came out of prison in 1933, he had decided to follow a life of crime. He formed the Dillinger Gang with people he had met in prison. [4] ＿＿＿＿＿＿＿＿＿ ＿＿＿＿＿＿＿＿＿＿ so long in prison, he would probably not have known so many other criminals! They carried out lots of violent bank robberies and killed a police officer in Florida. John Dillinger was Public Enemy Number One. Unfortunately for him, however, that made him a target for a new organization called the FBI, the Federal Bureau of Investigation. [5] ＿＿＿＿＿＿＿＿＿＿＿＿＿＿ following his gang, John Dillinger might have escaped. However, he was recognized by FBI agents as he left a theatre in Chicago and they shot and killed him.

only if, even if, unless, whether, if so 等

11 only if 和 if only

only if 用于强调特别重要的前提条件（1）。有时也把 only 用在主句的动词前（2）。短语 if and only if 的强调效果更突出，意为"仅在……这一种情况下"（3）。

1 *These can be used only if there is an emergency.* • *He'll come only if he's ordered to.*
2 *My children will only eat a breakfast cereal if they've seen it on TV first.*
3 *You broke the law if and only if the agreement formed a legal contract.*

表达愿望（4）或懊悔（5）时，可以在非真实条件句中使用 if only。

4 *If only I had an extra copy, I'd gladly give it to you.* （我希望我有一本多余的）
5 *If only she had been wearing a seat belt, she could have survived the crash.*

12 even if 和 even though

even if（"即使，纵然"）用于表达虽然某种情况有可能存在，但不会对主句所述的未来情况或可能发生的情况造成影响（6）。even though（"虽然，尽管"）用于谈论某种实际情况的存在不会影响主句所述的过去或现在的情况（7）。

6 *We'll have a great time even if it rains.* （可能会下雨，但并不会影响我们）• *Even if British History wasn't a required subject, I'd enjoy learning about it.*
7 *We had a great time even though it rained.* （当时下雨了，但并没有影响我们）• *Even though Matthew never studies, he passes all the tests.*

13 unless

unless 用于表达"除非在……条件下"，相当于 except if。它把前提条件作为特例来突出，有时含义等同于 if … not。

8 *He won't come unless you ask him.* （= *He won't come if you don't ask him.*）• *Unless there's a miracle, I'll have to ask for extra time to complete my report.*

与 if … not 相比，unless 的用法更有限。unless 不用于反事实条件句（9）。如果某情况出现的前提条件只能是否定意义的（不能理解为 except if）（10），或者主句以 then 开头（11），也不能用 unless。

9 *If we hadn't worked so hard, we would never have finished the project on time.*
10 *If he didn't have such a big nose, he'd be handsome.* （不说 ~~Unless he had such a big nose, …~~）
11 *If they cannot agree on the terms of the contract, then a strike is inevitable.*

14 whether (or not)

当条件句中有两种可能性（但不影响主句所述情况）时，可以用 whether 代替 if（表示"不管，不论"）（12）。如果一个选择与另一个选择相反，可以用 whether or not（13）。or not 常位于从句末尾，尤其当整个句子以 whether 开头时（14）。

12 *Whether we win or lose, we always enjoy playing.* • *I love soup, whether it's hot or cold.*
13 *They are going to send relief supplies whether or not the fighting has ended.*
14 *Whether it's raining or not, they're determined to play golf tomorrow.*

注意，也可以说：*If it's raining or not …* （不说 ~~If or not it's raining …~~）

15 if so, if not 等

如果想再次提及已经提过的事，可以简化 if 从句。有以下几种简化的方式。

15 *Some books may have missing pages. If so, they can be exchanged.*
16 *Rules really must be enforced. If not, they can easily be ignored.* （= *If the rules aren't enforced …*）
17 *I think you should take the job. If you do, I'll help you get started.* （= *If you do take the job …*）

→ 反事实条件句 186   even if / though 204   非真实条件句 186   whether 和 if 154, 161

P 完成下列句子，使其与所给句子的意思尽可能接近。

1 We'll have to leave without your friend if she doesn't come soon.
 Unless ....

2 We're going to start playing if Andy's ready or if he's not ready.
 Whether ....

3 If you aren't a registered student, they won't let you take books out of the library.
 They'll only ....

4 Our team played really well, but we didn't win the game.
 Even ....

Q 选择合适的词或短语填空（文本摘自一篇关于教学的文章）。

> only if ~~unless~~ even though if it isn't if only whether or not

♦ The style of teaching at universities has hardly changed in the past 1,000 years
 unless .... you count the invention of the blackboard 200 years ago.

1 Too many students leave the system thinking, ' .... I'd taken more practical
 courses.'

2 Colleges still rely on exams .... it is well-known that exams measure a very
 small part of a person's abilities.

3 Lectures are still the preferred teaching medium of professors .... they are of
 any real benefit to most students.

4 The system will change .... forces from the outside make it change.

5 .... a required course, then it has little chance of attracting high enrolment.

R 并非只有 if 从句可用于陈述条件。将下列句子中表示条件的标志性词语填到下面 A，B，C
三组的横线处。如有必要请查词典。

1 **Assuming** the information is correct, we have to reconsider our plans.
2 **Given** clear weather and good winds, the flight may arrive early.
3 **Providing (that) / Provided (that)** everyone is available, the next meeting will be on Monday.
4 Start slowly; **otherwise**, you won't be able to make it to the end.
5 **Suppose** your PC crashes, how will you recover your files?
6 **Supposing** you won the lottery, what would you do?
7 You can keep playing your music **as long as / so long as** no one complains.
8 **What if** I sent the file by email – could you look at it before tomorrow's meeting?
9 **With** a little help, we could make this school a much better place.
10 **Without** your advice, I wouldn't have known how to do it.

A 一般条件（表示 if this is the case）： _1 Assuming,_ ....
B 独有条件（表示 **only if** this is the case）： ....
C 特例条件（表示 **if** this is **not** the case）： ....

测验

A 选出最恰当的词或短语完成下列句子。

1 What's a miracle? Well, popcorn's a miracle if you _____ know how it's made.
a didn't **b** don't **c** won't **d** wouldn't

2 Some of you may have already completed section one. _____, you can go on to section two.
a If so **b** If you do **c** If you may **d** If not

3 In summer, if my dad finished work early, he _____ sometimes take us swimming.
a is **b** was **c** will **d** would

4 If you don't mind, I _____ finish my coffee before we leave.
a would **b** would have **c** would like **d** would rather

5 If they'd _____ Justin more time, he'd have been able to do a better job.
a give **b** giving **c** given **d** gave

B 从每句标有下划线的部分（A，B，C，D）中选出错误的一项。

1 If I <u>were</u> late, they usually <u>made</u> me <u>stay</u> after school and I <u>had</u> to do extra homework.

2 We <u>must</u> maintain a system of law, and <u>support</u> a police force. If we <u>don't</u>, the criminals <u>would</u> soon be in charge.

3 I'm not the kind of person who <u>goes</u> around <u>thinking</u> if only I <u>have</u> done this or that. I just <u>feel</u> lucky.

4 Things <u>will be</u> better if I <u>will get</u> a job and <u>earn</u> some money so I <u>don't have</u> to live with my parents.

5 The Czech Republic's top general <u>once warned</u> staff officers <u>they will lose</u> their jobs <u>if only</u> they <u>don't learn</u> English, according to a story in the news.

C 在每空填入一个合适的词，补全下面关于语言学习的建议。

Spend some time in a country where people speak the language. For example, [1] _____ you go to Paris, you [2] _____ learn French more quickly than if you [3] _____ classes at home. But it's better to go alone. If you [4] _____ with your friends in a group, you're more likely to speak your native language with them.

Try to find a job. If you [5] _____ in a restaurant in Salamanca, you [6] _____ have to speak Spanish to the customers all day. You could also think about who you live with. Imagine how fantastic your Spanish would be by the time you went home if you [7] _____ with Spanish people!

D 完成下列句子，使其与所给句子意思尽可能接近。

1 The party is not likely to happen because no one is willing to help.
Unless ....

2 She didn't escape injury; she wasn't wearing a crash helmet.
If only ....

3 I still loved her despite the fact that she could be very difficult.
Even though ....

4 We're leaving tomorrow if you like the idea or if you don't like the idea.
Whether ....

5 I arrived late; the traffic was so bad.
I'm sorry, but if ....

E 选择合适的从句填空。

whether you're getting an error message	if your queue gets bogged down
if you have received no error messages	if you are still having a problem
even if your printer is an older model	if any print jobs are on hold
if they just stop working	if your printer won't print
if it's a wireless model	if necessary

Printers are great when they do their job quietly and efficiently, but
1 ...., it can be a very frustrating experience.

What should you do 2 ....?

3 .... or your printer simply won't respond, you

should take a deep breath and follow these basic steps.

First, 4 ...., check to be sure that the printer is still

connected via USB or, 5 ....,

that you are connected to the right network. Check the print queue to find out

6 .... 7 ....,

it can cause the printer to grind to a halt. 8 ....,

you should still be able to print from a mobile device.

9 ...., go to the troubleshooting section in the User

Manual, or, 10 ...., contact Technical Support.

16 状语从句（adverbial clause）

状语从句通常以 **although, because, when** 等连词（conjunction）开头。连词可体现出状语从句与句子其他部分的关系（*Although the sun's shining, it's freezing outside this morning. I'm not going out because it's so cold.*）。

状语从句（*I might go out when it gets warmer.*）可用于提供关于某行为或情况的附加信息，用法类似于副词（*I might go out later.*）和介词短语（*I might go out in the afternoon.*）。

A 阅读下面的文章，在每段中找出一个状语从句。

A After her husband passed away, Emily Armstrong continued to take care of the special garden he had created in front of their small house. She imagined that Harry was 'up there' and looking down from time to time, so she 5 tried to take good care of his proud creation.

B Before he began his career with the national weather service, Harry had studied geography and art. Although he'd had to 10 give up his artistic ambitions, Harry still managed to find ways to be creative in his spare time. He had designed and created something unique in their front garden.

C It wasn't a garden in the usual sense. 15 There were no plants. Emily had tried to put in some flowers around the edges, but they always died. Her neighbour, Mrs Blair, said it was probably because there was all that cement in the soil. Harry hadn't 20 known, when he was mixing the cement, sand and water, then pouring it out into the wooden frame, that his concrete map would end up as the only thing in the garden, apart from the weeds that grew in 25 small cracks in the river valleys.

D When there was a spell of warm summer weather, the weeds would spread out from the cracks, especially in the south around the London area. Before Emily could get to 30 them, they would almost be in Wales, a wild patch of green in the pale grey expanse of the rest of the country.

E The busiest time was autumn, when Emily had to go out and sweep the whole country 35 every morning. If it wasn't wet, she could just use a brush to push the leaves down through England and sweep them away in the general direction of France. When it rained a lot, she would stand inside, watching the leaves pile 40 up in a soggy mess over most of Scotland.

F Even though it wasn't really cold during most of the winter, there would occasionally be freezing days of snow and sleet, after which Harry's concrete map would be transformed 45 into a shining sculpture of pure ice. The rough edges of Britain would change into smooth glistening lines and the country would become an abstract shape, as if it had been carved from a large flat slab of marble 50 by an expert hand. On a cold clear December morning, Emily would look out at the sculpture in her garden with a strong sense that, at that very moment, Harry was also looking down and enjoying the scene. He had 55 used weather to create art from geography.

B 根据上面的文章，判断下列表述是正确的（T）还是错误的（F）。

1 Harry Armstrong had studied art before he worked for the national weather service.   T / F
2 When Harry died, his wife created a concrete map of Britain in their front garden.   T / F
3 While he was mixing the concrete, Harry decided that his map would be the only thing in the garden.   T / F
4 Weeds grew in the cracks because the flowers Emily planted always died.   T / F
5 If the weather was dry, Emily could brush the leaves off the map.   T / F
6 When the weather was freezing in winter, the map looked like an ice sculpture.   T / F

状语从句和连词

1 状语从句

可将状语从句（如 **before he left**）像副词（如 **earlier**）或介词短语（如 **at ten o'clock**）那样用作句子的一部分。

1　*I talked to William before he left. = I talked to William earlier. = I talked to William at ten o'clock.*

状语从句通常位于主句之后（2）。如果把状语从句放在主句之前，则用逗号隔开（3）。

2　*You won't pass the test if you don't study.* • *We had to turn on the heating because it was cold.*
3　*If you don't study, you won't pass the test.* • *Because it was cold, we had to turn on the heating.*

有时一个句子中包含不止一个状语从句。

4　*Don't touch the paint before it has dried + because bubbles may form + if anything touches it.*

2 连词

可使用某些从属连词（subordinating conjunction），如 **after** 和 **while**，将状语从句和主句连接起来，并体现出两个分句在意思上有何关联。

5　*After you have a rest, you'll probably feel better.* • *I can't listen to music while I'm studying.*

其他从属连词如：**as, as if, as soon as, if, in order that, since, so, so that**。

将状语从句与主句连接起来时，只用一个连词（6）。状语从句不能用作独立的句子（7）。

6　*Because there were no lights, I couldn't see anything. It was dark so I couldn't do any work.*
　　（不说 *Because there were no lights, so I couldn't do any work.*）
7　*We couldn't use our computers because there was no electricity this morning.*
　　（不说 *We couldn't use our computers. Because there was no electricity this morning.*）

有些词，如 **after, before** 和 **than**，既可用作连词，引导状语从句，也可用作介词，后接名词短语（8）。在连词后使用主格人称代词（如 **we** 和 **they**）加动词（9）；在介词后使用宾格人称代词（如 **us** 和 **them**）（10）。

8　*I'll talk to you after I get out of my next meeting. = I'll talk to you after the meeting.*
9　*Anthony had arrived before we got there.* • *We had more money than they had.*
10　*Anthony had arrived before us.* • *We had more money than them.*

有些引导状语从句的连词（如 **because, although, while**）与引导名词短语的介词（如 **because of, despite, during**）含义相近。

11　*There were delays because the weather was bad. = There were delays because of bad weather.*
12　*Although she's old, Agnes still plays tennis. = Despite her age, Agnes still plays tennis.*
13　*He got injured while we were playing. = He got injured during the game.*

C 在第 **196** 页的文章中找到与下列短语含义相近的状语从句。

1　After her husband's death: _____
2　During warm summer weather: _____
3　Despite the usually mild winter weather: _____
4　Like a carving: _____

when, while, as 引导的时间状语从句

可以用 when 引导状语从句来描述一段时间（1）或一个时间点（2）。

    1 *When I was young, we didn't watch TV.* • *Most people don't have cars when they're students.*
    2 *When we heard the news, we were delighted.* • *I'll check the email when I get to work.*

注意，不要在 when 引导的从句中用 will。（不说 ~~I'll check the email when I will get to work.~~）

以 when 开头的从句还可用于描述在主句所述之事后马上发生的事情（3），或使主句所述之事中断的事情（4）。还可以用 when 谈论"每当"某事发生时的情况（5），类似于在事实条件句中使用 if。

    3 *We had just reached the shelter when the rain started pouring down.*
    4 *I was sleeping like a baby when the alarm went off.*
    5 *When demand increases, prices rise.* • *The roof used to leak when we had heavy rain.*

可用 while（"在……期间"）或 when 引导的从句描述一段时间，并用主句描述在该时间段内某个时间点发生的事（6）。如果两个分句所述之事在整段时间内同时发生，通常用 while 连接这两个分句（7）。

    6 *While / When you were out, your mother called.* • *I fell asleep while / when I was reading.*
    7 *There was nowhere to park, so I just drove round in the car while Tim was in the bank.*

as 可以像 when 和 while 一样引导一段时间，之后跟主句来描述在这段时间内发生的事（8）。as 或 just as（不用 ~~while~~）可用于聚焦某事发生的准确时间点（9）。as 还可用于说明随着时间推移而发生的一种变化与另一种变化的关联（10）。

    8 *As / When / While I was getting ready to leave, I heard that my flight had been cancelled.*
    9 *As I walked out of the hotel, a gust of wind blew my hat off. It happened just as I stepped outside.*
   10 *As I get older, I care less about what other people think.* （不说 ~~While I get older, I care less …~~）

D 完成下列句子，使其与所给句子的意思尽可能接近。

1 I watched Nick drive by in his new car while I was standing at the bus stop in the rain.
    When _____

2 You'll know that the fruit is getting ripe when the skin starts to turn yellow.
    As _____

3 We shouldn't talk about anything to do with work during lunch.
    While _____

4 I was getting out of the shower when my phone rang in the other room.
    Just as _____

E 根据第 196 页的文章提供的信息，在下列句子中选出恰当的连词，答案可能不止一个。

1 When / While Harry started working for the national weather service, he'd given up his artistic ambitions.

2 When / While it was wet during the autumn months, Emily couldn't brush the leaves away.

3 As / While the weather got warmer, weeds would spread out from the cracks.

4 As / When / While Emily looked at the sculpture on a cold clear December morning, she had a sense that Harry was doing the same thing.

→ as 200—201   事实条件句 185   just as 200   when 和 whenever 180   while 197, 204

after, before, until, since 等引导的时间状语从句

如果主句描述的事发生在状语从句所述情况之后，用 **after**（"在……后"）引导从句（1）。
如果主句描述的事发生在状语从句所述情况之前，用 **before**（"在……前"）引导从句（2）。
after 常与一般现在时或现在完成时（不与 ~~will~~）连用来说明已完成的行为（3）。

1 *After they left, we cleaned up and went to bed.* • *What will you do after you graduate?*
2 *Before he leaves, I'll ask him about the money.* • *They had eaten breakfast before we got up.*
3 *I'll help you after I write / have written my report.* （不说 *after I will write my report*）

until（"直到……时"）用于引起对某事的终点或结果的关注（4）。**since**（"自从……以来"）
用于谈论主句所述之事的起始点，这件事在那之后发生或依然是事实（5）。

4 *We'll wait until you're ready.* • *Heat the wax until it melts.* （不说 *Heat the wax before it melts.*）
5 *How long is it since you've been there?* • *I've lived here since I was ten.* （不说 *… after I was ten.*）

since 引导的从句用现在完成时或一般过去时（不用一般现在时）（不说 *since I'm ten*）。

once（"一旦，一经"）可引导描述主句行为或情况的起始点的从句。和 **after** 一样，**once** 从
句在把某事当作已发生的情况描述时，常使用一般现在时或现在完成时。

6 *Once you've seen Ani, you won't forget her.* • *Everyone likes it here once they get used to it.*

如果想表达一件事在另一件事之后很快就发生，可以用 **as soon as** 和 **immediately** 引导先发
生的事（7）。**the instant / minute / moment / second (that)** 等短语也可以这样用（8）。

7 *I came as soon as I heard the news.* • *Immediately I saw him, I recognized his face.*
8 *There are some students who rush out of the room the minute (that) class ends.*

F 选择合适的词填空，完成下列描述。如有必要请查词典。

blender	postscript	prediction	skewer	after	before	until	while

1 A _____ is a statement about an event _____ it happens.

2 A _____ is a wooden or metal stick pushed through pieces of meat or vegetables
   to hold them _____ they are cooking.

3 A _____ is extra information added _____ a letter or story is
   complete.

4 A _____ is a machine for chopping or mixing bits of food _____
   they become a liquid.

G 用 have ('ve) been 或 will ('ll) be 填空。

♦ Where will the refugees go after the camps *have been* _____ closed?

1 I'm sorry about the delay, but I _____ back as soon as I have checked this.

2 My back still hurts and it will soon be two weeks since I _____ at work.

3 I'm sure we _____ in London in August before we go to the Edinburgh Festival,
   so we can visit your new house then.

4 The moment we hear that the airport is open, relief supplies _____ loaded on to
   the waiting aircraft.

5 New students should not register for classes until they _____ given their
   registration numbers.

6 Once you _____ here for a few weeks, you won't want to leave.

7 The children _____ hungry when they come back from swimming this morning.

→ after, before 127，197 since 127，197，201 until 127

as, as if, as though 等引导的方式状语从句

可以用由 as（"像……一样；按……的方式"）（1）或 just as（"正像……一样；正如……"）（2）引导的方式状语从句来描述某事是怎样的或者是如何完成的。

1 *The film depicts life as it was in 1900. • Complete each exercise as I showed you.*
2 *I wrote the note just as you told me to. • Everything happened just as my mother had predicted.*

用在 feel, look, seem, sound, taste 等动词后时，引导方式状语从句的 as if 和 as though 含义相同（3）。在 act, behave, talk 等动词后，也可用 as if 或 as though 从句来描述行为举止（4）。

3 *Can I help you? You look as if you're lost. • He sounds as though he might be getting a cold.*
4 *She always tries to act as if she's my boss. • They talked about it as though it was worthless.*

在 as if 或 as though 从句中，有时用 were 构成虚拟语气：*He treats me as if I were a child.*

在非正式语言中，有时用 like 代替 as 或 as if。

5 *No one will ever love you like I do. • It feels like winter has suddenly arrived.*

注意，like 常用作介词：*It feels like winter.*（不说 ~~It feels as winter.~~）

as ... as（"像……一样……"）用于说明两种行为或情况在某方面相似（6）。在两个 as 中间可以用形容词或副词（7），或 many, much 等数量词（8）。

6 *Is Max still funny in the same way that he used to be? → Is Max still as funny as he used to be?*
7 *The weather isn't as hot as it was last year. • We didn't play as well as we did against France.*
8 *Were there as many problems as you anticipated? • It didn't cost as much as he said.*

有时也使用 not so ... as 构成否定式：*Ben is not so naive as you think.*

H 为问题（1—4）选择合适的答语（a—d），并在横线处补充 as 或 as if。

1 Did she seem afraid?   (.....)
2 Had she changed much?   (.....)
3 Did she fit in well?   (.....)
4 Did she write it correctly?   (.....)

a No, she was just _____ you had described her.
b Yes, she did it _____ she was supposed to.
c Yes, she looked _____ she had seen a ghost.
d Not really, because she acted _____ she was better than us.

I 选择合适的分句填空，分句须用 as though, just as 或 as ... as 引导，如有必要可作其他修改。

~~everyone has been saying~~	it really is	the guidebook had described it
I remembered it	it was made yesterday	they have done
nothing had happened		

◆ Is the new Italian restaurant *as* good *as everyone has been saying* ?
1 No one talked about it. They all behaved _____
2 I went to see my old school and it hadn't changed. It was still _____
3 This tea is terrible. It tastes _____
4 When you emulate someone successful, you try to do well _____
5 We found the little church hidden in the forest, _____
6 If you underestimate the cost of something, you think it isn't much _____

→ as 198, 201   (not) as ... as 120   many, much 90   just as 198   虚拟语气 167, 186

because, as, since 等引导的原因状语从句

because 用在从句开头，引导某事发生的原因或理由（1），或用于证明前面分句中的说法（2）。

1 *Because there had been an accident, we all arrived late.* • *I didn't eat because I wasn't hungry.*
2 *He says he didn't drive through a red light, but he's lying, because I saw him do it.*

as 和 **since** 有时可代替 because 引导原因状语从句（3）。**as** 和 **while** 可用于引导既说明时间段又表明原因的从句（= while and because）（4）。**since** 可用于引导既说明起始时间又表明原因的从句（= from that time and because）（5）。

3 *As it was late, we decided to stop working.* • *Since she knew Latin, I asked her to translate it.*
4 *As / While we're on the subject of money, I'd like to ask about next year's budget.*
5 *Since his wife left him, he's been depressed.* • *Since it's been snowing, we've stayed indoors.*

与 **since**（= from that time and because）类似，**now (that)**（"既然，由于"）可用于引导解释当前某个情况的从句。**now (that)** 引导的从句通常采用一般现在时或现在完成时。

6 *Now (that) we're married, we never go out.* • *I enjoy opera now (that) I've learned more about it.*

在正式语言中，有时用 **for**（7），**in that**（8）等连词代替 because，为前面的陈述引出原因或理由。

7 *It would be wise to save some of the money, for there may be unexpected expenses later.*
8 *We definitely have a problem in that there are more students than we have room for.*

---

1 完成下列句子，使其与所给句子的意思尽可能接近。

1 All the banks will be closed on Monday. It's a holiday.
As ....

2 She has had to use crutches. She had an operation on her foot.
Since ....

3 We're all together today. We should decide on a date for the Christmas party.
While ....

4 I wonder what he'll do next. He has finished his exams.
Now that ....

2 将第一组（1—4）与第二组（a—d）中含义相近的句子匹配起来，并用 as if 或 because 填空。

◆ I'd love to go out more, but I haven't had much free time lately.   (*e*)
1 It's more expensive to eat in a restaurant, but I don't like to cook.   (.....)
2 If I wanted to avoid doing something, I pretended to be ill.   (.....)
3 The cost of meat is higher now, but I don't eat it, so my food bill hasn't increased.   (.....)
4 No matter what the discussion is about, no one ever pays attention to my suggestions.   (.....)

a .... I'm a vegetarian, I'm spending less than other people these days.
b I acted .... I wasn't feeling well when I didn't want to do things.
c I spend more money on meals .... I don't make them myself at home.
d They always treat me .... I have nothing useful to say.
e I haven't been to a film or a play in ages *because* .... I've been busy at work.

→ because (of) 197   since 127, 197, 199   while 197—198

so that, in order that 等引导的目的状语从句

目的状语从句用于描述某种行为的目标或意图实现的结果。**so that**（1）和 **in order that**（2）可用于引导目的状语从句，且常与 **can**（此时主句使用现在时态）或 **could**（此时主句使用过去时态）等情态动词连用。在非正式语言中，通常单独使用 **so**，不加 **that**（3）。

1 *I'm going early so that I can find a good seat. • I'll take my umbrella so that I won't get wet.*
2 *Her father had worked hard for many years in order that they could have a better life.*
3 *I'm going early so I don't have to stand in a queue.*（不说 ~~… in order I don't have to stand …~~）

常常使用简单的动词不定式来表达目的（如 **to clean**）（4）。在正式语言中也使用短语 **in order to**（5）或 **in order not to**（6）。目的状语有时也用在句子开头（7）。

4 *Just use soap and water to clean it. • I think the boy fell when he was running to catch the bus.*
5 *They recommend using bleach in order to clean it thoroughly. • You must fight in order to win.*
6 *I'll clean the grill outside in order not to make a mess in here.*（不说 ~~… in order to not make …~~）
7 *In order to / To prevent vandalism, all doors and windows must be locked securely.*

有时用 **so as to** 和 **so as not to** 引导目的状语。

8 *It's designed that way so as to let in more light. • I'll put it near the door so as not to forget it.*

如果想说明动词不定式的主语，可以在不定式前面使用 **in order for** + 名词短语（9）/ 代词（10）。

9 *In order for the team to succeed, they must work together.*（不说 ~~In order to succeed the team,~~）
10 *In order for you to win, we will need to pray for a miracle.*（不说 ~~In order you to win, …~~）

L 完成下列句子，使其与所给句子的意思尽可能接近。

1 You should plan to leave early tomorrow. You'll avoid traffic jams on the way to the airport.
In order to _____

2 We had to account for every penny we spent so that no money would be wasted.
In order that _____

3 There must be a good source of light or plants won't grow indoors.
In order for _____

4 We waited a few minutes until the rain stopped. We didn't want to get wet.
So as _____

M 改正下列句子中的错误。

1 Mrs Peters slipped quietly into the room at the back that nobody would notice her.

2 I don't like it when they spray those chemicals all over the place for kill insects.

3 In order to care people about another person, they must feel connected to that person.

4 I didn't say anything about Nathan's coming in late so as to not get him in trouble.

5 A stepladder is made of two parts joined at the top in order it can stand on its own.

6 We must keep our new designs secret in order not our competitors find and copy them.

→ 动词不定式和动名词 139 情态动词 29 so (… that) 203

so, so … that, such … that 引导的结果状语从句

so 引导的结果状语从句可用于描述某事的影响或非计划中的结果。结果状语从句放在主句之后（1），在正式用法中经常用逗号把它与主句隔开（2）。

1　*I'm tired so I'm going to bed. • He missed the bus this morning so he was late for work again.*
2　*There has been a reduction in the oil supply and increased demand, so prices have risen.*

在正式语言中，有时用 **so that** 而非 **so** 引导结果状语从句。结果状语从句中的 **so that**（表示"所以"，相当于 as a result）与目的状语从句中的 **so that**（表示"以便，为了"，相当于 in order that）含义不同。

3　*A tree had fallen during the storm, so that the road was blocked and we couldn't go anywhere.*
　　（不说 *… in order that the road was blocked …* ）

可以在 **so** 和 **that** 之间加入形容词（4）、副词（5）或表示数量的词和短语（包含 **few, little, many, much** 等词）（6），之后用结果从句。在非正式用法中常省略 **that**。

4　*It was so nice (that) we ate lunch outside. • The puppy was so cute (that) she picked it up.*
5　*The lecturer talked so fast (that) none of us could understand him.*
6　*There were so many people (that) we had to wait. • I ate so much (that) I could hardly move.*

还可以在 **such** 和 **that** 之间使用名词短语（如 **nice weather**），之后用结果从句（7）。在非正式语言中常省略 **that**，但某些固定表达（如 **in such a way that**）中的 **that** 不可省略（8）。

7　*It was such nice weather (that) we ate lunch outside. • I got such a shock (that) I was speechless.*
8　*Try to think about these problems in such a way that you don't exaggerate their importance.*
可以说：*It's so nice that …* 或 *It's such nice weather that …* （不说 *It's so nice weather that …* ）

Ⓝ 把每组句子改写为一句话，用 so 引导结果状语从句。

1　They were feeling really tired. They went to bed early last night.
....

2　I wasn't able to do the homework. I forgot to take my textbook home with me.
....

3　Maddie is in a popular TV show. People recognize her when she's out shopping.
....

4　We had to drink bottled water. They said the tap water wasn't safe to drink.
....

Ⓞ 选择合适的分句填空，分句中须加入 so … that 或 such … that。

That class was early	We had a wonderful time on holiday
The fire spread rapidly through their cabin	Emilia's children had bad colds this morning
~~The fog was thick~~	You and I don't have much money

◆　*The fog was so thick (that)* ....　you couldn't see your hand in front of your face.
1　..　they couldn't save any of their belongings.
2　..　she couldn't let them go to school.
3　..　we can just throw it away carelessly.
4　..　we didn't want to come home.
5　..　everyone had trouble staying awake in it.

→ few, little 92　many, much 90　so 作结果连接词语 214　so that 202

although, though, even though 等引导的对比状语从句

可以用 **although** （"虽然，尽管"）引导从句，该从句包含的信息与主句所含信息形成对比，以表明主句所述内容是出人意料或令人惊讶的。

1　(The sun was shining. I expected it to be warm.) *Although the sun was shining, it was cold.* •
(James is ill. I expect he doesn't have to go to work.) *James has to go to work although he's ill.*

也可用 **but** 表示对比，但不能与 **although** 一起使用：*James is ill, but he has to go to work.*（不说 ~~Although James is ill, but he has to go to work.~~）

在非正式语言中经常用 **though** 代替 **although**（2）。**though**（不是 ~~although~~）还可用在被移到句首的形容词或副词之后（3）。

2　*Though Kate's clever, she isn't doing very well at school.* • *He has to go to work though he's ill.*

3　<u>Though the test was difficult</u>, we all passed. → *Difficult though the test was, we all passed.*

在正式语言中，**as** 也可用于这种结构：*Difficult as the test was, we all passed.*

如果想要强调反差，可以用 **even though** 谈论过去或现在的情况（4），用 **even if** 谈论未来或有可能发生的情况（5）。**even** 不与 **although** 连用，也不能单独用作连词。

4　*William kept playing golf even though it was raining.*（不说 *... ~~even although it was raining.~~*）

5　*William would play golf even if it was snowing.*（不说 *... ~~even it was snowing.~~*）

在 **even if** 引导的从句中，有时会使用 **were** 构成虚拟语气：*He would play even if it were snowing.*

在正式语言中，有时也用 **whereas**（6）和 **while**（7）等其他连词来表达两个分句间的对比。短语 **much as** 与 **like**, **hate**, **want** 等动词连用，也可用于构成对比从句（8）。

6　*In the past, boys were encouraged to be adventurous whereas girls were always told to stay clean.*

7　*While no one doubts his ability, his arrogant attitude has been difficult to accept.*

8　*Much as I like music, I can't listen to some operas for long.* • *Much as I want to, I can't help you.*

可用 **despite the fact that** 代替 **although** 引导对比从句（9）。还可用介词 **despite** 或 **in spite of** 引导动名词，代替 **although** 从句（10）。

9　*Despite the fact that he had lots of friends, he still felt really lonely sometimes.*

10　*Despite studying hard, I failed the test.* • *She wasn't satisfied in spite of being paid extra.*
（不说 ~~Despite I studied hard, I failed.~~ • ~~She wasn't satisfied in spite of she was paid extra.~~）

P　完成下列句子，使其与所给句子的意思尽可能接近。

1　I disagree with his point of view, but I understand why he thinks that way.
Although ....

2　Jack is still unemployed in spite of applying for about a dozen different jobs.
Though ....

3　While most people agreed that the car was a bargain, none of them wanted to buy it.
Even ....

4　Though it seems unlikely, the children may not want to go to the zoo on Saturday.
Unlikely ....

5　The old people didn't have very much money, but they were really generous.
Despite ....

简化的状语从句 (reduced adverbial clause)

由动词的分词构成的状语结构被称为简化的状语从句 (1)。由现在分词构成的简化状语从句的否定形式是在现在分词前加 **not** (2)。简化的状语从句也叫分词分句 (participle clause)，常用在正式语言中。

1　When he looked outside, he saw the police car. → *Looking outside, he saw the police car.*
2　Because she didn't feel very well, she sat down. → *Not feeling very well, she sat down.*

having + 过去分词构成的简化状语从句可用于描述先前已发生的行为，通常用于代替使用过去完成时的状语从句 (3)。**being** + 过去分词可用于代替使用被动式的从句 (4)。

3　After he had retired, Cecil decided to travel. → *Having retired, Cecil decided to travel.*
4　I was really quite flattered at first, because I was asked to work with one of the professors.
　　→ *I was really quite flattered at first, being asked to work with one of the professors.*

通常，只有在主句和状语从句的主语相同时才可使用简化的状语从句 (5)。当主语不同时，应避免使用简化的状语从句 (6)。

5　Because <u>it</u> was barking loudly, <u>the dog</u> scared us. → *Barking loudly, the dog scared us.*
6　Because <u>it</u> was barking loudly, <u>we</u> were scared.（不说 *Barking loudly, we were scared.*）

将 **before, as if** 等从属连词与现在分词连用也可构成简化的状语从句。

7　Before you leave, switch off all the lights. → *Before leaving, switch off all the lights.*
8　He stood there, as if he was waiting for someone. → *He stood there, as if waiting for someone.*
注意，不能这样用 **because**。（不说 *He stood there, because waiting for someone.*）

although, though, when, while 等从属连词可直接与形容词、介词短语 (9) 或表示被动含义的过去分词 (9) 连用，此时省略主语 + be。

9　*Although (they are) small, terriers are tough.* • *Freddie studied Greek while (he was) at Oxford.*
10　*Though (it had been) broken, it still worked.* • *When (it is) seen from space, the earth is blue.*
有时也可省略连词，只用过去分词：*Seen from space, the earth is blue.*

Q 选择合适的状语从句并使用其简化形式填空（文本改编自一篇谈论伦敦地铁系统的报纸文章）。

although it manages	as if they were trying	
until they make sure	~~while they waited~~	
although they were frustrated	once it has been broken	since it opened

◆　*While waiting* in line for buses during a recent one-day train strike, London's commuters displayed remarkable patience with their struggling Underground.

1　_____, most people just shrugged and went back to their newspapers, _____ to ignore this latest inconvenience.

2　_____ in 1863, the Underground has grown into a sprawling network of tracks, some of which are in desperate need of repair.

3　_____ to cover its operating costs from fares, the Underground never seems to have enough money for long-term investment and maintenance.

4　The government's argument is that, _____ into several private companies, each of the system's smaller parts will be better able to attract new investment.

5　Opponents of the government's plan to sell parts of the Underground say that they should not be allowed to proceed _____ that all existing lines are safe for passengers.

→ because 201　被动 57　是动名词还是现在分词？ 139　简化的关系从句 176

测验

A 选出最恰当的词或短语完成下列句子。

1. Players may not leave the area without permission _____ the game is being played.
   a despite **b** during **c** much as **d** while

2. Remember to wear a helmet _____ your head is protected.
   a in order that **b** so as **c** that **d** to

3. _____ they had been waiting in line all night, I was sure they'd get tickets.
   a As though **b** Because of **c** Since **d** Until

4. Amelia said it was _____ lovely weather they all went swimming.
   a as **b** as if **c** so **d** such

5. Once you _____ into a routine, you'll find the work is quite easy.
   a are settling **b** have settled **c** settled **d** will settle

B 从每句标有下划线的部分（A，B，C，D）中选出错误的一项。

1. They <u>didn't</u> think he <u>had been</u> to <u>visit</u> his birthplace since he <u>is</u> a small child.
   A B C D

2. Some British people put a 'GB' plate on the back of their car <u>so that</u> to show <u>that</u> the car is from Great Britain <u>when</u> they drive to other countries, <u>even though</u> it seems rather odd.
   A B C D

3. <u>When cooking</u> previously frozen vegetables, use about half as much time <u>as you would</u> for fresh vegetables <u>because becoming</u> softer <u>after they have been kept</u> in a freezer.
   A B C D

4. <u>For</u> it was late, they stopped near a stream <u>in order to</u> rest the horses and <u>so as not to</u> get lost <u>while</u> riding through the forest.
   A B C D

5. <u>Much as</u> I liked her paintings, I couldn't act <u>as</u> she was Picasso or someone like that <u>when</u> she clearly was a beginner, <u>though</u> very good for a beginner, of course.
   A B C D

C 选择合适的词填空。

> after   as   because   to   when (×2)

In Britain, ¹ _____ you need legal advice, you go to see a solicitor. Solicitors spend most of their time in their offices ² _____ their work mostly involves preparing legal documents, especially those involved in buying a house. They can, ³ _____ necessary, go to court with you, but, ⁴ _____ taking down details of a serious legal matter, they will often contact a barrister ⁵ _____ represent you in court. ⁶ _____ you may have seen in films or on TV, barristers wear white curly wigs and black robes in court.

完成下列句子，使其与所给句子的意思尽可能接近。

1 It was late and I was exhausted, so I went straight to bed.
Because _____.

2 There will have to be a change in his attitude or he won't continue to work here.
In order for _____.

3 From the way he talked, I thought he owned the restaurant.
He talked _____

4 Finish your homework, then you can go out.
You can't _____.

5 I know he's your friend, but he can't sleep here.
Even _____.

6 We left half an hour earlier than necessary because we didn't want to be late.
So as _____.

在每对词或短语中选择合适的一个填空。

although	as easy as	as if	just	as much	despite	so that	though
and so	so easy	if	just as	as much as	despite the fact	whereas	even

1 _____ a lot has been written and said about class differences in British society, they no longer mean 2 _____ they used to. Traditionally, the upper classes were wealthy and powerful 3 _____ the lower or working classes were poor. Nowadays, some of the upper classes may still seem to behave and speak 4 _____ their social status continues to be 5 _____ it was for their aristocratic ancestors, but it is no longer based on exclusive wealth and power. Maintaining large houses with lots of servants is not 6 _____ it used to be and, strange 7 _____ it may seem, some new owners of those large British country houses in fact come from halfway across the world. 8 _____ that their parents may have been middle or working class, many of today's wealthy Britons achieved success based on education and enterprise, not birth and inheritance.

连接词语（connector）和焦点结构（focus structure）

连接词语是用来连接分句或句子的单词（如 **consequently, however, so**）和短语（如 **in addition, in fact, for example**）。（*The Japanese economy has been very strong and consequently the yen has risen in value. In addition, the dollar has continued to show weakness. The pound, however, has remained steady.*）

焦点结构也用于将不同的句子衔接起来。有一种焦点结构叫前置（fronting）。在前置结构中，句子的一部分被移至句首，从而使关注点集中于此处。（*I can't eat asparagus. → I can eat broccoli and carrots. Asparagus I can't eat.*）

还有一种焦点结构是分裂句（cleft sentence）。分裂句突出句子的一部分，而把其他部分都放在另一个分句中。分裂句可以以 **it**（*It's asparagus I can't eat.*）或 **what**（*What I can't eat is asparagus.*）开头。

A 阅读下文，在每段中找出一个连接词语。

A All those people who say that the weather hasn't been normal recently are right. However, since there is really no such thing as normal weather, they probably mean
5 something else. If they mean that average summer temperatures have been getting warmer, then they are certainly correct. In fact, it is not just the summer temperature, but the general average temperature of the
10 whole world that has been steadily moving up.

B The signs are everywhere. There are small signs. For example, butterflies in North America have moved about 60 miles north of where they used to live. There are also very large
15 signs. Huge masses of ice in mountain glaciers and the Arctic are melting. The famous snow cap on Africa's Mount Kilimanjaro has almost disappeared. Actually, ice or snow doesn't really disappear, it turns into water, flows into the
20 ocean and causes sea levels to rise.

C Why is this happening? One answer is that it could simply be part of a natural process. After all, there have been long periods of warmth in the past. So we could just be

25 experiencing another warming trend. This kind of answer had more supporters in the past. What scientists now believe is that human activity is the cause. For more than two hundred years, humans have been
30 gradually changing the atmosphere, mainly as a result of industrial pollution. We have created an atmosphere around the earth that, like a giant glass container, lets heat from the sun through and holds it inside.

35 **D** Will temperatures and sea levels keep rising? Should we just move to higher ground and throw away our winter coats? The answer depends on where you live. If you live on the coast of Florida, the answer is a definite
40 yes. However, if you live in northern Europe, your temperatures may soon be on the way down. All that fresh water pouring into the Atlantic will change the circulation patterns in the ocean. As a consequence, the current
45 of air that flows towards Europe will become much cooler. According to one prediction, winter in London is going to become much more like winter in Copenhagen.

B 选择合适的句子作为上文各段（A—D）的结尾句，将对应段落的字母序号填入括号。

1 It may be a good idea to hold on to your coat. (.....)
2 It's known as the greenhouse effect. (.....)
3 It's called global warming. (.....)
4 As a result, small islands in the Pacific are going under. (.....)

连接词语和焦点结构的类型

1 起连接作用的副词

最常见的连接词语是 **however** 和 **then** 之类的副词，可用于连接前后两个句子（1）或分句（2）。

> 1 *We wanted to rent a flat near the university. However, they were all too expensive.*
> 2 *The old woman poured two cups of tea, then I asked her if she remembered my grandparents.*

此类副词还有：**actually, also, finally, instead, later, meanwhile, secondly, so, therefore**。

通常把用作连接词语的副词放在句子或分句句首（3）。连接词语中，只有 **as well** 和 **too** 不可置于句首。它们和其他一些连接词语可用在句尾（4）。连接词语也可用在句子中间，在系动词 **be** 或其他助动词之后（5），在主要动词之前（6）。不是所有连接性副词都可用在以上任意位置。

> 3 *I've been to Morocco several times. Actually, I've just come back from there.*
> 4 *I spent a few days in Casablanca. I visited Rabat and Tangier as well.*
> 5 *Don't forget your raincoat. You are also going to need an umbrella.*
> 6 *Dave and Alice arrived with steaming hot coffee. They also brought fresh rolls.*

一般不把连接词语置于动词和它的宾语之间。（不说 *They brought also fresh rolls.*）

2 起连接作用的短语

一些介词短语可用作连接词语，通常位于句首（7），但有时也位于句中（8）或句尾（9）。并不是所有起连接作用的介词短语都可用在以上任意位置。通常，使用逗号将此类短语与句子其他部分隔开。

> 7 *The doctor will see you soon. In the meantime, could you please complete these forms?*
> 8 *We have your application, but it's incomplete. You didn't, for example, include a photograph.*
> 9 *One man lied about having a degree in English. He had never been to university, in fact.*

此类介词短语还有：**as a result, for a start, in addition, in conclusion, in other words, on the other hand**。

to begin with 之类的不定式短语也可用作连接词语，通常位于句首。

> 10 *I had a summer job in a factory, but I didn't enjoy it. To begin with, I had to start at six, which meant I was always tired.*

此类不定式短语还有：**to conclude, to start with, to summarize, to sum up**。

3 焦点结构

可用焦点结构增强句子之间的衔接。可把句子的某部分移到句首，使这个句子与前一句更紧密地连接起来。这种语法结构即前置。

> 11 *I'd rather visit Paris than London these days. I don't like London as much as I used to.*
> → ... *London I don't like as much as I used to.*

也可用焦点结构强调句子的一部分，通常是为了与前句信息形成对比或就前句信息进行补充。这类句子以 **it**（12）或 **what**（13）开头，被称为分裂句。

> 12 *I didn't eat the strawberries. Jack ate them.* → ... *It was Jack who ate them.*
> 13 *We didn't like the way he spoke. We didn't like his rude behaviour.* → ... *What we didn't like was his rude behaviour.*

C 从第 **208** 页的文章中找出符合下列要求的例子。

1 所含连接词语位于句中的句子：...
2 以 **what** 开头的焦点结构：...

→ 副词 116，118　助动词 17　分裂句 217　前置 216　介词短语 125

连接词语、介词和连词

4 用连接词语还是介词？

一些连接词语（如 **as a result, in addition**）看起来像复杂介词（如 **as a result of, in addition to**）。有时可以不用连接词语（1）而在句首用复杂介词加名词（短语）（2）或代词（3）。

   1 *As a result, sea levels are rising. In addition, they discussed the situation in the Pacific.*

   2 *As a result of these changes, sea levels are rising.*（不说 *As a result of sea levels are rising.*）

   3 *In addition to that, they discussed the situation in the Pacific.*（不说 *In addition that, …*）

此类复杂介词还有：**as an example of, in comparison to, in comparison with, in contrast to**。

在句尾，也可使用复杂介词加名词（短语）或代词（4），或与该介词相似的连接词语（5）。

   4 *Paul went to Cambridge. Sarah chose Oxford instead of Cambridge.*

   5 *He went to Cambridge. She chose Oxford instead.*（不说 *… Oxford instead Cambridge.*）

5 用连接词语还是连词？

连接词语 **also** 和 **however** 的用法分别与并列连词 **and** 和 **but** 相似。若想强调某信息与前面的信息是何种关系，如补充（6）或对比（7），使用连接词语。

   6 *Lucy's doing great these days. She's living in the country. She also has a new boyfriend.* •
      She's living in the country and she has a new boyfriend.

   7 *I sometimes drink coffee in a restaurant. However, I prefer tea most of the time.* •
      I sometimes drink coffee in a restaurant, but I prefer tea most of the time.

若想强调某分句与前面的分句是何种关系，如因果（8）或对比（9），有时可在该分句开头先使用并列连词再使用连接词语。

   8 *She didn't sign the contract and consequently it isn't legal.*（不说 *… consequently and …*）

   9 *They were trapped for two days, but nevertheless they survived.*（不说 *… nevertheless but …*）

并列连词之后的分句有时可以简化，但连接词语之后不可简化。

  10 *The show was supposed to start early, but didn't.*（不说 *… however didn't.*）

虽然连接词语和连词都可用于连接句子内的分句，但通常用连词来连接同一个句子里的分句（11），用连接词语来连接不同的句子（12）。

  11 *You can stay here and help me or you can go inside, but you can't just sit watching TV.*

  12 *We were working outside all day. Meanwhile, he was sitting inside watching TV.*

so 和 **though** 既可作连接词语，也可作从属连词。作连词时，引导作为句子一部分的状语从句（13）；作连接词语时，连接两个句子（14）。

  13 *It was an interesting offer, though I couldn't accept it, so I said nothing.*

  14 *I'm sure it was her car outside. So she must have been at home.* • *We really liked their new flat. It was lovely. It was very expensive, though.*

D 根据第 **208** 页的文章中的信息，用合适的连接词语、介词或连词补全下列句子。

1   .... industrial pollution, the atmosphere has gradually changed.

2   .... small changes such as butterflies moving north, there are large changes such as glaciers melting .... flowing into the ocean. Sea levels are rising ....

→ 状语从句 197　复杂介词 125　并列连词和从属连词 12

E 在每对短语中选择合适的一个填空。文本选自一篇关于历史的文章。

> in addition   in contrast   for example   as a result
> in addition to   in contrast to   as an example of   as a result of

The Spanish-American war was fought between Spain and the United States in 1898. There were several reasons for US involvement. [1] _____, American investors were losing money because of Spanish policies in Cuba. [2] _____ the Spanish forces, the US navy was very modern and powerful. [3] _____ the war, Cuba became independent from Spain. [4] _____, the United States gained control of Puerto Rico.

F 选择合适的词或短语填空，补全这段描述。

> also   and   as a result   but   however   so

The Titanic was considered to be the fastest and most modern passenger ship of its day. It was [1] _____ believed to be unsinkable. During its first voyage in 1912, [2] _____, the ship hit an iceberg [3] _____ sank. While the ship was slowly sinking, there was time for the passengers to escape, [4] _____ there were not enough lifeboats, [5] _____ hundreds of people drowned in the disaster. [6] _____, tough new laws were introduced to make ships much safer.

G 为左侧的句子和分句（1—4）选择合适的下文（a—d），再选择合适的词填空。

> and   but   instead   or   so (×2)   though

1 We loved playing in the snow.   (......)   a _____ some of the students did.
2 I liked the car _____ my wife loved it.   (......)   b _____ we went by train _____.
3 I didn't think the test was long   c _____ we bought it.
   _____ difficult,   (......)   d It was really cold, _____.
4 There wasn't a flight available.   (......)

H 改正下文中连接词语用法有误的地方。

My friend Kazuko sometimes helps me with my English writing. She was born in Japan, ~~however,~~ but she spent part of her childhood in America consequently her English is really good. She isn't like an American, although. Americans seem to be very direct, in contrast this Kazuko is very indirect. As example, she never tells me that I have made a mistake. Instead that, she points to a line and takes a deep breath. She makes also a small 'tsss' sound. Alternatively, or she may say some part needs 'special attention'. For her, nothing is ever wrong; it is simply 'not finished yet'. As a result this, I have not only learned English from her, but I have also learned how to be helpful and patient. Nevertheless that, I think that she will have to take a few deep breaths when she reads this. In other word, it is not finished yet.

表示补充和表示对比的连接词语

6 表示补充的连接词语：**also, as well, too** 等

想表示自己在补充信息时，可把 **also** 用在句首（1）或句中（2），但通常不用在句尾。在句尾可以用 **as well** 或 **too**（3）。

1 *You mustn't forget to include the postcode. Also, make sure you provide a return address.*
2 *Carl is good at French. He's also studying French cooking. I think he also speaks Italian.*
3 *He speaks a little Spanish as well / too.*（不说 *He speaks a little Spanish also.*）

在正式语言中，可用其他连接词语（一般放在句首）引入关于前文的补充信息（4）或支撑信息（5）。

4 *We are sending food and water. In addition, they will need things like tents and blankets.*
5 *If you're ready, you should go ahead without me. Besides, I'd rather stay at home tonight.*

可用于正式语言的此类连接词语还有：**furthermore, indeed, likewise, moreover, similarly**。

表示要换一种方式表述前文信息时，可在句首用 **in other words**（6）或 **that is (to say)**（7）。

6 *It's described as downsizing. In other words, people are losing their jobs.*
7 *He told me he wanted to join the army. That is (to say), he wanted to wear a uniform.*

表示自己在补充更加具体的信息时，可以在句首、句中或句尾使用 **in particular**（8），**for example** 或 **for instance**（9）之类的连接词语。

8 *I enjoyed the book. In particular, I liked the details of life in Japan as it used to be.*
9 *William doesn't help with the housework. He has, for example, never washed the dishes.* •
  This study of smoking habits is incomplete. There's no mention of teenagers, for instance.

7 表示对比的连接词语：**however, instead** 等

however 和 **instead** 可用于表示对比关系，引出出人意料的或与前文矛盾的信息。**however**（10）和 **instead**（11）通常用在句首，但也可用在句中和句尾（12）。

10 *She had hoped Daniel would stay all weekend. However, he had to leave on Saturday.*
11 *He was supposed to stay here and help us move things. Instead, he went off to play golf.*
12 *Extra security precautions had been proposed earlier. They were, however, considered too costly at the time. A tightening of existing security measures was undertaken instead.*

可用于正式语言的此类连接词语还有：**in contrast, nevertheless, on the other hand, rather, yet**。

8 表示补充或对比的连接词语：**actually, in fact, after all**

在引入新信息来进行补充说明时——往往是为证明前面所述内容（13），或者在给出与预期大不相同的信息时（14），可使用 **actually** 和 **in fact**。它们通常用在句首，但也可用在句末或句中（15）。

13 *I've known Henry Martin for years. Actually, we went to the same school.*
14 *Everyone thought the exam would be difficult. In fact, it turned out to be quite easy.*
15 *We went to the same school, in fact.* • *It actually turned out to be quite easy.*

after all 可表示"（用于解释）别忘了，毕竟"，可用在句首或句尾来补充信息，以提醒他人某一事实（16）。**after all** 还可表示"还是，终究"，通常用在句尾来引入与预期有反差的信息（17）。

16 *I don't have to tell my parents everything. After all, I am over 21. / I am an adult after all.*
17 *When I saw the rain, I didn't think we could go for a walk. Anthony convinced me to go with him and we saw a beautiful rainbow. I'm so glad we decided to do it after all.*

→ besides 133   in addition (to) 125，210   instead (of) 125，210

I 选择合适的词或短语填空，补全下文中的释义。如有必要请查词典。

> facelift (×2)　forklift　lift (×2)　also (×2)　for example　similarly　that is

A ¹＿＿＿＿＿＿＿＿＿, which is ²＿＿＿＿＿＿＿＿＿ known as an elevator in the USA, is a machine that you stand in to go up and down inside a building. This word is ³＿＿＿＿＿＿＿＿＿ used for the action of taking someone somewhere in a car, described as 'giving someone a ⁴＿＿＿＿＿＿＿＿＿'. Something rather different is meant by a ⁵＿＿＿＿＿＿＿＿＿, which is an operation to make someone look younger by, ⁶＿＿＿＿＿＿＿＿＿, removing fat or pulling the skin tighter. ⁷＿＿＿＿＿＿＿＿＿, the process of improving the appearance of the outside of a building can be described as 'giving it a ⁸＿＿＿＿＿＿＿＿＿'. A ⁹＿＿＿＿＿＿＿＿＿ is a vehicle with special equipment, ¹⁰＿＿＿＿＿＿＿＿＿, two long metal prongs sticking out in front, which is used for lifting and moving heavy things.

J 为每段文本（改编自一篇杂志文章）添加一组连接词语（不一定按词语的原顺序添加）。

> ~~also~~ / however / in other words　indeed / in fact / too　actually / also / in particular

also

A　Roger Goodman was really fit when he played rugby in school. He stayed in good shape through university. Once he started working, things changed. He began eating a lot more and exercising a lot less. After a few years, his clothes were feeling tight and he was breathing really hard after running up stairs. He was 'out of shape'.

B　Roger didn't think he had time for outdoor activities, so he decided to join a health club. Like a lot more men these days, he started thinking about cosmetic surgery to improve his appearance. He wanted to get rid of some of the wrinkles around his eyes. Cosmetic surgeon Dr Khalid Idris of Body Image in Highbury says, 'Our clients used to be mostly women. Now we have more men than women coming in for certain types of surgery.'

C　The number of men seeking help from surgeons like Dr Idris has increased dramatically in recent years. It's a trend that started in the USA where cosmetic surgery is a $500 million business. The emphasis on looking young isn't limited to facelifts, but has created a huge demand for dental improvements and hair transplants.

K 改正下面句子中连接词语用法有误的地方。

1　I'm still studying European History. I'm hoping as well to take a British History class.

2　I'd rather have chicken than fish if that's okay. I don't like actually fish very much.

3　I don't mind correcting students' homework. It's part of my job after all that.

4　I wouldn't say that Adam is the best student. In addition, he's certainly not the worst.

5　Recycling has been successful in schools. On the other hand, young children now automatically put their empty bottles in the recycling bin, not the dustbin.

引导结果和表示时间的连接词语

9 引导结果的连接词语：**so, therefore** 等

可在句首用 **so**，表示后面的事情是前面所述事件的结果，或者是由该事件引起的（1）。如果想强调按照逻辑会产生或必然造成某结果，可用 **therefore**（2）。**therefore** 比 **so** 更正式。

1　*We were moving some things out of the house when it started pouring with rain. So everything got very wet.*

2　*The woman killed her husband and she intended to do it. Therefore she is guilty of murder.*

在正式语言中，通常可以在句首用 **as a result**，表示某事是前面所述事件的直接结果。

3　*There has been an increase in population and a shortage of housing. As a result, rents have gone up and fewer students can afford to live within walking distance of the college.*

可用于正式语言的此类连接词语还有：**accordingly, as a consequence, consequently, hence, thus**。

10 表示时间的连接词语：**then, afterwards** 等

then 可用作连接词语，通常位于句首，表示按照时间顺序（4）或逻辑顺序（5），一个行为或情况发生在另一个行为或情况之后。**then** 有时也用在分句开头，强调后面所述事件是前面的 **if** 分句所述事件合乎逻辑的结果（6）。

4　*We had unpacked everything for the picnic and had just sat down. Then it started to rain.*

5　*Perhaps you could hire a car for a few days. Then you'd be able to go wherever you wanted.*

6　*If we allow the terrorists to succeed, then no one will ever feel safe again anywhere.*

表述两个句子在时间上的关系时，也可在句首或句尾使用其他连接词语，如 **afterwards**。

7　*The film was based on Harris' first novel. Afterwards, the book became a bestseller.*

此类连接词语还有：**earlier, later, previously, subsequently**。

meanwhile 可表示"与此同时"，用于说明在一段时间内同时发生了两件事（8）；该词还可表示"在此期间"，用于谈论在两个时间点之间发生的事（9）。**meanwhile** 通常用在句首。

8　*My sister finished high school and got a good job. Meanwhile, I remained a poor student.*

9　*Let's meet again tomorrow. Meanwhile, I'll get in touch with Sebastian about your proposal.*

此类连接词语还有：**in the meantime**（"在此期间"），**simultaneously**（"同时地"）。

L 为左侧的句子和分句（1—6）选择合适的下文（a—d），并在横线处补充 so 或 then。

1　We got stuck in a bad traffic jam.　（＿＿）

2　I know you don't like green peppers.　（＿＿）

3　If our operating budget is cut by 10%,　（＿＿）

4　It was a terrible morning, with a lot of problems in the office.　（＿＿）

5　A lot more people came to the meeting than they expected,　（＿＿）

6　The children have to do their homework every afternoon when they come home.　（＿＿）

a　＿＿＿＿＿ at lunchtime I spilled some tomato soup down the front of my white shirt.

b　＿＿＿＿＿ they can play or watch TV.

c　＿＿＿＿＿ when we arrived, it had already started.

d　＿＿＿＿＿ we really will have to reduce services.

e　＿＿＿＿＿ I didn't put any in the salad.

f　＿＿＿＿＿ the room was very crowded.

→ 结果状语从句 203　so 202—203，210　用在 if 从句后的 then 189　时间状语从句 198—199

用于列举的连接词语

first（或 **firstly**），**second**（或 **secondly**）等词用在句首，可表示列举的事物或一连串事件的顺序。有时也用 **then** 或 **next** 来代替 second(ly)、third(ly) 等。

1 *We really have to clean the house. First, we have to take out the rubbish. Then / Second, we'll have to wash all the dishes piled up in the kitchen sink. Thirdly / Next we really need to scrub the floor because it's so dirty.*

在句首可用 **for a start** 代替 first(ly)，表示下文要开始列举一串理由来证明或解释前面陈述的内容（2）。可在句首用 **finally** 表示这是列举事项的最后一项（3）。

2 *I hated working there. For a start, everyone else was much older than me.*

此类连接词语还有：**first of all, in the first place, to begin with, to start with**。

3 *Finally, I must thank my parents for their years of patience and support.*

可用短语 **to sum up** 表示接下来将对已提出的观点进行概括、总结。

4 *To sum up, they liked our ideas, but they want to know more about the costs involved.*

此类连接词语还有：**in brief, in conclusion, in short, in summary, to conclude, to summarize**。

A 将所给连接词语添加至以下食谱中的恰当位置。

> finally   first   second   then (×2)

To make hot-baked chips for two, you'll need four large potatoes, the white of one egg, a quarter teaspoon of cayenne pepper and a pinch of salt. Slice each potato lengthwise, cut each slice lengthwise into long sticks. Mix the egg white, cayenne and salt in a bowl. Stir the potato sticks round in the mixture. Spread the coated potato sticks on a greased baking sheet and bake them in the oven at 170° for 35 minutes.

B 选择合适的连接词语填空（文本改编自教科书上的文章），有的句子也可不用连接词语。

> as a result   ~~for a start~~   in short   secondly   so   then

◆ _____ Animal communication is different from human communication in two ways.

◆ *For a start,* ∧Animal signals are always restricted to what is happening here and now.

1 _____ When your dog comes to you and says, 'Woof!', it always means, 'I'm woofing now.' It doesn't mean, 'I woofed last night.'

2 _____ However, humans can easily talk about last night and things that happened years ago.

3 _____ They can go on to talk about what they'll be doing tomorrow or next year.

4 _____ Humans are also capable of talking about what doesn't even exist.

5 _____ They can refer to things like heaven and hell without ever having seen them.

6 _____ Animal communication consists of a fixed number of signals and each signal is used for one particular thing or occasion.

7 _____ Human communication, on the other hand, is very creative and humans are able to invent new words, as illustrated by 'woofing' in the last paragraph.

8 _____ Human communication has special properties not found in animal communication.

焦点结构：前置和倒装（inversion）

把句子的一部分（如宾语）前移至句首，可促使他人更关注该部分，或起到强调作用。这叫"前置"。通常在正式语言中，可以通过前置来强化一个句子与前一个句子之间的联系（1）或突出对比效果（2）。

1 She was coughing, sneezing and shivering. He recognized these symptoms immediately.
→ … *These symptoms he recognized immediately.*

2 We met the Greens. We liked Mrs Green, but we really didn't care for her husband.
→ … *Mrs Green we liked, but her husband we really didn't care for.*

在被前置的成分后，常把动词或助动词置于主语之前。这被称为"倒装"。倒装结构通常用在句首的介词短语（3）或 **here, there** 这类副词（4）之后，把描述姿势或运动的动词置于主语之前。

3 I was told to sit on a chair in the middle of the room. An old woman stood behind the chair.
→ … *Behind the chair stood an old woman.* • *Into the room walked two men wearing sunglasses.*

4 *Here comes the bride.* • *There goes my bus.* （不说 ~~There my bus goes.~~）

还可把否定词（如 **neither, nor**）（5）、以 **not** 开头的短语（6）以及 **scarcely, seldom** 这类副词（7）放在前面，之后使用倒装结构。

5 *I don't like it. Neither do my parents. Nor does anyone else that I've asked.*

6 *Not until later did we notice the broken glass.* • *Not only was the car old, it had no windows.*

7 *Scarcely had he sat down when the doorbell rang.* • *Seldom have I heard such nonsense.*

only 与表示时间的词语（8）或其他介词短语（9）连用并位于句首时，之后用倒装结构。

8 *Only after the test will we know if it worked. Only then can we decide what to do next.*

9 *I've looked for it in other places. Only in Italy can you find this special kind of ice cream.*

当分词结构被移到句首时，后面也要用倒装结构。这种用法常见于故事的叙述中。

10 *The bedroom was empty. Lying on the bed was a parcel. Attached to it was a small note.*

O 选择合适的表达填空。

did she	is it	it was	she was	she would	was something
had she	it is	here comes	was she	would she	was part

Only occasionally [1] _____ find herself reading someone else's newspaper, over their shoulder, as she sat in the station waiting room. Mostly [2] _____ just not very interested, nor [3] _____ willing to risk getting caught. Why [4] _____ so embarrassing to get caught doing that, she wondered to herself. It isn't against the law or anything. But facing her today [5] _____ that really caught her attention. One of our greatest fears in modern life, the headline said, was having to speak in public. The article offered ways to develop your confidence. Seldom [6] _____ ever had to speak to an audience, but [7] _____ her turn to give a ten-minute presentation in her Spanish class that afternoon. Not only [8] _____ have to speak to an audience, [9] _____ have to do it in a foreign language. She felt the room getting hotter as she leaned forward to get a closer look. Suddenly blocking her view [10] _____ of a large black beard and the big nose of the newspaper's owner. 'Oops. Oh, [11] _____ my train,' she said quickly, as she stood up and stumbled towards the door. Public speaking isn't scary, she thought to herself, [12] _____ public reading that makes me really nervous.

→ 否定词后的倒装 48

焦点结构：分裂句

想让他人更关注句子的一部分（或想强调此部分）时，可以使用被称为"分裂句"的特殊结构。在分裂句中，句子被分为两部分，重点落在其中一部分。这部分在说话时通常重读。一些分裂句以 **it** 开头，称作 **it** 分裂句（1）；另一些以 **what** 开头，称作 **wh-** 分裂句（2）。

1　Martin + ate your pizza. → *It was Martin who ate your pizza.*
　　Martin ate + your pizza. → *It was your pizza that Martin ate.*
2　Anna really likes + chocolate ice cream. → *What Anna really likes is chocolate ice cream.*

❶ it 分裂句

it 分裂句的结构一般是：**it + be + 强调部分 + who**（3）或 **that**（4）引导的关系从句。其中关系从句中的关系代词有时可省略（5）。

3　Someone said Ali phoned earlier. ~ Ali didn't phone. Alex phoned. → … ~ *No, it wasn't Ali who phoned. It was Alex.*
4　I'm not interested in anyone else. I love you! → … *It's you that I love!*
5　Don't you like vegetables? ~ No, I like most of them. I hate onions. → … *It's onions I hate.*

it 分裂句通常用于强调句子中的名词或代词，但也可用于强调其他部分，如副词（6）或状语从句（7）。

6　You were supposed to be here yesterday. → *It was yesterday that you were supposed to be here.*
7　Things got worse after Elaine left. → *It was after Elaine left that things got worse.*

❷ wh- 分裂句

wh- 分裂句的结构一般是：**what** 从句 **+ be +** 强调部分。强调的部分可以是名词短语（8）或名词性从句（9）。

8　I can't stop yawning. I need a cup of coffee. → … *What I need is a cup of coffee.*
9　They don't know if Richard's planning to stay here. They're hoping that he'll leave soon.
　　→ … *What they're hoping is that he'll leave soon.*

wh- 分裂句也可用于强调动词短语。此时，**what** 从句中通常会用到动词 **do** 的某种形式，而被强调的动词短语中常常用动词原形（10）。如果 **what** 从句含有 **to do**，则后面被强调的动词短语中有时用带 **to** 的动词不定式（11）。

10　Alice has an unusual job. She repairs old clocks. → … *What she does is repair old clocks.*
11　David is ambitious. He wants to study law. → … *What he wants to do is (to) study law.*

有时可以用 **all**（在此处表示"唯一"）代替句首的 **what**。

12　I'll stop yawning soon. I just need a cup of coffee. → … *All I need is a cup of coffee.*

P 完成下列分裂句，对标有下划线的部分作出强调，使所写句子与所给句子的意思尽可能接近。

1　The cigarette smoke is irritating my eyes.
　　It _____.
2　We had to clean up all the mess.
　　It _____.
3　Jimmy watches TV in his room instead of studying.
　　What _____.
4　Scientists now believe that human activity is the cause.
　　What _____.

→ 状语从句 197　动词不定式 139　名词性从句 161　关系从句 173

测验

A 选出最恰当的词或短语完成下列句子。

1　These plants usually flower in spring, _____ won't if there is frost.
　　a but　**b** however　**c** nevertheless　**d** otherwise

2　I enjoyed reading the story. It was rather sad, _____.
　　a also　**b** but　**c** so　**d** though

3　Jasmine is working as a dental assistant. What she does is _____ people's teeth.
　　a clean　**b** cleans　**c** cleaning　**d** to clean

4　Tickets are required for admission. _____, those who don't have a ticket won't get in.
　　a Consequently　**b** Rather　**c** Similarly　**d** Subsequently

5　Desert flowers can be invisible for years _____ appear suddenly after heavy rain.
　　a actually, but　**b** alternatively or　**c** consequently and　**d** nevertheless, so

B 从每句标有下划线的部分（A，B，C，D）中选出错误的一项。

1　To begin with, she insisted that, in addition to her children, she should be allowed to bring their
　　A　　　　　　　　　　**B**
　　pets; that is, she wanted as well to bring a dog and two cats.
　　C　　　　　**D**

2　For many years, coal was not only readily available, but it was also very cheap in comparison
　　　　　　　　　　　　A　　　　　　　　　　　　　　　**B**　　　　　**C**
　　other types of fuel and consequently it was used in all the factories.
　　　　　　　　　　D

3　As a matter of fact, we had just heard about the problem and, because of that, we didn't stay
　　A　　　　　　　　　　　　　　　　　　　　　**B**
　　actually in London very long afterwards.
　　C　　　　　　　　　　**D**

4　In conclusion, the new rules state that, in accordance with our agreement, workers who
　　A　　　　　　　　　　　　　**B**
　　previously did extra work without extra pay must now receive overtime pay. As a result that
　　C　　　　　　　　　　　　　　　　　　　　　　　　　　　　　**D**
　　those who are asked to do extra work will receive additional payment.

5　In the meantime, some of us had to stay in the old building, though it was rather primitive.
　　A　　　　　　　　　　　　　　　　　　　　　　　**B**
　　For a start, there was no hot water. In addition to there were cockroaches everywhere.
　　C　　　　　　　　　　　　**D**

C 选择合适的词或短语填空。

after all　　for example　　in addition　　in the meantime　　so

The difficulty of getting people to pay attention to the problem of rising sea levels
is that it often has to compete with, [1] _____, news of rising food
prices or an increase in violent crime. [2] _____, you are unlikely
to worry about flooding in the future if, [3] _____, you can't afford
to eat or you're about to be shot. [4] _____, most of us don't live
anywhere near the sea. [5] _____ why should we worry about it?

D 完成下列句子，使其与所给句子的意思尽可能接近。

1 There wasn't any butter. We used margarine instead.
   Instead ....

2 You can only get dishes and bowls with this design in Poland.
   Only ....

3 We didn't discover the mistake until much later.
   Not ....

4 Flooding causes most of the damage in spring.
   It's ....

5 She left because he was so unpleasant.
   It was ....

6 I know that the main road is blocked.
   All ....

7 He went to the party by himself.
   What he ....

8 Rose is hoping to travel across Canada by train.
   What ....

E 从每对词或短语中选择恰当的一个填空。

afterwards	as a result of	in contrast	similarly
next	the result is	in particular	it's the same

that	in the beginning	what
that is	to begin with	why

[1] .... I'd like to do today is introduce some important terms that you will become familiar with during this class. [2] ...., there is the term 'greenhouse effect'. A greenhouse is a building with glass sides and a glass roof which trap heat from the sun and hold it inside the building. [3] ...., the polluted atmosphere surrounding the earth is now trapping and holding the heat of the sun, causing temperatures to rise. [4] ...., the polluted atmosphere is having the same kind of effect as a greenhouse. [5] ...., there is the term 'greenhouse gases'. These are the gases which are polluting the atmosphere. [6] ...., one gas called carbon dioxide, which is produced when things like coal and oil are burned, accumulates in the atmosphere and is a direct cause of the greenhouse effect. [7] .... the greenhouse effect, we are now experiencing a phenomenon known as 'global warming', which is a more general term for increased world temperatures.

1 句子（sentence）

A* 1 He was unconscious. **(line 17)**
OR Police praised the young teacher's quick thinking. **(line 24)**
OR The bus driver never regained consciousness. **(line 27)**
OR He was later pronounced dead at East Surrey hospital. **(line 28)**
OR That's a terrible tragedy. **(line 33)**
OR A local driving school has also offered him six free driving lessons. **(line 38)**

2 A young English teacher saved the lives of 30 students **when** he took control of a bus **after** its driver suffered a fatal heart attack. **(line 1)**
OR Harvold, **who** has not passed his driving test, said, 'I realized (that) the bus was out of control **when** I was speaking to the students on the microphone.' **(line 11)**

B 1 after (OR when)
2 suffered (OR had)
3 hit (OR collided with)
4 before
5 died
6 but
7 was
8 praised
9 and
10 offered

C 1 He **was** unconscious. **(line 17)**
OR That**'s** a terrible tragedy. **(line 33)**
2 If he **hadn't reacted quickly (line 25)**
OR He **was later pronounced** dead at East Surrey hospital **(line 28)**
OR He **had worked regularly** with the school **(line 29)**
3 there **could** have been a terrible accident **(line 25)**
OR I hoped the driver **would** survive **(line 32)**

D 1 I was so relieved that **no one** else was hurt **(line 31)**
2 (he) was very well regarded by **staff (line 30)**
OR He had worked regularly with the **school (line 29)**

E 1 won't be easy
2 Was *Lord of the Flies*
3 has pockets
4 doesn't interest me
5 isn't going to
6 None of you are
7 have I had
8 wasn't about dancing
9 Is Statistics

10 aren't made

F 1 was (c)   3 is (a)   5 are (b)
2 was (e)   4 is (d)

G 1 orchestra have   5 Darts has
2 everybody has   6 teachers has / have
3 Nobody … has   7 police have
4 committee have   8 eggs has

H 1 holdall
2 carry things
3 travel
    (OR are travelling)
4 hinge
5 swings
6 closes
7 hallucination
8 seeing things
9 hypocrite
10 pretends
11 behaves
12 hijacker
13 seizes
14 go
15 demand things

I 1 take (b) put it in
2 like (c) going to
3 wait (d) shivering
4 heard (a) believe it

J 1 gets, moves
2 rest, nap (OR nap, rest)
3 hibernate, eat
4 lie, fall
5 talks, happens
6 sing, go
7 snore, breathe

K 1 She whispered 'Good luck' to him.
2 The judge fined her £700 for speeding.
3 The farmer refused us permission to walk across his field (OR refused to give us permission OR refused to give permission to us)
4 James confessed (to me) that he took (OR had taken) Caroline's book.

L 1 reserved … keeping it for
2 transmitted … spread them to (OR spread … transmit them to)
3 retrieved … found them for (OR found … retrieved them for)
4 transferred … sells him to (OR sold … transfers him to)
5 required … offer them to

M She ~~explained us~~ > explained to us (OR explained) gave the following ~~information half~~ of the husbands > information to half
Your wife has ~~described you a holiday trip to China~~ > described a holiday trip to China to you
One of her friends ~~told to her~~ > told her

---

* 此类题目（从文章中找相应例子）的参考答案给出了一些具代表性的例子，但文中也可能存在其他符合要求的例子。

You ~~think sounds~~ like a really good idea > think (that) it sounds

you ~~ask to her~~ some questions > ask her (OR ask)

Your wife has ~~suggested you a holiday trip to China~~ > suggested a holiday trip to China to you

You ~~don't like~~ > don't like it

You ~~believe is a~~ really bad idea > believe (that) it is a

you ~~ask some questions her~~ > ask her some questions (OR ask some questions)

The researcher didn't ~~tell to the wives~~ > tell the wives

the ~~wives she said~~ to the husbands > wives what she said

~~decide the husbands~~ thought it was a good idea > decide if (OR whether) the husbands

N 1 look*(**f**)　　3 appear (**b**)　　5 taste (**c**)
　　2 feel (**e**)　　4 sound* (**a**)

* 第 1 题的 look 和第 4 题的 sound 可互换。

O 1 smelled OR tasted
　　2 tasted OR smelled
　　3 get
　　4 seemed to make
　　5 become
　　6 looked
　　7 appeared to be
　　8 turned
　　9 get
　　10 feel
　　11 stay
　　12 turn

P It ~~appeared a~~ big problem > appeared to be a (OR seemed (to be) a)

She ~~went to be crazy~~ > went crazy

she just decided to ~~make blonde her hair~~ > make her hair blonde

her hair ~~turned into~~ bright orange > turned

~~It also became orange her face~~ > Her face also turned orange (OR It also made her face orange OR Her face also became orange)

she ~~looked like~~ really strange > looked

Mona ~~looked an~~ orange balloon > looked like an

Mona ~~got to be~~ very upset > got

I just ~~kept to be~~ quiet > kept

make it ~~look like~~ better > look

Q 相同的主语 [3]
　　相同的主语和动词 [5]
　　相同的主语和助动词 [4]
　　相同的动词和宾语 [7]
　　与后面重复的宾语和 / 或介词短语 [6]
　　补充 [8]
　　选择 [11]
　　并列 [9]
　　否定意思的并列 [10]
　　关系从句 [14]
　　名词性从句 [13]
　　状语从句 [15]
　　后面加一个逗号 [16]

R 1 (**c**) or … and
　　2 (**d**) or (OR and)
　　3 (**a**) but … and
　　4 (**b**) and

S 1 we talked, he got
　　2 she came, talked
　　3 It seemed, got, had
　　4 came, we had
　　5 it stopped, seemed

T 1 heartbeat　　6 heart-throb　　11 which
　　2 or　　　　　7 who　　　　　12 and
　　3 as　　　　　8 and　　　　　13 Heartburn
　　4 Heartbreak　9 whom　　　　14 which
　　5 because　　10 heart attack

U 1 who　　4 tell　　7 but
　　2 live　　5 if　　8 because
　　3 and　　6 see　　9 don't like

测验

A 1 d　　2 b　　3 b　　4 d　　5 c

B 1 C (contained)
　　2 C (prefers)
　　3 D (put £20 in …)
　　4 D (show it to me OR show me it)
　　5 C (made all the young people happy)

C 1 begins in November
　　2 include fever
　　3 catch the flu
　　4 give it
　　5 sneezes

D 1 Nick admitted to one of the detectives that he had taken the cash box.
　　2 The police persuaded us that it was too dangerous and we were convinced.
　　3 The frog suddenly turned into a prince after the princess kissed him.
　　4 He told us that two hours wouldn't (OR won't) be enough to finish the job.
　　5 Someone painted the wall white yesterday.

E 1 were ready
　　2 seemed quite satisfied
　　3 stood alone
　　4 is better
　　5 became clear

2 时态（tense）

A 1 For several years he will have **been** trying to turn a good idea … (**line 4**)
　　OR He won't **be** doing anything special … (**line 6**)
　　2 For several years he will **have** been trying … (**line 4**)
　　OR … his business venture won't **have** made any money for most of the past year. (**line 8**)

B 1 B　　2 E　　3 D　　4 A　　5 C

C 从下列每项的例子中任选一个。

祈使语气或动词不定式: turn (**A**), celebrate (**A**), do (**A, B, C**), pay (**B, D**), make (**B, D, E**), become (**B**), Imagine (**C**), write (**C**), get (**C**), download (**C**), be (**D**), create (**D**), work (**E**)

一般现在时（动词原形）: need (**C**)

一般现在时（第三人称单数形式）: is (**A**), wants (**D**), has (**E**)

现在进行时: are applying (**C**), am writing (**C**), is (always) counting (**E**), is having (**E**)

现在完成时: has asked (**C**), have known (**C**), has thought (**E**)

现在完成进行时: have been trying (**C**)

一般过去时: started (**B**), sold (**B**), met (**B**), showed (**B**), created (**B, E**), established (**B**), set (**B**), found (**C, E**), needed (**C**), were (**D**), didn't think (**D**), discovered (**D**), turned (**D**), tried (**D**), had (**D**), didn't (really) make (**D**), did (**E**), went (**E**)

过去进行时: were starting (**B**), were looking (**C**), weren't learning (**C**), was working (**D**), was doing (**D**)

过去完成时: had seemed (**B**), had used (**B**)

过去完成进行时: had been writing (**B**), (had been) selling (**B**), had been creating (**B**)

表示将来: will (soon) need (**A**), won't be (**E**)

将来进行时: won't be doing (**A**)

将来完成时: won't have made (**A**)

将来完成进行时: will have been trying (**A**)

D A 1 tell   2 says   3 has   4 is
  B 5 look   6 are   7 live   8 move   9 resemble
  C 10 'm (OR am) looking   11 isn't   12 Do … know
    13 're (OR are) repairing   14 's (OR is) using

E 1 has won … has said … hat-trick
  2 also-ran … has taken … has not finished
  3 has heard … has-been … has trained
  4 no-show … has bought … hasn't come

F 1 have … known (**c**) 've (OR have) been
  2 (**b**) 've (OR have) … been swimming
  3 Have … completed (**d**) 've (OR have) … done
  4 Have … shown (**a**) 's (OR has) been reading

G ~~She is living~~ here since 2012 > She's (OR She has) lived OR She's (OR She has) been living
  ~~she has been going~~ back > she's (OR she has) gone
  ~~She's having~~ an accent > She has
  people who ~~are coming~~ from France > come
  ~~I never ask her~~ > I've (OR I have) never asked her
  if she ~~is speaking~~ French > speaks
  She ~~is really liking~~ to go to the theatre > really likes
  ~~she is inviting~~ me > she's (OR she has) invited OR she invited
  In the short time ~~I'm knowing~~ her > I've (OR I have) known
  ~~we become~~ good friends > we've (OR we have) become

H A 1 came   2 said   3 were making
  B 4 broke   5 stole   6 was teaching   7 saw
  C 8 explained   9 understood   10 was talking

D 11 didn't get   12 missed   13 was wondering
    (OR wondered)

I 1 had planned (OR had been planning)
  2 had been
  3 had broken
  4 had caught
  5 had been living (OR had lived)
  6 had been taking (OR removing)
  7 had made
  8 had … removed (OR taken)
  9 had … had

J ~~we sometimes stop~~ > we sometimes stopped (OR we would sometimes stop)
  If it wasn't ~~rain~~ > raining
  ~~we just sleep~~ outside > we just slept (OR we would just sleep)
  We really ~~enjoying~~ that > enjoyed
  If it ~~was rain~~ > was raining (OR rained)
  and ~~crawl~~ inside > crawled
  while we ~~sleep~~ in the tent > were sleeping
  I ~~think~~ > thought
  the ground ~~moving~~ under me > was moving (OR moved)
  I ~~sit~~ up > sat
  and I ~~realize~~ > realized
  the tent ~~was try~~ to move > was trying
  ~~was hold~~ it in place > was holding
  When we ~~get~~ outside > got
  we ~~discover~~ > discovered
  that we ~~stand~~ > were standing
  our tent ~~slowly floats~~ away > was slowly floating
  ~~we really surprised~~ > we were really surprised
  then we ~~think~~ > thought
  it ~~is~~ very funny > was

K A 1 started   2 've (OR have) … met
  B 3 Have … heard   4 have … become   5 had
  C 6 told   7 've (OR have) had   8 hasn't come

L 1 asked   6 didn't know
  2 were   7 didn't call
  3 didn't seem   8 've (OR have) had
  4 did … say   9 haven't eaten
  5 told   10 's (OR has) made

M 1 needed (**b**) gave
  2 said (**a**) had talked
  3 came (**d**) hadn't finished
  4 (**c**) had worked

N 1 was   7 went
  2 had … reached   8 didn't eat*
  3 were   9 was
  4 hadn't … locked   10 had cooked
  5 didn't lock   11 have gone
  6 hadn't eaten*   12 explained

*第 6 题和第 8 题答案可互换。

O 给出或询问与将来有关的信息 [2]
  未来可能出现的行动 [1]

将来某特定时间正在进行的行为 [5]
计划或打算 [4]
已经完成 [7]
从某一时间开始一直持续到该时间 [6]
根据过去的经验或已有知识作出的预测 [10]
用在预测条件句中 [9]
根据现在的感受或想法作出的预测 [8]
在过去作出的预测 [11]
已经作好的决定 [12]
当时作出的决定 [13]
按计划表、时间表将会发生的事 [16]
将来的行为 [15]
已经计划好或安排好将要做的事 [14]

P 1 will be (**b**) 'll (OR will) have been
2 will (**d**) Will … be
3 will be (**a**) 'll (OR will) have been
4 will be (**c**) 'll (OR will) have been

Q 1 wasn't going to stop (OR wouldn't stop)
2 don't start
3 'll be (OR 'm going) to be
4 'll give
5 make

R 1 or ~~I report~~ you > or I'll (OR I will) report
2 Let's get together for lunch sometime, ~~will~~ we? >
shall
3 '~~I do it!~~' > I'll do
4 Matt McGuire ~~will spend~~ five years > will have spent
5 ~~I'm~~ going to work > I was
6 Do you think she'll ~~go~~ to bed already? > have gone
7 I guess ~~it's raining~~ later > it'll rain (OR it's going to
rain)
8 those that we think ~~about to~~ be available > are about
to (OR will OR are going to)
9 you'll ~~sit~~ on a plane > be sitting
10 If ~~I'll find~~ > I find
~~I download~~ them > I'll download
11 ~~Will Stefan to get~~ these boxes later > Is Stefan to get
(OR Will Stefan get)
~~is to take~~ them now? > is he to take (OR will he take
OR is he taking)
12 before ~~it'll close~~ > it closes
or the parcel ~~doesn't~~ arrive > won't

测验

A 1 c   2 a   3 d   4 b   5 a

B 1 D (is having)   4 A (make)
2 A (used)   5 C (had put)
3 C (knew)

C 1 was walking   5 saw
2 thinking   6 whispered
3 were looking   7 wasn't wearing
4 had decided   8 hadn't changed

D 1 By the time we sell the car, we will have spent £300
on repairs.
2 This is the first time I have (ever) had to think about
my health.
3 Juliet has been working (or has worked) here
for about six years.
4 It's even worse than I thought it would be.
5 It was Christmas when I (last) talked to my parents.

E 1 is … happening   7 have created
2 have been   8 lets
3 be experiencing   9 holds
4 had   10 Will … keep
5 believe
6 have … been changing OR have
been … changing

3 情态动词（modal）

A 1 should never (**line 6**)
OR won't (**line 65**)
2 We **may** be told, for example, that we **should** never
open an umbrella indoors because that **will** bring
bad luck. (**line 6**)

B 1 E   2 C   3 D   4 A   5 B

C We aren't told why or what kind of bad thing **might**
happen to us, but few of us **are going to** try to find out.
(**line 8**)
Others **will** say that seeing a black cat **is supposed to**
be lucky. (**line 38**)
This is usually heard when people talk about their good
luck or when they are hoping that they **will be able to**
get or do something they want. (**line 54**)

D 1 be … have
2 be … be
3 be … have
4 have … have been

E 1 预测: But we would probably have been asked to
leave the restaurant.
2 意愿、习惯和偏好: I would have hated to have to
buy a new one.
3 能力: We could easily have chatted for another hour.
4 许可: Children may not be left alone in the
playground.
5 可能性: I was glad that my old laptop could be
repaired.
6 必要性: They must be accompanied by an adult.
7 推论: I guess he must have forgotten about it.
8 义务和建议: He should be helping you clear out the
garage.

F 1 going to (**c**) must be
2 can't (**b**) must have
3 ought (**a**) won't
4 may have been (**d**) able to

G 1 advisable, shouldn't
2 inevitable, will

3 reluctant, wouldn't
4 inconceivable, can't
5 hypothetical, might

H I ~~didn't could~~ do that > couldn't
I knew I ~~will~~ have to quit my job > would
I ~~have~~ much less money > would have
I ~~don't should~~ give up such a good job > shouldn't
I couldn't ~~decided~~ > decide
what I ~~ought do~~ > ought to do
she ~~should go~~ to university > should have gone
I ~~should to give~~ it a try > should give
I ~~didn't should~~ be afraid > shouldn't
she ~~may can~~ help me pay > might be able to

I 1 would
2 I'd
3 I'm going to
4 would have
5 I was going to
6 Shall
7 you'll
8 won't
9 I'll

J 1 wouldn't start … pushed
2 'd (OR would) like … 'd (OR would)… have
3 'd (OR would) …play … will … stay
4 'll (OR will) …be … 'd (OR would) hate
5 won't (OR will not) need … 'll (OR will) have eaten (OR eat)
6 would be … wouldn't say

K 1 can't (OR cannot OR aren't able to) fly … can (OR are able to) … swimming
2 unflappable … can (OR is able to) stay
3 numb … couldn't (OR wasn't able to) feel
4 illiterate … can't (OR cannot OR aren't able to) read
5 successful … been able to … tried OR has tried
6 managed … were able to … difficult

L 1 couldn't
2 could
3 could
4 can

M 1 be allowed to (**f**)
2 Can (**a**)
3 be allowed to (**e**)
4 can (OR may) (**b**)
5 be allowed to (**d**)

N Of course, you ~~could~~ > can
she ~~isn't being able to~~ do her own work > isn't able to (OR can't)
she ~~can have said~~ > could have said (OR can say)
Sorry, but you ~~can not~~ > can't / cannot
how ~~do they could~~ do their work > could they (OR can they)
I knew that I ~~can~~ have tried > could
I didn't think ~~I'll can~~ change how she behaved > I could

O 1 may be … disqualified
2 undecided … may … may not
3 potential … might not
4 may not … feasible
5 theoretical … might

P 1 can't imagine

2 could be
3 couldn't be sent
4 could have been avoided
5 could have been saved

Q 1 They ~~can~~ be going to > may / might / could
2 George ~~can~~ still need > may / might / could
3 You ~~may~~ be hanged > might / could
4 These people ~~can~~ have > may / might
5 ~~May~~ someone tell me > Can / Could
6 we really ~~might not~~ believe > can't / cannot / could not / couldn't
7 if you ~~may~~ be willing > might
8 the weather ~~can~~ be > may / might / could
9 ~~May~~ the children > Could

R 1 step … have to
2 fruit … mustn't
3 must / have to … command
4 obligation … don't have to
5 duty-free … don't have to
6 taboo … mustn't
7 evil … have to

S 1 needn't have … unnecessary
2 mustn't … allowed
3 need to … official
4 having to … significant
5 must … impossible

T 1 so you ~~mustn't~~ clean them > don't have to
2 Everyone will ~~have got to~~ go > have to
3 I'll ~~need get~~ some aspirin > need to get (OR have to get)
4 I ~~must to~~ find a replacement > must (OR have to)
5 customers ~~needn't to~~ leave > don't need to (OR needn't)
6 we ~~had got to~~ take a taxi > had to
7 the one ~~to must have to~~ tell him > to have to (OR who must (OR has to))
8 you ~~don't need be~~ over 21 > don't need to (OR have to) be
9 we ~~must~~ go > had to
10 we ~~needn't have to wait~~ > needn't have waited (OR didn't need to wait)

U 1 (**d**) must
2 (**c**) must be
3 (**e**) must have
4 (**a**) can't have
5 (**b**) can't

V 1 must have taken
2 must have been
3 couldn't have done
4 couldn't have carried (OR couldn't carry)
5 must have put
6 must be losing

W 1 had better
2 umbrella
3 shouldn't
4 ladder
5 should be
6 should have

7 shoulder
8 ought not
9 mirror
10 cat
11 is supposed to

测验

A 1 d   2 a   3 a   4 c   5 a

B 1 A (may)
2 D (ought not to be)
3 D (would)
4 C (can)
5 A (had)

C 1 may not be familiar
2 can be used
3 must be paid
4 won't be required
5 will be charged

D 1 Students are not allowed to park here. (OR Students are not permitted to park here.)
2 His trip may have been cancelled at the last minute.
3 She didn't enjoy having to get up at five o'clock every morning.
4 He couldn't have committed the crime, according to the report.
5 This shirt shouldn't have been (OR ought not to have been) put in the washing machine.

E 1 might*
2 couldn't
3 was able to
4 would
5 be able to
6 would*
7 be willing to
8 had to
9 should
10 was … going to
*第 1 题和第 6 题答案可互换。

4 否定句（negative）和疑问句（question）

A 1 Is there anything else? (**line 29**)
OR Is it a weapon? (**line 44**)
2 She **wasn't** seriously injured, but it really frightened her and she **wouldn't** go out alone. (**line 4**)

B 1 G*   2 E   3 H*   4 F   5 D
*第 1 题和第 3 题答案可互换。

C 1 She wasn't seriously injured, but it really frightened her and she **wouldn't** go out alone. (**line 4**)
OR For example, women with longer hair are more likely to be attacked than women whose hair is shorter or in a style that **can't** be grabbed. (**line 25**)

2 We advise people **not to go** alone to parking areas and garages … (**line 38**)
3 **Who** can take part? (**line 11**)

D Well, it isn't much of a weapon, **is it?** (**line 45**)

E 1 isn't … non-resident
2 not … non-event
3 Non-refundable … doesn't
4 nondescript … no
5 non-stop … won't

F 1 Why don't
2 Where did
3 What do
4 When were
5 Whose … are

G we ~~didn't really could~~ say much > really couldn't (OR couldn't really)
What ~~you think~~ is the best pet? > do you think
I ~~not care~~ about pets > don't care
Why ~~we have~~ pets? > do we have
We ~~not need~~ them for anything > don't need
~~don't~~ we? > do
some people think dogs ~~not clean~~ > aren't clean
so ~~they not~~ good pets > they're not (OR they aren't)
~~does he~~? > do they
He didn't ~~answered~~ > answer
she ~~could have not~~ a cat > couldn't have (OR could not have)
Why ~~do some people can't~~ have pets? > can't some people
~~Do~~ some pets more expensive to keep > Are
How ~~will be trained the pet~~? > will the pet be trained
Who ~~is take care~~ of the pet? > takes care (OR will take care)

H 1 (**c**) none   3 No (**a**) not
2 (**d**) none   4 not (**b**) no

I 1 doesn't   5 not   9 never
2 carefree   6 invisible   10 indifferent
3 nothing   7 no one   11 no
4 careless   8 infallible

J 1 There has (OR There's) never been a better chance to make money on the stock market.
2 We didn't notice until the next morning that she hadn't come home. (OR We didn't notice that she hadn't come home until the next morning.)
3 No one (OR Nobody) warned us at any time about polluted water. (OR No one / Nobody warned us about polluted water at any time.)
4 The janitor will say, 'Don't smoke in here,' won't he?

K 1 had I   5 I had   9 did I
2 Not only   6 nothing   10 Not until
3 were they   7 no idea   11 did we
4 they were   8 Nor

L 1 (**d**) Which   3 (**a**) What   5 (**b**) Which
2 (**f**) What   4 (**c**) What   6 (**e**) Which

M 1 How often (**C**)
   2 What … from (**A**)
   3 With whom (**C**)
   4 Which of (**B**)
   5 Where … from (**A**)
   6 Who … by (**C**)
   7 What … for (**C**)

N 1 Who else
   2 What … about
   3 Whatever
   4 Where
   5 How long
   6 Where exactly
   7 Which … in
   8 Where … from
   9 How ever

O 1 Who do you believe is responsible for the current conflict?
   2 Where did her father think she might have gone?
   3 When did the weather forecaster say the rain should stop?
   4 What do you imagine their new house is going to look like?

P 1 (**c**) Who
   2 (**e**) Do … Why
   3 (**d**) didn't … did
   4 (**b**) How
   5 (**a**) Does … which

Q 1 He's   5 you're   9 he did
   2 Is he   6 you don't   10 I do
   3 he was   7 was he   11 don't you
   4 do I   8 did he

测验

A 1 b   2 a   3 d   4 c   5 a

B 1 C (did he ask)
   2 D (no longer take)
   3 D (didn't you)
   4 C (do they)
   5 B (not an)

C 1 Aren't   3 no   5 Can't
   2 what   4 I'm not

D 1 Not only was the room cold, it was also very damp.
   2 Who did your sister say she gave the money to?
   3 What does Andreas think has been stolen?
   4 She said, 'Why don't you (OR Why not) take the train instead of driving?'
   5 They asked me what his name was and where he lived.

E 1 Nothing
   2 never
   3 no
   4 What … YZ-23

5 Why … Leisure
6 Who … Somebody else
7 Did … Yes
8 which … London
9 Where … New York
10 How … None

5 被动（passive）

A will find (**line 30**); were found (**line 45**)
have been moving (**line 25**); had been moved (**line 17**)

B 1 have been … injured
   2 have been left
   3 was hit
   4 were (OR have been) destroyed
   5 were (OR have been) buried / trapped
   6 have blocked
   7 have had to be flown in
   8 are going to be felt

C 1 … the apple blossoms that **are** always **shaken** loose from the trees … (**line 4**)
   OR … and (**are**) **blown** along the country roads. (**line 5**)
   OR The scenes of devastation this morning **are described** by one rescue worker as 'like the end of the world'. (**line 22**)
   2 The names of all victims **are being withheld** until their families can be notified. (**line 50**)
   3 … small towns … **have been hit** by storms every spring. (**line 1**)
   OR … the roads **have been blocked** by dozens of fallen trees. (**line 28**)
   OR About 100 people **have been** seriously **injured** … (**line 54**)
   OR … more than 1,000 **have been left** homeless. (**line 55**)
   4 … the Clintons **were found** alive by rescuers this morning. (**line 45**)
   OR Tragically, they **were** both **killed** when part of a wall crashed through the floor on top of them. (**line 48**)
   5 Other buildings where tractors and equipment **were being stored** seem to have been completely blown away. (**line 18**)
   6 Herds of cattle that **had been moved** into barns for safety are nowhere to be seen, nor are the barns. (**line 16**)

D 1 to be (**e**)   3 been (**f**)   5 been (**b**)
   2 be (**d**)   4 be (**a**)

E 1 are expected
   2 were left
   3 are blocked (OR were blocked OR have been blocked)
   4 were knocked
   5 was flooded (OR is flooded)
   6 to be rescued
   7 are closed

8 were injured (OR have been injured OR are injured)

9 were reported (OR have been reported)

F 1 The house can't be seen from the street.

2 He said our papers wouldn't (OR won't) be corrected before Friday.

3 The towels must have been taken out of the dryer.

4 Your books aren't going to be stolen from this room.

5 I didn't enjoy being told what to do all the time.

G 1 is also called

2 is believed

3 may have been convicted

4 have been shown

5 had been sentenced

6 was released

7 has also been used

8 would never have been solved

H 1 Erin was seen outside the theatre as she was waiting to go in. She had a new hairstyle.

2 Karen feels sad because she wasn't promoted (OR hasn't been promoted) and she has to carry on as if nothing happened.

3 The ball is thrown to Evans (OR Evans is thrown the ball). Evans tries to go past Jennings, but he is stopped (by Jennings). It's a foul.

I 1 impossible (**a**)

2 inexplicable (**b**)

3 knowledgeable (**b**)

4 illegible (**b**)

5 inaudible (**a**)

6 unspeakable (**b**)

7 reusable (**a**), (**b**)

J just after my younger sister ~~born~~ > was born

Lots of people ~~were come~~ > came

I ~~gave~~ the job > was given

As each guest ~~was arrived~~ > arrived

I ~~handed~~ boxes > was handed

which ~~filled~~ with things > were filled

that ~~wrapped~~ in Christmas paper > were wrapped

I ~~told~~ which ones > was told

and which ones ~~had to be place~~ > had to be placed (OR I had to place)

So many presents ~~brought~~ for us > were brought

the experience of ~~given~~ so much > being given

K 不关注这一行为的施动者 [1]

不知道是谁实施了这些行为，或认为该信息不重要 [2]

受某行为影响的人或事物 [3]

两个或更多个句子谈论的主题 [5]

对同一个主语造成影响的多个行为 [4]

规则和警告 [9]

描述步骤，特别是用于研究报告 [7]

正式书面报告中 [8]

避免提出针对个人的命令 [11]

不想表明所说之事只与说话者自身或个人行为有关 [10]

由他人作出的陈述、提出的问题 [13]

给出的命令和要求 [12]

撇清自己和所述信息的关系 [14]

可以将……用在这种结构中 [15]

不清楚所述的当前事件真实与否 [17]

如果是过去的事，……完成式 [18]

L You can only consult reference books in the library.

You must obtain special permission to use them outside the library.

You should return all books on time or you will have to pay a fine.

If you do not pay the fine, you will lose borrowing rights.

You may not borrow library books for others or give them to others.

If you lose a book, you must pay the cost of replacement.

M 1 are (OR were) said to be

2 were told not to use

3 is (OR was) reported to have died

4 wasn't mentioned … were received

N It has been claimed that tasks cannot be used successfully with beginner-level students.

The following study was designed so that that claim could be investigated.

Two groups of students were created, each with different proficiency levels.

They were given a task in which they were shown a set of pictures and asked to tell a story. (OR A task was given to them … a set of pictures was shown to them … they were asked …)

They were recorded as they spoke and then their stories were examined.

O 1 is considered by

2 was established by

3 are filled with

4 are performed … were experienced by

5 were not written by

P 1 were defeated (**d**) reacted

2 were smashed (**c**) were stolen

3 get caught (**b**) get beaten up

4 were treated (**a**) were reported

Q 1 opened

2 stopped

3 crashed

4 was knocked

5 was carried

6 ran

7 exploded

8 shook

9 was handed

10 get … injured

施动者: (**5**) the surging crowd, (**6**) I, (**9**) the old woman

测验

A 1 d   2 a   3 c   4 c   5 c

B 1 C (married)
   2 D (crashed)
   3 B (had been locked with a special key)
   4 C (being repaired OR which were being repaired
      OR which had been repaired)
   5 B (was (OR is) located)

C 1 is experienced
   2 was believed (OR considered)
   3 were bitten by (OR had been bitten by)
   4 could be cured by
   5 was … recommended by
   6 is … considered (OR believed)
   7 may (OR might) be said

D 1 There's a saying that Rome wasn't built in a day.
   2 The tests have been collected and the answers (have been) checked.
   3 Death is more likely to be caused by a bee sting than a snake bite these days.
   4 There were reported to be serious problems with the new design.
   5 We weren't given instructions or shown what to do. (OR We weren't given any instructions … OR We were given no instructions nor shown …)

E 1 n   3 o   5 h   7 i
   2 b   4 c   6 l   8 e

6 冠词（article）和名词（noun）

A 1 True   4 8 million   7 80 per cent
   2 True   5 False   8 True
   3 False   6 True

B 1 an accident (**line 22**)
   2 the United States (**line 9**)

C 从下列每项的例子中任选一个。
   1 Europe (**line 8**)
   2 a … crash (**line 10**), a (…) flight (**lines 15, 16**), a factor (**line 18**), a smoke hood (**line 32**), a fire (**line 33**)
   3 the airport (**line 5**), the flight (**lines 6, 17**), the chance (**line 9**), the (…) exit (**lines 23, 25, 26**), the number (**line 24**), the … door (**line 27**), the … person (**line 28**), the plane (**line 32**), the hood (**line 33**)
   4 car (**line 4**)
   5 the … forms (**line 1**), The … planes (**line 7**), the … jets (**line 7**), the … airlines (**line 8**), the … parts (**line 14**), the people (**line 19**)
   6 … jets (**line 1**), … planes (**lines 11, 12**), accidents (**line 13**), seats (**line 25**), clothes (**line 28**), … fibres (**line 29**), … materials (**line 30**), … gases (**line 34**)
   7 The duration (**line 17**), the dark (**line 26**), the skin (**line 31**)

8 Flying (**line 1**), transportation (**line 2**), travelling (**line 3**), air (**line 3**), survival (**line 21**), cotton (**line 29**), wool (**line 30**), smoke (**line 34**)

D 用 a / an 来表达它们所属的类别 [1]
   用 the 来明确地指出该对象 [2]
   用于将所谈论的事物分类 [3]
   谈论某类事物中的任意一例 [4]
   工作 [6]
   信仰 [5]
   按定义对事物进行分类 [9]
   描述某种特征 [8]
   该类事物中的一例 [7]
   日常生活中的 [11]
   自然界中的 [10]
   职业 [12]
   某种独一无二的社会角色 [14]
   用在表示专业机构的名词前 [13]
   发明物、乐器 [16]
   泛指某类人、事物或动物 [15]
   含 of 的介词短语 [19]
   关系从句 [18]
   形容词最高级和强调形容词（如 main, first）之前 [17]

E 1 the   7 the   13 a
   2 the   8 an   14 a
   3 –   9 a   15 a
   4 –   10 the   16 –
   5 the   11 the   17 –
   6 the   12 the   18 –

F 1 (f) the   3 (a) the   5 (c) a
   2 (d) a   4 (e) the   6 (b) the

G 1 a   6 –   11 –
   2 the   7 a   12 –
   3 a   8 the   13 –
   4 the   9 –   14 the
   5 the   10 a   15 a

H I was starting to ~~learn the English~~ > learn English
   He was from Cardiff ~~in the Wales~~ > in Wales
   He was always ~~making the jokes~~ > making jokes
   One day he ~~wrote words~~ > wrote the words
   ~~on blackboard~~ > on the blackboard
   I offered to ~~answer question~~ > answer the question
   changed ~~to the A~~ > to A (OR to an A)
   that ~~was good answer~~ > was a good answer
   he ~~changed letter~~ > changed the letter
   happy ~~with new spelling~~ > with the new spelling
   ~~With the absolute confidence~~ > With absolute confidence
   I looked round ~~in the confusion~~ > in confusion
   it ~~needed second M~~ > needed a second M
   it should have ~~the M~~ too > an M
   nodded with ~~the smile~~ > a smile
   I still ~~remember terrible feeling~~ > remember the terrible feeling
   feeling ~~of the embarrassment~~ > of embarrassment

I

1 a	6 a	11 a
2 a	7 a OR –	12 a
3 a	8 –	13 –
4 one	9 a	14 –
5 One	10 –	15 an

J

1 an	11 –	21 –
2 –	12 –	22 –
3 –	13 a (OR the)	23 –
4 –	14 –	24 a
5 –	15 the	25 the
6 an	16 the (OR –)	26 the
7 –	17 –	27 –
8 a	18 –	28 –
9 a	19 the	29 the
10 a	20 the	30 –

K

1 –	11 the	21 a
2 –	12 a (OR the)	22 one (OR –)
3 a	13 the (OR a)	23 the
4 a	14 a	24 an
5 one	15 the	25 an
6 one	16 the	26 the
7 an (OR –)	17 the	27 the
8 –	18 a	28 the
9 a (OR one)	19 the	29 –
10 one	20 the	30 –

L

人、生物、物体 [1]
行为、事件 [2]
物质和材料 [5]
抽象的概念、品性和状态 [4]
活动 [3]
单个事物 [7]
一种物质或笼统概念 [8]
不可数名词 [9]
可数的名词短语 [10]

M

1 government	7 a mixture
2 a country	8 cereal*
3 a … piece	9 nuts*
4 toast	10 – … fruit
5 – … bread	11 milk
6 soup	12 breakfast

* *第 8 题和第 9 题答案可互换。*

N

1 outskirts … are (e)	4 Binoculars are (a)
2 press is (d)	5 is (c) fortnight
3 Mathematics is (b)	

O

为某个特定的人或物所有 [1]
不表示所有关系 [2]
人或其他生物 [5]
团体或机构 [6]
时间 [7]
地点 [4]
将抽象的概念当作人来看待 [8]
将一个物体描述为某事物的"所有者" [9]
知道某名词所有格后面的名词是什么 [11]
非某特定个体的形式出现 [10]
当某事物是另一事物的一部分时 [13]
正在描述过程、想法或行为时 [12]
当所有者以一个长短语表示时 [14]
应用对象 [16]
构成材料 [18]
具体工作 [15]
所属类型 [17]
发生或应用的地点或时间 [19]
使用连字符（ - ） [20]

P

1 Life's troubles
2 worries of each day
3 morning's special news
4 world's problems
5 woman's love
6 Mother's Day

Q 第一部分

1 consumer groups
2 credit cards
3 college student
4 credit card offers
5 application forms
6 give-aways
7 T-shirts
8 bottom line
9 high-risk borrowers
10 credit rating
11 interest rates
12 sense of responsibility
13 money matters
14 buy-now-pay-later world

第二部分
parents' willingness; children's credit card debt

R

1 a … job … an … restaurant … the pay
2 an … bicycle … The shop owner
3 the teacher … the board
4 a film … The price

S

1 The	5 The	9 a
2 the	6 the	10 the
3 –	7 a	11 the
4 –	8 the	12 the

T

1 a (d) the	5 a (a)	9 – (b)
2 – (j) the	6 a (h)	10 – (e) a
3 the (f)	7 A (c)	
4 one (g) –	8 a (i) –	

U 4 – 2 – 1 – 5 – 3 – 6 – 9 – 8 – 7

测验

A 1 d   2 b   3 c   4 b   5 b

B
1 B (is)
2 D (tennis)
3 B (research)
4 C (pairs of trousers)
5 C (devices)

C 1 the   5 the   9 an   13 the
     2 a   6 –   10 –   14 –
     3 the   7 the   11 –   15 the
     4 the   8 a   12 –   16 the

D 1 Yesterday, a masked man robbed a woman outside a (OR the) post office.
     2 In business news, the Bank of England is raising (OR will raise) interest rates by 1.5 per cent (OR %).
     3 Yesterday's news of the murder of a priest in Kent (has) shocked the community.
     4 Reviewers have criticized a new account of Scottish history by an English writer.

E 1 the middle of the century
     2 The urgency of the challenges
     3 the authors of the report (OR the report's authors)
     4 Sims' (OR Sims's OR The Sims) organization
     5 the health of the earth
     6 the group's latest report
     7 the world's population (OR the population of the world)
     8 the destruction of the environment

7 限定词（determiner）和数量词（quantifier）

A 1 all these changes (**line 27**)
     2 all cars (**lines 11, 18, 53**)

B 1 C   2 E   3 D   4 A   5 B

C 1 that car (**line 17**)
     this area (**line 20**)
     those old farms (**line 23**)
     these changes (**line 27**)
     OR those Saturday trips (**line 37**)
     2 从下列五组例子中任选四组，每组任选一个例子。
     my grandfather (**lines 1, 5, 30, 39**) OR my grandmother (**lines 2, 7, 27**) OR my eyes (**line 3**) OR my grandparents (**lines 19, 26**) OR my driveway (**line 50**)
     their voices (**line 4**) OR their lifetimes (**line 20**)
     our return (**line 37**) OR our accident (**line 38**) OR our driveway (**lines 42, 45**)
     his thoughts (**line 43**) OR his window (**line 48**)
     your house (**line 51**)

D 1 a little, much
     2 each, every, one
     3 a few, both, many, several, ten

E 从下列例子中任选四个。
     a lot of other cars (**line 8**)
     Both of my grandparents (**line 19**)
     lots of new houses (**line 23**)
     one of them (**line 26**)
     some of the problems (**line 32**)
     one of those Saturday trips (**line 37**)

F A 1 these   2 my   3 those   4 his

     B 5 this   6 that   7 our   8 a few
     C 9 much   10 the   11 his   12 some
     D 13 some   14 30   15 most   16 a little
     E 17 a   18 both   19 each   20 half

G 1 maximum … much
     2 quota … many
     3 unanimous … every
     4 lottery … any
     5 majority … most

H ~~One of boys~~ fell > One of the boys
     ~~twisted the ankle~~ badly > twisted his ankle
     ~~Most them~~ stayed > Most of them
     ~~with injured~~ boy > with the injured
     while ~~two the older boys~~ left > two of the older boys
     ~~this two boys~~ didn't know > these two boys
     walking round ~~in big circle~~ > in a big circle
     for ~~a few hour~~ > a few hours
     back with ~~his friends~~ > their friends
     ~~each boys~~ had brought some water > each boy (OR each of the boys)
     ~~all them~~ managed to survive > all of them (OR they all)

I 与复数名词和不可数名词连用 [1]
     用作代词 [2]
     谈论具体的人或物 [3]
     肯定句 [5]
     期望得到肯定回答的提问或主动提议 [4]
     含有否定意思的句子 [7]
     不期望得到具体回答的问句 [6]
     if 从句 [9]
     表达 "任何一个，无论哪个" [8]
     一个相当大的数量 [10]
     一个大约的数字或百分比 [12]
     身份或名称不详的人、地点或事物 [11]
     强调 "not any" [13]
     用 no, 不用 not any [14]
     用在单数形式或复数形式的名词之前 [16]
     用作代词, 且可与 of 短语连用 [15]

J 1 (c) any   3 (b) no   5 (a) some
     2 (f) any   4 (e) any   6 (d) some

K 1 There was some woman here yesterday asking if we had any old clothes, but I told her we didn't (have any).
     2 Some (OR Some of the) information in that newspaper article was incorrect. There aren't any wolves or bears in Scotland.
     3 I've managed to find some dry paper to start a fire, but I can't light it. Don't you have any matches?
     4 I'm sure I made some mistakes when I was typing. If you find any mistakes, please correct them.

L 1 no   4 any   7 any
     2 any   5 no   8 no
     3 some   6 some   9 any

M 1 empty … none
     2 uninhabited … some … none

3 some … any … extinct
4 no … scoreless
5 dead … no

N 1 (b) whole   3 (a) both
   2 (d) half   4 (c) All

O 1 no   4 Both of   7 half
   2 none of   5 both   8 whole
   3 one of   6 all of   9 one of

P 1 twins … neither   4 quarterly … every
   2 choice … either   5 doubles … each
   3 couple … neither

Q 1 There hasn't been much discussion of the new road, but (many (of the)) older village residents are against it.
   2 Did you ask how much these postcards cost? How many (of them) are you going to buy?
   3 I'll be (much) later today because I have so many different places to go to and there's so much traffic in town.
   4 I asked my classmates if they did much (of the) homework and many (of them) said they didn't do much (of it) unless there was a test.

R 1 Many   4 Many … much
   2 much of   5 many of
   3 many of

S 1 (d) most of   4 most (c) most
   2 (f) more of   5 most of (b)
   3 more (a) more 6 (e) more of

T 1 many   4 more
   2 more   5 more
   3 many   6 much

U 1 few (d) a few   4 few (a) little
   2 a little (e) a few of 5 a little (c) a few
   3 (b) a little of

V 1 a quarter of   4 twice as
   2 Once a   5 twenty per cent of the
   3 two-fifths of an 6 four times the

W 1 little   4 fewer
   2 a few   5 fifty per cent
   3 fewest

测验

A 1 c   2 c   3 b   4 c   5 c

B 1 D (some of their friends)
   2 C (either colour OR either of the colours)
   3 C (a little information OR some information)
   4 A (all of them OR they all)
   5 A (most of Europe)

C 1 a lot of   3 some   5 the
   2 both   4 neither 6 a little

D 1 Not many people are willing to help others.
   2 Half the report (OR Half of the report) has been written already.
   3 No explanation was given (to us) for the delay.
   4 All of us want to live forever.

E 1 a great deal of
   2 many
   3 more
   4 little
   5 no
   6 Most of
   7 88 per cent
   8 51 per cent of
   9 twice
   10 most

8 代词（pronoun），代替（substitution）和省略（ellipsis）

A 1 **it's** as if you've known each other all your lives (**line 26**)
   OR She took his right hand and placed **it** against hers, palms touching (**line 33**)
   2 She took his right hand and _ placed it against hers, palms touching. (**line 33**)
   OR She matched left hands now and _ fell sideways to the bed laughing. (**line 44**)

B 1 D   2 C   3 E   4 A   5 B

C 1 they, we (**C**)
   2 hers, mine, yours* (**E**)
   * *注意 E 篇第一行中 his right hand 的 his 是限定词而非代词。见第 83 页。*

D You meet **someone** for the first time, and it's as if you've known each other all your lives. (**line 25**) **Everything** goes smoothly. (**line 27**)

E 1 yours   3 his   5 that … this
   2 they   4 it … him

F 1 You know that you shouldn't use a phone while you're driving.
   2 I heard that they're going to demolish this old factory so (that) they can build a new school.
   3 If you're self-indulgent, you allow yourself to do or have too much of what you like.
   4 I think that we shouldn't criticize when we're not sure of our facts. (OR I think that you shouldn't criticize when you're not sure of your facts.)

G 1 A disguise … something … no one
   2 Camouflage … something … everything
   3 A mirage … something … nothing

H she ~~played it~~ (OR ~~she played it~~)> played them for ~~we~~ to learn the words >us

hers favourite songs > her
no really understood the words > no one (OR nobody)
but every talked > everyone (OR everybody)
about different something > something different
in his groups > their
And no ones were trying > no one (OR nobody) was
to practise his English > their
one song that went like that > this
what your want > you
what your need > you
That was interesting words > Those were
I did learn somethings > something (OR some things)

I 1 (c) himself
2 (a) yourself (OR yourselves)
3 (d) myself
4 (b) them

J 1 yourself   5 ourselves
2 it   6 they
3 itself   7 themselves
4 we

K 1 by herself   4 with me
2 about himself   5 near you
3 for themselves

L 1 each   5 each*   9 one
2 other   6 other's*   10 another
3 yourself   7 one*   11 each
4 you   8 another's*   12 the other
* 第 5 题、第 6 题的答案组合 each other's 可与第
7 题、第 8 题的答案组合 one another's 互换。

M 1 express themselves
2 hurt herself
3 blamed each other (OR blamed one another OR each blamed the other)
4 agree with each other (OR agree with one another)
5 meet each other's (OR meet one another's)

N 1 It really annoys everyone that Anthony never helps with the cleaning.
2 It can be a big disadvantage not having a car.
3 It's very important in my job to see potential problems in advance.
4 It was a complete mystery why she left so suddenly.
5 It must have been a shock to discover that your passport was missing.
6 It always amazes me that people can eat such unhealthy food and live so long.

O 1 there was snowing > it was snowing (OR there was snow)
2 It isn't much time left > There
3 There certain to be questions > There are certain
4 It was said to be hundreds of people stranded > There were said to be hundreds of people stranded (OR Hundreds of people were said to be stranded)
5 A lot of fat and sugar is in pies > There's a lot of fat and sugar in pies

6 Everyone found very amusing > found it very amusing
7 They viewed it offensive > viewed it as offensive
8 there were found no survivors > no survivors were found (OR there were no survivors found)

P 1 (d) any
2 ones (c) ones
3 some (b) them
4 one (a) it

Q they started looking for it > one
some ones were really expensive > some
But she kept looking for it > one
She eventually found a second-hand > a second-hand one
so she bought right away > bought it right away
every had fallen for the same trick > every one
(OR everyone OR each one)

R 1 so … so   3 does so   5 to do so
2 so … do it   4 done it

S 1 so   3 –   5 ones
2 –   4 one   6 –

T 与前面重复的主语 [5]
重复的主语和助动词 [4]
重复的主语和动词 [6]
省略重复的主语 [8]
主语（和助动词等）通常不省略 [7]
宾语 [10]
介词短语 [9]
使用宾格代词而不是省略宾语 [11]
重复的动词短语 [13]
重复的形容词和介词短语也可以省略 [12]
动词不定式的 to [15]
或 not to [14]
还可以省略 to [16]
重复的动词可以省略 [17]
保留重复的动词 [18]
提出问题 [19]
转述问题 [20]

U 1 Litter   6 –   11 Rubbish
2 –   7 –   12 they
3 –   8 Pollution   13 –
4 Waste   9 –   14 them
5 them   10 them

V 1 train
2 Boston
3 no one was
4 wouldn't tell us what
5 the others hadn't
6 didn't
7 I sat in the back
8 she didn't want to

W He put the money on the table and ~~he~~ sat down. He sat in his hot clothes and ~~he~~ felt heavy. The woman looked over at him and ~~she~~ smiled. Her smile said she was in charge and she could take his money if she wanted ~~to take his money~~. Of course she could ~~take his money~~, he thought, but obviously she didn't want to ~~take his money~~ yet. The smile lingered for a moment or two longer, then ~~it~~ disappeared and ~~it~~ was replaced by a dark stare.

'I asked you to pay me a thousand and you agreed ~~to pay me a thousand~~. This is only five hundred.'

'You'll get your thousand. I'll give you half ~~of your thousand~~ now and I'll give you the other half ~~of your thousand~~ later when I get the orchid.'

'I could get the orchid and ~~I could~~ find someone else who'd want to buy it.'

'You won't ~~find someone else who'd want to buy it~~. Nobody else is even looking for this orchid.'

The dark stare wanted to stay, but ~~it~~ was slowly replaced by half a smile. It said she would give him half of the smile now and the other half ~~of the smile~~ later.

测验

A 1 d   2 b   3 b   4 c   5 c

B 1 B (her)
2 C (the other)
3 D (she tastes it)
4 B (regarded it as an opportunity)
5 B (a knife was discovered)

C 1 do something   3 someone else
2 them myself   4 do it

D 1 It should have been useful having wealthy parents, but they didn't actually support her.
2 They don't like each other. (OR They don't like one another.)
3 I'm sure there will be someone at the airport to meet you.
4 It would not be a good idea to go swimming out in the ocean by yourself.
5 There were said to be thousands of people affected by the rail strike.

E 1 she   5 anyone   9 one
2 me   6 ours   10 anywhere
3 myself   7 that   11 it
4 him   8 himself

9 形容词（adjective）和副词（adverb）

A 1 very important (line 15)
OR really bad (line 34)
2 large heavy wooden wardrobes (line 33)

B 1 very (OR really)
2 important

3 diagonally
4 directly
5 horizontal
6 small
7 large (OR heavy OR wooden)
8 pointed
9 Blue
10 soft
11 natural

C 限定：main (line 16)
强化：perfect (line 5)

D 从下列每项的例子中任选一个。
看法：comfortable, harmonious, beneficial, important, best, better, easier, bad, vulnerable, restless, negative, soothing, peaceful
大小：small, large
物理特性：heavy, soft
年龄、存在时间或所处时间：ancient, modern, contemporary
形状：pointed, horizontal
颜色：blue, brown

E 从下列每项的例子中任选一个。
所在位置：outdoor
起源或来源：Chinese
材料：wooden
类型：agricultural, physical, horizontal, natural
用途：relaxing

F ancient Chinese OR large wooden OR heavy wooden OR soft natural

G 1 The flags of Britain and the USA both have red, white **and** blue designs.
2 He described the wonderful, friendly, outgoing people who worked in the little Italian café.
3 You immediately notice the large plastic vases with pink **and** purple flowers on every table.
4 There are many industrial **and** agricultural applications of the new chemical compounds.
5 What are the cultural, religious **and** historic origins of these current regional conflicts?

H 1 The entire German team played well.
2 The wine made a small red stain.
3 There's nothing new in the main Christian values.
4 You'll need comfortable leather hiking boots.
5 It has a long pointed stem with tiny pink flowers.
6 The windows are in huge circular wooden frames.
7 They are the major northern industrial nations.
8 ✓
9 They found a beautiful antique rocking chair.
10 Her mother was alone in the total chaos.
11 ✓
12 We don't understand recent American economic policies.

I
1. large
2. rare
3. black
4. white
5. similar
6. small
7. hard
8. shiny white*
9. bluish-grey*
10. great
11. thin*
12. sharp*
13. cool
14. northern
15. large
16. tropical
17. juicy
18. yellow
19. prickly

* 第 8 题和第 9 题答案可互换，第 11 题和第 12 题答案可互换。

J
1. great little outdoor
2. carefree, crazy, happy（任意顺序均可）
3. older English
4. southern European
5. cheap Spanish
6. big square plastic
7. sour and twisted (OR twisted and sour)

K
1. irritating (d)
2. worried (c)
3. exhausted (b)
4. astonishing (a)

L
1. interesting
2. annoying
3. amazed
4. interested
5. annoyed
6. amazing
7. boring

M
1. home-made
2. long-distance
3. peace-keeping
4. never-ending
5. well-educated
6. funny-looking
7. white-washed

N The situation is ~~appalled~~ > appalling
without seeing ~~a homeless~~ > a homeless person (OR the homeless)
The ~~unemployeds~~ stand around > unemployed
The old and sick ~~receives~~ no help > receive
Why are we no longer ~~shocking~~ > shocked
~~Does~~ the Japanese > Do
and the ~~Canadian~~ have the same problems > Canadians
The unthinkable ~~have~~ happened here > has

O
1. We thought we had started our hike early, but other people had already left the campsite (OR had left the campsite already).
2. The workers usually get paid weekly, but they haven't been paid for last week yet (OR they haven't yet been paid for last week).
3. The students still hadn't completed all their work when they had to leave here yesterday.
4. Alice lived here recently, but she doesn't live here any more.
5. We used to hardly ever hear them (OR We hardly ever used to hear them), but they've become really noisy lately (OR but lately they've become really noisy).

P
1. only
2. outside
3. today
4. no longer
5. twice
6. sometimes
7. recently
8. ever
9. yet

Q
1. The couple had got married very recently (OR had very recently got married).
2. The baby looks exactly like her mother.

3. He isn't only an athlete, he's a scholar too!
4. Wait for us, we're coming now.
5. Lunch is almost ready.
6. Wear this silly hat. It's only for fun.

R
1. I completely forgot my brother's birthday yesterday. (OR Yesterday I completely forgot my brother's birthday. OR I forgot my brother's birthday completely yesterday.)
2. The piano is really large and our doorway isn't wide enough.
3. We enjoyed the trip very much (OR We very much enjoyed the trip), but it was too expensive.
4. I'll read the report carefully tomorrow. (OR I'll carefully read the report tomorrow. OR Tomorrow I'll read the report carefully. OR Tomorrow I'll carefully read the report.)

S
1. Traditionally (c) completely
2. only (a) of course
3. carelessly (e) even
4. Individually (f) enough
5. casually (b) very
6. extremely (d) angrily

T
1. Actually
2. certainly
3. very*
4. seriously
5. unfortunately
6. completely*
7. of course
8. probably
9. uncontrollably
10. still
11. Apparently
12. nervously

* 第 3 题和第 6 题答案可互换。

U
1. longer … more likely (OR likelier) … best
2. oldest (OR eldest) … taller … fast
3. new … better-behaved (OR more well-behaved) … earlier
4. best-known … shorter … easier (OR most beautiful … more different … quicker)
5. different … most beautiful … quickest (OR short … well-known … easiest OR easy … well-known … shortest)
6. well … worst … least skilled

V
1. the best
2. as quickly as
3. more easily
4. faster
5. better
6. less beneficial*
7. more wasteful*
8. smaller
9. the most important
10. puzzled

* 第 6 题和第 7 题答案可互换。

W they put the ~~good-looking~~ of all the people > best-looking
were ~~not attractive~~ as those > not as (OR so) attractive
the people in Group A were ~~warm~~ > warmer
~~kind~~ > kinder
~~exciting~~ > more exciting
and ~~sensitive~~ than those in Group B > more sensitive
Group A would find ~~high-paid~~ jobs > higher-paid
have ~~successful~~ marriages > more successful
and lead ~~happy~~ lives than Group B > happier

to have ~~appealing~~ personalities > more appealing
and to be ~~socially~~ skilled than the Group B women >
more (OR better) socially
but also to be ~~vain~~ > vainer (OR more vain)
~~materialistic~~ > more materialistic
~~snobbish~~ > more snobbish
and ~~likely~~ to get divorced than them > more likely
Group A would be ~~bad~~ parents than Group B > worse

测验

A　1 c　　2 b　　3 b　　4 a　　5 c

B　1 D (six feet deep)
2 B (some soldiers who were afraid)
3 C (I usually drink)
4 A (~~very~~)
5 B (Italians)

C　1 already … never　　4 Eventually … easier
2 just … further　　5 Suddenly … short
3 longer … reading　　6 round black

D　1 Everyone thought the event was well-organized and exciting.
2 The earlier you leave here, the quicker you'll get there.
3 Mark is not as good a cook as David.
4 I'm looking for a fairly long green woollen scarf.

E　1 only　　　　6 young
2 earlier　　　7 Japanese
3 yet　　　　8 coloured
4 acutely　　　9 certainly
5 pleased　　10 far

10 介词 (preposition)

A　从下列例子中任选四个。
At the same time (**line 11**)
in the Christmas break (**line 17**)
at night (**line 30**)
during the weekend (**line 31**)
until 3 a.m. (**line 34**)
on Friday and Saturday nights (**line 34**)

B　1 during
2 in exchange for (OR for)
3 in
4 for
5 than
6 at
7 during
8 with
9 according to
10 of

C　1 we talked to (**d**)
2 of them (**a**)
3 apart from working (**b**)
4 in which today's (**c**)

D　1 at six in the morning
2 on her birthday next Saturday
3 in September every year
4 at night in winter
5 on Christmas Day in the past
6 at four o'clock on Friday afternoon
7 at 65 in 2015
8 on the 4th of July in 1776 (OR on the 4th of July, 1776 OR in 1776 on the 4th of July)

E　1 Expiry date　　5 by　　　　8 at
2 during　　　　6 Curfew　　9 until
3 Deadline　　　7 after　　　10 in
4 in

F　1 ~~waiting since an hour~~ > waiting for an hour (OR waiting an hour)
~~till~~ his next meeting > before
2 My sister ~~works~~ > has worked (OR has been working) since ~~after 2013~~ > 2013 (OR before 2013)
3 received in this office ~~until~~ 9 a.m. > by (OR before)
~~in~~ the first of March > on
4 appointments ~~in every morning~~ > every morning
see you ~~on next Monday morning~~ > next Monday morning

G　1 on (**d**) in　　　　3 in (**a**) at
2 at (**c**) in　　　　4 on (**b**) in

H　1 The meeting focused **on** economic problems **in** developing countries **in** South-East Asia.
2 You can either stand **at** the bar or sit **at** a table **in** most pubs **in** Britain.
3 We were depending **on** my brother to meet us **at** the exit door after the concert.
4 The children were laughing **at** something they had seen **in** a cartoon.

I　1 overpopulation among
2 overlap between
3 overalls over
4 above … overflow
5 below … overhead

J　1 from　　　　5 along
2 out of　　　6 to
3 towards　　7 past
4 across

K　1 through … to
2 along … towards
3 out of … from

L　1 over　　　　5 from
2 on　　　　　6 into
3 through　　7 towards
4 along

M　1 of the door with a screwdriver
2 with American history by reading
3 with some friends of ours
4 by scoring … of the match

5 by taxi … with her
6 with the yellow lampshade … with a cheque

N 1 omelettes without
2 fish besides
3 meal except
4 fruit except for
5 ice cream with
6 bread without
7 pizza, minus

O 1 You have to fill in this form and send it back with your payment.
2 My dad has given up his attempt to get the university to do away with tuition fees.
3 We had to cut back on our spending after we found out that our rent was going up.
4 Please go along with local customs at the temple and take off your shoes (OR take your shoes off) before going in.

P 1 Stand up
2 raise … up*
3 breathe out
4 bend … down
5 breathe in
6 lift … up*
7 go back

* 第 2 题和第 6 题答案可互换。

Q 1 B 3 B 5 A 7 A OR B
2 A 4 B 6 A 8 B

测验

A 1 a 2 a 3 c 4 d 5 c

B 1 C (instead of)
2 C (~~on~~)
3 B (in)
4 D (over)
5 D (out of OR in)

C 1 away 3 to 5 out of
2 from 4 in 6 for

D 1 During August this building will be closed for renovation.
2 Besides shopping, what else did you do when you were in Rome? (OR Besides shopping when you were in Rome, what else did you do?)
3 Apart from the apple I gave you earlier, haven't you eaten anything else today?
4 Without more financial support we won't be able to do much.

E 1 By 5 towards 8 of
2 past 6 with 9 along
3 At 7 into 10 across
4 under

11 动词不定式（infinitive）和动名词（gerund）

A helped hundreds of people to stop **smoking** (**line 11**)
and **avoiding** social situations (**line 17**)
situations that will make her want **to smoke** (**line 18**)
many people continue **smoking** (**line 22**)
Encourage her **to avoid** stressful situations (**line 24**)

B 1 kick the habit (**line 5**)
2 doing yoga (**line 26**)
3 (going) cold turkey (**line 33**)
4 over the counter (**line 41**)

C 1 want to become (2)
2 makes them experience (3)
3 to stop doing (1)
4 for controlling (2) (OR of treating (3) OR without needing (4))

D 1 to be … having
2 to have … being
3 to have … having
4 to have … to be

E 1 to have finished (4)
2 to be studying (1)
3 to have been living (2)
4 to be done (4)
5 to have been constructed (3)
6 having slept (1)
7 being killed (2)
8 having been built (3)

F 1 Your homework was supposed to have been (OR to be) done before you went out.
2 I wanted to thank her for having taken (OR for taking) the time to help me.
3 They complained about not having been (OR not being) told about the changes.

G 1 travelling
2 meeting
3 to have visited
4 to have been doing
5 being held
6 to have been based
7 to be using
8 to be burning
9 to have been built
10 not to have seen

H 1 hope (OR am hoping) to visit
2 invited … to stay
3 wants … to spend
4 enjoy taking
5 imagine … making
6 love to be

I 1 allow … to take
2 forget to send

236

3 meant to tidy
4 prefer not to talk (OR prefer not talking)
5 avoid trying to drive
6 forced ... to stop playing

J encouraged me ~~take~~ > to take
advised me ~~remember~~ > to remember
remember ~~clean~~ the bathrooms > to clean
likes ~~clean~~ bathrooms > cleaning (OR to clean)
I didn't mind ~~do~~ it > doing
I was first starting ~~learn~~ > to learn
I could practise ~~speak~~ English > speaking
I enjoyed ~~try improve~~ my English > trying to improve
I didn't want ~~work~~ > to work
I don't regret ~~do~~ it > doing
I decided ~~study~~ harder > to study
and try ~~get~~ a different job > to get

K 1 It's essential to plan ahead in my kind of job. (OR It's essential in my kind of job to plan ahead.)
2 Jessica was disappointed not to see any of her friends at the shopping centre.
3 It was so good of Christopher to come to our rescue when our car broke down.
4 Those huge buses aren't easy to drive along narrow winding roads.

L 1 plan ... to take
2 problem keeping
3 place to stay
4 information ... reserving
5 task ... to call
6 someone to ask
7 cost ... renting

测验

A 1 d   2 c   3 b   4 a   5 d

B 1 A (learning)
2 D (refused to help)
3 B (tell us to wait)
4 A (visiting)
5 D (of doing)

C 1 assumed to be
2 heard ... sneeze (OR sneezing)
3 remembered ... telling
4 allowed to go
5 smell ... burning

D 1 A place to park is sometimes hard to find.
2 Is it really necessary to keep all these old files?
3 It would be a mistake for him to buy a new car now.
4 Amy still remembers being bitten by a dog when she was very young.
5 The boy denied having done anything wrong.
(OR The boy denied doing anything wrong.)

E 1 trying
2 to look
3 to do
4 to regain
5 stopping
6 to keep
(OR to have kept)
7 starting
8 losing
9 putting
10 going

12 转述 (reporting)

A 1 He would just nod and **say**, 'Thanks for coming round,' ... (**line 56**)
2 ... those who had opinions mostly **said** that it was a strange story ... (**line 50**)

B 1 C   2 D   3 B   4 F   5 A   6 E

C 1 put (**line 11**) (OR call out (**line 13**))
2 grumbled (**line 22**)

D 1 comma
2 quotation mark
3 comma
4 quotation mark
5 quotation mark
6 quotation mark

E 'Susanna,' Mrs Alder called out, 'I'd like you to come and meet Michael.' A girl appeared in the doorway. 'How do you do?' she said. 'Nice to meet you,' he mumbled. 'Please don't call him "Michelle" or "Mikey" or any other silly names,' warned Mrs Alder as she swept out of the room. 'Have you read "Harry Potter"?' Susanna suddenly said. 'What one?' he asked. 'Oh, no, you little Mickey Mouse,' she said as she came into the room, 'you must say "Which one?", not "What one?", if you're going to survive here.' (OR ... into the room. 'You must ...')

F 1 He said that he left (OR had left) his jacket there the day before (OR the previous day).
2 The reviewer wrote that Carlin's new book was the funniest thing he or she had ever read.
3 She said that they wouldn't eat it then, but they might have it for lunch the next day (OR the following day).
4 He advised us that we should take as much water as we could carry.
5 You told me that you had to (OR must) get something to eat or you would faint.
6 CompCo is reporting that demand for new PCs in the UK is declining.
7 She asked if she should get rid of those old boxes in the cupboard.

G 1 could
2 is
3 has
4 are
5 can't
6 won't
7 would
8 will
9 live
10 can
11 lived
12 were
13 had

H 1 I mentioned to Mr Brody that there was something wrong with the lights.
2 I reminded Julia that she and her friends had to tidy up after the party.

3 He warned me (OR you / him / her / us / them) not to touch any of the wires.

4 He denied doing anything wrong. (OR He denied that he had done anything wrong. OR He denied that he did anything wrong. OR He denied having done anything wrong.)

I
1 had mentioned   5 told
(OR mentioned)   6 explained
2 wondered   7 claim
3 talk   8 begged
4 asked   9 thought

J I can't ~~agree them~~ > agree with them
and offered ~~me to help~~ > to help me
I ~~explained them~~ > explained
that I ~~can't~~ get the wheel off > couldn't
One of them ~~told that~~ > told me that (OR said that)
and ~~assured that~~ > assured me that
He even suggested ~~me to stand~~ > standing (OR that I (should) stand)
~~warned me watch out~~ > warned me to watch out
(OR warned (me) that I should watch out)
~~joked~~ the small wheels > joked about
~~I spoke them thanks.~~ > I thanked them. (OR I told them, 'Thanks.' OR I said, 'Thanks' to them.)
They ~~refused take~~ > refused to take
I ~~offered pay them~~ > offered to pay them

K
1 One of the defendants called out that he (OR she) was not guilty.
2 Her statement that she'd been adopted really surprised us.
3 I agree with the students' argument that the cost of tuition has increased too much.
4 No one believed his claim that he was not a thief. (OR … his claim not to be a thief.)

L
1 (c) whether   3 (d) where
2 (a) who   4 (b) that

M
1 One of the visitors asked about whether there would be a fridge in the hotel room. (OR … asked if there would be … OR … asked whether there would be …)
2 He asked me why I did that (OR why I was doing that OR why I had done that OR why I had to do that) and I pointed out that it was part of my job.
3 She asked me what to do next (OR what she should do next) and my response was that she should (OR could) get some more chairs.
4 Her explanation that no one asked her (OR had asked her) whether or not she had a degree (OR if she had a degree or not OR whether she had a degree or not) was incredible.

N
1 why she wasn't sleeping
2 that there was a 'moster' under her bed
3 what a 'moster' was
4 if (OR whether) she had seen the monster
5 (that) she hadn't, but (that) she knew it had big teeth
6 where it had come from

O
1 The professor asked her students not to eat or drink during lectures. (OR The professor asked her students if they would not eat or drink during lectures.)
2 The guard ordered the prisoner to stand up when the judge came in.
3 The worker asked to leave early on Friday. (OR The worker asked (his boss) if he could leave early on Friday.)
4 Scott's mother recommended applying to several universities. (OR Scott's mother recommended (that) he (should) apply to several universities.)

P
1 to place her napkin in her lap (OR that she should / must place her napkin in her lap OR that she place her napkin in her lap)
2 not to rest her elbows on the table (OR that she should / must not rest her elbows on the table OR that she not rest her elbows on the table)
3 to chew her food with her mouth closed (OR (that) she should / must chew her food with her mouth closed)
4 not to talk with her mouth full (OR (that) she shouldn't / mustn't talk with her mouth full)
5 not to put a lot of food on her plate all at once (OR that she shouldn't / mustn't put a lot of food on her plate all at once OR that she not put a lot of food on her plate all at once)
6 not to take more food until it is offered (OR that she shouldn't / mustn't take more food until it is offered OR that she not take more food until it is offered)
7 should / must ask somebody
8 if they would (please) pass the salt (OR to (please) pass the salt)

Q
1 recommendation that we (should) take the early flight to Glasgow
2 belief that a perfect life can be achieved
3 diagnosis … that I had an ear infection
4 sorry that she lost her temper
5 positive that we would all pass the exam
6 aware that dogs weren't allowed there

测验

A 1 b   2 d   3 b   4 c   5 a

B
1 D (would be able)
2 C (agreed with me)
3 C (encouraged her not to quit)
4 A (inquired about whether)
5 B (offered to bring OR offered to bring us)

C
1 tell   5 hadn't spoken
2 asked   6 replied*
3 explained*   7 pointed out
4 hadn't said   8 talk (OR talked)
* 第 3 题和第 6 题答案可互换。

D 1 Mrs Dalloway said she would buy the flowers herself.

2 She asked Henry if he had left (OR left) his keys in the door.

3 There was an announcement that the strike was over.

4 His only comment was that he would return the following day (OR the next day OR the day after).

5 His statement that he wouldn't do it surprised us.

6 I remember one time when my aunt told me not to talk with my mouth full. (OR … my aunt told me that I mustn't (OR shouldn't) talk with my mouth full.)

7 They invited me (OR us) to stay at their house.

E 1 (that) he would be here by eight o'clock

2 if she knew where Rob was

3 (that) she thought he had gone out about half an hour earlier

4 apologized (OR said that he was sorry)

5 that he had forgotten that he had promised to take his mother into town that morning

13 名词性从句 (noun clause)

A 1 One of the individuals typically insists **that** he or she will not stop doing something despite the fact **that** it is a source of conflict. (**line 46**)

OR Sometimes one of them will say **that** he or she actually prefers it **that** the other has separate interests. (**line 48**)

*NOT: ~~On the basis of their study, the researchers have concluded that a modern marriage may begin with passionate love, but its survival depends a lot on 'companionate love', a feeling that includes affection, caring and friendship.~~ (**line 62**)

* 该句中的第二个 *that*（＝which）是关系代词，引导的是关系从句，不是名词性从句。见**第 164 页**。

2 It makes you wonder **if** getting married is worth the effort. (**line 7**)

B 1 T 2 T 3 F 4 F 5 F 6 F

C 1 that it was one of their best memories (**line 33**)

OR that he or she will not stop doing something (**line 46**)

OR that he or she actually prefers it that the other has separate interests (**line 49**)

2 **the case** that marriage has become a gamble (**line 9**)

OR **one indication** that the couple speaks with a single voice (**line 24**)

OR **the fact** that it is a source of conflict (**line 48**)

3 **likely** that a marriage will end in divorce (**line 5**)

OR **delighted** that so many of their couples stayed together (**line 20**)

OR **obvious** that these individuals had really different views about marriage (**line 57**)

4 what advice they would give to younger people thinking about getting married (**line 51**)

5 **to** what makes a successful marriage (**line 13**)

D 2 We **learned** that pineapples don't grow on trees. (**7**)

3 No one **noticed** that the keys were missing. (**7**)

4 She could never **anticipate** what he might want. (**8**)

5 I'll **show** you how it works. (**10**)

6 He **screamed** that he hated school. (**9**) (OR She **said** that she felt that everyone was against her. (**9**) OR He **told** me that he loved me. (**10**))

7 Ewan **suggested** that we should leave early. (**8**)

8 They **consider** it an offence when women go out in public without covering their heads. (**12**) (OR We **thought** it odd that no one called us. (**13**) OR Many people **regard** it as a really bad idea that the police have started carrying guns. (**14**))

E 1 It doesn't surprise me at all that they don't have any money left.

2 It just astonishes me that children would rather sit watching TV instead of playing outside.

3 It has never been explained why the government didn't act immediately to stop the movement of all animals.

4 It wasn't clear whether Nicole's father had been for or against her marriage, but he did participate in the wedding ceremony.

F 1 what   4 that   7 Whether
2 it   5 it   8 that
3 that   6 that   9 where

G 1 **That** Mr Baker complained about the noise was predictable, but we assured **him** (**that**) it wouldn't happen again. (OR It was **predictable that** Mr Baker complained about the noise, but we assured **him** (**that**) it wouldn't happen again.)

2 The headmaster warned **us** (OR **me** OR **you**) during our meeting **that** some teachers wouldn't like **it that** (OR **the fact that**) their classrooms had suddenly been changed.

3 They told me about **what** Sam had said in the meeting, but I thought **it** strange (**that**) he hadn't mentioned money.

4 The police regarded **it as** suspicious **that** the dead woman's husband had recently taken out a life insurance policy in her name.

5 The prosecutor showed the jury how **the crime could** have been committed by Feldman, but he didn't convince **them** (OR **the jury**) that Feldman was guilty.

H 1 His explanation that he had been stuck in traffic for over an hour didn't sound right.

2 Their discovery that the boy suffered from asthma changed their attitude.

3 The belief that there are aliens from outer space living among us is quite widespread.

I 1 with the view that
 2 to the fact that
 3 conclusion was (that)
 4 against the idea that
 5 example of
 6 Despite the fact that
 7 belief that
 8 in agreement that

J 1 premonition … that … which
 2 Scepticism … that … that
 3 superstition … that … which
 4 Déjà vu … that … which
 * 本题旨在考查对名词性从句和关系从句的辨别，以上答案中的 which 实际上也可换为 that。

K raise ~~issues how~~ equality can be > issues of (OR about OR with regard to) how
 ~~the fact which~~ women don't have > the fact that
 based on ~~the belief people's~~ attitudes can be changed > the belief that people's
 ~~the assumption other~~ peaceful changes > the assumption that other
 ~~in spite of it is~~ largely controlled by men > in spite of the fact that it is

L 1 We were afraid (that) our old car might break down.
 2 I was completely surprised that (OR when OR by the fact that) Karen suddenly decided to quit her job.
 3 Sean was absolutely sure (that) the test would be easy.

M 1 unlikely (that)
 2 aware of how
 3 surprising when
 4 glad (that)
 5 embarrassed by what
 6 amazed (that)

N 现在虚拟语气 [1]
 把 not 放在动词前 [2]
 替代现在虚拟语气 [3]
 （表示）命令（的动词后面）[6]
 （表示）规定（的动词后面）[5]
 （表示）建议（的动词后面）[4]
 可用于转述命令、指示 [7]
 不能用于转述陈述 [8]
 （表示）命令（的名词后面）[11]
 （表示）规定（的名词后面）[10]
 （表示）建议（的名词后面）[9]
 表示必要性的形容词 [12]

O 1 crucial (d) (should) not be disturbed
 2 stipulates (OR stipulated) (c) (should) have
 3 recommends (OR recommended) (f) (should) spend
 4 suggestion (a) (should) be given
 5 requirement (b) (should) be worn
 6 insists (OR insisted) (e) (had) arrested

P A 1 what they're thinking
 2 what happened that day
 3 who their best friends are
 B 4 that women are less likely than men
 5 that men get the impression
 6 that women never tell jokes

C 7 if women and men talk equally
 8 people think
 9 the women talked more
D 10 that men think
 11 women talk a lot
 12 that they hear women

Q 1 that there was another world
 2 (that) Columbus reached Iceland
 3 he could reach China
 4 that Columbus wasn't the first European
 5 (that) Columbus's visit to Iceland gave him the confidence
 6 there would eventually be a place to land

测验

A 1 c 2 d 3 a 4 d 5 b

B 1 A (That Amber … OR The fact that Amber …)
 2 D (that)
 3 A (that the director said)
 4 B (like it that OR like the fact that)
 5 B (remind us (OR me OR you) that)

C 1 idea of **how** categorization works
 2 we take it for granted **that** categories have
 3 and **that** all members of a given category
 4 we see **that** it is
 5 it is not surprising **that** we hold

D 1 He didn't conceal the fact that his parents weren't English.
 2 It has always been a big mystery to me why anyone would want to jump out of a plane and put their trust in a parachute.
 3 Our expectation was that no one would be there.
 4 Bridget was sorry that her comments had upset Mark's mother.
 5 Despite the fact that these apples don't look very nice, they're delicious.

E 1 noticed (that)
 2 know if
 3 reason to when
 4 argue (that)
 5 concedes that
 6 That emotion
 7 rule out that
 8 view that
 9 feel (that)
 10 unfair that

14 关系从句 (relative clause)

A A which sank in 1718 (**line 6**)
  OR who was the most notorious pirate of his day (**line 7**)
 B whose real name was Edward Teach (**line 9**)
  OR whatever they captured from these enemies of the queen (**line 15**)
 C when the European powers declared peace (**line 17**)
  OR what they knew best (**line 21**)
  OR which had the speed and power (**line 25**)
  OR which they renamed 'Queen Anne's Revenge' (**line 28**)

D that he needed (**line 35**)
  OR whose huge black beard was twisted into long
    tails (**line 38**)
  OR who carried several guns and swords in belts
    (**line 40**)
  OR (which were) slung across both shoulders (**line 41**)
  OR that he could use (**line 43**)
E when he was killed in a sea battle with two British
  ships (**line 46**)
  OR which had been sent (**line 47**)
  OR (that) we still have today (**line 52**)

B 1 who   5 which
   2 that (OR which)   6 when
   3 who (OR whom)   7 that (OR which)
   4 that (OR which)   8 – (OR that OR which)

C (that) he needed (**line 35**)
   (that) he could use (**line 43**)

D 限制性的: which had the speed and power (**line 25**)
   which had been sent (**line 47**)
   非限制性的: which sank in 1718 (**line 6**)
   which they renamed 'Queen Anne's Revenge' (**line 28**)

E 1 who   4 (that)   7 who
   2 that   5 who   8 that
   3 which   6 which   9 whom

F 1 that (OR which) uses exaggerated actions, often
     involving accidents
   2 who controls a sports game
   3 in which each competitor takes part in three
     different sports
   4 from whom you rent a room or flat (OR that (OR who)
     you rent a room or flat from)
   5 , the largest part of which is below the surface of the
     water,
   6 , some of which are poisonous,
   7 , which consists of nine islands,
   8 , whom (OR who) most people know as Mark Twain,

G a letter said I had been terminated > a letter that
   (OR which) said
   the letter, that came from the university, > which
   termination (means 'the end') > which means
   which it felt really weird > which felt
   that I could be fired from it > that I could be fired from
   (OR from which I could be fired)
   I was just a student didn't have a job > a student who
   (OR that) didn't
   it was an error had been caused > an error that
   (OR which) had
   I wasn't the only one had been terminated > the only
   one who (OR that) had
   A lot of other people didn't have jobs > other people
   who (OR that) didn't

H 1 Lacrosse … played … using
   2 mermaid … having
   3 jigsaw … printed … cut

4 shadow … caused … standing

I 1 parked outside … sitting in it
   2 standing on the bed … covered with feathers
   3 starting at 8 p.m. … based on a true story
   4 accused of crimes committed during the war

J For all you food-lovers ~~who will be~~ sitting at home and
   ~~who will be~~ looking for something ~~that is~~ interesting
   on TV this afternoon, there's a fabulous new show
   ~~which is~~ called 'The Asian Kitchen', ~~which has been~~
   created and ~~which has been~~ produced by Mary Sah,
   ~~which begins~~ **beginning** at 4.30 this afternoon. Among
   the dishes ~~which will be~~ featured will be Saucy Tofu,
   ~~which consists~~ **consisting** of tofu squares ~~which have~~
   ~~been~~ dipped in a special batter, ~~which have been~~
   deep-fried and ~~which have been~~ covered in a creamy
   peanut sauce, and Evil Shrimp, ~~which is~~ made with hot
   peppers ~~which have been~~ sautéed with other vegetables
   and ~~which are~~ served with shrimp ~~which are~~ sizzling in
   a shallow pool of red curry. It's the most delicious thing
   on TV today!

K 人 [1]
   组织 [3]
   地点 [2]
   某物的一部分 [4]
   属于某物的事物 [5]
   在名词后使用 of which [7]
   将名词加 of 放在从句末尾 [6]
   人称代词 [9]
   不定代词 [8]
   后面可接 who 或 that 引导的关系从句 [12]
   省略关系代词或使用简化的关系从句 [11]

L 1 whose parents are dead
   2 who doesn't care about money
   3 whose wood (OR the wood of which OR of which the
     wood) is strong and durable
   4 from whose upper windows (OR from the upper
     windows of which) large flags were hanging
   5 who have completed their questionnaires
   6 many of whose paintings look like large comic strips

M 1 before which you must complete something
   2 for whose moral education you have promised to
     be responsible (OR whose moral education you have
     promised to be responsible for)
   3 whom (OR who) you look up to
   4 through which you look (OR which you look through
     OR that you look through OR you look through)

N about ~~a situation which~~ those > a situation in which
   (OR a situation where)
   ~~those want~~ to fight > those who want
   a person ~~who the~~ house > whose
   house is made of glass, ~~it's~~ something > which is
   ~~something is~~ easily broken > something which (OR that)
   is

241

the person you threw the stone at him > the person at whom you threw the stone (OR the person whom you threw the stone at OR the person (who) you threw the stone at)

the meaning of it I looked up > the meaning of which (OR whose meaning)

similar to you have > to those you have (OR to those that you have OR to those which you have)

for anyone is critical > anyone who is

O 1 when   3 how   5 how
   2 where   4 what   6 why

P 1 Prison … where
   2 motive … why
   3 crime … which
   4 Revenge … that … what
   5 Quarantine … when

Q 1 **(d)** however   4 **(e)** whichever
   2 **(c)** whatever   5 **(b)** whoever
   3 **(a)** whenever

R 1 that   4 what   7 how
   2 where   5 when   8 why
   3 which   6 whichever

测验

A 1 a   2 b   3 c   4 d   5 b

B 1 C (who had … 因为不能用 that 引导描述人的非限制性关系从句)
   2 C (along which something)
   3 C (that OR when 因为 every time 后不使用 when)
   4 C (which made 因为不能用简化的关系从句表述突然发生的行为)
   5 D (that was left 因为把数量词用作代词时, 后面不能用 which)

C 1 whose   4 What
   2 that OR which   5 which
   3 where OR in which

D 1 Elizabeth is the name from which Betty is derived. (OR Elizabeth is the name (that / which) Betty is derived from.)
   2 India is where her parents were born. (OR India is the place / country where / in which her parents were born.)
   3 Hemingway is the author whose short stories I liked best.
   4 Whatever I do, her parents will never like me.
   5 I was at the first lecture, during which he talked about humanism. (OR I was at the first lecture, when / where / in which he talked about humanism.)

E 1 (that is / which is) often told to children
   2 who sells a cow
   3 (which / that) his mother thinks are worthless

4 which grow very quickly
5 (that is / which is) called a beanstalk
6 where (OR in which OR above which) he discovers a giant
7 from whom he steals some things (OR that / who he steals some things from)
8 suspecting (OR who suspects) something is wrong
9 which he then cuts down
10 who is chasing him

15 条件句（conditional）

A 1 If she caught a cold (**line 50**)
   2 if I put a huge swimming pool in front of my house (**line 30**)
     OR If I went to all that trouble (**line 33**)
     OR If you were in my situation (**line 45**)

B 1 (Cathy)   3 (Anna)   5 (Bea)
   2 (Erin)   4 (Dave)

C 1 If she has a cup of coffee, she always wants to smoke a cigarette. (**line 7**)
     OR If she catches a cold, she goes to bed immediately. (**line 53**)
   2 … if she had a cigarette in her hand, she was cool. (**line 3**)
   3 If you are successful, it will be because of hard work. (**line 12**)
     OR If you don't have a struggle, you won't experience the triumph. (**line 20**)
     OR If you build it, they will come. (**line 26**)

D 1 was (f)   3 is (a)   5 don't (b)
   2 come (d)   4 is (e)   6 is (c)

E 1 … if I put a huge swimming pool in front of my house, people would think I was crazy. (**line 30**)
     OR If I went to all that trouble, I would put the pool at the back of my house. (**line 33**)
     OR If I were you, I would sell it. (**line 36**)
     OR If you were in my situation, I would help you out! (**line 45**)
   2 If he had wanted to sell his car, he would have done that already. (**line 39**)
     OR If he had worked harder at school, he would have had some kind of career by now. (**line 42**)

F 1 If I knew Jason's phone number, I could tell him what happened.
   2 If she had prepared for the test, she would (OR could OR might) have passed.
   3 If you had warned us about the bad weather, I would (OR could OR might) have brought a raincoat.
   4 If I was (OR were) in your situation, I would (OR might) start looking for another job.

G 1 would start
   2 wanted*
   3 could do
   4 started
   5 would contribute
   6 had started
   7 could have paid*
   8 would have contributed*
   9 decided*
   10 would cost
   11 would end up

* 第 2 题和第 9 题答案可互换，第 7 题和第 8 题答案可互换。

H he ~~always fall~~ asleep > always fell (OR would always fall OR always used to fall)

his feet ~~are~~ near the fire > were

his slippers ~~start~~ to smoke > started (OR would start)

my grandmother ~~has to~~ rush over > had to (OR would have to)

my father ~~sit~~ in that chair > sits

he immediately ~~go~~ to sleep > goes

and ~~start~~ snoring > starts

My mother ~~get~~ really annoyed > gets

if that ~~happen~~ > happens

if I ~~take~~ ... ~~happen~~ to me > take ... will happen (OR took ... would happen OR were to take ... would happen)

I ~~don't~~ have this dilemma > wouldn't

my older brother ~~didn't move~~ away > hadn't moved

If he ~~stays~~ > had stayed

he ~~is~~ given the chair > would have been

and I ~~am not faced~~ with the problem > wouldn't be faced (OR wouldn't have been faced)

If I ~~move~~ > moved

the chair ~~fit~~ > would (OR could) fit

~~Do~~ I really have a problem > Would

if I ~~settle~~ > settled

and ~~give~~ in > gave

But who ~~wake~~ me ... if my slippers ~~catch~~ > would wake ... caught (OR will wake ... catch)

I 1 he ... rather
   2 he ... prefer
   3 he'd ... have
   4 he ... wants
   5 he'd ... chase

J A number of idioms have come from the game of cricket. If something is described as *not cricket*, it means that it is not fair or honourable. If someone is *on a sticky wicket*, they are in a difficult situation. (OR Someone is *on a sticky wicket* if they are in a difficult situation.) This is because balls do not bounce very well if the ground near the wicket is sticky (wet and muddy). If it is said that someone had *a good innings*, it means they had a long life or career.

K 1 hadn't eaten
   2 isn't
   3 didn't watch
   4 took
   5 has completed
   6 wouldn't be
   7 would stay
   8 would have arrived

a If they took the test earlier today, they won't get the results until tomorrow.

b If it isn't going to be a problem, I'd like to leave my bike in the hallway tonight.

c If William sent the parcel last week, it would have arrived by now, I'm sure.

d If it was a terribly cold day outside, we would stay in bed until noon.

e If the neighbour's dog hadn't started barking at 4 a.m., I wouldn't be so tired now.

f I wouldn't feel so full now if I hadn't eaten so much at lunch.

g If Sarah has completed all her work already, we can let her leave early today.

h If you didn't watch television as a child, you probably won't know why some of these people from old TV programmes are famous.

L 描述现在 [1]
过去 [2]
谈论规则 [5]
习惯 [4]
因果关系（如科学现象）[3]
主句可以用祈使句 [6]
表达计划 [8]
预测 [9]
询问将来的事 [11]
提出请求 [10]
纯粹的想象 [14]
某种做法可能产生的结果 [15]
做某事的意愿，虽然实际上并没有能力去做 [13]
表达懊悔 [17]
进行指责 [18]

M 1 预测, 9
   2 事实, 3
   3 假设, 15
   4 事实, 5
   5 反事实, 16
   6 事实, 6
   7 假设, 13
   8 反事实, 18

N 1 had asked (c)
   2 was (a)
   3 don't want (e)
   4 hadn't forgotten (b)
   5 need (d)

O 1 if the times hadn't been so hard
   2 If he had found a job
   3 If his father hadn't told
   4 If he hadn't spent
   5 If FBI agents hadn't started

P 1 Unless she comes soon, we'll have to leave without your friend. (OR Unless your friend comes soon, we'll have to leave without her.)

   2 Whether Andy's ready or not, we're going to start playing. (OR Whether or not Andy's ready, we're going to start playing.)

   3 They'll only let you take books out of the library if you're a registered student.

   4 Even though our team played really well, we didn't win the game.

Q 1 If only
   2 even though
   3 whether or not
   4 only if
   5 If it isn't

R A 一般条件: 2 Given, 5 Suppose, 6 Supposing, 8 What if, 9 With

B 独有条件: 3 Providing (that) / Provided (that), 7 as long as / so long as

C 特例条件: 4 otherwise, 10 Without

测验

A 1 b   2 a   3 d   4 d   5 c

B 1 A (was)   3 C (had)   5 C (if)
  2 D (will)   4 B (get)

C 1 if   4 go   6 will
  2 will   5 work   7 lived
  3 take / have

D 1 Unless someone is willing to help, the party is not likely to (OR will not) happen.
  2 If only she had been wearing (OR had worn) a crash helmet, she would (OR might OR could) have escaped injury.
  3 Even though she could be very difficult, I still loved her.
  4 Whether you like the idea or not, we're leaving tomorrow.
    OR Whether or not you like the idea, we're leaving tomorrow.
  5 I'm sorry, but if the traffic hadn't been so bad, I wouldn't have arrived late.

E 1 if they just stop working
  2 if your printer won't print
  3 Whether you're getting an error message
  4 if you have received no error messages
  5 if it's a wireless model
  6 if any print jobs are on hold
  7 If your queue gets bogged down
  8 Even if your printer is an older model
  9 If you are still having a problem
  10 if necessary

16 状语从句 (adverbial clause)

A A so she tried to take good care of his proud creation (**line 5**)
  B Before he began his career with the national weather service (**line 7**)
    OR Although he'd had to give up his artistic ambitions (**line 9**)
  C when he was mixing the cement, sand and water, then … frame (**line 20**)
  D When there was a spell of warm summer weather (**line 26**)
    OR Before Emily could get to them (**line 29**)
  E when Emily had to go out and sweep the whole country every morning (**line 33**)
    OR If it wasn't wet (**line 35**)
    OR When it rained a lot (**line 38**)

F Even though it wasn't really cold during most of the winter (**line 41**)
  OR as if it had been carved from a large flat slab of marble by an expert hand (**line 48**)

B 1 T   2 F   3 F   4 F   5 T   6 T

C 1 After her husband passed away (**line 1**)
  2 When there was a spell of warm summer weather (**line 26**)
  3 Even though it wasn't really cold during most of the winter (**line 41**)
  4 as if it had been carved from a large flat slab of marble by an expert hand (**line 48**)

D 1 When I was standing at the bus stop in the rain, I watched Nick drive by in his new car.
  2 As the skin starts to turn yellow, you'll know that the fruit is getting ripe.
  3 While we're eating (OR having OR at) lunch, we shouldn't talk about anything to do with work.
  4 Just as I was getting out of the shower, my phone rang in the other room.

E 1 When   3 As
  2 When OR While   4 As OR When OR While

F 1 prediction … before   3 postscript … after
  2 skewer … while   4 blender … until

G 1 'll be   5 've been
  2 've been   6 've been
  3 'll be   7 will be
  4 will be

H 1 (c) as if   3 (d) as if
  2 (a) as   4 (b) as

I 1 They all behaved as though nothing had happened
  2 It was still just as I remembered it
  3 It tastes as though it was made yesterday
  4 you try to do as well as they have done
  5 hidden in the forest, just as the guidebook had described it
  6 you think it isn't as much as it really is

J 1 As it's a holiday, all the banks will be closed on Monday.
  2 Since she had an operation on her foot, she has had to use crutches.
  3 While we're all together today, we should decide on a date for the Christmas party.
  4 Now that he has finished his exams, I wonder what he'll do next.

K 1 (c) because   3 (a) Because
  2 (b) as if   4 (d) as if

L 1 In order to avoid traffic jams on the way to the airport, you should plan to leave early tomorrow.
  2 In order that no money (would) be wasted, we had to account for every penny we spent.

3 In order for plants to grow indoors, there must be a good source of light.

4 So as not to get wet, we waited a few minutes until the rain stopped.

M 1 ~~that~~ nobody would notice her > so (OR in order) that
2 ~~for~~ kill insects > to
3 ~~In order to care people~~ about another person > In order for people to care
4 ~~so as to not~~ get him in trouble > so as not to
5 ~~in order it can stand~~ > in order that it can stand (OR in order for it to stand)
6 ~~in order not our competitors find~~ > in order that (OR so that) our competitors don't find

N 1 They were feeling really tired, so they went to bed early last night.
2 I forgot to take my textbook home with me, so I wasn't able to do the homework.
3 Maddie is in a popular TV show, so people recognize her when she's out shopping.
4 They said the tap water wasn't safe to drink, so we had to drink bottled water.

O 1 The fire spread so rapidly through their cabin (that)
2 Emilia's children had such bad colds this morning (that)
3 You and I don't have so much money (that)
4 We had such a wonderful time on holiday (that)
5 That class was so early (that)

P 1 Although I understand why he thinks that way, I disagree with his point of view. (OR Although I disagree with his point of view, I understand why he thinks that way.)
2 Though he has applied for about a dozen different jobs, Jack is still unemployed.
3 Even though most people agreed that the car was a bargain, none of them wanted to buy it. (OR Even though none of them wanted to buy it, most people agreed that the car was a bargain.)
4 Unlikely though it seems, the children may not want to go to the zoo on Saturday.
5 Despite the fact that the old people didn't have very much money, they were really generous. (OR Despite not having very much money, the old people were really generous.)

Q 1 Although frustrated … as if trying
2 Since opening
3 Although managing
4 once broken
5 until making sure

测验

A 1 d   2 a   3 c   4 d   5 b

B 1 D (was)
2 A (~~so that~~ OR in order)
3 C (because they become)

4 A (Because)
5 B (as if OR as though)

C 1 when   3 when   5 to
2 because   4 after   6 As

D 1 Because it was late and I was exhausted, I went straight to bed.
2 In order for him to continue to work here, there will have to be a change in his attitude.
3 He talked as if (OR as though) he owned the restaurant.
4 You can't go out until you finish (OR have finished) your homework.
5 Even though he's your friend (OR Even though I know he's your friend), he can't sleep here.
6 So as not to be late, we left half an hour earlier than necessary.

E 1 Although   5 just as
2 as much as   6 as easy as
3 whereas   7 though
4 as if   8 Despite the fact

17 连接词语（connector）和焦点结构（focus structure）

A A then (**line 7**) OR In fact (**line 7**)
B For example (**line 12**) OR also (**line 14**) OR Actually (**line 18**)
C After all (**line 23**) OR So (**line 24**)
D However (**line 40**) OR As a consequence (**line 44**)

B 1 D   2 C   3 A   4 B

C 1 There are **also** very large signs. (**line 14**)
2 **What** scientists now believe is that human activity is the cause. (**line 27**)

D 1 As a result of (OR Because of OR As a consequence of)
2 In addition to (OR As well as) … and … as a result (OR as a consequence OR as well OR too)

E 1 For example   3 As a result of
2 In contrast to   4 In addition

F 1 also   3 and   5 so
2 however   4 but   6 As a result

G 1 (d) though   3 or (a) but
2 and (c) So   4 (b) So … instead

H ~~in America consequently her English~~ > in America. Consequently, her English (OR in America and consequently her English OR in America, so consequently her English)
She isn't like an American, ~~although~~ > though
seem to be ~~very direct, in contrast this Kazuko~~ > very direct. In contrast, Kazuko (OR very direct. In contrast to this, Kazuko OR very direct, but in contrast, Kazuko)
~~As example~~ > For example
~~Instead that~~ > Instead (OR Instead of (doing) that)

She ~~makes also~~ a small > also makes
a small 'tsss' ~~sound. Alternatively, or she~~ may say >
sound or she (OR sound. Alternatively, she OR sound.
Or she)
~~As a result this~~ > As a result (OR As a result of this)
~~Nevertheless that~~ > Nevertheless (OR Despite that OR In
spite of that)
~~In other word~~ > In other words

I
1 lift
2 also
3 also
4 lift
5 facelift
6 for example
7 Similarly
8 facelift
9 forklift
10 that is

J
A **However,** once he started working, things changed.
(OR Once he started working, **however,** things
changed. OR Once he started working, things
changed, **however.**)
In other words, he was 'out of shape'. (OR He was, **in
other words,** 'out of shape'. OR He was 'out of shape',
in other words.)

B **Also,** like a lot more men these days, he started
thinking about cosmetic surgery … (OR Like a lot
more men these days, he **also** started thinking about
cosmetic surgery …)
In particular, he wanted to get rid of some of
the wrinkles around his eyes. (OR He wanted, **in
particular,** to get rid of some of the wrinkles around
his eyes. OR He wanted to get rid of some of the
wrinkles around his eyes, **in particular.**)
Actually, now we have more men than women
coming in for certain types of surgery. (OR Now we
actually have more men than women coming in
for certain types of surgery. OR Now we have more
men than women coming in for certain types of
surgery, **actually.**)

C *__Indeed,__ the number of men seeking help from
surgeons like Dr Idris has increased dramatically in
recent years. (OR The number of men seeking help
from surgeons like Dr Idris has *__indeed__ increased
dramatically in recent years.)
*__In fact,__ the emphasis on looking young isn't limited
to facelifts, but has created a huge demand …
(OR The emphasis on looking young isn't limited to
facelifts, but *__in fact__ has created a huge demand …
OR The emphasis on looking young isn't limited to
facelifts, but has *__in fact__ created a huge demand …)
… but has created a huge demand for dental
improvements and hair transplants **too.**
* *indeed* 和 *in fact* 可互换位置。

K
1 I'm hoping ~~as well to take a British History class.~~ >
to take a British History class as well
2 ~~I don't like actually fish very much.~~ > Actually, I
don't like fish very much (OR I don't actually like fish
very much OR I don't like fish very much, actually)
3 It's part of my job ~~after all that.~~ > after all

4 ~~In addition,~~ he's certainly not the worst. > However,
(OR Nevertheless, OR On the other hand, OR Yet)
5 ~~On the other hand,~~ young children now
automatically put their empty bottles in the
recycling bin, not the dustbin. > For example
(OR For instance OR In particular OR In fact)

L
1 (c) So   3 (d) then   5 (f) so
2 (e) So   4 (a) Then   6 (b) Then

M To make hot-baked chips for two, you'll need four large
potatoes, the white of one egg, a quarter teaspoon of
cayenne pepper and a pinch of salt. **First,** slice each
potato lengthwise, **then** cut each slice lengthwise into
long sticks. **Second,** mix the egg white, cayenne and
salt in a bowl. **Then** stir the potato sticks round in the
mixture. **Finally,** spread the coated potato sticks on a
greased baking sheet and bake them in the oven at 170°
for 35 minutes.

N
1 – (OR So when your dog comes to you …)
2 –
3 Then(,) they can go on to talk about what they'll be
doing tomorrow or next year.
4 –
5 As a result, they can refer to things like heaven and
hell …
6 Secondly, animal communication consists of a fixed
number of signals …
7 –
8 In short, human communication has special
properties …

O
1 *did she
2 she was
3 was she
4 is it
5 was something
6 had she
7 it was
8 *would she
9 she would
10 was part
11 here comes
12 it is
* 第 1 题和第 8 题答案可互换。

P
1 It's the cigarette smoke that's irritating my eyes.
2 It was us who (OR that) had to clean up all the mess.
3 What Jimmy does is watch TV in his room instead
of studying.
4 What scientists now believe is that human activity is
the cause.

测验

A 1 a   2 d   3 a   4 a   5 a

B
1 D (a dog and two cats as well)
2 C (in comparison to OR in comparison with)
3 C (actually stay in London)
4 D (As a result, OR As a result of that,)
5 D (In addition to that, OR In addition,)

C
1 for example
2 After all
3 in the meantime
4 In addition
5 So

D 1 Instead of (using) butter, we used margarine.
2 Only in Poland can you get dishes and bowls with this design.
3 Not until much later did we discover the mistake.
4 It's flooding that causes most of the damage in spring. (OR It's in spring that flooding causes most of the damage.)
5 It was because he was so unpleasant that she left.

6 All I know is that the main road is blocked.
7 What he did was go to the party by himself.
8 What Rose is hoping to do is to travel across Canada by train.

E 1 What
2 To begin with
3 Similarly
4 That is
5 Next
6 In particular
7 As a result of

下列各段中均有四处空格。

为每处空格选出一个最佳答案（a，b，c 或 d）。

1 After police arrested a man for breaking into a supermarket, they discovered that the thief was actually a teenage girl dressed as a man. Although they informed [1] _____ she didn't have to [2] _____ them anything, the girl confessed [3] _____ she had done it [4] _____ her family because they had no money and they were hungry.

1 a) *her that*	b) *that*	c) *that her*	d) *to her that*
2 a) *admit*	b) *explain*	c) *report*	d) *tell*
3 a) *that*	b) *that to them*	c) *them that*	d) *them to that*
4 a) *by*	b) *for*	c) *that*	d) *to*

2 It was [1] _____ late and I was beginning to [2] _____ tired, so I asked Rachel to finish her drawing and tidy up. She held the drawing up for me to see. It [3] _____ a big black dog that [4] _____ sitting at a table.

1 a) *becoming*	b) *being*	c) *getting*	d) *going*
2 a) *feel*	b) *feel as*	c) *feel it*	d) *feel to be*
3 a) *looked*	b) *looked as*	c) *looked for*	d) *looked like*
4 a) *seemed*	b) *seemed like*	c) *seemed to be*	d) *seemed was*

3 The residents of Montclair valley are [1] _____ only upset about some recent changes, but they're also very angry because [2] _____ consulted. Some families have lived and [3] _____ crops in the valley for many years, [4] _____ now their way of life is being threatened by developers who plan to build hundreds of new houses in the area.

1 a) *both*	b) *either*	c) *neither*	d) *not*
2 a) *wasn't*	b) *weren't*	c) *it wasn't*	d) *they weren't*
3 a) *grew*	b) *grow*	c) *growing*	d) *grown*
4 a) *after*	b) *before*	c) *but*	d) *or*

4 Because it [1] _____ a lot recently, I [2] _____ out as much and I suspect you will have been [3] _____ why I haven't been in touch. I'm sorry about the long silence, but I [4] _____ to phone you this week and maybe we can arrange to meet for lunch on Friday or Saturday.

1 a) *has been raining*	b) *is raining*	c) *rain*	d) *rains*
2 a) *am not going*	b) *don't go*	c) *haven't gone*	d) *never go*
3 a) *believing*	b) *knowing*	c) *realizing*	d) *wondering*
4 a) *am promising*	b) *have been promising*	c) *have promised*	d) *promise*

5 My grandfather said that when he ¹ _____ up, he lived on a farm. During the summer, he ² _____ to get up early every morning and work all day on the farm. He said that most people ³ _____ to go away on holiday, as they do now. But he ⁴ _____ feeling unhappy or deprived or anything like that because all of his friends were in the same situation.

1 a) *had been growing*   b) *had grown*   c) *was growing*   d) *was grown*
2 a) *had been*   b) *has*   c) *was having*   d) *would have*
3 a) *didn't use*   b) *haven't used*   c) *wasn't used*   d) *weren't used*
4 a) *didn't remember*   b) *hadn't been remembering*   c) *hadn't remembered*   d) *wasn't remembering*

6 As soon as the war was over, the refugees ¹ _____ to go back to the villages they ² _____ about five years earlier. When they arrived, they ³ _____ that other groups from the east had moved into the ruined houses and ⁴ _____ rebuilding them.

1 a) *have tried*   b) *had tried*   c) *tried*   d) *were tried*
2 a) *have left*   b) *had left*   c) *leave*   d) *were left*
3 a) *have found*   b) *had found*   c) *found*   d) *were found*
4 a) *are*   b) *have*   c) *had*   d) *were*

7 Paul and Jack meet in the corridor as Jack is locking his office door.

Paul: Oh, hello. I ¹ _____ put this report in your in tray, but perhaps you'd rather take it now.

Jack: Oh, thanks. Actually, I ² _____ have lunch right now, but if you put it in my in tray, I ³ _____ it as soon as I ⁴ _____ back.

1 a) *'ll*   b) *'m going to*   c) *shall*   d) *was going to*
2 a) *'ll*   b) *'m going to*   c) *shall*   d) *would*
3 a) *'ll be reading*   b) *'ll have read*   c) *'ll read*   d) *read*
4 a) *get*   b) *'ll be getting*   c) *'ll get*   d) *'ll have got*

8 I'm not sure where Karen is. She ¹ _____ have been waiting outside her house this morning so that we ² _____ give her a lift to work, but she wasn't there. Of course, she might ³ _____ sleeping and didn't hear us. If she had decided to take the bus, she ⁴ _____ arrived by now. I hope she isn't sick.

1 a) *may*   b) *must*   c) *ought*   d) *should*
2 a) *can*   b) *can be*   c) *could*   d) *could have*
3 a) *be*   b) *been*   c) *have*   d) *have been*
4 a) *will be*   b) *will have*   c) *would be*   d) *would have*

9 Don't you hate it when people say things like 'Let's be careful, ¹ _____ we?'? It always sounds to me as if two of us ² _____ to do something together, but in fact the other person ³ _____ doing anything. ⁴ _____ prefer it if they just said, 'You should be careful', because that's what they really mean.

1 a) *will*   b) *would*   c) *shall*   d) *should*
2 a) *are going*   b) *will*   c) *will be*   d) *would*
3 a) *won't*   b) *won't be*   c) *won't have*   d) *won't to*
4 a) *I'd*   b) *I'll*   c) *I'm*   d) *I've*

10 The best summer holiday I ¹ _____ was when I was ten and I went to stay with my grandparents for a few weeks. At that time they were living in the country and ² _____ still go for long walks through the woods. I ³ _____ to climb trees and run around with their dog. I ⁴ _____ go near the lake by myself, but my grandfather sometimes took me fishing there.

1 a) *am remembering* b) *can remember*   c) *must remember*   d) *was remembering*
2 a) *can*   b) *could*   c) *may*   d) *might*
3 a) *could*   b) *could be*   c) *could have*   d) *was able*
4 a) *can't*   b) *may not*   c) *might not*   d) *wasn't allowed to*

11 Tommy, ¹ _____ better slow down and wait for the rest of us. I'm sure we have lots of time, so we ² _____ to run. We don't ³ _____ stop and buy tickets and there are still lots of people on the platform, so the train ⁴ _____ come yet.

1 a) *you'd*   b) *you'll*   c) *you're*   d) *you've*
2 a) *aren't need*   b) *don't need*   c) *needn't*   d) *needn't have*
3 a) *have to*   b) *have got to*   c) *must*   d) *must have to*
4 a) *can't*   b) *can't be*   c) *can't have*   d) *couldn't*

12 Joe has just returned to the school computer room where Sam is working.

Joe: Who ¹ _____ been using my computer?

Sam: I have ² _____ idea. But these computers are for any student who wants to use them, ³ _____?

Joe: Of course. But ⁴ _____ you see me doing my work on that one before lunch? I hope I remembered to save it.

1 a) *has*   b) *has he*   c) *have*   d) *have they*
2 a) *no*   b) *no longer*   c) *not*   d) *not an*
3 a) *aren't they*   b) *can't it*   c) *don't they*   d) *isn't it*
4 a) *aren't*   b) *didn't*   c) *don't*   d) *haven't*

3 Liz is helping Lucy clean out her flat.

Liz: Did you want to keep all these old books or [1] ....?

Lucy: I'm not sure. They look interesting, but [2] .... of them would be worth anything.

Liz: So, [3] .... of them do you think [4] .... going to keep?

1 a) *no*	b) *none*	c) *not*	d) *nothing*
2 a) *none*	b) *no one*	c) *not any*	d) *nothing*
3 a) *for what*	b) *for which*	c) *what*	d) *which*
4 a) *are*	b) *are you*	c) *you*	d) *you are*

4 The Star Tree hotel chain is in financial trouble and some of their smaller hotels are going to have [1] .... Rising costs [2] .... for recent losses and many smaller hotels [3] .... to have been losing money for many years. No buyer has yet [4] .... for the properties.

1 a) *been sold*	b) *being sold*	c) *sold*	d) *to be sold*
2 a) *are being blamed*	b) *blamed*	c) *have blamed*	d) *to be blamed*
3 a) *are reported*	b) *are reporting*	c) *been reported*	d) *have reported*
4 a) *been found*	b) *being found*	c) *found*	d) *to be found*

15 'The Waste Land' is [1] .... title of [2] .... poem by T.S. Eliot, first published in 1922. [3] .... style of the poem has had a great influence on [4] .... modern poetry.

1 a) *a*	b) *an*	c) *the*	d) –
2 a) *a*	b) *an*	c) *the*	d) –
3 a) *A*	b) *An*	c) *The*	d) –
4 a) *a*	b) *an*	c) *the*	d) –

16 'I don't call this [1] .... progress,' says Rob Harding, owner of [2] .... small business in the city centre. He complains that an hour and fifteen minutes [3] .... become his typical commuting time every morning. 'It used to take only twenty minutes. There's just too much [4] .... now.'

1 a) *a*	b) *one*	c) *the*	d) –
2 a) *a*	b) *an*	c) *the*	d) –
3 a) *are*	b) *has*	c) *have*	d) *is*
4 a) *car*	b) *cars*	c) *motor*	d) *traffic*

17 I'm really enjoying my new job. All of [1]_____ people I work with are friendly and I haven't had [2]_____ problems so far. The best part is that I get paid [3]_____ two weeks instead of waiting [4]_____ month between pay days like in my last job.

   1 a) *that*   b) *the*   c) *them*   d) –

   2 a) *any*   b) *much*   c) *some*   d) *no*

   3 a) *all*   b) *both*   c) *each*   d) *every*

   4 a) *a whole*   b) *the whole of*   c) *whole*   d) *whole of*

18 Last year we had [1]_____ more rain in the early spring and it made [2]_____ in the garden grow better. We probably had three or four [3]_____ strawberries as we're getting this year. I checked the strawberries in the garden this morning, but there [4]_____ that were ripe.

   1 a) *a large number of*   b) *a lot of*   c) *many*   d) *much*

   2 a) *all*   b) *each*   c) *every*   d) *everything*

   3 a) *time as many*   b) *time as much*   c) *times as many*   d) *times as much*

   4 a) *was only a little*   b) *was only little*   c) *were only a few*   d) *were only few*

19 I was sitting at my desk when there was a loud crash as something came flying through the window. At first I thought it was a rock, but then I realized it was a cricket ball. I picked up the ball and put it on the desk beside [1]_____. Two young boys appeared outside the broken window. They said they were sorry, but then they started arguing, with each blaming [2]_____ for causing the accident. Then suddenly one of them asked if [3]_____ could have the ball back. I said, 'I don't think [4]_____. Not until you pay for this broken window.' They looked at me, then at each other, and then they both started running.

   1 a) *me*   b) *mine*   c) *my*   d) *myself*

   2 a) *another*   b) *one other*   c) *other*   d) *the other*

   3 a) *it*   b) *then*   c) *they*   d) –

   4 a) *it*   b) *so*   c) *that*   d) –

20 Although they were described as the [1]_____ designs in many years, there isn't [2]_____ about the latest line of shoes from Santorelli. As one of the most famous designers [3]_____ Italy, Salvatore Santorelli is expected to do [4]_____ simply repeat the previous year's successful formula of 'smart casual' sandals.

   1 a) *first Italian new*   b) *first new Italian*   c) *new first Italian*   d) *Italian first new*

   2 a) *anything new very* b) *anything very new*   c) *new anything very*   d) *very new anything*

   3 a) *by*   b) *in*   c) *of*   d) *to*

   4 a) *as much as*   b) *more than*   c) *the best*   d) *the most*

1 I remember when we stayed [1] .... New York [2] .... a few days [3] .... last summer. It was really hot, even [4] .... night, and I just felt miserable.

1 a) *at*   b) *in*   c) *into*   d) *–*
2 a) *by*   b) *during*   c) *for*   d) *in*
3 a) *at*   b) *on*   c) *in*   d) *–*
4 a) *at*   b) *by*   c) *during*   d) *in*

22 When we were students, my friends and I rented a cabin [1] .... the mountains so that we could go hiking. It only cost us £55 for the whole week, not [2] .... food, of course. One day, my friend Daniel got tired and stopped to rest, saying he'd catch [3] .... later, but when he still hadn't returned to the cabin [4] .... late afternoon, we started getting worried. Luckily, he met some men who lived in the area and they brought him back to the cabin before it got dark.

1 a) *above*   b) *in*   c) *on*   d) *over*
2 a) *include*   b) *included*   c) *includes*   d) *including*
3 a) *up us*   b) *up with us* c) *us up*   d) *with us up*
4 a) *by*   b) *during*   c) *in*   d) *since*

23 When I visit big cities like Paris, I usually avoid [1] .... to the most famous places because I really hate crowds. But it was no use [2] .... that to my friend Tatjana because she was really eager [3] .... the *Mona Lisa* in the Louvre and she refused [4] .... outside while she went in.

1 a) *go*   b) *going*   c) *gone*   d) *to go*
2 a) *trying explain* b) *trying to explain* c) *to try explaining* d) *to try to explain*
3 a) *for see*   b) *to see*   c) *in seeing*   d) *seeing*
4 a) *letting me to wait* b) *letting me wait* c) *to let me to wait* d) *to let me wait*

24 At a time when it has become so important [1] .... in school, we shouldn't be [2] .... to learn that more students are cheating than ever before. With so many of them anxious about [3] ...., students also now seem to believe that those who cheat are unlikely [4] ....

1 a) *succeed*   b) *succeeding*   c) *success*   d) *to succeed*
2 a) *surprise*   b) *surprised*   c) *surprises*   d) *surprising*
3 a) *fail*   b) *failed*   c) *failing*   d) *to fail*
4 a) *to catch*   b) *to be catching* c) *to be caught* d) *to have caught*

25 There was one student who asked about [1] .... it was okay to use a dictionary during the exam and I had to tell her [2] .... it. Then she started arguing [3] .... me that her teacher always allowed her to use it in class. I had to remind [4] .... was an exam, not a classroom exercise.

1 a) *if*   b) *that*   c) *whether*   d) *why*
2 a) *don't use*   b) *no use*   c) *no using*   d) *not to use*
3 a) *about*   b) *for*   c) *to*   d) *with*
4 a) *her it*   b) *that*   c) *that it*   d) *–*

26 Andrew Murphy, former managing director of Delco Electronics, has pleaded 'Not Guilty' to charges [1] .... £5 million from the company. He claims not to know where [2] .... He has suggested that an accountant [3] .... the money. Investigators consider [4] .... anyone else in the company could have committed the crime.

1 a) *stealing*   b) *that he stole*   c) *to have stolen*   d) *which he stole*
2 a) *did go the money*   b) *did the money go*   c) *the money went*   d) *went the money*
3 a) *is taking*   b) *should take*   c) *takes*   d) *took*
4 a) *it unlikely that*   b) *that it unlikely*   c) *that unlikely*   d) *unlikely that*

27 I've been looking for a special kind of brown cheese [1] .... made in Norway, but [2] .... name I can't remember. There was one woman I talked [3] .... in the Gourmet Experience shop on King Street [4] .... said they could order it for me if I could give her more information about it.

1 a) *it*   b) *that's*   c) *was*   d) *which*
2 a) *what*   b) *which*   c) *where*   d) *whose*
3 a) *to*   b) *to her*   c) *to whom*   d) *–*
4 a) *what*   b) *who*   c) *whom*   d) *–*

28 The term 'organic' can only be used to describe food [1] .... in situations [2] .... no artificial chemicals have been used. Anyone [3] .... fertilizer [4] .... containing chemicals to make tomatoes grow bigger, for example, is certainly not growing them organically.

1 a) *grown*   b) *that growing* c) *where growing* d) *which grown*
2 a) *how*   b) *that*   c) *where*   d) *which*
3 a) *use*   b) *used*   c) *uses*   d) *using*
4 a) *what*   b) *when*   c) *which*   d) *–*

29 [1] .... their hair wasn't actually very long, rock groups such as the Beatles and the Rolling Stones were often criticized as 'long-haired' or 'needing haircuts' when they first became popular during the early 1960s. At that time men were sometimes considered effeminate if they [2] .... long hair. The opposite was true for men who grew a beard [3] ...., of course, it was allowed to grow too long. Beards grow faster than hair and need more care. In fact, if the average man never trimmed his beard, it [4] .... to nearly ten metres in his lifetime. Now, that's a lot of hair!

1 a) *Even though*   b) *If only*   c) *Unless*   d) *Whether*
2 a) *had*   b) *have*   c) *will have*   d) *would have*
3 a) *if*   b) *if not*   c) *only if*   d) *unless*
4 a) *grew*   b) *has grown*   c) *will grow*   d) *would grow*

30 I'm still waiting to find out if I passed the entrance exam. Perhaps I'll get the news later today when I [1] .... to school. I promise I [2] .... you as soon as I get the news. It's three weeks [3] .... I took the exam, but my teacher warned me that they sometimes don't announce the results until more than a month [4] ....

1 a) *go*   b) *have gone*   c) *going*   d) *will go*
2 a) *call*   b) *called*   c) *'ll call*   d) *'m calling*
3 a) *later*   b) *once*   c) *since*   d) *when*
4 a) *has passed*   b) *is passing*   c) *passed*   d) *will pass*

31 [1] .... in most other sports players are usually trying to get the most goals or points [2] .... win, the opposite is true in golf. In a game of golf, it is the lowest score that wins. Each player must try to get his or her ball in the hole [3] .... as few shots as possible. For each hole there is a given number of shots called 'par'. [4] .... a player uses one shot less than par, it's called a 'birdie' and one more than par is called a 'bogey'.

1 a) *Even although*   b) *In spite of*   c) *Instead of*   d) *Whereas*
2 a) *for*   b) *in order to*   c) *so that*   d) *such that*
3 a) *use*   b) *uses*   c) *used*   d) *using*
4 a) *As*   b) *Since*   c) *When*   d) *While*

32 [1] .... our flight from London to Toronto was delayed because [2] .... bad weather, we missed our connection to Vancouver and had to spend six hours in the airport [3] .... for the next flight. [4] .... being delayed, we still had a good trip and didn't feel too jet-lagged when we arrived.

1 a) *After*   b) *Although*   c) *If*   d) *So that*
2 a) *it*   b) *of*   c) *the*   d) *–*
3 a) *have waited*   b) *waited*   c) *waiting*   d) *were waiting*
4 a) *Although*   b) *As*   c) *Despite*   d) *Unless*

33 What the recent use of DNA testing has shown [1]........................ eyewitness testimony may not always be reliable. [2]........................, an eyewitness testified that he saw Arthur Medeiros with Annie Anderson shortly before the young woman was murdered and, [3]........................ that testimony, Medeiros was convicted and sent to prison. Not until much later [4]........................ discovered through DNA testing that someone other than Medeiros had been responsible for Anderson's death.

1 a) *is it*   b) *is that*   c) *it is*   d) *that is*
2 a) *For example*   b) *In addition*   c) *On the other hand* d) *Therefore*
3 a) *afterwards*   b) *as a consequence* c) *as a result of*   d) *subsequently*
4 a) *it was*   b) *they*   c) *was*   d) *was it*

34 Do you sometimes feel anxious or irritable when you're driving? It may be the smell inside your car [1]........................ is determining how you feel. A recent study of American drivers found that the smell of peppermint or cinnamon improved their performance by reducing anxiety more than 20 per cent. Alertness [2]........................ increased by almost 30 per cent. [3]........................, the smell of cakes or fast food made drivers more irritable and caused them to speed, probably because those smells stimulate hunger [4]........................ make drivers more anxious to get where they're going sooner.

1 a) *it*   b) *that*   c) *what*   d) *which*
2 a) *also*   b) *as well*   c) *besides*   d) *moreover*
3 a) *In conclusion* b) *In contrast*   c) *In other words*   d) *In particular*
4 a) *and*   b) *as a result of*   c) *consequently and*   d) *however didn't*

位于答案之后括号中的数字表示所考查语法点的相关信息所在的页码。

1 1 a (8)
   2 d (8)
   3 a (8)
   4 b (8)

2 1 c (10)
   2 a (10)
   3 d (10)
   4 c (10)

3 1 d (12)
   2 d (12)
   3 d (12)
   4 c (12)

4 1 a (18)
   2 c (18)
   3 d (17, 18)
   4 d (18)

5 1 c (20)
   2 d (20)
   3 a (20)
   4 a (20)

6 1 c (22, 23)
   2 b (22, 23)
   3 c (22, 23)
   4 d (20)

7 1 d (24, 32)
   2 b (24, 32)
   3 c (24)
   4 a (24)

8 1 d (30)
   2 c (29, 34)
   3 d (30)
   4 d (30)

9 1 c (32)
   2 a (32)
   3 b (32)
   4 a (33)

10 1 b (34)
   2 b (34)
   3 d (34)
   4 d (35)

11 1 a (41)
   2 b (38)
   3 a (38)
   4 c (40)

12 1 a (45)
   2 a (45)
   3 a (46)
   4 b (46)

13 1 c (48)
   2 a (48)
   3 d (50)
   4 d (52)

14 1 d (58)
   2 a (57, 58)
   3 a (57, 63)
   4 a (57, 58)

15 1 c (78)
   2 a (70)
   3 c (70)
   4 d (72)

16 1 d (74)
   2 a (74)
   3 b (75)
   4 d (74)

17 1 b (83, 84)
   2 a (86, 90)
   3 d (84)
   4 a (88)

18 1 d (90)
   2 d (88, 89, 98)
   3 c (93)
   4 c (92)

19 1 a (100)
   2 d (100)
   3 c (97)
   4 b (105)

20 1 b (111, 112)
   2 b (112, 118)
   3 b (120)
   4 b (120)

21 1 b (128, 130)
   2 c (126, 127)
   3 d (126)
   4 a (126, 127)

22 1 b (128, 129)
   2 d (125)
   3 b (134)
   4 a (126, 127)

23 1 b (142)
   2 b (145)
   3 b (144)
   4 d (139, 143)

24 1 d (144)
   2 b (144)
   3 c (144)
   4 c (140, 144)

25 1 c (154)
   2 d (156)
   3 d (152)
   4 a (152)

26 1 b (164)
   2 c (161)
   3 d (161, 167)
   4 a (162)

27 1 b (173)
   2 d (178)
   3 a (173, 179)
   4 b (173)

28 1 a (176)
   2 c (180)
   3 d (176, 178)
   4 d (176)

29 1 a (192)
   2 a (185)
   3 d (192)
   4 d (186)

30 1 a (185)
   2 c (199)
   3 c (198, 199)
   4 a (199)

31 1 d (204)
   2 b (202, 203)
   3 d (205)
   4 c (198, 201)

32 1 a (197, 199)
   2 b (197)
   3 c (205)
   4 c (204)

33 1 b (217)
   2 a (212)
   3 c (210, 214)
   4 d (216)

34 1 b (217)
   2 a (212)
   3 b (212, 215)
   4 a (210)

规则动词

通常，在规则动词的动词原形后加 -ed（1）或 -d（2）即可构成其一般过去式和过去分词。

1 *I asked him, but he hasn't answered yet. • We wanted to know. • I have waited patiently.*

2 *They agreed that it was a good idea. • That's why we have continued. • She hasn't smiled much.*

有些动词须先双写词尾的辅音字母（位于重读音节中一个单独的元音字母之后），再加 -ed。

3 *She had planned to visit us and regretted that poor health had stopped her.*

此类动词还有：**dragged, occurred, permitted, preferred, ripped, robbed, slipped, trimmed**。

注意，英国英语中的 cancelled, travelled 等在美国英语中拼写为 canceled, traveled 等。

有些动词须先把词尾的 -y（位于辅音字母之后）变为 -i-，再加 -ed。

4 *Have you tried to get a scholarship? ~ I applied for one, but they haven't replied yet.*

此类动词还有：**carried, copied, cried, hurried, identified, implied, studied, testified, worried**。

不规则动词

有些动词的一般过去式形式比较特殊。

5 *We saw Jack Brown yesterday. • I forgot I had your keys. • They understood what I taught them.*

有些动词是通过在动词原形后加 -en（6）或 -n（7）构成过去分词。

6 *Where have you been? • Have you eaten anything? • I had hidden it, but it had fallen out.*

7 *I haven't seen that film. • Have you known him a long time? • They've driven up from London.*

有些动词的一般过去式和过去分词的拼写方式与其动词原形相同。

8 *Yesterday I hit my forehead on the shelf and cut it, but it hasn't hurt too badly today.*

此类动词还有：**bet, burst, cost, forecast, let, put, quit, ride, set, shut, split, spread, thrust**。

有些动词的一般过去式和过去分词既有规则形式，也有不规则形式。

9 *Have you burned / burnt the toast? • I dreamed / dreamt about you. • He spilled / spilt some milk.*

此类动词还有：**kneeled / knelt, leaped / leapt, learned / learnt, lighted / lit, speeded / sped**。

注意，使用此类有两种形式的动词时，-ed 形式正变得越来越常见，尤其在美国英语中。

常见的不规则动词

动词原形	一般过去式	过去分词
be	was, were	been
become	became	become
begin	began	begun
bend	bent	bent
bet	bet	bet
bite	bit	bitten
blow	blew	blown
break	broke	broken
bring	brought	brought
build	built	built
burst	burst	burst
buy	bought	bought
catch	caught	caught
choose	chose	chosen
come	came	come
cost	cost	cost
cut	cut	cut
dig	dug	dug
do	did	done
draw	drew	drawn
drink	drank	drunk
drive	drove	driven
eat	ate	eaten
fall	fell	fallen
feed	fed	fed
feel	felt	felt
fight	fought	fought
find	found	found
fly	flew	flown
forget	forgot	forgotten
forgive	forgave	forgiven
freeze	froze	frozen
get	got	got
give	gave	given
go	went	gone
grow	grew	grown
have	had	had
hear	heard	heard
hide	hid	hidden
hit	hit	hit
hold	held	held
keep	kept	kept
kneel	knelt	knelt
know	knew	known
lay	laid	laid
lead	led	led
leave	left	left
lend	lent	lent
let	let	let
lie	lay	lain

动词原形	一般过去式	过去分词
light	lit	lit
lose	lost	lost
make	made	made
mean	meant	meant
meet	met	met
pay	paid	paid
put	put	put
read	read	read
ride	rode	ridden
ring	rang	rung
rise	rose	risen
run	ran	run
say	said	said
see	saw	seen
sell	sold	sold
send	sent	sent
set	set	set
shake	shook	shaken
shine	shone	shone
shoot	shot	shot
show	showed	shown
shut	shut	shut
sing	sang	sung
sink	sank	sunk
sit	sat	sat
sleep	slept	slept
slide	slid	slid
speak	spoke	spoken
spend	spent	spent
spit	spat	spat
split	split	split
spread	spread	spread
stand	stood	stood
steal	stole	stolen
stick	stuck	stuck
strike	struck	struck
swear	swore	sworn
sweep	swept	swept
swim	swam	swum
take	took	taken
teach	taught	taught
tear	tore	torn
tell	told	told
think	thought	thought
throw	threw	thrown
understand	understood	understood
wake	woke	woken
wear	wore	worn
win	won	won
write	wrote	written

下面列出了语法术语和相关解释。释文（不包含例句）中的蓝色粗体词表示它们本身是语法术语，可在本术语表中找到。释文后的数字表示正文页码，在该页可找到关于该术语的更多信息。

action verb 行为动词：用于描述做了什么或发生了什么的动词（**verb**）（*I ate lunch.*）。请比较：**state verb 状态动词**。3

active 主动：动词（**verb**）的主动形式用于描述主语（**subject**）的行为动作（*A thief stole my car.*）。请比较：**passive 被动**。57

adjective 形容词：new, good-looking 之类用于修饰名词（**noun**）的词（*Charlotte's new boyfriend is good-looking.*）。111—112，114

adverb 副词：really, recently 之类用于修饰动词（**verb**）、形容词（**adjective**）、副词（**adverb**）或句子（**sentence**）的词（*I met him recently and he's really good-looking.*）。116，118

adverbial 状语：在分句（**clause**）或句子（**sentence**）（*I'll meet you in town later after I finish work.*）中用于补充信息的副词（**adverb**）（*later*）、介词短语（**prepositional phrase**）（*in town*）或状语从句（**adverbial clause**）（*after I finish work*）。3

adverbial clause 状语从句：从句（**clause**）的一种，通常由从属连词（**subordinating conjunction**）引导（*because*），用于提供某事发生的时间或原因等信息（*I can't go out because I have to study.*）。197

agent 施动者：实施或引起某行为的人或物，通常在主动（**active**）句中作主语（**subject**）（*Dickens wrote Oliver Twist.*）。64

article 冠词：在名词（**noun**）之前用作限定词（**determiner**），包括定冠词（**definite article**）（*the*）和不定冠词（**indefinite article**）（*a / an*）（*The car had a flat tyre.*）。69—70

attributive adjective 定语形容词：用在名词（**noun**）之前的形容词（**adjective**）（*She had red hair and green eyes.*）。请比较：**predicative adjective 表语形容词**。112

auxiliary verb 助动词：动词 be, do, have 的某种形式或情态动词（**modal**）。它们与主要动词（**main verb**）连用可构成不同的时态、否定句和疑问句（*Have you eaten yet?*）。3，17

bare infinitive 不带 to 的动词不定式：= **base form** 17

base form 原形：动词（**verb**）的基础形式，如 be 和 eat，同词典中给出的形式。17

clause 分句；从句：包含一个主语（**subject**）和一个动词（**verb**）的一组词，构成一个简单句（**simple sentence**）（*She left yesterday.*），或构成主从复合句（**complex sentence**）（*She left before you came.*）或并列复合句（**compound sentence**）（*She left and I'm glad.*）的一部分。3，12

cleft sentence 分裂句：该句型把一个句子（**sentence**）（*I'm not supposed to drink coffee.*）分为两部分，强调其中的一部分，包括 it 分裂句（**it-cleft**）（*It's coffee that I'm not supposed to drink.*）和 wh- 分裂句（**wh-cleft**）（*What I'm not supposed to drink is coffee.*）。217

collective noun 集体名词：= **group noun** 75

common noun 普通名词：不表示任何人或事物的名称的名词（**noun**）（*The car had a flat tyre.*）。请比较：**proper noun 专有名词**。69

comparative 比较级：通常通过在形容词（**adjective**）或副词（**adverb**）的词尾加 -er（*healthier*）或在前面加 more / less（*less expensive*）构成，后面通常跟 than，用于对两个对象在某方面的情况进行比较（*Fish is **healthier** and **less expensive** than meat.*）。请比较：**superlative** 最高级。120

complement 补语：用在系动词（**linking verb**）之后的单词或短语，通常用于描述主语（*She is a **student** so she isn't **rich**.*）。10

complex preposition 复杂介词：由两个或更多单词构成的介词（**preposition**）（*In addition to me, there were three other people waiting in front of the entrance.*）。请比较：**simple preposition** 简单介词。125

complex sentence 主从复合句：由两个或更多分句（**clause**）组成的句子（**sentence**），分句之间由 because, before 等从属连词（**subordinating conjunction**）连接（*I went to bed because I was tired.*）。请比较：**compound sentence** 并列复合句。12

compound adjective 复合形容词：由用连字符连接的两个单词组成的形容词（**adjective**）（*a **good-looking** person, a **home-cooked** meal*）。114

compound noun 复合名词：由两个或更多单词构成的名词（**noun**），指人或事物（*a **bus driver**, an **application form***）。76

compound sentence 并列复合句：由两个或更多分句（**clause**）组成的句子（**sentence**），分句之间由并列连词（**coordinating conjunction**）（*and, but, or*）连接（*Dave read a magazine **and** I went to bed.*）。请比较：**complex sentence** 主从复合句。12

compound-complex sentence 并列-主从复合句：由三个或更多分句（**clause**）组成的句子（**sentence**），连接分句的既有并列连词（**coordinating conjunction**）又有从属连词（**subordinating conjunction**）（*Dave read a magazine **and** I went to bed **because** I was tired.*）。请比较：**complex sentence** 主从复合句，**compound sentence** 并列复合句。12

conditional 条件句：包含一个条件从句（**clause**）和另一个分句的句型。条件从句通常以 if 开头，构成另一个分句（**clause**）所述之事发生的条件（*If I have time, I'll help you.*）。185—186，188

conjunction 连词：and, but, or 等用于连接单词、短语或句子的词（*It's late **and** I want to go home.*）。2，197，210

connector 连接词语：通常用于连接句子（**sentence**），有时也用于连接分句（**clause**）的单词（*however*）或短语（*in addition*）（*They didn't win. **However**, they played better than last week. **In addition**, they scored two goals.*）。209—210

continuous 进行时：动词（**verb**）的一种形式，由 "be ＋ 现在分词（**present participle**）" 构成（*The baby **is sleeping**.*）。17

contracted form 缩约形式：单词的缩短形式（*I've, he's, she'd, we'll, they won't*）。24，29

coordinating conjunction 并列连词：常见的并列连词有 and, but, or（*I'll write **or** I'll call you.*）。请比较：**subordinating conjunction** 从属连词。12

copula / copular verb 系动词：= **linking verb** 10

countable noun 可数名词：既有单数形式（*book, child*）也有复数形式（*books, children*）的名词（**noun**），用于指被视为单独个体的人或事物。请比较：**uncountable noun** 不可数名词。74

counterfactual conditional 反事实条件句：非真实条件句（**unreal conditional**）的一种，用于谈论两个未曾发生过的事件之间的假想的联系（*If you had been born in the Middle Ages, you would have had a harsh life*）。186

defining relative clause 限制性关系从句：一种关系从句（**relative clause**），用于对人或事物作出辨认或加以分类（*Do you know the man who lives upstairs?*）。请比较：**non-defining relative clause 非限制性关系从句**。174

definite article 定冠词：the（*Can you see the moon?*）。请比较：**indefinite article 不定冠词**。69—70

demonstrative pronoun 指示代词：包括 this, that, these, those，用于代替名词短语（**noun phrase**）（*I like these better than those.*）。83，98

demonstrative 指示词：包括 this, that, these, those，可以在名词（**noun**）之前用作限定词（**determiner**）（*this book*），也可以用作代替名词短语（**noun phrase**）的代词（**pronoun**）（*I don't like that.*）。83，98

determiner 限定词：用在名词（**noun**）之前的单词，如冠词（**article**）（*a / an, the*）、指示词（**demonstrative**）（*this, that, these, those*）和物主词（**possessive**）（*my, your, his, her, its, our, their*）（*A friend sent me this funny card for my birthday.*）。83

direct object 直接宾语：受动词（**verb**）所示行为影响的对象（*I dropped the ball.*），可以是单词或短语。请比较：**indirect object 间接宾语**。8

direct speech 直接引语：在转述时所引用的说话人的原话，通常放在引号（**quotation marks**）内（*He said, 'I'm tired.'*）。请比较：**indirect speech 间接引语**。149

ellipsis 省略：省去某些词或短语而不重复它们（*Lucy came in and _ sat down.*）。106

empty object *it* 形式宾语 it：位于直接宾语（**direct object**）的位置，不代指任何事物的 it（*I hate it when I miss the bus.*）。102，162

empty subject *it* 形式主语 it：位于主语（**subject**）的位置，不代指任何事物的 it（*It was nice to go for a walk even though it was raining.*）。102，162

empty subject *there* 形式主语 there：位于主语的位置，不代指任何事物的 there（*There isn't any food left.*）。103

equative 同级：用于 (not) as ... as 结构中的形容词（**adjective**）或副词（**adverb**）。这一结构用于表示某事物在某方面与另一事物一样（或不一样）（*Your jacket is as big as my coat.*）。120

ergative 作格动词：一种后面不带宾语（**object**）的动词（**verb**），一般用于说明某事只是单纯地发生了，并没有施动者（*The door suddenly opened.*）。这类动词拥有相应的（词形、词义相同）及物动词（**transitive verb**）。许多语法书将作格动词与那些只有不及物用法的动词一同视为不及物动词（**intransitive verb**）。64

factual conditional 事实条件句：真实条件句（**real conditional**）的一种，用于表述两件事之间在现在、过去或一直存在的固定关联（*If the fruit is soft, it's ready to eat.*）。185

first conditional 第一条件句：= **predictive conditional** 185

focus structure 焦点结构：前置（**fronting**）和分裂句（**cleft sentence**）之类的结构，用于使他人更关注句子的某一部分（*Tea I can drink. It's coffee I'm not supposed to drink.*）。216—217

fraction 分数：half, two-thirds 之类的单词或短语，与 of 连用，在限定词（**determiner**）或代词（**pronoun**）之前作数量词（**quantifier**），用于描述某事物的一部分（*Two-thirds of the students are from Europe.*）。93

fronting 前置：将句子（**sentence**）（*I can't drink coffee.*）的一部分前移至句首的句型（*Coffee I can't drink because it gives me a headache.*）。216

generic noun 泛指名词：用于对某类人或事物作笼统表述，而不专指某个具体例子的名词（**noun**）（*Women live longer than men.*）。75

generic pronoun 泛指代词：one, they, we, you 等用于泛指"人们"的代词（**pronoun**）（*They say you can't teach an old dog new tricks.*）。97

gerund 动名词：与现在分词（**present participle**）形式相同，但用作名词（**noun**）（*I enjoy walking.*）。139

group noun 集体名词：表示由一群人组成的集合体的名词（**noun**），如 committee 和 team（*The Olympic committee chooses the national team.*）。75

hypothetical conditional 假设条件句：非真实条件句（**unreal conditional**）的一种，用于表达某种远离现实、不大可能发生的情况，即谈论两个假想事件之间的联系（*If I had a lot of money, I'd buy a Mercedes.*）。186

imperative 祈使语气：动词（**verb**）的形式为原形（**base form**），通常用于给出命令（*Stop!*）。17

indefinite adverb 不定副词：anywhere, everywhere 之类的副词（**adverb**），用于非常笼统地谈论地点（*I've looked everywhere, but I can't find my notebook anywhere.*）。98

indefinite article 不定冠词：a / an（*Would you like an apple or a banana?*）。请比较：**definite article 定冠词**。69—70

indefinite pronoun 不定代词：someone, anything 等用于非常笼统地谈论人和事物的代词（**pronoun**）（*Someone called earlier, but they didn't say anything.*）。98

indirect object 间接宾语：用在 give, send 等动词（**verb**）之后的单词或短语，表示接受某事物的人（*I gave Rob some money. I sent a letter to them.*）。请比较：**direct object 直接宾语**。8

indirect question 间接疑问句：转述他人提出的问题但不引用原话，而是用名词性从句（**noun clause**）来转述 wh- 疑问句（**wh-question**）（*He asked what we were doing.*）或 yes / no 疑问句（**'yes / no' question**）（*He asked if we were from Sweden.*）。52，154

indirect speech 间接引语：转述别人说的话但不引用原话，而是用名词性从句（**noun clause**）进行表述（*He said that he was tired.*）。请比较：**direct speech 直接引语**。150

infinitive 动词不定式："to + 动词（**verb**）原形（**base form**）"的形式（*I'm hoping to win.*）。139

-ing form -ing 形式：参见 **gerund 动名词**和 **present participle 现在分词**。17，139

intransitive verb 不及物动词：后面不接宾语（**object**）的动词（**verb**）（*I can't sleep.*）。请比较：**transitive verb 及物动词**。6

inversion 倒装: 把动词（**verb**）或助动词（**auxiliary verb**）置于主语（**subject**）之前的结构（*Into the room **walked** two men.*）。216

inverted commas 引号: = **quotation marks** 149

it-cleft it 分裂句: 把一个句子（**sentence**）（*I'm not supposed to drink coffee.*）分为两部分的句型，第一部分为"it ＋ be ＋ 强调部分"，第二部分为一个关系从句（**relative clause**）（*It's coffee [that] I'm not supposed to drink.*）。请比较：*wh-cleft* **wh- 分裂句**。217

linking verb 系动词: be, become, seem 等与补语（**complement**）连用的动词（**verb**），通常在描述主语时使用（*She is / seems unhappy.*）。10

linking word 起连接作用的词: = **connector** 209

main verb 主要动词: 分句（**clause**）中的动词（**verb**）（*Did you **follow** that? I **understood** what she said.*）。请比较：**auxiliary verb 助动词**。45—46

mass noun 不可数名词: = **uncountable noun** 74

mixed conditional 混合条件句: 条件句（**conditional**）的一种，两个分句（**clause**）的时态（**tense**）搭配与通常情况不同（*If you saw the film, you'll remember the battle scene.*）。188

modal 情态动词: 助动词（**auxiliary verb**）的一种，包括 can, could, must 等，与动词（**verb**）原形（**base form**）连用，表示可能、许可、必要性等（*You **must** leave now.*）。请比较：**phrasal modal 短语情态动词**。29

multiplier 乘数: twice, five times 之类的单词或短语，用在限定词（**determiner**）之前作数量词（**quantifier**），可说明某事发生的频率或两个事物之间的倍数关系（*They pray **five times** a day.*）。93

negative 否定句: 包含助动词（**auxiliary verb**）、not / n't 和主要动词（**main verb**）的句子（**sentence**）或分句（**clause**）（*I **don't** care.*）。45

negative adverb 否定副词: never, no longer 等用作副词的单词或短语（*He **never** studies.*）。45，48

nominal clause 名词性从句: = **noun clause** 161—162

non-count noun 不可数名词: = **uncountable noun** 74

non-defining relative clause 非限制性关系从句: 用于补充额外信息的关系从句（**relative clause**），通常用逗号把它与其他部分隔开（*My friend John, **who lives upstairs**, has a cat.*）。请比较：**defining relative clause 限制性关系从句**。174

non-finite form 非限定形式: = **base form** 17

noun 名词: 用于表示人或事物的单词，包括普通名词（**common noun**）（*book, courage*）和专有名词（**proper noun**）（*Shakespeare, Denmark*）。69

noun clause 名词性从句: 功能相当于名词短语（**noun phrase**）的 that 从句（*that-clause*）（*I know **that it's late**.*）或 wh- 从句（*wh-clause*）（*I didn't know **what you were doing**.*）。161—162

noun phrase 名词短语: 中心词是名词（**noun**）的一组词，用作主语（**subject**）或宾语（**object**）（*Their new flat is really big so they're having **a party for 60 people on Saturday night**.*）。4

object 宾语：用作直接宾语（**direct object**）（*He took the money.*）、间接宾语（**indirect object**）（*I gave him the money.*）或位于介词（**preposition**）之后（*He took it with him.*）的名词（**noun**）、名词短语（**noun phrase**）或代词（**pronoun**）。8，125

object pronoun 宾格代词：用作宾语（**object**）的人称代词（**personal pronoun**）（*me, you, him, her, it, us, them*）（*James gave them to me, not her.*）。97

pair noun 双数概念的名词：表示由两个相配部分组成的物品的名词（**noun**），例如 scissors 或 trousers。75

parenthetical noun clause 作插入语的名词性从句：用在名词（**noun**）之后补充信息的名词性从句（**noun clause**），通常用逗号、破折号或括号将该从句隔出来（*His first suggestion, that we should go to Manchester, wasn't very popular.*）。164

participle 分词：动词（**verb**）的一种形式，包括现在分词（**present participle**）（*breaking, repairing*）和过去分词（**past participle**）（*broken, repaired*）。17

participle adjective 分词形容词：来源于现在分词（**present participle**）（*surprising*）或过去分词（**past participle**）（*shocked*）的形容词（**adjective**）（*She seemed shocked by the surprising news.*）。114

participle clause 分词分句：= **reduced adverbial clause** 205

particle 小品词：与动词（**verb**）搭配构成短语动词（**phrasal verb**）的词，有些也是介词（**preposition**）（*on*），有些也是副词（**adverb**）（*away*）（*He put on his jacket and walked away.*）。134

passive 被动：动词（**verb**）的被动形式由"be + 及物动词（**transitive verb**）的过去分词（**past participle**）"构成，用于说明主语（**subject**）承受的动作（*My car was stolen.*）。请比较：**active 主动**。57

past continuous 过去进行时：动词（**verb**）的一种形式，由"was / were + 现在分词（**present participle**）"构成（*The baby was sleeping.*）。17，20

past participle 过去分词：指 broken, repaired 这类动词（**verb**）形式，用于构成完成时（**perfect**）（*I had broken my watch.*）和被动式（**passive**）（*It was repaired.*）。17

past perfect 过去完成时：动词（**verb**）的一种形式，由"had + 过去分词（**past participle**）"构成（*Had you forgotten anything?*）。17，20

percentage 百分比：ten per cent（10%）之类的短语，与 of 连用，在限定词（**determiner**）或代词（**pronoun**）之前作数量词（**quantifier**），用于描述某事物的一部分（*Ten per cent of the population is living in poverty.*）。93

perfect 完成时：动词（**verb**）的一种形式，由"have + 过去分词（**past participle**）"构成（*Have you forgotten anything?*）。17

personal pronoun 人称代词：任意一个主格代词（**subject pronoun**）（*I, you, he, she, it, we, they*）或宾格代词（**object pronoun**）（*me, you, him, her, it, us, them*）。97

personification 拟人化：将抽象的概念或事物当作人来看待（*Death's cold hand touched his shoulder.*）。76

phrasal modal 短语情态动词：用法相当于情态动词（**modal**）的短语，如 be able to, be going to, have to（*We have to wait for Cathy.*）。请比较：**modal 情态动词**。29

phrasal verb 短语动词：由"动词（**verb**）＋ 小品词（**particle**）"构成的词组，例如 sleep in 或 put on（*He put on his shoes.*）。134

pluperfect 过去完成时：= **past perfect** 20

possessive determiner 物主限定词：my, your, his, her, its, our, their。请比较：**possessive pronoun 物主代词**。83

possessive noun 名词所有格：名词（**noun**）后加 "'s"（*Lee's car*）或只加 "'"（*Jones' house*）的形式。76

possessive pronoun 物主代词：mine, yours, his, hers, ours, theirs。请比较：**possessive determiner 物主限定词**。97

possessive 所有格；物主词：用在名词（**noun**）前的限定词（**determiner**），如 my, your, their 等（*my chair, your money*）；用于代替名词短语（**noun phrase**）的代词（**pronoun**），如 mine, yours, theirs 等（*I found mine, but I couldn't find yours.*）。名词所有格（**possessive noun**）也是一种所有格形式。76，83，97

predicative adjective 表语形容词：用在系动词（**linking verb**）之后的形容词（**adjective**）（*Her hair was red and her eyes were green.*）。请比较：**attributive adjective 定语形容词**。112

predictive conditional 预测条件句：真实条件句（**real conditional**）的一种，用于表达一件事与另一件可能会发生的事之间可能存在的联系（*If I have time, I'll help you.*）。185

preposition 介词：用在名词（**noun**）、名词短语（**noun phrase**）或代词（**pronoun**）之前，构成介词短语（**prepositional phrase**）的单词（*at, on*）和短语（*in front of*）（*I'll meet you at noon on Friday in front of the library.*）。125

prepositional phrase 介词短语：结构为"介词（**preposition**）＋ 名词（**noun**）/ 名词短语（**noun phrase**）/ 代词（**pronoun**）"的短语（*on the table, in front of me*）。125

present continuous 现在进行时：动词（**verb**）的一种形式，由"am / is / are ＋ 现在分词（**present participle**）"构成（*The baby is sleeping.*）。17—18

present participle 现在分词：动词（**verb**）的一种形式，如 sleeping，用于构成进行时（**continuous**）（*Is he sleeping?*）。请比较：**past participle 过去分词**。17

present perfect 现在完成时：动词（**verb**）的一种形式，由"has / have ＋ 过去分词（**past participle**）"构成（*Have you forgotten anything?*）。17—18

progressive 进行时：= **continuous** 17

pronoun 代词：用于代替名词（**noun**）或名词短语（**noun phrase**）的词，如 she, anything, herself（*Molly is very old and she can't do anything by herself.*）。97—98，100

proper noun 专有名词：首字母大写，用于表示人或事物名称的名词（**noun**）（*Elsa is from Switzerland.*）。请比较：**common noun 普通名词**。69

quantifier 数量词：many, some 之类的单词或 a few, a lot (of) 之类的短语，用于谈论数量（*Some people have a lot of money.*）。84

question 疑问句：一种助动词（**auxiliary verb**）位于主语（**subject**）和主要动词（**main verb**）之前的句子（**sentence**），包括 wh- 疑问句（*wh-question*）（*When did he leave?*）和 yes / no 疑问句（*'yes / no' question*）（*Did he leave?*）。45

question tag 附加疑问句，疑问尾句：附加在陈述句之后的，由助动词（**auxiliary verb**）和主格代词（**subject pronoun**）构成的简短疑问句（**question**）（*He hasn't left yet, has he? He's still here, isn't he?*）。46

quotation marks 引号：成对的标点符号（'...' 或 "..."），用于标示直接引语（**direct speech**）、具有特殊含义的单词或短语、标题等（*'I'm tired,' he said. · Have you read 'Animal Farm'?*）。149

real conditional 真实条件句：条件句（**conditional**）的一种，描述的事情在现在或过去是事实，或者有可能会发生。（*If I open the door, the cat will run out.*）。请比较：**unreal conditional 非真实条件句**。185

reciprocal pronoun 相互代词：each other 和 one another。100

reduced adverbial clause 简化的状语从句：由分词（**participle**）或 "从属连词（**subordinating conjunction**）＋ 分词（**participle**）" 构成，作用相当于状语从句（**adverbial clause**）（*[Before] leaving the house, he switched off the lights.*）。205

reduced negative 简化的否定句：否定句（**negative**）的简化形式，通常由连词（**conjunction**）加 not 构成（*Do you want this or not? If not, can I have it?*）。48

reduced relative clause 简化的关系从句：由分词（**participle**）构成且不含关系代词（**relative pronoun**），作用相当于关系从句（**relative clause**）（*I saw some people waiting outside.*）。176

reflexive pronoun 反身代词：myself, yourself, himself, herself, itself, ourselves, yourselves, themselves。100

relative clause 关系从句：从句（**clause**）的一种，通常由关系代词（**relative pronoun**）引出，用于给前面分句（**clause**）中的名词短语（**noun phrase**）提供更多信息（*I was in a bus which was packed with children who were making a lot of noise.*）。173—174

relative pronoun 关系代词：用于引出关系从句（**relative clause**）的 who, whom, whose, which, that（*I have a friend who can fix computers.*）。在表示时间的名词后面，用 when 引出关系从句。在表示地点的名词后面，用 where 引出关系从句（*We met in Sydney, where I was working for a year.*）。在名词 reason 后面，有时用 why 引出关系从句。173

reported speech 间接引语：= **indirect speech** 150

reporting verb 转述动词：say, reply 这类用于直接引语（**direct speech**）（*He said, 'Hello.'*）或间接引语（**indirect speech**）（*I replied that I was busy.*）中的动词（**verb**）。149—150, 152

rhetorical question 修辞性疑问句：形式上是疑问句但用来表达陈述语义的句子（*Who cares?*）。52

second conditional 第二条件句：= **hypothetical conditional** 186

simple preposition 简单介词：单个的介词（**preposition**），如 at, during, in, without。请比较：**complex preposition 复杂介词**。125

simple sentence 简单句：由一个主语（**subject**）和一个动词（**verb**）构成的单独分句（**clause**）（*Mary sneezed.*），句中也可能包含宾语（**object**）和状语（**adverbial**）（*We ate lunch in a café.*）。请比较：**compound sentence 并列复合句**，**complex sentence 主从复合句**。3

split infinitive 分裂不定式：在 to 和动词（**verb**）之间插入副词（**adverb**）的不定式（**infinitive**）（*I want **to really understand** him.*）。139

state verb 状态动词：用于描述状态而非行为的动词（**verb**）（*I **know** that he has a lot of money.*）。请比较：**action verb 行为动词**。3

subject 主语：一般用在动词（**verb**）之前的名词（**noun**）、名词短语（**noun phrase**）或代词（**pronoun**），说明动词所述动作的执行者（***Anthony** lost his keys and **I** found them.*）。4

subject pronoun 主格代词：用作主语（**subject**）的人称代词（**personal pronoun**）（*I, you, he, she, it, we, they*）（***He** wants to get married and **she** doesn't.*）。97

subject-verb agreement 主谓一致：指动词（**verb**）应在单复数形式上与主语（**subject**）保持一致（***He is** eating lunch.* • ***They are** eating lunch.*）。4

subjunctive 虚拟语气：名词性从句（**noun clause**）中动词（**verb**）原形（**base form**）的一种特殊用法，有时也叫作现在虚拟语气（**present subjunctive**）（*They have proposed that taxes **be** increased.*）。在动词 wish 后的名词性从句（**noun clause**）（*I wish I **were** older.*）或假设条件句（**hypothetical conditional**）（*If I **were** you, I'd complain.*）中，were 的特殊用法也属于虚拟语气，有时也叫作过去虚拟语气（**past subjunctive**）。167，186

subordinating conjunction 从属连词：用于引出状语从句（**adverbial clause**）（*because*）、名词性从句（**noun clause**）（*that*）或关系从句（**relative clause**）（*who*）的单词或短语（*I didn't know **that** you were the person **who** called me **because** you didn't leave your name.*）。请比较：**coordinating conjunction 并列连词**。12，197

substitution 代替：使用 one, ones, so 和 do so 等词代替重复出现的单词、短语或分句（**clause**）（*I have a black pen, but I need a red **one**.*）。104

summary report 总结性转述：用一个动词（**verb**）来总结他人所说话语的简短转述（*He **apologized**.*）。152

superlative 最高级：通常通过在形容词（**adjective**）或副词（**adverb**）词尾加后缀 -est（*fast**est***），或在词前加 "the + most / least" 构成（***most** expensive*），用于表示某事物在某方面程度最高或最低（*He wants to get **the fastest** and **most expensive** car in the world.*）。请比较：**comparative 比较级**。120

tag question 附加疑问句，疑问尾句：= **question tag** 46

tense 时态：动词（**verb**）形式与动词所描述的行为或状态发生的时间之间的关系。17

***that*-clause that 从句**：一种由 that 引导的名词性从句（**noun clause**）（*I thought **that** I had made a mistake.*）。161

third conditional 第三条件句：= **counterfactual conditional** 186

three-word verb 三词动词：由 "短语动词（**phrasal verb**）+ 介词（**preposition**）" 构成的动词形式（*You should **hold on to** that book.*）。134

transitive verb 及物动词：后面接宾语（**object**）的动词（**verb**）（*I **dropped** the ball.*）。请比较：**intransitive verb 不及物动词**。6

two-word verb 双词动词：= **phrasal verb** 134

uncountable noun 不可数名词：只有单数形式、与单数动词连用的名词（**noun**），用于指活动（*research*）、概念（*honesty*）、物质（*rice*）等事物，但不能指单独的个体。请比较：**countable noun 可数名词**。74

unreal conditional 非真实条件句：条件句（**conditional**）的一种，非真实条件句中的事件是实际上没有发生过的、不太可能发生的或想象的（*If you had asked me earlier, I would have helped you.*）。请比较：**real conditional 真实条件句**。186

verb 动词：在分句（**clause**）中用于描述主语（**subject**）的行为（*eat, steal*）或状态（*belong, understand*）的词（*He stole something that belonged to me.*）。3

verb with object 接宾语的动词：= **transitive verb** 6

verb without object 不接宾语的动词：= **intransitive verb** 6

***wh*-clause wh- 从句**：一种由 what, whether 等 wh- 疑问词（*wh*-word）引导的名词性从句（**noun clause**）（*I don't know **what** she wants.* • *I can't remember **whether** she likes tea or coffee.*）。161

wh*-cleft wh- 分裂句**：把一个句子（**sentence**）（*I'm not supposed to drink coffee.*）分为两部分的句型，一部分通常是以 what 开头的分句（**clause**），另一部分为"be ＋ 强调部分"（*What I'm not supposed to drink is coffee.*）。请比较：it*-cleft it 分裂句**。217

***wh*-question wh- 疑问句**：以 what, who, when, how 等词开头的疑问句（**question**）（*When did he leave?*）。请比较：**'yes / no' question yes / no 疑问句**。45

***wh*-word wh- 疑问词**：what, who, where, how 等用在 wh- 疑问句（*wh*-**question**）或 wh- 从句（*wh*-**clause**）开头的单词（*Where have you been?* • *I don't know what's wrong.*）。45，161

'yes / no' question yes / no 疑问句：以助动词（**auxiliary verb**）或 be 开头的疑问句（**question**），通常用 yes 或 no 回答（*Did he leave?*）。请比较：***wh*-question wh- 疑问句**。45

zero conditional 零条件句：= **factual conditional** 185